Laws and Societies in the Canadian Prairie West, 1670-1940

LAW AND SOCIETY

Law and Society Series
W. Wesley Pue, General Editor

The Law and Society Series explores law as a socially embedded phenomenon. It is premised on the understanding that the conventional division of law from society creates false dichotomies in thinking, scholarship, educational practice, and social life. Books in the series treat law and society as mutually constitutive and seek to bridge scholarship emerging from interdisciplinary engagement of law with disciplines such as politics, social theory, history, political economy, and gender studies.

A list of the titles in this series appears at the end of this book.

Edited by Louis A. Knafla and Jonathan Swainger

Laws and Societies in the Canadian Prairie West, 1670-1940

UBCPress · Vancouver · Toronto

15 14 13 12 11 10 09 08 07 06 05   5 4 3 2 1

Printed in Canada on ancient-forest-free paper (100% post-consumer recycled) that is processed chlorine- and acid-free, with vegetable-based inks.

Library and Archives Canada Cataloguing in Publication

Laws and societies in the Canadian prairie west, 1670-1940 / edited by Lou Knafla and Jonathan Swainger.

(Law and society)
ISBN-13: 978-0-7748-1166-8 (bound); 978-0-7748-1167-5 (pbk.)
ISBN-10: 0-7748-1166-8 (bound); 0-7748-1167-6 (pbk.)

1. Law – Social aspects – Prairie Provinces – History. 2. Sociological jurisprudence – History. 3. Law – Prairie Provinces – History. 4. Prairie Provinces – History. 5. Northwest, Canadian – History. I. Knafla, Louis A., 1935- II. Swainger, Jonathan Scott, 1962- III. Series: Law and society series (Vancouver, B.C.)

KE394.L42 2005   340'.115'09712   C2005-904391-1   KF345.L42 2005

Canada

UBC Press gratefully acknowledges the financial support for our publishing program of the Government of Canada through the Book Publishing Industry Development Program (BPIDP), and of the Canada Council for the Arts, and the British Columbia Arts Council.

Printed and bound in Canada by Friesens
Set in Stone by Artegraphica Design Co. Ltd.
Copy editor: Dallas Harrison
Proofreader: Deborah Kerr

UBC Press
The University of British Columbia
2029 West Mall
Vancouver, BC V6T 1Z2
604-822-5959 / Fax: 604-822-6083
www.ubcpress.ca

Contents

Illustrations

Photographs

Maps

Figures

Preface

The writing of Canadian legal history has been a patchwork affair. When a large group of legal-historical scholars met at the University of Manitoba in 1997 for a "Special Conference on Canada's Legal History: Past, Present, and Future," concerns about the lack of literature on the country's legal history across its geographical regions were met with comments ranging from "it can't be done" to "it should not be done." While the Osgoode Society continues to publish its important *Essays in the History of Canadian Law,* its eastern, or central, bias combined with a fragmented approach leave the broader outlines of our legal-historical record still untouched. The only sustained work in the country is that of the Canadian State Trials series originated by the late Murray Greenwood and Barry Wright, which Professor Wright is continuing to this day. This lack of what one may hesitate to call a "national" overview of how law works on the ground has also led to the neglect of larger regional, legal identities outside of Ontario and Quebec, of which the Prairies are a major element.

The advent of the UBC Press Law and Society Series in 2001 provided Canadians with an important impetus to the writing of their legal-historical record, one with which this collection is proud to be associated. The view that the history of the law must be written from a broad perspective of peoples, communities, and states within a larger global context is one that will mark the twenty-first century. Too often the "west" is seen as an appendage of central Canada, rather than as a region that developed its own culture, society, and institutions from a broader mosaic that was Native, European, and North American. This volume attempts to speak on issues and problems in Canada's Prairie West with that larger goal in mind, as well as continuing to develop the fascination with its people and events.

Laws and Societies in the Canadian Prairie West, 1670-1940

1
Introduction: Laws and Societies in the Anglo-Canadian North-West Frontier and Prairie Provinces, 1670-1940

Louis A. Knafla

Prologue

Nearly a quarter of a century ago, David Flaherty defined a new age for Canadian legal history. Writing an introduction for the first volume of the Osgoode Society's *Essays in the History of Canadian Law,* he proposed that there were two kinds of legal history, internal and external, and that the future lay with the latter.[1] Flaherty's view was that legal history was a branch of history that must focus on the general relationships between law and society. It must be systematic and dynamic, proceed on a sound theoretical basis, and explore the provocative questions. Legal history must go beyond the internal history of a topic. It must seek to understand the fundamental assumptions upon which law was made, how it interacted with people, and what creative forces resulted. In addition, legal history must be comparative. In the case of Canada, it must be studied and written within the context of France, Great Britain, and the United States.[2]

The present volume features a number of junior and senior authors who have been brought up in that comprehensive and comparative mind-set that Flaherty identified in 1981. They believe that legal history counts and that it can advance the knowledge of our history and its development. They believe that legal history must be broadly based, taking into consideration all relevant aspects of life and the societies and institutions that it spawns. They also believe that it is significant to research and write the legal history of perhaps the most neglected region of Canada, the Prairies. Stretching from the Canadian Shield to the Rocky Mountains, it comprises approximately one-half of Canada and one-quarter of the land mass of North America.

The term "North-West Frontier" is employed for the early contact history of the Prairies in four senses. First, it contains theoretically what Richard White has expressed as the middle ground between the European colonial rulers and their legal constructs and the Native peoples who originally inhabited the land, a ground that must engage both of these cultures. Second, it represents chronologically the second phase of European sovereignty to be established in Canada. It came after the French creations of New France and Acadia and before the eighteenth- and nineteenth-century colonies founded by Great Britain in the east and far west. Third, it is bounded geographically on the east by the Maritime colonies, Quebec, and Ontario, and on the west by British Columbia and the Yukon. And fourth, in comparative terms, it bears a kinship relationship to the American Northwest Territories and Great Plains below that developed under the flag of the United States.

The purpose of this introduction is to place the essays that follow in a comprehensive and comparative construct that provides an interpretive platform representing the best of modern historiography.[3] Thus, it attempts to fulfill two goals simultaneously. On one level, it provides a survey of the region's legal history that is constructed around the major themes of the essays in this volume. And on another level, it summarizes the findings of the essays as they pertain to those major themes by weaving them into the legal-historical narrative. The major themes that emerge from the essays are as follows: the role of discretion in dealing with Native peoples and immigrants; activist post commanders, magistrates, and judges who see themselves as independent of central authority; a devotion to English common law in litigating traditional legal actions; a willingness to use the experiences of non-Canadian common law jurisdictions in settling legal matters unique to the Prairies; the nurturing of principles of individualism and the free flow of capital; and an embedded social conservatism that forms a background for judicial conservatism on social issues in the midst of pressures to adapt more quickly to issues of modernity. According to two of the major legal historians of western Canada, "legal history that neglects the wider context risks misunderstanding or ignoring altogether the forces that shaped both the legal rules and the events to which they were applied."[4] This includes identifying the continuities of the region, exploring its contingencies, and interpreting their significance in comparative contexts. The essays here have been organized into two sections: First Nations and First Peoples, and Adaptations to Modernity. Of all the regions for Canadian legal history, the Prairies is the least developed. But it is also one of the most promising as it engages issues and questions that remain at the forefront of society today.

This introduction first assesses the European origins of the Prairies and its historiography, and then surveys the history of the region through its initial context of European laws and indigenous peoples to the various pre-Confederation frontiers from colonial America to Prince Rupert's Land from 1670 to 1870. Four essays are concerned directly with this era – those of Hamar Foster, Sidney Harring, Russell Smandych, and Paul Nigol, and two are underpinned by its concepts – Greg Marquis and Roderick Martin. The introduction then surveys the interaction of law and society in the post-

Confederation era from 1870 to 1940. This era engages Harring and the latter two essays and more particularly those of Zhiqiu Lin and Augustine Brannigan, Tristan Goodman, Janice Erion, and John McLaren. All of them, however, explore a myriad of issues and problems beyond the scope of this introduction, and they should be read to be enjoyed.

A number of conclusions emerge. Not surprisingly, the influences that shaped the various meanings of law in the region were as numerous as the cultures that came together on the interior plains and the northern barrens. British, Canadian, and American perspectives on the nature of law, disorder, punishment, and recompense all flavoured the regionalized legal culture. No matter how novel the situation encountered, the newcomers inevitably drew upon the well of their own personalized experiences and the knowledge of how disputes had been settled at "home." Yet, at the same time, the law ways of the indigenous peoples and the realities of local circumstances precluded the blanket impositions of foreign legal structures. Indeed, as Foster argues, the law of necessity ensured that local practice and discretion remained an integral aspect of the region's legal culture. Thus, the comparative focus is critical to any understanding of legal developments in the Prairies. Ultimately, the ongoing tension between how neatly these local methods fit – or to the degree that they fit at all – into the imported norms was at the core of the region's legal experiences and stands as the battleground on which the themes of these essays and the history they explore are formed.

Historiography

The themes in these essays form part of a new legal historiography that seeks to understand the law in a more dynamic role in pluralistic societies. Legal history in North America in the past half-century was predominantly viewed as the study of law as it related to the history of social development.[5] Law was seen as constant change often obscured by forms, technicalities, and fictions. In North America, in particular, it had been increasingly doctrinal, pinned to the rise of the modern state and its institutions, with an emphasis on theory. Recently, it has also adopted a European concern for the "margins" of history, focusing on children, women, immigrants, unskilled workers, the poor, and indigenous peoples. Thus, the examination of how law works in society has been as important as the study of its institutions.[6]

Most of the factors above have marked research on the Prairies since the mid-1970s, attesting to the quality of its historical-legal scholarship. Moreover, some of the prominent writers of the region are featured in this volume. While most of the collected essay volumes of the Osgoode Society for Canadian Legal History, for example, have ignored the geographical middle ground of the country,[7] its general historiography has had a rich tradition.[8]

According to an easterner, "after industrialization the most important aspect of Canadian history between 1867 and 1920 was the expansion of western settlement."[9] In contrast, legal-historical writing on this crucial period has been piecemeal, apart from that concerning the Riel Rebellions and the North-West Mounted Police (NWMP). Nonetheless, the region has emerged from "a scholarly void to a lively branch of social and intellectual history."[10]

In "Toward a Legal History of the Great Plains," John Wunder has observed the strength of regional history and case studies of communities in exploring the historiography of the "New Western History."[11] Studying ten states and three provinces – Texas to New Mexico, Missouri to Colorado, North Dakota to Montana, and Manitoba to Alberta – Wunder notes how little has been written on the large issues of the area concerning Native-white relations, discrimination against minorities, the development of large corporations and monopolistic practices, and the exploitation of the land. Lacking as we do a Willard Hurst or a Morton Horwitz, the role of law in displacing the Plains Indians and aggrandizing water and mining rights stands out for major study.[12] So too do the subjects of race, gender, class, community, economic dependency, and the environment.[13]

Kermit Hall has emphasized the significance of this region in his examination of "The Legal Culture of the Great Plains."[14] Hall found no more than six articles and no books written on the subject in the United States in the past twenty years. As in Canada, legal history and culture are written primarily from the view of the east and anecdotally from the far west. The myth of lawlessness on the Plains south of the forty-ninth parallel, like that of its pristine serenity northward, has been due to a legal historiography "chained by environmental determinism."[15] Too often legal history assumes that the richest regions and states produce the richest legal environment and national prominence.

The exception was Walter Prescott Webb, writing more than a century ago.[16] Webb saw all institutions and laws change once immigrants crossed the ninety-eighth meridian into the Great Plains. Geodemographic circumstances led to new property laws for land, livestock, and water, fencing laws to resolve conflicts between farmers and ranchers, and a strong strain of individualism that led to more democratic political institutions and women's suffrage. These developments, in turn, underwent a transformation in the later decades of the nineteenth century with the advent of banks, corporate farms, and commercial and industrial development. What Webb saw for the Great Plains has much currency for the Prairies.

Hall has documented the problems of the Plains myth. For violent crime, he suggested that lawlessness was more random than systematic and that homicide rates were at the bottom of the state tables. For women, he argued that economic necessity led to better dower provisions, more matrimonial and alimony cases, and more divorces, with women gaining the right to sit on juries and vote in elections. For the economy, he saw a Third World economy exploited by eastern railways, banks, and manufacturers, which led to the Granger and Populist Movements of the 1870s and 1890s. The People's Party Convention was in Omaha, Nebraska, in 1890, and William Jennings Bryan carried all the Great Plains states except North Dakota in the election of 1896. Many of their platform planks were incorporated into later legislation, including regulatory and antitrust laws, graduated income tax, postal savings banks, public utilities, the initiative, and the referendum. Given a diverse legal culture, Hall argued for a more pluralistic view of its internal and external relations.[17] It is this pluralistic view that can be used to illuminate for the Prairies the internal and external relations of the law that Flaherty proposed for Canadian legal history nearly twenty-five years ago.

The portrait of the North-West Frontier drawn by Foster, Harring, Smandych, and Nigol depicts a battleground between the forces of English and Native legal cultures and private and public law. The contest between the forces of English and Native cultures has been eloquently described by Richard White in environmental terms: Europeans were the sea, Natives the rocks. The land witnessed a constant storm, the sea pounding and wearing down the rocks, but it could never absorb the remains. These cultures subverted the middle ground between assimilation and "otherness." In the end, the Native populations would diminish, as did the buffalo. But in the process, these varied cultures became more like each other, an acculturation that formed a middle ground that forged its own collective identity.[18] This middle ground also hosted numerous legal systems – those diverse indigenous legal orders and English customary and positive law.[19] Because it underwent the cultural process that engaged its founding peoples, the Prairies developed a unique legal system.

The common law tradition of British colonies was not unlike that of the mother country. Until the nineteenth century, the common law of England was largely for the landed aristocracy – the law of the elite practised in the central courts at Westminster.[20] Even then, however, it was not unified or uniform. One could sue for different, or conflicting, remedies across the hall in courts of both common law (Common Pleas, Exchequer, and King's Bench) and equity (Chancery and Admiralty). It was in the customary and statutory local courts in towns, ports, boroughs, and counties where most litigation took place.[21] This amalgam of legal traditions was a separate sphere, called customary or municipal law, and was understood by the phrase "the custom [or course] of the common law."[22] Comprising sublegal cultures, it was not the "high" law of Coke or Blackstone. It was, however, good law.[23] Customary law gave a quintessential pluralistic basis to English law and was not dissimilar to the local law practised in the colonial courts of England's colonies. Colonial judges in the communities knew of Coke and Blackstone and may have read some of their works. But in court, they often referred to their personal copies of Richard Burn's *Justice of the Peace,* in which municipal law and its formularies were prevalent, as did their English contemporaries.[24]

North-West Frontiers, 1670-1870

European Laws and Indigenous Peoples

European states enforced their wills on indigenous peoples on the basis of the international law of conquest.[25] The classical argument was posed in the early seventeenth century by the author of modern international law, Hugo Grotius, in his "just war" theory. According to Grotius, a conquest replaced the former political state with that of the conqueror, making its previous rights extinct. Monarchs must have absolute power, and the rights of the conqueror were unlimited.[26] This concept was a reiteration of the Spanish concept of a "holy war" derived from the medieval Crusades and used in the conquest of Mexico in the sixteenth century. Conquest, colonization, and confiscation were based on natural and divine law.[27] Later a revisionist argument was made by Richard Zouche and Samuel Pufendorf, who held that while states must accept the results of war they were not bound by "unjust wars."[28] This position was based on the earlier writings of Franciscus de Vitoria, who argued that Amerindians had princes, rights, and duties that could not be abrogated without careful scrutiny by the conquerors.[29] Pufendorf's position was expanded in the Enlightenment by Jean-Jacques Rousseau, who argued that unjust treaties or wars did not settle questions of rightful possession. Wars were between states.[30]

The major writer of the Enlightenment on this question was Emmerich de Vattel. Agreeing with Rousseau on the limitations of conquest, he went on to discuss how positive law did not distinguish between just and unjust wars. The laws of war protected the rights of individuals as well as the rights of states and accepted the law of prescription (title held uninterrupted for a long time) as well as that of conquest. However, since international law demanded stability, the results of wars had to be observed. Thus, the victors had to enter into treaties with those who were defeated, and the terms of treaties were indisputable facts that had the force of law even though they might be biased in favour of the victors.[31] This led to a Eurocentric positivist school of international law in the nineteenth century, justifying the dispossession of Amerindian as well as all Aboriginal peoples.[32]

According to Harring, "in tribal society, culture, law and politics are an indivisible part of the whole life of a people."[33] Since European society's relationship with tribal society was colonial and imperialistic, Europeans forced their institutions upon the Natives, changing their traditional legal orders. Tribal law became more centralized, moving from the level of the community to the tribe or tribal nation. Sovereignty became critical for their own protection and for their negotiations with neo-European bodies. As Harring explains, their legal culture then became deeply entwined with tribal sovereignty and notions of law and legality more deeply engrained in their culture.[34]

In England, the early explorations of North America in the late sixteenth century were clearly designed for trade, land, and settlement. The elder Richard Hakluyt appealed to Christianity and commerce with his advice to plant them, man them, and keep them. He held that "good" Christian monarchs had the duty to colonize, settle, and profit from these lands, exercising control over their peoples.[35] Queen Elizabeth's title, moreover, should rightfully extend over North America from the West Indies to the Arctic Circle.[36] The territories, once documented in official correspondence, legal transactions, and charters, would then be English by law. However, this jurisdiction was not based on conquest, as common law admitted the practice of local customs where they were well established in communities as part of the municipal law of the land. These practices are explored by Nigol in his essay on fur trade and Native societies in the Prairies. (See Map 1.1.)

The key to British acceptance of indigenous law was proof of its continuity over time: the peoples' identities, territorial foundations, and judicial precedents. In the imperial period (presettlement), local municipal laws were accepted as an early concept of legal pluralism. Coke said that England and its possessions were governed by their municipal (internal) laws.[37] The legal rules governing their interaction were derived from the "law in dominions," later called the law of empire or imperial law.[38] Since most of the law's principles were from custom and judicial precedent, not statutes or prerogative law, it was an "imperial common law." In countries uninhabited by Europeans, settlers had their municipal law by "birthright," parallel to the local customs of indigenous peoples.[39] This arrangement led to the common law doctrine of Aboriginal rights.[40] In inhabited countries taken by conquest, the Eurocentric school of legal thought applied, and local law was in force only until altered or abrogated by the Crown.[41] This appears to be the position adopted by the NWMP in their early years that is noted by Marquis' essay. One can find both schools of thought in Martin's examination of the Territorial judges from 1887 to 1907. The conflict between those schools, however, can be seen most clearly in the earlier history of the British Australian frontier.

The British Australian Frontier

The application of British "imperial common law" with the inclusion of Aboriginal rights had its origins in Australia, where a colonial administration developed earlier than on the Canadian Prairies. There the English colonial administration accepted that indigenous legal systems would operate parallel to the English ones. They did so for eastern parts in 1788, Western Australia in 1829, South Australia in 1836, and New South Wales by 1842, where colonial judges and governors held that Aboriginals could not be tried for criminal offences under English law.[42] The Supreme Court of South Australia ruled that Aboriginals could be subject to English law only if they "have in some degree acquiesced in our dominion." When the governor had the police apprehend Aboriginal leaders suspected of killing English survivors of a shipwreck, they were subjected "to summary justice" and executed.[43] The Colonial Office sent a rebuke. The judicial view in New South Wales that was conveyed to the judges of South Australia in 1840-41 was that the courts should not interfere in indigenous disputes. However, when the secretary of state for the colonies was asked for a formal legal opinion from Westminster, he declined to give one because he did not want to offend his colonial governors.

This reluctance, however, changed by 1870. Harring explains how an Aboriginal was tried and convicted in a common law court for the murder of another.[44] The period in which this took place, 1835-70, was critical for the history of the North-West Frontier. As Smandych observes in his essay here, humanitarian concerns over indigenous peoples in England led in 1835 to the creation of the Aborigines Protection Society and the Select Committee of the House of Commons on Native Inhabitants of British Settlements. The committee's report recognized that Aboriginals were allowed to have their own laws in Australia, South Africa, and the Canadas.[45] Thus, there were now "aboriginal protectors" in the Australian colonies.[46]

The report, penned by the great statesman William Gladstone, formally recognized Aboriginal law and made possible its absorption into the common law. Smandych explains how Sir James Stephen, a key figure, was raised in the West Indies as a passionate defender of Aboriginal rights. Becoming permanent undersecretary of the Colonial Office in 1836, he prepared the *Colonial Evidence Act* of 1843 that allowed Natives to give evidence, including unsworn testimony, in colonial British courts. These legal rights enabled Sir George Grey, the famous colonial law reformer and governor of South Australia, and later New Zealand and Cape Colony, to bring Aboriginal law within the customary law ambit of the common law, thereby providing for its amalgamation. As a legal theorist, Grey also brought it under the scrutiny of English positive law. Thus, by 1870, the colonial administration considered Native customary law as absorbed into English common law wherever it was invoked. The change can be seen in the courts of British Columbia by 1884 and, as Martin shows, in the Supreme Court of the North-West Territories by 1907. Lacking the voice of the Natives, the "empire of law" had superseded the "empire of history."[47]

In Western Australia, there were no reported decisions in the early years. Governor Hutt considered the use of English law against Aboriginals unjust and said so to Lord Glenelg, secretary of state for the colonies, in 1839. Hutt wanted these people to have a modified English law: evidence without oaths and judges without juries. He was, however, quite firm in his pessimistic view of Aboriginal justice: Aboriginals follow "no rule but the impulses of their own caprice and passions, blood for blood being their law, and every man the judge, jury and executioner in his own quarrel."[48] Nonetheless, it was clear that the view from London was not always practised in the colonies and that local discretion (or necessity, as Foster put it) was the guiding policy. This policy, essentially British in its origins,[49] became the guiding principle in the legal history of the Prairies and is present in most of the essays in this volume. In addition, as we will see below, Australian developments in the private law area found their way into the Canadian Prairies through Westminster, Ottawa, and San Francisco. But the doctrines on which colonial policy and law in the Prairies were based evolved on the British American frontier from the seventeenth through the nineteenth centuries.

The British American Frontier

Common law doctrines lived in the courts and not in the theatre of politics and empire. The European invasion of North America in the seventeenth century was based on the ideology of the medieval Crusades: the fruits of conquest were legitimate if its cause was just in the eyes of their God. They had the heathen for their inheritance and the Earth for their possession. Racism grew out of this feudal ideology.[50] In North America, the Europeans invaded a widowed land. In New England alone, an estimated Native population of 72,000 by 1600 was perhaps only 10,000 by 1670. Some demographers argue that the Native population of North America north of the Rio Grande about 1600 was ten to twelve million but was reduced to fewer than one million by the time of the Hudson's Bay Company (HBC) charter in 1670. Europeans, incapable of conquering the wilderness, were quite capable of conquering those who could.[51]

From the 1680s to 1763, the First Nations generally were loyal to the French, but in the course of time they gradually lost the power to force Europeans to the middle ground. The American Revolution choreographed the term "Indians,"[52] moved them from the upper to the middle ground, and created the image of an exotic society of the past. The Natives, in turn, began to see themselves more often as people of the dead, trapped in the dreams of the mind but not in the reality of life. Thus, it was no coincidence that they were significantly reduced in numbers at the hands of neo-Europeans just as they themselves had pushed the buffalo to the brink of extinction.[53]

According to our current vision of the "old north-west," the region was a land of moving borders, parted by the peregrinations of peoples who collectively followed the biological diversity of the land with the seasons. The advent of British colonies, and the empowering of the new republic, were derived at the expense of the Indians. The original North-West Territories were created to institutionalize the Indians of the region, giving them an identity in European terms that in the future could be constrained, assimilated, or exterminated.[54] Imperial control was established in 1755, when Britain handed over the control of Aboriginals to the Indian Department.

The Royal Proclamation of 1763, however, restated former policy. It set the western boundaries of the colonies at the height of the Appalachians, reserving the rest of the land to the Mississippi River for the Indians subject to future treaties.[55] This Indian country was confirmed by Britain in the *Quebec Act* of 1774.[56] In the meantime, the Treaty of Fort Stanwix (1768) enlarged the boundaries of the Indian country from the Mississippi east to the Ohio River. These developments, however, would be short-lived. Future treaties with the new republic would undo what had been accomplished.[57]

The American War of Independence changed the geopolitical landscape forever.[58] The Anglo-American Treaty of 1783 gave the new republic all land west to the Great Lakes and the Mississippi, violating the spirit of 1763, 1768, and 1774 and English common law precedent. On 13 July 1787, *An Ordinance for the Government of the Territory of the United States North West of the River Ohio* created the first neo-European entity in the northwest. It established a colonial government on the Ohio frontier to protect its property interests and promote settlement, with eventual self-government and statehood. The ordinance of 1787 was a charter that provided terms for future territorial and state government. It also confirmed Indian rights to their lands and liberties, but under the authority of Congress, which was authorized to make laws for them and, if necessary, wage just wars against them.[59] The Six Nations Iroquois Confederacy was split during the American Revolution. Their annexation was one aim of the War of 1812. Indian lands and rights were restored in the Treaty of Ghent of 1814 but under American sovereignty.[60]

In the decades that followed, Indians migrated north of the Great Lakes as the rest of their societies were forcibly relocated west of the Mississippi and greatly reduced by armies after the Civil War. Once north of the Great Lakes, they were under the jurisdiction of Upper Canada. Harring has explained how the government of the Canadas bought their land through treaties, resettled them on reserves, and tried to make them farmers. Other historians have chronicled the failure of this accommodation.[61] A precedent, drawn from the United States, had been made in the Canadas. These events developed as part of a new capitalist spirit that emerged in the United States in this era.[62] According to a Supreme Court decision in 1850,[63] the ordinance of 1787 extinguished Native land titles, established private property and the law of descent, and extended the "inalienable" rights won by "Americans" in the War of Independence to all land west of the Ohio.[64] In

Canada, as Harring notes, these concepts would be exported to the Prairies in the 1870s.

Issues concerning Native rights were discussed in Britain during the House of Commons debates on the *Quebec Act* in 1774. Both Solicitor General Alexander Wedderburn and Attorney General Edward Thurlow argued that conquered peoples deserved to be left in possession of their municipal laws, customs, and religions.[65] This view was later solidified in a parliamentary report of 1837 that followed judicial precedent. It recommended that the British concept of "venue" be used to define the extent of British jurisdiction. The queen's law, and the queen's peace, extended only to places where British subjects resided.[66] The Colonial Office then made this the basis of its policy for applying British law in the colonies.

The continental European view, however, emphasized the political will of sovereignty in the conquest of non-Christian peoples. Official letters of state from France in 1540, and to Canada and Acadia in 1603, held that Indian lands could be taken over by treaty, colonization, or conquest.[67] This view continued into the nineteenth century, when the rights of "savages" allowed them to engage in treaties and be bound to the land.[68] In the United States, it was found in Chief Justice John Marshall's judgment that Indian title could be extinguished by conquest.[69] Marshall, citing de Vitoria, held that Indian tribes had a minimal sovereignty as "domestic dependent nations" that allowed the federal government to extinguish their title.[70] But he also used English law to defend the rights of the Cherokees in Georgia in the famous Cherokee Nations cases of 1832-33.[71] "Civilizing" the "barbarians" was a European doctrine that became part of the American concept of "manifest destiny" in subsequent decades that stretched across the Great Plains to the California and Oregon Trails.[72] The extension of federal power over Amerindian culture, law, and land, and congressional allowance of acts to override treaties, marked the republic's "New Colonialism" in the second half of the nineteenth century.[73] But Canada's western frontier would develop more autonomously due to the unique legal position and experiences of the Hudson's Bay Company.

The HBC Frontier

The Prairies was "discovered" first by the French and then by the English. Bounded by the Red River and Hudson Bay in the east, it stretched west to the Rocky Mountains. Embracing the lower part of the Hudson Bay drainage, its major arteries were the North and South Saskatchewan Rivers. This excluded the northern rivers of the Athabasca and the Peace, which flowed into the Mackenzie to the Arctic Ocean, and the drainage of the Missouri and Mississippi Rivers, which flowed south to the Gulf of Mexico. These rivers, and their drainage, were recorded by French explorers who mapped the area.[74] (See Map 1.2.)

The first English incursion into the bay was Henry Hudson's sail of 1610, landing on the shore of James Bay in the autumn. Hudson named it after his king, James VI of Scotland and I of England, and the larger bay after himself. His trade of two deerskins for an axe in the following spring became part of Cree folklore, recited in the 1740s.[75] The British north-west was originally European. Its early merchants and explorers came from Prague, Avignon, and London, operating through English joint stock companies. Concentrating on the Saskatchewan River system, London financiers fed the political interests of Prince Rupert that led to the inaugural voyage of the *Eaglet* and the *Nonsuch* from Gravesend on 3 June 1668 to Hudson Bay, returning in October 1669 with 3,000 pounds of beaver furs that sold for £1,379 6s. 10d.[76] This was followed immediately with a charter that Charles II signed for the Adventurers into Hudson's Bay in 1670 as part of a new royal policy to create Crown colonies in North America. Most of the early posts, however, were in French hands until the efforts of Pierre Radisson of Trois Rivières and John Churchill placed them in company hands by 1697.[77] Some contemporaries and modern scholars have argued that the charter may have been illegal. But as Foster has observed, "necessity" gave it the force of law.

The law of Rupert's Land, according to the HBC charter of 1670, was the law of England insofar as it applied to those people who did not live under the authority of other previously established nations in the region.[78] In practice, the company accepted the rule of Aboriginal law for the domestic concerns of Native people. A number of indigenous legal customs accepted by the company are explained in Nigol's essay. Such usage was confirmed much later when the Court of Queen's Bench of Quebec upheld Native customs as they applied to actions of company employees.[79] This was also upheld later by the Supreme Court of the North-West Territories.[80]

Nigol provides a study rich in archival materials from the Hudson's Bay Company to demonstrate just how much discretion was used by the chief factors of the company. Drawing from naval, master-servant, and private company law, they relied on whatever tools they had acquired from their professional backgrounds. Thus, an Orkney Scot such as Joseph Isbister, who came from the British navy, treated his post at Albany like a ship. He used a strict military style for corporal punishment at will without any semblance of legal process. Regarding Natives as fugitives from a foreign ship, he treated them as enemies. He swapped blood for blood, imposing legal sanctions and capital punishment. He also denied his men any contact with Native women. James Isham, however, at York Factory, had been a bookkeeper. Lenient toward his men, he tried to use company policy in handling them. Generous and paternalistic, he believed in Native rights and fathered a mixed-blood son. He also held that the company had no jurisdiction in the lands of First Nations. Sexuality, like positive law, had twin faces of prescription and practice.[81]

In the end, Nigol shows how the company officers used a mixture of private and public law at their posts. Because they lacked any knowledge of formal law, their rule was characterized by discretion. Isbister's method resulted in conflict and poor trade. Isham's method led to a collegial atmosphere in which there were few breaches of order and a successful level of trade. Natives who dealt with Isbister would have had little interest in English common law. Those who dealt with Isham must have seen it as customary practices not unlike their own. There were two chief factors and two legal systems at work. One succeeded; the other did not. One revealed the king of England as a great white father, the other as the devil in waiting. Each one, in Foster's terms, military or civil, drew on the "law of necessity." Lacking a court of appeal for "long-distance justice," the two societies had formed different laws and customary practices in a conflict of laws situation that could only be resolved with compromise.

The Cree retained control of the middle ground, especially along the North Saskatchewan River, in spite of perhaps 500 *coureurs* living on the land of its drainage system.[82] From 1670 to 1740, preferring to trade with the French, they worked the French and English against one another to obtain the highest prices for their furs and exploited English traders to the bay. Since most of the incoming technology fit into their social structure, the Cree had to make minimal adjustments. The Europeans, however, were forced for survival to adopt Native dress, style, and trading habits.[83] Nigol explains how company factors had to disregard instructions in allowing indigenous traders access into the posts. Foster suggests that the fur trade law that evolved in these centuries became a unique amalgam of English, Scottish, French, and Native legal cultures. Eventually, however, the Cree would lose their middle ground in the company's ascendant monopoly of 1821-40.[84]

The original Northwest was Aboriginal, comprising those First Peoples who populated North America before the European incursions and settlements and who were recognized, under European law, as sovereign states with their own customary laws. Named by Americans and English-speaking Canadians as Indians, they had their own voices, their own histories, and their own understandings of themselves. In the early period of contact, relations between First Peoples and a European culture that forged national and regional identities[85] were not always cordial. Smandych reveals how Upper Canadian and Ontario judges were "sublimely ignorant" of British policy on Natives and their lands and "arrogantly indifferent" to their rights and traditions. In spite of this, First Nations such as the Cree and Ojibwa were tenacious in maintaining their legal traditions in the face of incoming settlers.[86] As Harring demonstrates, they had to be. Dependent upon the land as they were, their prime directive was to preserve the customary practices that sustained their communities. (See Map 1.3.)

Various jurisdiction acts attempted to settle the parameters of the company's authority. Britain's *Canada Jurisdiction Act* of 1803 gave parties in the "Indian Territories" recourse to the courts of Lower and Upper Canada, authorizing the governor of Lower Canada to appoint justices of the peace and commit persons for trial.[87] Badly flawed, the act did not define the Territories, and non-British subjects were excluded from its jurisdiction. When violence erupted between the North-West Company (NWC) and the Hudson's Bay Company in 1812-16, the ensuing prosecutions and trials were described as "perfect chaos."[88] As Foster writes, the attorney general appealed to positive law, and the jurors acquitted on local circumstances. According to officers of the North-West Company, Lord Selkirk's colony of Assiniboia was based on a defective title. His "buccaneers" maintained by force a monopoly of land that infringed the Indian Territories and sought "to sanction injustice and legalize oppression." In their opinion, the creation of the colony was in violation of the Proclamation of 1763.[89] The *Civil and Criminal Jurisdiction Act* of 1821 clarified the company's authority, but it was seldom used. It provided Foster's characterization of long-distance justice.[90] Instead, the company and its courts used a mixture of discretion, Native custom, and private and public law to resolve disputes.

Common Law Courts and Conflicts

A formal legal system was established in the district of Assiniboia in 1835 with a governor, council, and general quarterly court. Civil and criminal codes were drafted, and in 1851 at Fort Garry the law of Assiniboia was declared to be the law of England at the accession of Queen Victoria in 1837. The history of the first court's recorder, Adam Thom (1840-51), has been plagued with controversy. Legal improprieties, questionable judgments, and insensitivity to Natives, Métis, and country-born led to his dismissal. A recent study, however, finds that settlers, parties, and witnesses brought a large body of evidence to the court that jurors heard carefully before rendering their verdicts. It suggests that the records of the court deserve more study than the edicts of its recorder.[91] Thus, in Assiniboia, as in other districts of Rupert's Land, questions of law, class, and race caused the Hudson's Bay Company to act carefully until the transfer of its charter to the Crown in 1869.[92]

Smandych explores the 1845 trial and execution of Capinesseweet, a Saulteaux Indian charged with and found guilty of murdering a Sioux. An act of revenge, the homicide seemingly fell outside the presumed boundaries of English law. Examining both the colonial and the local contexts, Smandych contends that Recorder Adam Thom's belief that Native peoples were within his jurisdiction can be seen as an evolution in his mind of

British colonial policy. Foster sharpens that outlook by explaining how Thom viewed the application of English positive law to such circumstances as "repugnant to justice." Thus, while Natives were systematically discouraged, on the one hand, from resorting to traditional means of dispute resolution, on the other they were encouraged to embrace the alleged benefits of English law and the quality of its protection.

Hence, in the famous *Connolly* case, English law applied only in the trading posts and did not abrogate the laws and customs of Native communities. As Foster notes, mixed marriages became the universal "custom of the country" even though, as Nigol explains, the company's instructions had forbidden them. Justice Monk's decision in 1867 (later upheld) was that Cree law was valid in Prince Rupert's Land in 1803 because it was a custom under private international law, and there had been no legal document changing Cree custom after the Proclamation of 1763.[93] In the *Mohegan* case, the Privy Council held that the "nation" had a separate system of municipal law.[94] Thus, Cree customs were part of the imperial law. In the *Tanistry* case, the court held that by *Calvin's Case* local customs agreeable to English law could continue in force after either conquest (Ireland) or unification (Wales), as the law of gavelkind in Kent.[95] Thus, Native law was recognized under English municipal common law. The question was whether Native custom was part of English municipal law or a municipal law of its own under imperial common law.[96]

The problem was that Coke also said that upon conquest all "infidel" law was void.[97] While modified in England, this view was used by nineteenth-century American judges to hold that tribal customs were barbarous and thus incapable of recognition at common law. It was against the earlier legal tradition and early writings on international law. Grotius believed that giving subjected people their own laws and government was an act of humanity, prudence, and good legislative policy (not really a law of the *jus gentium* or "law of nations").[98] Many contemporary observers saw the continuity principle as part of the law of nations in Canada at the conquest of Quebec,[99] and later in the *Connolly* case.[100] Engrained in English common law from time immemorial,[101] only the legislative power of a sovereign state could change municipal law.[102] Thus, the survival of a pluralistic system of municipal laws with the positive law of courts and legislatures was compatible with the British concept of sovereignty.

The legal history of the Hudson's Bay Company had been fraught with conflict since the early nineteenth century. Much of this violence, however, was isolated. Foster suggests that company lawyers were always fearful of the possible consequences of litigation and believed that the company had no jurisdiction over First Nations. But the problems were sufficient to bring complaints to Britain's House of Commons, create royal commissions, and pose questions on the legality of the charter. The company, as Nigol explains, controlled its men by economic pressure, physical intimidation, and tolerance of "recreational" violence.[103] Thus, it is not surprising that Thom would attempt to create a regime of law and order in Assiniboia even if it involved the use of official lawlessness, and that officials in the western expanses of Rupert's Land would continue using force with discretion to maintain order in fur trade society.[104] Thom's regime was later legitimated, as Foster explains, when the Supreme Court of Manitoba upheld his trial of capital offences in Rupert's Land. Later the dominion government would sanction the HBC to exercise federal jurisdiction in all criminal matters in the Arctic.[105]

For British law, the local customs practised in Rupert's Land were deemed in the 1860s to have been incorporated inclusively into common law.[106] Mixed-blood marriages were upheld by the courts under private international law because those customs had not been changed by statute since British sovereignty was claimed in 1763. Colonial courts must, therefore, enforce local customs under British imperial law.[107] In the settlement era of the colonial period, Native sovereignty co-existed with British or American territorial sovereignty. In the United States, however, Indians were deemed incapable of incorporation. They were aliens, and their laws foreign, as long as they held their lands. Even after treaties and settlement into reserves, state courts applied Aboriginal custom or Native customary law as elements of a foreign legal system.[108] In "exclusive continuity," local law was a distinct municipal legal system outside the imperial constitution; under "inclusive continuity," it was within that constitution. When the British had sovereignty over European peoples, the British lived in those lands under the local municipal system. But for non-Christian lands, nineteenth-century courts held that settlers within their enclaves had their own law, creating two parallel municipal systems. As we have seen above, the first British Empire had a proliferation of distinct nations, laws, and customs, with English settlers bringing their own municipal laws with them. This has become the principle of continuity establishing the common law doctrine of Native rights in later Canadian history.[109] It also formed the guidelines for the pluralistic legal system that developed with the growth of a modern, capital, and natural resource economy and society that followed the folding of Britain's Prince Rupert's Land into the Canadian North-West Territories.

Laws and Societies in the Anglo-Canadian North-West, 1670-1940

Custom and English Municipal Law

Virtually all the essays in this volume rely to some extent on the role of common law custom in law and society relationships in settled communities of the Prairies. The factory posts of the Hudson's Bay Company, the Métis, Doukhobors, and mining communities, the problems of law enforcement, and the extent to which the law governs human relationships in the family, and corporate ones in the community, all invoked customary rights as well as those restrictions placed upon them by statute and judicial precedent.

In theory, the law of the state replaced the law of the community in Canada in the course of the nineteenth century. But in practice, as Martin observes, the judges of the Prairies exercised judicial discretion broadly to include principles of customary rights that extended back to the pluralistic regime of fur trade society and into the deep recesses of the common law legal tradition. The inclusion of customary rights in a legal regime is what Foster calls a recognition of law as local knowledge. Citing Clifford Geertz and Justice Oliver Wendell Holmes, Foster suggests that the cultural exponent of law is found in its living experiences. Working out the tension between customary and positive law gives us "justice."

English customary law had its origins in Anglo-Saxon customs: the customs and laws of the "folk" supplemented by royal and ecclesiastical decrees.[110] This tradition of common law as custom is at the heart of a concept of English common law that is based on the customs of the people and not on the dictates of the sovereign. In the early modern period, which corresponds to the era of the early discoveries and contact with Native peoples, Sir Edward Coke gave lip service to this concept.[111] The link between Anglo-Saxon England and the sixteenth century was made by the first legal scholar of ancient English customs, William Lambarde, who edited the early laws[112] and outlined the codification process of existing customs from the Anglo-Saxons.[113] Its fullest exposition as legal precedent was by Sir John Davies, who held that custom, agreeable to people for "time out of mind," had the force of law. Called the *"jus commune"* ("common law"), it was *"jus non scriptum"* ("unwritten"), better than any law in the world.[114] The concept was enforced by common law jurists such as Sir Henry Finch and Sir Matthew Hale, who authored the term "municipal law" as an original part of the common law of England.[115]

The Scottish and English who managed and served the Hudson's Bay Company were familiar, as was their legal counsel,[116] with the common law tradition of local customary or municipal law. Customary law remained vibrant in England to the late seventeenth century and in Scotland to the late eighteenth century. Its significance for English trading companies since the later middle ages, as well as for the HBC, is documented by Nigol. It was imported wholesale into the North American colonies in the seventeenth century and engrained in the minds of its judges and legal officials on both sides of the border.[117] It was also brought westward and northward from New England by those immigrants who replicated their culture in the lands across the Appalachians[118] and from the Maritime colonies across the Canadian Shield.[119] For Rupert's Land, Martin notes its efficacy for the common law courts. Elements can also be seen in the essays of Foster, Smandych, and Goodman. A contemporary quoted from the epistles of Horace to explain this legacy: "They changed their skies, but not their minds who sailed across the sea."[120] As early American colonists, they brought their law along with their cows and furniture.[121]

The legal history of First Nations has received little detailed examination north of the forty-ninth parallel. Their law was bound up with family, community, religion, culture, and economy. When written in the historical discourse of neo-Europeans, it was structured by racism and ethnocentrism. No Natives, for example, could understand how their lands could have been sold by the Hudson's Bay Company for £300,000. In 1867, Canada created an "Indian" policy to replace the colonial one. Treaties 1-7 were framed by the treaty model of Ontario. Implemented by the NWMP and stipendiary magistrates from 1873, the policy soon degenerated into oppression, land theft, and starvation with the demise of the Plains buffalo. Following the resistance of 1870, the results, as Harring relates, included frequent conflict and the rebellion of 1885. It took extrajudicial power, Ontario-style, to bring Natives and Métis within the framework of Canadian law. Disregarding their rights at trial, mistranslating treaties, creating fraudulent acts, restricting Natives to reserves, prohibiting the exercise of their tribal cultures, and imposing an authoritarian legal order, official lawlessness replaced the unofficial version.[122]

The common law world, however, could have provided for a different outcome had that notion of common law as custom been applied by the rulers of the day. According to Kent McNeil, if common law courts had applied the rules of real property law at the point where First Nations had been integrated into the empire, Natives would have had their land in fee simple.[123] Relying primarily on positive law, McNeil has shown how case law can be worked to provide for the integration of disparate people provided they wish to be integrated into a neo-European society. Harring argues that they did not. When First Nations did enter into treaty negotiations on "white man's terms," they were intentionally misled. Similar problems confronted the waves of immigrants who poured into the Prairies in the late nineteenth and early twentieth centuries. Riding the rails into a region that was nursed by imperial corporate interests for its fur-bearing resources, those peoples would have to develop a legal system that would accommodate settling and using the land with the capital interests required to develop and exploit it. (See Map 1.4.)

Agricultural and Industrial Capitalism

The history of the Prairies has been characterized by three eras: the fur trade era of 1640-1840, the market economy of the 1840s-90s, and the agricultural and industrial capitalism of 1900-40. In geo-economic terms, the region was marked by three geological planes that cut across it: the southern flat plains, the narrow middle parkland with rolling hills, and, for Europeans, the large and impenetrable northern boreal forest. The rivers flowed north and east, facilitating transportation from the Prairies to Hudson Bay. Since each territorial district and later province was carved from south to north, plain, parkland, and forest were linked into the economies of each region. Spanning 1,500 kilometres from east to west, and even more from south to north,[124] the region mirrored for Canada in size and role the Great Plains below it.

The settlement of the Canadian Prairies was seen traditionally as following the template of the Great Plains.[125] The land acquired from the Hudson's Bay Company in 1870 was a national inheritance subject to the national agenda, like the Louisiana and Gadsden purchases of the United States. Parliament's creation of the Canadian Pacific Railway (CPR) in 1880, with its massive land grants and subsidies, was a corollary of the Illinois Central Railway of 1850-57. By 1893, nearly half of the agricultural land of the Prairies was in the hands of ten railway companies and their subsidiaries (31.8 million acres). Moreover, 89 percent of the land grants were in Saskatchewan and Alberta. The railways, however, drafted their own colonization plans and sold land cheaply to prospective settlers. By 1927, the CPR alone had sixty-eight colonization offices in Britain, Europe, and the United States. In addition, the HBC had 6.6 million acres, and land reserved for school belts was 9.4 million acres. After land reserved for towns and woodlands, a maximum of 23 percent of agricultural land was left for homesteading.[126]

The settlement of the Prairies was made possible by two developments legislated in tandem, the *Indian* and *Homestead Acts*. As Harring has documented, the *Dominion Indian Acts* of 1869 and 1876 placed Native peoples in the legal position of children, and the acts of 1884 and 1895 struck at the foundations of their culture. Treaties 1-7, signed between 1871 and 1878, ended the region as a multi-use habitat. It was clear, as Harring reveals, that the Native leaders did not understand the treaties (which were poorly translated) in the same way, and many communities did not sign them. In addition, the oral promises of the dominion that the Natives considered as part of the treaties were later disavowed. "The queen's promises," encapsulated in Native oral tradition since the eighteenth century, were to be no more. Like the nonconforming European sectarian immigrants who succeeded them, as McLaren documents, they would be hounded into assimilation.

The *Dominion Lands Act* of 1872 provided for the disposition of Prairie land remaining after grants to the HBC and the CPR. It was seen as a corollary of the United States *Homestead Act* of 1862. Chester Martin went so far as to call it Lincolnian, diffusing wealth and strengthening democracy. The age of the homesteader began at eighteen, and women were eligible if sole head of the family. John A. Macdonald's "National Policy" brought the "Empire of Dominion Lands" to Rupert's Land, isolated from the east by the Precambrian Shield and the Laurentian barrier. The land given, however, was small, 160 acres per family compared to 640 acres in most of the Plains states. Applicants had to be naturalized or declare their intention.[127] The land given, moreover, was also restricted. The 1872 act introduced, as Goodman explains, the dominion's control of water rights that would shape the economic development of the land.

The framework for the settlement of the North-West Territories was provided in the *Homestead Acts* of 1875-80. In 1875, the dominion Parliament gave the Territorial Council limited powers over property, wills, and descent.[128] These powers were expanded to those of a province in 1877,[129] providing direct power without the intervention of Ottawa by 1886.[130] The acts of 1878-79 were designed to protect family property at the desertion or death of the husband.[131] The Territories gained more autonomy and distinction when the *Real Property Act* of 1886 introduced the Robert Torrens land title registration system.[132] Its significance to contemporaries was revealed in Herbert Jones' history of the system published in that year.[133] Originally Australian, as Goodman explains, it was adopted by western and Rocky Mountain states. Its popularity was seen in protecting property rights from "invisible clouds."[134] But the Canadian government, like that of the United States, reserved Crown lands to itself outside the Torrens system even after the creation of the provinces of Alberta and Saskatchewan in 1905 and the transfer of Crown lands in 1930.[135]

The purpose of the National Policy was to develop the industrial economy of eastern Canada by exploiting the natural resources of the Prairies. As Foster observes, and Goodman and Erion document, the National Policy built on the great fur trade companies of the colonial era to promote giant corporations with exclusive monopolies. Natural resources such as water were reserved to the Crown for the promotion of agriculture and industrial capital formation. Visioning an economic hinterland, the policy gave rise to entrepreneurs such as Max Aitken, who obtained through his Royal Securities Company massive financial investment from London, New York, and Montreal to develop an agricultural, industrial, and commercial infrastructure for the region.[136] (See Map 1.5.)

The era of 1896-1914 was one of capital formation on the Canadian Prairies, bringing it into the forefront of the North American economy.[137] Lawyers such as James Lougheed and Richard Bennett made their fortunes by assisting the wheels of capitalism through the creation of oligarchies and monopolies in transportation, banking, irrigation, grain elevators, wholesaling, and retail merchandising. They drew up articles of incorporation, assisted in the business plan, forged amalgamations, and defended their clients' interests to the highest level of judicial appeal.[138] The association between law and commercial development in North America was never closer than that achieved in this region.

Prairie society was very mixed by 1914. Manitoba was more populous and stable than the Territories, but its European and Métis communities adapted more slowly to social and economic changes than those of the previous Territories. By surname, fewer than half of the Prairie population were British, with 20 percent each western and eastern European. The major nationalities were British, European, and American.[139] This agrarian society was focused on grains and cattle. Financed by London and eastern Canadian capital, it had the means to create one of the fastest-growing regions of the country until the advent of war and depression.

By 1930, of the ninety-nine million acres for homesteading, only 59 percent had been entered or patented, and 41 percent of that had been cancelled. Other sources of land use were grazing leases and forest reserves. It took twelve years for the dominion government to work out the transfer of unalienated lands to the Prairies. With preemptions, military scrip, and half-breed grants, by 1930 less than 12 percent of the land was left, and most of that was unusable for subsistence farming.[140] Federal land use policy was pervasive. It intruded into every aspect of Prairie life. Constantly in flux, its rules and regulations were not always well known or clarified, making standard practices and enforcement difficult to maintain.[141] As Goodman and Erion suggest, this practice of ambiguity served well the interests of corporations founded to exploit the natural resources of the region.

Natural resources were jealously guarded by the dominion government. While given away to Manitoba in its creation as a province in 1870, nearly 60 percent of its lands had been reserved or complicated by the dominion. All natural resources, however, were withheld from the North-West Territories and the subsequent provinces of Saskatchewan and Alberta. In addition, some twenty-five million acres were reserved for the dominion in each province in 1905, which were used as a "compensation fund" for subsidies to the provinces. Alberta, which at the time had 87 percent of the country's coal reserves, and perhaps 90 percent of its oil and gas reserves, had a natural resource industry based on federal leases. Water power also was in the hands of the dominion. By 1930, over one million acres of prairie were reserved for irrigation under lease by the dominion. Control was in the hands of the Department of the Interior, created in 1873 largely for the management of the region's natural resources.[142] Soon, however, this control came into the hands of private and public corporations such as the Canadian Pacific Railway, Calgary Power, and the Royal Securities Company, which represented the interests of imperial and local entrepreneurs and financiers.

Corporate Law

The distinction between private and public lands and interests has not been clear in North America's historical past. In *Who Controls Public Lands?* it was argued that private industries that utilized public lands such as mining, forestry, and animal husbandry exercised a control over those lands that has been detrimental to the public interest.[143] This thesis can also be applied to public water and the hydroelectric industry on the Prairies. The traditional interpretation of state or provincial regulatory bodies is that they were created to protect consumers against monopoly powers and high user rates. Recent work, called the "Chicago School," suggests that state regulatory policy actually benefited utilities and was essentially "captured" by business interests. The regulation era in the United States dates from 1905 to 1924,[144] coinciding with Erion's study of Calgary Power in these years.

One of the more fascinating areas of legal-historical scholarship in recent years that intersects the private-public domain has been water rights. Concerned initially with Native peoples,[145] it has since expanded to the centre of the legal history of natural resources.[146] According to some historians, the problem of "eastern"-driven historical and legal professions has stymied the growth of scholarship in this area. The wet and humid east had no interest in the subject of water apart from how to get rid of it;[147] in the west, water rights were originally fluid, "first come, first served," and never fixed. Riparian rights could be upheld by the courts, but there were no legal principles to govern the quantities that could be used or diverted. As Goodman explains, a whole new water law was required due to the environmental differences that existed in the North American west.

The dominion Parliament responded with the *North-West Irrigation Act* of 1894. Originating in Australia in the 1840s, and adopted by California, Utah, and Wyoming, this legislation placed all water rights in the hands of the Crown.[148] Goodman's analysis of the legislation and debates shows how the prior allocation system was crafted out of the Australian and western American experiences. This "western" solution to water rights was designed to allow the Crown to promote agriculture and industry by selling or leasing such rights to those who would make the best economic use of them. It enabled the government to patronize large corporations for the development of irrigation, hydroelectric, forestry, and energy projects in the Territories. It had, however, a devastating effect on the lands and resources of Native peoples and isolated immigrant communities in semi-arid areas that are still largely unexamined in the legal-historical literature.[149]

Water was essential for the growth of agriculture and industry in the southern Prairies. Goodman notes how the "irrigation block" of the CPR in 1903 was the largest irrigation project in North America. Attacked by some smaller landowners, its negation of riparian water rights was still being litigated in the 1980s. Erion depicts how Calgary Power developed a monopoly of water power in southern Alberta and used that monopoly to influence and control the regulatory powers of the provincial government,

1910-28. Using private and public papers, she details the ways in which the company gained control of all the water sources for the production of hydroelectric power and became the sole supplier for the city of Calgary. The entrepreneurial financier Max Aitken and the monopolist Herbert Holt were able to replicate in Calgary what they had fashioned in Montreal: the rise of Montreal Light and Power, 1900-6. Their local icon was the young lawyer from Nova Scotia, Richard Bennett, counsel for the CPR and its vast irrigation company. Bennett knew water.

The story of the Calgary Power Company is a history in microcosm of the agricultural and commercial capitalism of the Prairies. The Aitken-Holt model was concocted in the Caribbean, where the Royal Securities Company created its first monopolies of utilities with the aid of London and New York money. Once bond holders had the track record of excellent profits at the hands of this accomplished team, they would follow it to the western Canadian frontier. Preferential tariffs made Prairie agriculture and ranching profitable. They enabled entrepreneurs to gain control first of the water supply and then form combinations to exploit the market for cement, pipe, lumber, agricultural machinery, and grain elevators. Government-appointed regulatory bodies proved unequal to the task of protecting consumers.

The secret of water use was to gain control of the federal licences, build the dams and the hydroelectric facilities, and offer low prices to stave off competition. The federal government and the courts used the principle of the "common good" to allow the development of large hydroelectric projects over the interests of individuals.[150] Calgary Power applied this legal principle to its profitable use. The low water rates of 1912 were raised in 1920 and raised higher in 1928. The Public Utilities Board created to regulate them met largely in private. Empowered with the regulation of electric and natural gas utilities, as well as telephone, it was saddled with multiple administrative tasks and devoted most of its energy to approving the sale of public land, securities, municipal contracts, and local government borrowing. Erion relates a Great Plains success story in which state regulatory policy benefited utilities that were "captured" by private business interests.[151] The Chicago-Illinois experience, 1914-24,[152] bears a close resemblance to that of Calgary-Alberta. It became the model of capital formation for utilities in the region. The issue of "control" in the marketplace was not, however, isolated. It was also at the heart of a rapidly growing and diverse society concerned with social control and criminality.

Law Enforcement and the Courts

The problem of control in ordering the economic life of the region for the capital formation of eastern interests, as we have seen above, was also evidenced in the area of law enforcement. While the HBC can be seen in business terms as the precursor of the CPR, Canada Cement, the Alberta Pacific

Grain Elevator Company, and Calgary Power, it can also be seen in legal terms as the precursor of the North-West and Royal Canadian Mounted Police. In ways more subtle than Macdonald's Conservative government may have perceived, the task of bringing order to the Prairies was based on the Anglo-American tradition of mercantilism. The vast expanse of this sparsely populated, multiracial region required multidimensional corporate identities sufficiently powerful to withstand the vicissitudes of an unyielding prairie environment.

Legal conflict in Prince Rupert's Land before 1870 was based on the initial contact between Native peoples and merchant capitalism; after 1870, it was between merchants and consumers, farmers and bankers, employers and employees, and the perpetrators of personal and property crimes and their victims. The critical transition period was from the 1830s to the 1880s. As we have read, it was not a peaceful environment. The HBC in the past had often ignored violence and allowed extralegal solutions to thefts and killings associated with the fur trade. Thus, with the transfer of Rupert's Land to the dominion in 1870, Prairie society was not at peace.[153] The introduction of arable and husbandry farming by immigrants did not produce tranquility. A more recent study of the ranching community in southern Alberta at the grassroots level depicts a rural society that suffered violence and death with little outside protection down to 1914.[154]

Harring paints a challenging view of the arrival of the NWMP in 1873. It was accompanied over time with the disappearance of the buffalo, the advent of the *Indian Act,* the loss of Natives' collective commons, treaty negotiations, the institution of a pass system, and a legal assault on indigenous culture. What that culture received, on the basis of the white man's story, was a "legally structured frontier." According to Marquis' essay, the structure was a buffer between the Métis and Natives on one side and immigrant settlers on the other. Once occupied with treaty making, First Nations brought their own agendas to the table. They believed that their rights, as understood by their representatives, were protected. They were not. For example, when they turned to the Territorial Council to protect the remaining buffalo, the dominion government vetoed the ordinance. Thus, subsequent relations between Natives and neo-Europeans were poisoned, culminating in the rebellion of 1885.

The portrait of a more violent west has been crafted quite recently.[155] This view has been corroborated by Justice J.W. McClung, who, in an entertaining study titled *Law West of the Bay,* has used episode after episode to document the culture of violence that marked the North Saskatchewan River valley from 1778 to 1900. Edmonton becomes the "murder capital" of Prince Rupert's Land and law the work of vendetta, siege, and trophy scalp.[156] Captain William Butler's report of his winter journey from Fort Garry to Rocky Mountain House in 1870-71 recorded rampant crime and massacres and led to the establishment of mounted police and civil magistrates and the extinguishment of Native lands for settlement along the North and South Saskatchewan Rivers.[157] This view has been advanced by Robert Waite for the Idaho Territory, Warren Elofson for Montana and Assiniboia in the same period, and Jonathan Swainger for the Peace River country afterward.[158] In these regions, lawlessness was rampant, violent crime increased with the growth of modernity, and law enforcement was ineffective. And, as Lesley Erickson has shown for women on the Prairies, it was not just a problem caused by Natives, immigrants, and working-class men.[159]

According to Robin Fisher, the Prairies were peaceful compared to British Columbia,[160] and the Canadian stereotype of the peaceful west was based on the Prairie experience. This traditional view was also espoused by Wilbur Bowker, who believed that the great dedication and efficiency of the NWMP and the stipendiary magistrates pacified the region by the 1880s with "Expeditious Justice: Western Style."[161] A more judicious perspective of this stereotype has been put forward by a historian of the NWMP, Rod Macleod.[162] The archival evidence, both qualitative and quantitative, supports the view that violence was an integral part of the Prairie historical experience from the eighteenth through the early twentieth centuries.[163] McLaren suggests here that changes in the *Criminal Code* that expanded crimes such as vagrancy and criminalized other nonviolent actions may have contributed to this development. According to Lin and Brannigan, the seeds of violence were being sown in taverns, pool and dance halls with alcohol, gambling, prostitution, and fisticuffs. What distinguished the Prairies from the Great Plains below was the absence of armed troops to extinguish the Native population and the criminal activities of corporations and organized vigilantes.

The few historic confrontations of organized violence, such as the Riel Rebellions, the Cypress Hills Massacre, and the Winnipeg General Strike, were due perhaps to a combination of racial and economic forces. Land speculators, and the actions of Natives, Métis, and later European immigrants, were prominent players in those events. Crossing the Prairies was not unlike crossing the Great Plains. For Native migrations as well as settler incursions, many a man, woman, and child would have "seen the elephant."[164] Many would turn back, and many would die. Hardship was endemic to their existence, and the sharp appearance of economic forces that threatened that existence may have been the breaking point. As McLaren reveals, Liberal federal governments promoted their pilgrimages. And provincial police forces, according to Lin and Brannigan, identified them as "dangerous classes." Thus, on one level, the dissidents who took part in organized violence may be seen as the Canadian section of the American "Civil War of Incorporation."[165]

The continuing threat of organized violence was met by quasi-military forces. The military model was as important in the Prairies after Confederation and the transfer to Canada as before, as witnessed in the alternatives assessed by Nigol that faced the chief factors of the Hudson's Bay Company. The North-West Rebellion of 1885 has long been viewed as a defining moment in the history of the new Territories between Native and Métis and immigrant societies.[166] Wandering Spirit's jailhouse interview of 26 November 1885 recalled how Louis Riel had dispatched his messengers to the camps of the Cree to rise up with him and destroy the Canadians, whose government had reneged on its promises and treated them badly.[167] The federal government saw the issue as one of the survival of a settler's west, an issue that it had accused the HBC of fomenting in the "insurrection" of 1875.[168] The victory of the militia spelled the end of the First Nations as a political and military force in the region.

The NWMP became the rock of law enforcement. Created for the Prairie environment, they became the Royal North-West Mounted Police in 1904 and the Royal Canadian Mounted Police in 1919, with the added duties of security and intelligence. On the Prairies, they were seen as a symbol of Canadian sovereignty in an area threatened by Indian Wars and American expansion as well as an institution that would facilitate settlement.[169] Harring reveals further the extent to which their extraordinary delegated judicial powers enabled them to control and settle the frontier on Ottawa's terms, especially with regard to Métis and Native peoples. Lin and Brannigan note that they served as a model for the creation of the Alberta and Saskatchewan provincial police forces in 1917. In the Yukon, the NWMP became an institution of Canadian imperialism.[170] While politics was an important element in the history of the Mounted Police, other elements were equally important. Marquis, Canada's historian of the police, suggests that policing must be studied within a comparative context and, in this volume, demonstrates why.[171]

Marquis, comparing the NWMP with the Royal Irish Constabulary, provides an analysis of what each was supposed to be and what each became. The Mounted Police were projected to be a multiracial force. Circumstances surrounding the resistance of 1870 caused them to be predominantly Anglo-Celtic. Physical stature and military experience were deemed to be crucial. Yet nearly 70 percent of them were skilled workers, farmers, and clerks, many of whom could not ride. Advancement was to be by merit, but politics proved to be more important. They were encouraged to protect the Natives, which they accomplished to a significant degree. However, by 1900 they were arresting more whites per capita than Natives and Métis. By 1914, the force had become bushwhackers, colonizing agents, roving bureaucrats, and sometimes policemen. And by 1921, when the Royal Irish Constabulary was being disbanded, there were orders not to hire them because they were perceived as unsuited to the role of a Canadian policeman.

The test of the NWMP as law enforcers can be seen most graphically in the trials of the Riel Rebellion of 1885. The subject has a considerable literature,[172] but one topic that has not been fully explored is that of language. We tend to forget that First Nations' understanding of the treaties in the 1870s was different from that of those who had drafted them. Canadians are well aware of such misunderstandings caused by language. It has beset the history of Anglo-French relations since the Conquest of New France in 1760. As Harring has demonstrated, it has also coloured some of the great trials in the region.[173] In the 1885 trials, he found that the evidence was weak, the defence counsel perfunctory, and jurors and judges biased. Native people's stories were never admitted into court in their own words. Some recalled the woeful translation given to One Arrow in 1870: that he had knocked off the queen's bonnet and struck her in the rear with his sword.[174] Smandych notes here how such trials were primarily for Ottawa and local spectators. (See Map 1.6.)

A major distinction between law enforcement in rural and urban areas was the "enforcers." Mounted Policemen ruled the grassland, parkland, and small towns, assisted by local militia. The larger towns and cities, however, were searching for a system of law enforcement that was closer to the needs and agendas of their communities. Saddled with the NWMP, who drew their authority from Ottawa, fast-growing and populous communities were looking to local forces who would have a shared responsibility in the collectivity of the town environment. Perhaps they were aware of the limitations of the dominion police in shouldering that collective responsibility. Once they could afford their own police, they did not hesitate to create them under provincial statute. Thus, the police magistrate became a key figure in the law enforcement scene from the turn of the century.

In their study of crime in Calgary, 1882-1939, Thomas Thorner and Neil Watson have made a quantitative analysis of crime rates per capita in the city. The crime rate was high in the early years, dropped and remained relatively stable for several decades, and fell sharply during the First World War. The rate rose from 1919 and then fell dramatically during the Great Depression.[175] In the rural judicial district of Hanna, the records for the common crimes of theft and drunkenness reveal that the crime rate per capita was less than half that of Calgary, and most thefts seem not to have been of a malicious intent or reflective of economic trends.[176] While hardly conclusive, this evidence suggests that reported crime was much more an urban than a rural Prairie phenomenon. Even then, however, criminal activity may have been largely unreported. David Bright, in a pathbreaking study of crime in Calgary in the interwar years, reveals that sexual crime was an enduring feature of civic life, state categorizations were not always relevant, prosecution was irregular, and conviction rates were low.[177]

One of the major reasons for the rise of crime rates in Alberta and Saskatchewan during the First World War was the creation of provincial police forces. The British Columbia Provincial Police were founded in 1858, and Manitoba had a force since 1880, but the other two Prairie provinces did not adopt them until 1917. Lin and Brannigan examine the history of these two forces and present their findings with an elaborate method of qualitative and quantitative research. These forces were created in part because the dominion government could no longer afford an increase in enforcement during the financial exigencies of the war, and in part because the provinces wished to expand the enforcement of new liquor control and public order offences that were part of the moral reform movement of the era. The law of the local community was resurfacing as European immigrants replaced Native peoples and Métis as the non-Anglo-Canadian peoples.

The result was a paradigm shift in enforcement. First, there was a shift from class control involving Natives, Métis, and non-English-speaking immigrants to public order crime control. By the late 1920s, there were more arrests under provincial statutes than there were for crimes under the *Criminal Code* of Canada. Drunkenness and vagrancy were given more prosecutorial energy than major personal and property crimes. With the social gospel, prohibition, and women's rights movements, foreign immigrants became the target of provincial policing. Striking miners and communist leaders were also selected. The problem was that convictions did not match arrests. Witnesses were unwilling to give evidence for such offences, and juries were reluctant to convict the accused. Since the costs of provincial policing did not match the results, criticisms by stipendiary magistrates and justices of the peace (JP), coupled with the impact of the Great Depression, caused a crisis in legitimation that brought about their abolition in 1928-32.

Farther north, in the North-West Territories of the post-1870 period, policy choices in dealing with Native peoples fell into well-worn shoes. In some instances, the nonapplication of Canadian criminal law was deemed prudent, inasmuch as the Inuit were following traditional methods of dispute resolution and avoiding the excessive costs of formal investigations and trials. The advent of the RCMP brought increased trade and firearms but also disease, debt, and crime.[178] As Smandych and Foster note, in some quarters this arm of the law had run into arctic societies with the charter of 1670. Consequently, the presence or absence of Canadian law and legal officials could either reinforce traditional methods of dispute resolution or discourage them, while responding to the necessities of Canadian sovereignty in the north. The focus and success of prosecutorial energies depend in large part on the lawyers who litigate and the judges who determine them in the courts. Thus, the rise of a legal society of lawyers, magistrates, and judges from different regions, countries, and occupational backgrounds would affect significantly any attempts of the state, territory, or provinces to exercise successfully the kinds of control that were evidenced more frequently in eastern Canada, Great Britain, or the United States. While statute law was the law of the state, legal challenges and judicial interpretation remained buoyant in this youthful society.

Judges and the Law Profession

The history of legal society on the Prairies, and its ties to commercial activity, can be seen more fully in the activities of early legal practitioners. Most of the early professional lawyers in Manitoba, for example, 1870-1900, made their living not by legal practice but by "brokering." This meant acting as businessmen and drawing contracts for railways, banks, insurance companies, and real estate and acting as middlemen in such transactions.[179] The practice was equally matched in the North-West Territories from the 1890s to the 1920s. Those who were unwilling to develop business interests remained poor, retaining their hardy lifestyle and entertainments.[180] Richard Bennett counselled many prospective lawyers not to go west unless they were prepared to use their law for business practice and speculation.[181] Thus uniting with leading businessmen, lawyers helped to forge the credit networks that wrought the agricultural, industrial, and commercial enterprises of the region.[182] Lawyers who survived the postwar depression did so by being willing to undertake the collection of receivables, debt foreclosures, and civil actions under twenty-five dollars and by being tolerant of clients who did not pay their fees or did so in kind.[183]

The creation of the province of Manitoba and the North-West Territories in 1870 brought an odd collection of lawyers and judges to the Prairies. They came from all over: Great Britain, Ireland, Nova Scotia, New Brunswick, Quebec, and Ontario.[184] According to contemporaries, they were "characters" who were eclectic in their manners, jovial in their personal relationships, and unexpectedly learned in their craft.[185] The first generation of lawyers in Manitoba was rural, practising in small towns and communities. By 1910, most of these lawyers had left the small towns for the cities. Nonetheless, they did not give way to the large law firm in the manner that occurred in eastern Canada.[186] By 1910, at least half were still in small firms, and one-quarter were practising alone.[187] The conditions that prompted them to "go west" were largely unchanged from the 1870s.

The growth of the large corporation, however, redefined the role of the law profession. In a trend that started in Manitoba and moved west, lawyers were becoming less involved in litigation and more active in legal counselling. By the turn of the century, they were serving as "preventive technical legal counselors" to enable businessmen to avoid the costly and time-consuming nuisance of litigation.[188] Maintaining an essential service industry for banks, insurance companies, wholesalers, and retailers, they became community leaders who devoted considerable time to churches, schools, charities, and social and sporting clubs. For central Alberta, Jonathan Swainger has revealed how lawyers filled the gap in financial services by being lenders of first resort as well as agents for financial institutions.[189] In southern Alberta, Henry Klassen has revealed how they organized credit networks and became a conduit for the flow of capital into the region.[190] Later, in the interwar years, they would maintain these capital and credit functions in spite of meagre fees and bankruptcies during the Depression era.[191]

The legal profession was quite homogeneous in the late nineteenth and early twentieth centuries. Most lawyers and judges were British descendants, with a distinct number from the Maritimes and Ontario.[192] The Maritimes influence was prominent. Edward Wetmore came west to join the new Territorial Supreme Court in 1887 after directing the consolidation of the New Brunswick statutes. He later assisted in the consolidation of the Territorial statutes in 1898 and those of Saskatchewan in 1908.[193] Influential in cases upon appeal, his elegant judgments gave credibility to the precedents created. Lawyers who set up shop in places such as Moosomin and Fort Macleod established local customary law with their legal opinions. One would not often go to the Supreme Court *en banc* at Regina without "a Moosomin opinion."[194] They also did not hesitate to bring their culture with them. Like Charles Pringle Conybeare, they brought their clothes, furniture, social habits, and religion, and they replicated their orchards and gardens.[195]

Justices such as Charles Allan Stuart were keenly in tune with the mindset of a non-British immigrant society. During the First World War, when the United States and Canada were dealing with the problem of alleged subversion by Germanic immigrants, the Supreme Court of Alberta used a strict interpretation of "intent" to protect the civil liberties of central European immigrants from the suits of overzealous xenophobes. In 1917, in the midst of the worst years of the war, Stuart evolved a "clear and present danger clause" test for a flood of sedition charges.[196] He granted an appeal for the protection of individual rights on a thorough examination of English case law and legal treatises. This was two years before Justice Oliver Wendell Holmes Jr. adopted a similar test in the US Supreme Court.[197] Swainger's original study of this subject suggests a court that was on the cutting edge of civil rights.[198] Martin's analysis of the court's judicial tradition enables us to understand how such precedent-setting judgments occurred in Alberta.

The second generation of lawyers and judges learned their trade on the Prairies. One of the most outstanding lawyers of the 1920s-50s was James Milvain. His father, James, arrived in Lethbridge as a sixteen-year-old "remittance man" from Newcastle-upon-Tyne, England, as an apprenticed ranch-hand. Ranching on the Porcupine Hills, his son James was a lawyer from 1927 to 1959 and justice and chief justice of the Supreme Court's Trial

Division from 1959 to 1979. Approachable, personable, and community oriented, "Uncle Val" discussed cases in chambers as well as in the courtroom and listened to people outside as well as inside the courthouse. He went out of his way to resolve cases involving Native peoples out of court with local customary practices. As lawyer and judge, he believed that disputes were better served when resolved out of court rather than within.[199] Milvain was well nurtured in the municipal law tradition.

The judges of the first two generations of the Territories had the burden of creating a law that would facilitate the region's distinct and increasingly varied society. Martin has examined the 614 Supreme Court cases for 1887-1907 and produced an incisive analysis of the law and precedents that they made. The courts were awash in civil cases, many requiring homemade remedies. The result was a perusal of English, Canadian, or American precedents to fashion a law that would become unique to the Prairies. Some of the new substantive law that they carved can be seen in the subsequent discussion of private and public law. The process in which they engaged reveals the stresses and strains of a frontier settler society.

The bench was always mindful of English and Canadian precedents. But judges did not hesitate to identify and create accommodations for local circumstances within their judgments. Having to come to terms with Native peoples and immigrants, as discussed by Foster, Harring, and Smandych, they were careful in handling the tension that existed between rules and precedents articulated within the law. Foster observes that the settlement history of the Red River Colony could be told "solely through a narrative of the lawsuits and prosecutions that took place" between 1813 and 1873. Martin's analysis for the succeeding generation sketches the rules of a new society and the means by which they were hammered into shape.

Prairie judges saw themselves as exercising independent judgment in the best English common law tradition, relying on "the customs of the country," judicial precedents, federal and provincial legislation, and necessities of the age in a frontier society that was in the midst of an agricultural and industrial revolution. There were, however, cracks in their work. As we have seen, Natives, Métis, and non-British immigrants could and did suffer at the hands of the law owing to its inability to handle problems of language, culture, and religion. The essays of Foster, Harring, Nigol, and Smandych explore those problems in depth. The problems of law and justice, from the conflicts of 1812-18 to those of 1870 and 1885, were not easily eradicated in the era of 1886-1918 nor of 1918-40.

Nonetheless, judicially the North-West Territories was in the mainstream of the British common law tradition. Since many of its judges were from eastern Canada, they were deeply immersed in English law and the customary common law tradition. The list of British statutes in force at the creation of the Territories in 1870 (their reception date) was prodigious, as were those for Alberta and Saskatchewan in 1905.[200] No Supreme Court justice would lack knowledge of medieval statutes ranging from *Westminster I* (1275) to the *Statute of Uses* (1536). The same could be said for the judges of Manitoba.[201] The graphic picture of the work of the early judges presented by Martin provides the link between the British common law tradition in the Prairies and the modern history of the judiciary in its provinces.[202] The discretionary regime of law and justice that has been noted by Nigol and Smandych gave way to the need to establish certainty with firm precedents in a new positive law tradition unique to the region. And this new positive law tradition can be perceived in the development of several private law regimes.

Private Law

Lawyers were at the forefront of creating a new and unaffected legal system on the Prairies. Through advising governments and legislatures, and framing pleadings, they developed a simpler law of property and of drainage, matters crucial to the region's economic development, and less cumbersome forms of public boards, commissions, and municipal jurisdictions.[203] John Phillip Reid, writing about law on the Overland Trail, suggests that we can best understand a society from its civil behavioural patterns. Therefore, the onus on the legal historian is to research property dealings, debtor-creditor relations, and other common civil transactions to draw more far-reaching conclusions on the habits, actions, and values of society.[204] These are, unfortunately, among the least-studied areas in the history of the Prairies and thus still unknown. We can, however, piece together the ways in which private law regimes developed in the areas of family law, gender, and ethnicity.

The law of intestacy in Canada, drawn from English common law, had always favoured fathers at the expense of mothers and children. The North-West Territories, however, did not follow that practice. It favoured wives who came west to build their husbands' estates. Thus, the *North-West Territories Real Property Act* of 1886 gave provisions for wives and children and allowed illegitimate children and their children to inherit through their mother as if legitimate.[205] The legislation was designed to encourage prospective wives to come west and contribute to family structure. The legislation, however, was not original to the Canadian Prairies. It had been tested successfully in the Great Plains and other states south of the border from Massachusetts to California.[206] While later federal legislation placed limits on the disposition of estates,[207] the federal *Intestate Succession Act* permitted the Prairie provinces to amend it, allowing courts to alter the statutory distributions for spouses or children.[208]

A similar development occurred with dower and curtesy. Under dower, a wife could claim one-third of the family estate of the deceased husband,

and under curtesy the husband could claim all of his wife's lands at her death. On the Prairies, however, the Torrens system of registering land title abolished both dower and curtesy because they restricted the free transfer of land.[209] In Alberta and Saskatchewan, where the beneficiary died before the testator, the common law rule that there was no gift to the beneficiary's children was abolished, with the gift saved for both wife and children. Later, in the First World War, the Prairie provinces brought back dower acts in 1915-18 that gave wives life estates in their homesteads. Further, in Alberta, the legislation gave the wife a life interest in her husband's homestead on his death irrespective of his will.[210] (See Map 1.7.)

Life was not, however, always favourable to women in this region. Using the Supreme Court reports, and the archives of the attorney general, Allison Rankin has examined the history of divorce on the Prairies, 1905-30.[211] Young wives were expected "to haul a double load." Not receiving equal rights to guardianship, child custody, or alimony, they could obtain divorce only by an act of the dominion Parliament. Rankin explains how, in *Board v. Board* (1918), the celebrated judgment of the Supreme Court of Alberta that Britain's *Matrimonial Causes Act* of 1857 was received in the Territories as part of the law of England as of 1870 was not as pivotal as historians have claimed. While the court was the first one in Canada to allow divorce petitions to succeed, the result brought only partial relief for aggrieved women. Early cases were petitions brought by husbands, with most petitions by wives uncontested. The court's narrow definition of domicile that precluded applications from women whose husbands left them for other jurisdictions, and grounds for mental cruelty, were still restrictive and upheld by the Judicial Committee in Westminster Hall.

The pivotal, but limited, changes concerning the law of divorce and family relations in Alberta spilled over into Saskatchewan in the early twentieth century. The influences behind this change were not far from the Prairie provinces. The courts in Great Plains states such as Montana in the 1880s and 1890s allowed wives to petition for divorce based on mental cruelty and wilful neglect, and juries awarded dissolution. In the "single incident ruling," the Supreme Court held that a single slap, verbal abuse, or a threat was a ground for divorce.[212] Husbands were held to higher standards of moral behaviour in their matrimonial unions, a condition that led to the "companionate marriage" originating in California in the late nineteenth century. Whether middle or working class, judges and juries granted divorce at a high rate, reaching 70-80 percent in this era.[213] They accepted the principle of divorce where women became victims of selfish and tyrannical men in their failed personal and family relationships.[214] These developments led to a new sense of womanhood south of the border that was not without influence in the Prairie provinces. Women read these stories in newspapers and magazines and heard of them in their travels. Divorce petitions forced men to conduct themselves with higher moral standards. Judges, in raising the bar for the behaviour of husbands, were creating a new form of protection for the family called "judicial patriarchy."[215]

Gradually, these ideas and the precedents that developed from them brought change to family law on the Prairies through justices such as Stuart who were open to legal precedents from Maritime provinces and Great Plains states where divorce was attainable. Change, however, came slowly since judges were suspicious of a movement that struck at the foundation of private rights. Plains courts began to see parents as mere agents of the state to rear their children, creating a situation that undermined parental rights and empowered the state to legislate in areas of family and child welfare.[216] The situation also led to a form of consensual divorce in the late nineteenth century.[217] Alberta and Saskatchewan judges, however, did not go so far as to accept changes in family and private law areas where traditional and customary values were seen as essential to a stable society.

While the law was not favourable to women in the early twentieth century, neither was it favourable to groups who had been excluded from society because of nontraditional behaviour and beliefs. The Sons of Freedom were Doukhobors who refused to send their children to public schools, responding to a 1927 movement to require all education to be in English. In Yorkton, Saskatchewan, fifty-five Doukhobor adults and children were arrested on vagrancy charges for appearing nude in public. This mode of protest, matched by Sons in British Columbia, resulted in changes to the *Criminal Code* that increased the punishments for this offence. McLaren's essay, an exhaustive search of private and public records, relates the arrests, prosecutions, and convictions of these splinter ethnic groups.

Educational policy had become part of the "test" of the new immigrants of the 1920s and 1930s. The Russian language, in particular, was seen as the language of communism in this age of the "Red Scare" and the Sons of Freedom as Bolsheviks. Saskatchewan had become a centre of ethnic, cultural, and linguistic tension in the Prairies. Manitoba had passed through this phase, and Alberta was not there yet. The Saskatchewan situation was more volatile. A Ku Klux Klan rally at Moose Jaw in 1927 drew 10,000 spectators. Saskatchewan, unlike British Columbia, had no detention centres. Thus, it was ill equipped to deal with nude public protests in the streets. In the end, only arsonists were prosecuted, and few were sentenced. McLaren reveals the extent to which minorities were forced to comply with the law of the state. As in the earlier history of First Nations, common law was not always kind to those who represented minority interests and an alternative culture. But the legal system proved accommodative in absorbing local customs into positive law. Individuals were made examples of, and the big stick was used with discretion. Therefore, from First Peoples to later immigrants, legal pluralism was the glue that bound together a many-tongued, multicultural society.

Epilogue

The frontiers of English common law extended across the Canadian Prairies from the Great Shield to the Rocky Mountains. For the neo-Europeans, "colonists carry with them only so much of the English law as is applicable to their own situation ... What shall be remitted and what rejected, at what times and under what restrictions, must in case of dispute be decided in the first instance by their own provincial judicatures."[218] For the Natives, their law was incorporated into the imperial common law as common custom as they treatied to become part of the Canadian nation-state. Native peoples might retain their First Nations but as subdivisions of a common law state. For those Natives who did not enter into treaties, the law of the state bore only so much force as circumstances allowed. This has meant that much of the Prairies still lacks a law of the land that has reached a middle ground. The sea and remains of rock that were being crushed on the anvil of conflict and assimilation in the eighteenth, nineteenth, and twentieth centuries are still a focus of disputed territory at the dawn of the twenty-first.

These remains, in legal-historical terms, are those of English municipal law – a large, inland sea that still contains the conjunction of pluralistic legal systems. A more complex system than Native customary law, municipal law covered the whole range of customs operative in a common law world, from the unwritten to written positive law. It has become the structure for the study of the law of its mother and other common law countries.[219] Individual jurisdictions established their own rules and procedures, and high courts determined their legitimacy. The customs of local people and their communities were larger than the law practised in their courts, which itself was larger than the precedents that emanated from the highest bench of all. Positive law defined the law of the state, municipal law the practices of its people. When Natives referred to "the queen's promises," they envisioned no more than those with whom they treatied.

All the factors and situations above have been witnessed in the legal history of the Prairies. Its original Native peoples, successive waves of European immigrants, and the migration of neo-Europeans from east to west and from the southeast to the northwest, individually and collectively, have influenced the history of its law. Moreover, external factors are even more important than internal ones in the history of its peoples as well as its laws. As historians of imperial history have discovered, race and the quest for adaptation to modernity were instrumental in the formation of national identity and therefore an integral part of a country's legal culture.[220]

Philip Girard and Jim Phillips, writing in the Osgoode Society's volume on Nova Scotia, noted how different the legal history of the Maritimes was from the legal history of Ontario and Quebec and how different again both regions were from the Canadian west. They noted that two-thirds of the first essay collection on the Canadian west – *Law and Justice in a New Land* – were devoted to Aboriginal rights, natural resources, and law on the frontier.[221] We can now add to these differences new legal regimes for the end of riparian water rights, the privatization of public utilities, the rise of oligarchic and monopolistic forms of business organization, and the creation of pluralistic customary rights. The latter would assimilate Native peoples, Métis, and non-English-speaking immigrants into an Anglo-Canadian society that would look more to the British, the vision of Prince Rupert, and the Great Plains and Rocky Mountain states than to the eastern regions of the country for much of its inspiration and movement to modernity.

There is one area, however, in which the legal history of the Prairies reflects that of the Maritimes and bridges the thesis of David Flaherty with which this essay began: external legal history. The Girard and Phillips statement that a "subtle and complex mixture of English, American, and indigenous influences was at work in shaping and reshaping our legal order from the earliest times" can also be applied to the Prairies.[222] The difference was that the English influence was part of a larger British one that involved Scottish, colonial Australian, and western American influences. The results were shaped by similar concerns that cut across all regional boundaries of the country once the North-West Frontier entered into the mainstream of life in Confederation: a balance between progressive reform and an innate conservatism lodged in the customs and values of the past.

Comparative legal-historical writing was one of the great developments in the past century, especially in colonial legal experiences.[223] It has caught the imagination of scholars of the North American west and urges the necessity for cross-borderlands legal history.[224] For example, a recent study of settlement has observed that the process of immigration was similar on both sides of the Great Plains–Prairies border, from social relationships to the formation of communities.[225] And Donald Pisani's essays on public policy in the western states reveal clearly how their people feared centralized power whether it was federal or corporate, believed in practical local solutions, placed their trust in the marketplace, and respected the law to maintain social order.[226] Thus, a comparative examination of municipal law formation waits for its historian. Topics might include the multicultural discourse of conquest, Native, European, and neo-European cultural conflict, imperial-colonial relations, origins of regional identity, Native-state relations, criminal justice institutions, domestic violence and crimes against women, natural resources law, personal and corporate rights, consumer rights in the growth of a market economy, the rise of litigation in a pluralistic society, and the rule of law among the high priests of the judiciary.

Several common points of reference are prominent. In the Rocky Mountain area of the United States, the influence of the environment was pervasive, whether in mining, water, forestry, labour, or corporate law. There was little discussion of fundamental legal principles or "rights." There was, instead, an unfettered belief in private initiative, a suspicion of human behaviour, and skepticism of politicians and governments.[227] Frontiers were at the crossroads of Native-white relations.[228] Perhaps they were also at the intersection of law and society in the Great Plains and Prairies. Similarities between the legal culture of the Prairies, and that of the Great Plains and Rocky Mountains, are too strong to ignore.[229] They include the rise of corporate monopolies in an agrarian society, the organization of working men and strikes, the movement for women's rights and suffrage, the advent of women into the law profession and the magistracy, a romantic view of nature and the environment, and the ideals of freedom, personal rights, and rugged individualism.[230] In the end, what these essays demonstrate in their totality is that the North-West Frontier was shrouded by multiple frontiers and that the Prairie region had several legacies from Aboriginal, British, Canadian, and American influences that shaped it in a distinctive manner that is still undergoing historical reconstruction.

On New Year's Eve 1949, as Hamar Foster recalls, he travelled across a frozen river to a New Year's party at the Hudson's Bay Company post at Fort Vermilion, Alberta. He was wrapped in a bearskin, and his father wore the traditional buffalo coat that was standard issue for members of the Royal Canadian Mounted Police.[231] The buffalo had long been the symbol of the Prairies, and the "buffalo jump" is still a well-travelled spot on the visitor's itinerary. Foster states that culture is the essence of the law and that legal historians must give it the attention it deserves. By "essence" he means its customs, language, and behaviour. The Proclamation of 1763 embraced many language groups and dialects. Since then there are even more language groups across the country, increasing yearly. The bear and buffalo coats have largely disappeared, and the sheep and cattle that replaced them represent new cultural icons. The RCMP are still as large as life itself. But the law, and the new socioeconomic problems that it is called upon to adjudicate, spring from the ancient customary and positive law that have ruled us from the past.

Acknowledgments

I wish to thank Warren Elofson, Doug Harris, Betty Jamieson, Don Smith, Jewel Spangler, the contributors to this volume, and especially my co-editor Jonathan Swainger for their useful criticisms and suggestions, and my wife, Maggie, for her ever-patient questioning and editing. Some of the themes of this essay were put forward in short papers presented at the annual conferences of the American Society for Legal History in October 1999 and the Canadian Law and Society Association in June 2000. I also wish to thank those participants and the anonymous reviewers of the original manuscript for their additional comments, criticisms, and suggestions, and to acknowledge the resources provided by the British Library (London), the Institute of Advanced Legal Studies (London), the Huntington Library (San Marino), the Glenbow-Alberta Institute (Calgary), the Legal Archives Society of Alberta (Calgary), and the Mackimmie and Law Libraries of the University of Calgary.

Notes

1 David H. Flaherty, "Introduction," *Essays in the History of Canadian Law,* vol. 1, ed. David H. Flaherty (Toronto: Osgoode Society, 1981), 3-42, especially 3-19.

2 Jim Phillips and Philip Girard, eds., "Introduction," in *Essays in the History of Canadian Law,* vol. 3, *Nova Scotia* (Toronto: Osgoode Society, 1990), 7.

3 Keith Windshuttle, *The Killing of History* (New York: Free Press, 1996), 219-21.

4 Hamar Foster and John McLaren, "Hard Choices and Sharp Edges: The Legal History of British Columbia and the Yukon," in *Essays in the History of Canadian Law,* vol. 6, *British Columbia and the Yukon,* ed. Hamar Foster and John McLaren (Toronto: Osgoode Society, 1995), 5.

5 Lawrence Friedman, *A History of American Law* (New York: Simon and Schuster, 1973), 14-15.

6 Louis A. Knafla, "Legal History," in *Encyclopedia of Historians and Historical Writing,* vol. 1, ed. Kelly Boyd (London and Chicago: Fitzroy Dearborn, 1999), 700-1. The influence of the state has been even greater in the historiography of crime: see Louis A. Knafla, "Crime and Deviance," ibid., 259-60. For a more conservative view of legal-historical scholarship in North America, see Mark Tushnett, "Interdisciplinary Legal Scholarship: The Case of History-in-Law," *Chicago-Kent Law Review* 71 (1996): 909-35.

7 An exception has been British Columbia, namely the weighty *British Columbia and the Yukon,* ed. Foster and McLaren.

8 Bruce Braden Peel, comp., *A Bibliography of the Prairie Provinces to 1953,* 2nd ed. (Toronto: University of Toronto Press, 1973); Janice Dickin McGinnis, "Bibliography of the Legal History of Western Canada," in *Law and Justice in a New Land: Essays in Western Canadian Legal History,* ed. Louis A. Knafla (Toronto and Calgary: Carswell, 1986), 333-54.

9 See Jim Phillips, "The History of Canadian Criminal Justice, 1750-1920," in *Criminology: A Reader's Guide,* ed. Jane Gladstone, Richard V. Ericson, and Clifford D. Shearing (Toronto: Centre of Criminology, 1991), 65-124; and Jim Phillips, "Crime and Punishment in the Dominion of the North: Canada from New France to the Present," in *Crime Histories and Histories of Crime,* ed. Clive Emsley and Louis A. Knafla (Westport: Greenwood Press, 1996), 163-200, for additional ideas and work.

10 J.P.S. McLaren, "Meeting the Challenges of Canadian Legal History: The Alberta Contribution," *Alberta Law Review* 32 (1994): 423-35.

11 John R. Wunder, ed., *Law and the Great Plains: Essays on the Legal History of the Heartland* (Westport: Greenwood Press, 1996), 3-8.

12 For example, the equivalent of J. Willard Hurst's *Law and Economic Growth: The Legal History of the Lumber Industry in Wisconsin, 1836-1915* (Cambridge, MA: Harvard University Press, 1964).

13 See, in particular, Richard White, *"It's Your Misfortune and None of My Own": A New History of the American West* (Norman: Oklahoma University Press, 1991).

14 Kermit L. Hall, "The Legal Culture of the Great Plains," in Wunder, *Law and the Great Plains,* 9-28.

15 Ibid., 10.

16 Walter Prescott Webb, *The Great Plains* (Lincoln: University of Nebraska Press, 1931; reprint 1981).

17 Hall, in Wunder, *Law and the Great Plains,* 15-28.

18 Richard White, *The Middle Ground: Indians, Empires, and Republics in the Great Lakes Region, 1650-1815* (Cambridge, UK: Cambridge University Press, 1991).

19 Positive law is written law such as statutes and court decisions.

20 See, especially, Christopher Hill, *Liberty against the Law: Some Seventeenth-Century Controversies* (New York: Penguin, 1997).

21 Over 90 percent in the city of London: Penny Tucker, "London Courts in the Reign of Edward IV," in *Courts, Counties, and the Capital in the Later Middle Ages,* ed. Diana E.S. Dunn (New York, 1996). The role of the central courts declined further from the mid-seventeenth century to the mid-eighteenth century, a thesis of Christopher W. Brooks, *Lawyers, Litigation, and English Society since 1450* (London and Rio Grande: Hambledon Press, 1998).

22 Louis A. Knafla, "Common Law and Custom in Tudor England: or, 'The Best State of a Commonwealth,'" in *Law, Literature, and the Settlement of Regimes,* ed. Gordon J. Schochet (Washington, DC: Folger Institute, 1990), 171-86. The clearest contemporary explanation was made by Sir John Davies, *Le Primer report des cases in les courts del roy* (Dublin: J. Franckton, 1615), signatures iii-v.

23 Coke's view of common law as *jus scriptum* ("written law"), published in his *Reports for Calvin's Case,* was not the majority view as expressed by Chancellor Ellesmere, who published a separate report of the case with a much wider interpretation: Louis A. Knafla, *Law and Politics in Jacobean England: The Tracts of Lord Chancellor Ellesmere* (Cambridge, UK: Cambridge University Press, 1977), 216-24.

24 Richard Burn, *The Justice of the Peace and Parish Officer,* 30th ed., ed. J.B. Maule (London: Hodges, Foster, 1869). For the role of the JP in the legal system of the Canadian North-West, see David Carey, ed., *Carey's Manitoba Reports* (Calgary: Carswell, 1918), i-ix.

25 See, in general, the thoughtful work of Sharon Korman, *The Right of Conquest: The Acquisition of Territory by Force in International Law and Practice* (Oxford: Clarendon Press, 1996).

26 Hugo Grotius, *De Jure Belli ac Pacis* [1625], trans. Francis W. Kelsey (Oxford: Clarendon Press, 1925), book 3, chapter 6.

27 Robert A. Williams, Jr., "The Medieval Discourse of Crusade," in *Native American Law and Colonialism, before 1776 to 1903,* ed. John R. Wunder (New York and London: Garland Publishing, 1996), 77-122. Grotius assumed a world of independent states, a natural society of territorial nations that had the right to conquer nonterritorial ones.

28 See Richard Zouche, *Juris et Judicii Fecialis* (The Hague: Johannis Verhoeve, 1659); and Samuel Pufendorf, *De Jure Naturae et Gentium* [1688], trans. C.H. Oldfather and W.A. Oldfather (Oxford: Clarendon Press, 1934), book 3, chapter 8, section 1.

29 Franciscus de Vitoria, *De Indis et de jure belli relectiones* [1540], trans. J.P. Bate (Washington, DC: Carnegie Institute, 1917), book 1, chapter 9. De Vitoria acknowledged the right of conquest but only if Natives resisted "benign influences."

30 Jean-Jacques Rousseau, *The Social Contract and Discourses* [1762], trans. G.D.H. Cole (London: Dent, 1973 reprint), book 1, chapter 3.

31 Emmerich de Vattel, *The Law of Nations* [1758], trans. Joseph Chitty (Philadelphia: T. and J.W. Johnson, 1863), book 3, chapter 13.

32 See, in general, James Tully, "Aboriginal Property and Western Theory: Recovering a Middle Ground," *Social Philosophy and Policy* 11, 2 (1994): 153-80.

33 Sidney L. Harring, "Crazy Snake and the Creek Struggle for Sovereignty: The Native American Legal Culture and American Law," *American Journal for Legal History* 34, 4 (1990): 365.

34 Ibid., 365-80.

35 Richard Hakluyt, *A Particular Discourse Concerninge the Greate Necessitie and Manifolde Comodyties that Are like to Growe to This Realme of Englande by the Westerne Discoveries Lately Attempted* [1584] (London: Hakluyt Society, 1993), chapters 1, 3-4, 13-15, 20. See also Thomas J. Scanlan, *Colonial Writing and the New World 1583-1671* (New York: Cambridge University Press, 1999).

36 Hakluyt, *Particular Discourse,* chapter 18.

37 *Calvin's Case, 7 Coke's Reports,* 1a at 19b.

38 *Campbell v. Hall, 20 State Trials,* 239 at 264; *Process into Wales* (1668-74), 1 Vaughan 418; and *Campbell v. Hall* (1774), 1 Cowper 209-13.

39 CJ John Vaughan in *Craw v. Ramsey* (1670), Vaughan 274; William Blackstone, *Commentaries on the Laws of England,* vol. 1 (Oxford: Clarendon Press, 1765), 105-7. See, in general,

Thomas G. Barnes, "'As Near as May Be Agreeable to the Laws of This Kingdom': Legal Birthright and Legal Baggage at Chebucto, 1749," in *Law in a Colonial Society: The Nova Scotia Experience,* ed. Peter Waite, Sandra Oxner, and Thomas Barnes (Toronto: Carswell, 1984), 9-14.

40 See Brian Slattery, *Ancestral Lands, Alien Laws: Judicial Perspectives on Aboriginal Title* (Saskatoon: University of Saskatchewan Native Law Centre, 1983), 10-15; Geoffrey Lester, *Inuit Territorial Rights in the Canadian Northwest Territories* (Nunavut: Tungavik Federation of Nunavut, 1984); and Mark Walters, "*Mohegan Indians v. Connecticut* (1705-1773) and the Legal Status of Aboriginal Customary Laws and Government in British North America," *Osgoode Hall Law Journal* 33 (1995): 785-92.

41 *Calvin's Case,* 17v.

42 B. Bridges, "The Extension of English Law to the Aborigines for Offences Committed Inter Se, 1829-1842," *Journal of the Royal Australian Historical Society* 59 (1973): 264.

43 S.D. Lendrum, "The 'Coorong Massacre': Martial Law and the Aborigines at First Settlement," *Adelaide Law Review* 6 (1977): 26.

44 S.L. Harring, "The Killing Time: A History of Aboriginal Resistance in Colonial Australia," *Ottawa Law Review* 26 (1994): 405.

45 British Parliamentary Papers, *Report from the Select Committee on Aborigines (British Settlements),* c. 425, in the *Sessional Papers* (1837).

46 See Jean Woolmington, ed., *Aborigines in Colonial Society* (Melbourne: Cassell Australia, 1973), chapter 7.

47 *Mabo v. Queensland [No. 2]* (1992), 107 *Australia Law Reports* 1 at 42-44, 62-68, 144-48.

48 Quoted in Desmond Sweeney, "Australia's Forgotten Legal Pluralism: The Western Australian Experience under Governor Hutt," paper presented at the Australian and New Zealand Law and History Society Annual Conference, Melbourne, 4 July 1998. I wish to thank Dr. Sweeney for a copy of his paper.

49 Michael J. Braddick, *State Formation in Early Modern England c. 1550-1700* (Cambridge, UK: Cambridge University Press, 2000), 177-78, 379-80, 397-410.

50 Francis Jennings, *The Invasion of America: Indians, Colonialism, and the Cant of Conquest* (Chapel Hill: University of North Carolina Press, 1975), 3-14.

51 Ibid., 15-31.

52 See Karen Ordahl Kupperman, *Indians and English: Facing Off in Early America* (Ithaca: Cornell University Press, 2000); and Sherry L. Smith, *Reimagining Indians: Native Americans through Anglo Eyes, 1880-1940* (New York: Oxford University Press, 2000).

53 White, *The Middle Ground,* 518-23.

54 Francis Jennings, *The Founders of America* (New York: W.W. Norton, 1993), 318-19. I wish to thank Tony Hall for this reference and for his discussions on this subject. The first part of his major work has just been published: Anthony J. Hall, *American Empire and the Fourth World: The Bowl with One Spoon, Part One* (Montreal: McGill-Queen's University Press, 2003).

55 The text of this important document is in Ian A.L. Getty and Antoine S. Lussier, *As Long as the Sun Shines and the Waters Flow: A Reader on Canadian Native Studies* (Vancouver: UBC Press, 1983), 29-37.

56 Hilda Neatby, *The Quebec Act: Protest and Policy* (Scarborough: Prentice-Hall, 1973).

57 Dorothy V. Jones, *License for Empire: Colonialism by Treaty in Early America* (Chicago: University of Chicago Press, 1982), 58-91.

58 See, in general, Edward Countryman, "Indians, the Colonial Order, and the Social Significance of the American Revolution," *William and Mary Quarterly* 53 (1996): 342-62.

59 Peter Onuf, *Statehood and Union: A History of the Northwest Ordinance* (Bloomington: Indiana University Press, 1987), 58-66.

60 Alec R. Gilpin, *The War of 1812 in the Old Northwest* (Toronto: Ryerson Press, 1958).

61 Sarah Carter, *Lost Harvests: Prairie Indian Reserve Farmers and Government Policy* (Montreal: McGill-Queen's University Press, 1990).

62 Joyce Appleby, *Capitalism and a New Social Order: The Republican Vision of the 1790s* (New York: New York University Press, 1984).

63 *Strader et al. v. Graham,* 10 *Howard* 82 (1850), the judgment by Roger Taney (CJ).

64 Onuf, *Statehood and Union,* chapter 7 and 133-45.
65 The debates are quoted in Hilda Neatby, *Quebec: The Revolutionary Age, 1760-1791* (Toronto: McClelland and Stewart, 1966), 141.
66 *Report of the Select Committee of the House of Commons on Native Inhabitants of British Settlements* (London: n.p., 1837).
67 The documents are translated in M.F. Lindley, *The Acquisition and Government of Backward Territory in International Law: A Treatise on the Law and Practice Relating to Colonial Expansion* (London: Longmans, Green, 1926).
68 Namely, Hegel and Mill, who considered "despotism" a lawful means to deal with them, thus legitimating the violence of imperialism.
69 *Johnson and Graham's Lessee v. McIntosh* (1832), 21 U.S. [8 *Wheaton*] 543.
70 See Vine Deloria Jr., and Clifford M. Lytle, "American Indians in Historical Perspective," in Wunder, *Native American Law,* 128-30.
71 Joseph C. Burke, "The Cherokee Cases: A Study in Law, Politics, and Morality," in Wunder, *Native American Law,* 136-67; R. Kent Newmyer, *John Marshall and the Heroic Age of the Supreme Court* (Baton Rouge: Louisiana State University Press, 2001).
72 See Francis Parkman, *The California and Oregon Trail: Being Sketches of Prairie and Rocky Mountain Life* (New York: Putnam, 1849), ed. Charles H.J. Douglas (New York: Macmillan, 1910). See, more generally, Michael Howard, *The Lessons of History* (Oxford: Clarendon Press, 1991).
73 Wunder, *Native American Law,* preface.
74 Grace Lee Nute, *Caesars of the Wilderness: Médard Chouart, Sieur des Groseilliers, and Pierre Esprit Radisson, 1618-1710* (New York and London: D. Appleton-Century, 1943), 105-24.
75 Andrew Graham, *Andrew Graham's Observations on Hudson's Bay, 1769-1791,* ed. G. Williams and R. Glover (London: Hudson's Bay Record Society, 1969), 204.
76 The details from Captain Gillam's journal were published in *The English Pilot: The Fourth Book* (London: William Fisher, 1689).
77 Nute, *Caesars of the Wilderness,* 39-57, 286-351.
78 A copy of the original charter is in *The Canadian North-West: Its Early Development and Legislative Records,* vol. 1, ed. E.H. Oliver (Ottawa: Government Printing Bureau, 1915), 135-53.
79 *Connolly v. Woolrich* (1867), *Lower Canada Jurist* 11 (1866), 197-265, by Monk J.; and the appeal in *La Revue légale* (1869), 253-400. These reports contain a mine of valuable historical documentary evidence.
80 *R. v. Nan-E-Quis-A-Ka* (1889), 1 T.L.R. 211 (C.A.), by Wetmore J.
81 See Ronald Hyam, *Empire and Sexuality: The British Experience* (Manchester: Manchester University Press, 1990); and Anne McClintock, *Imperial Leather: Race, Gender, and Sexuality in the Colonial Context* (New York: Routledge, 1995). For the working relationships of Native women and fur traders, see the recent study of Bruce M. White, "The Woman Who Married a Beaver: Trade Patterns and Gender Roles in the Ojibwa Fur Trade," *Ethnohistory* 46 (1999): 109-57.
82 Nute, *Caesars of the Wilderness,* 287. For the successful adaptation of Native peoples to the fur trade, see Hugh Brody, *The Other Side of Eden: Hunters, Farmers, and the Shaping of the World* (New York: North Point Press, 2001).
83 Paul C. Thistle, *Indian-European Trade Relations in the Lower Saskatchewan River Region to 1840* (Winnipeg: University of Manitoba Press, 1986), chapter 2.
84 Ibid., chapters 3-4. For the problem of Native dependency in this period when profits were not forthcoming, see *Prophecy of the Swan: The Upper Peace River Fur Trade of 1794-1823,* ed. David V. Burley and J. Scott Hamilton (Vancouver: UBC Press, 1996), 126-36.
85 Martin Daunton and Rock Halperin, "British Identities, Indigenous Peoples, and the Empire," in *Empire and Others: British Encounters with Indigenous Peoples, 1600-1850,* ed. Martin Daunton and Rock Halperin (London: UCL Press, 1999), 1-18.
86 The thesis of Sidney L. Harring, *White Man's Law: Native People in Nineteenth-Century Canadian Jurisprudence* (Toronto: Osgoode Society, 1998). See, however, the massive study of Edward Lazarus, *Black Hills, White Justice: The Sioux Nation versus the United States, 1775 to the Present* (New York: Harper Collins, 1991).

87 43 George 3 (1803), c. 138.

88 J.M. Bumsted, *Fur Trade Wars: The Founding of Western Canada* (Winnipeg: Great Plains Publications, 1999), 198. This is the most recent account of the conflict (75-154) and the trials (195-216).

89 Alexander Greenfield, *A Narrative of Transactions in the Red River Country* (London: B. McMillan, 1819), the quotes at xiii, xi. These were trial notes from the law reports published after NWC men were acquitted of murders and robberies accused by Lord Selkirk.

90 Hamar Foster, "Long-Distance Justice: The Criminal Jurisdiction of Canadian Courts West of the Canadas, 1763-1895," *American Journal of Legal History* 34 (1990): 5. For trials under the statutes, see Hamar Foster, "Conflict Resolution during the Fur Trade in the Canadian North West, 1803-1859," *Advocate* 51, 6 (1993): 872-74.

91 Robert Baker, "Transplanting the Law to Rupert's Land 1835-51: Reassessing Canadian Frontier Legal History," *Law and History Review* 17, 2 (1999): 204-46.

92 See, in general, Louis A. Knafla, "From Oral to Written Memory: The Common Law Tradition in Western Canada," in *Law and Justice in a New Land: Essays in Western Canadian Legal History,* ed. Louis A. Knafla (Calgary and Toronto: Carswell, 1986), 31-77.

93 *Connolly v. Woolrich* (1867), 17 R.J.R.Q. 75; and *Johnstone v. Connolly* (1869), 17 R.J.R.Q. 266.

94 For North America, see Bruce Clark, *Native Liberty, Crown Sovereignty: The Existing Aboriginal Right of Self-Government in Canada* (Montreal and Kingston: McGill-Queen's University Press, 1990). For contemporaries, see G. Chalmers, ed., *Opinions of Eminent Lawyers, on Various Points of English Jurisprudence, Chiefly concerning the Colonies, Fisheries, and Commerce of Great Britain,* vol. 1 (London: C. Goodrich, 1814).

95 *Case of Tanistry* (1608), *Davies Irish Reports,* Davis 28-30.

96 For the cases, see Mark D. Walters, "The 'Golden Thread' of Continuity: Aboriginal Customs at Common Law and under Section 35(1) of the *Constitution Act, 1982.*" I wish to thank Dr. Walters for a draft copy of his essay.

97 *Calvin's Case* (1608), 7 *Coke's Reports,* 17v.

98 Hugo Grotius, *De Jure Belli ac Pacis* (1625), book 3, chapter 8, parts 1 and 4.

99 Sir James Marriott, *Plan of a Code of Laws for the Province of Quebec* (London: n.p., 1774), 12.

100 *Johnstone v. Connolly* (1869), 17 R.J.R.Q. 276-78.

101 Mathew Hale, *The History of the Common Law,* 4th ed. (London: T. Cadel, 1779), 77, 95.

102 *Buckley v. Rice Thomas,* 1 Plowden 118 (KB) at 126; *Dawes v. Painter* (1674), 1 Freem 175-76; and *Connolly v. Woolrich* (1867), 17 R.J.R.Q. 138.

103 See John Foster, "Paulet Paul: Métis or 'House Indian' Folk Hero?" *Manitoba History* 9 (1985): 2-8.

104 John Phillip Reid, "The Layers of Western Legal History," in *Law for the Elephant, Law for the Beaver: Essays in the Legal History of the North American West,* ed. John McLaren, Hamar Foster, and Chet Orloff (Regina: Canadian Plains Research Center, 1992), 45-55.

105 See Shelagh D. Grant, *Arctic Justice* (Montreal and Kingston: McGill-Queen's University Press, 2002).

106 As in *Connolly v. Woolrich* (1867), 17 R.J.R.Q. 75; and *Johnstone v. Connolly* (1869), 17 R.J.R.Q. 266.

107 *Connolly v. Woolrich* (1867), 96 and 138.

108 Alan Trachtenberg, *The Incorporation of America: Culture and Society in the Gilded Age* (New York: Hill and Wang, 1982); and the thesis of Walters, "The 'Golden Thread' of Continuity."

109 Slattery, *Ancestral Lands,* 10-15.

110 See, in general, Patrick Wormald, *The Making of English Law: King Alfred to the Twelfth Century,* vol. 1, *Legislation and Its Limits* (London: Blackwell Publishers, 1999), 93-101. For the wider European context, see the imposing collection on *Folk Law: Essays in the Theory and Practice of Lex Non Scripta,* ed. Alison Dundes and Alan Dundes (Madison: University of Wisconsin Press, 1995).

111 Sir Edward Coke, *The Fourth Part of the Institutes of the Laws of England: Concerning the Jurisdiction of Courts* (London: A. Crooke, 1669), 222-89 passim.

112 William Lambarde, *Sive de priscis Anglorum legibus libri* (London: John Day, 1568); and the revised edition by Abraham Whelock (Canterbury: Roger Daniel, 1644).

113 William Lambarde, *Archion: Or a Commentary upon the High Courts of Justice in England* (London: D. Frere, 1635); *The Edition from the Manuscripts,* ed. Charles H. McIlwain and Paul Ward (Cambridge, MA: Harvard University Press, 1957), 1-31; and William Lambarde, *Perambulation of Kent: Conteining the Description, Hystorie, and Customes of that Shyre* (London: R. Newberie, 1576; reprint Bath: Adams and Dart, 1970), passim. For a modern attempt to do this for the history of tribal customs in Kent from Æthelberht to Henry II, see Hiroshi Hayashi, *Essays in Anglo-Saxon Law and History II* (Tokyo: privately printed, 1994), 147-214.
114 Davies, *Le Primer report,* signatures iii-v.
115 See Louis A. Knafla, "Common Law and Custom in Tudor England: Or, 'The Best State of a Commonwealth,'" in *Law, Literature, and the Settlement of Regimes,* ed. Gordon J. Schochet (Washington, DC: Folger Institute, 1990), 171-86.
116 Glyndwr Williams, "Highlights of the First 200 Years of the Hudson's Bay Company," *The Beaver* supplement (1970): 70.
117 Zachariah Chaffee Jr., in the introduction to Julian Goebel, *Law Enforcement in Colonial New York: A Study in Criminal Procedure* ([1944]; Montclair, NJ: Patterson Smith, reprint 1970), xxii.
118 Andrew R.L. Cayton, "Radicals in the 'Western World': The Federalist Conquest of Trans-Appalachian North America," in *Federalists Reconsidered,* ed. Doron Ben-Atar and Barbara B. Oberg (Charlottesville: University of Virginia Press, 1998), 78.
119 Knafla, *Law and Justice in a New Land,* 53-54, 64, 73.
120 Zachariah Chaffee Jr., "Colonial Courts and the Common Law," in *Essays in the History of Early American Law,* ed. David Flaherty (Chapel Hill: University of North Carolina Press, 1969), 69.
121 See also Barnes, "Legal Birthright and Legal Baggage," 1-23. Jim Phillips and Philip Girard write in their *Essays in the History of Canadian Law: Nova Scotia* that such legal traditions may well account for "the high degree of local particularism that obtained in the legal affairs of the various provinces" (6). This is also the thesis of Andrew Cayton in "Radicals in the 'Western World'" for the early American colonists who moved west (78).
122 Harring, *White Man's Law,* passim.
123 The thesis of Kent McNeil, *Common Law Aboriginal* (Oxford: Clarendon Press, 1989), especially chapter 7.
124 See, in general, Gerald Friesen, *The Canadian Prairies: A History* (Toronto and London: University of Toronto Press, 1984), 3-9.
125 Chester Martin, ed., *Dominion Lands Policy* (Toronto: McClelland and Stewart, 1973), the major study of this vast subject. See, more recently, *Terra Pacifica: People and Place in the Northwest States and Western Canada,* ed. Paul W. Hirt (Pullman: Washington State University Press, 1998); and Randy William Widdis, *With Scarcely a Ripple: Anglo-Canadian Migration and the United States and Western Canada, 1880-1920* (Montreal and Kingston: McGill-Queen's University Press, 1998).
126 Martin, *Dominion Lands Policy,* 38-87, for the statistics above.
127 Kirk N. Lambrecht, *The Administration of Dominion Lands, 1870-1930* (Regina: Canadian Plains Research Center, 1991), 22.
128 (Canada 1875), 38 Victoria, c. 39.
129 (Canada 1877), 40 Victoria, c. 7, s. 3.
130 *Territorial Law Reports* (1886), xix.
131 *Homestead Exemption Act* (Canada 1878), 41 Victoria, c. 15; *Dominion Lands Act* (Canada 1879), 42 Victoria, c. 31.
132 49 Victoria, c. 26; R.S.C. (1886), c. 50.
133 Herbert C. Jones, *The "Torrens System" of Transfer of Land* (Toronto: Carswell, 1886).
134 Sandra Petersson, "Something for Nothing: The Law of Adverse Possession in Alberta," *Alberta Law Review* 30, 4 (1992): 1291-1323; and Bruce H. Ziff, "Matter of Overriding Interest: Unregistered Easements under Alberta's Land Titles System," *Alberta Law Review* 29, 3 (1991): 718-23, where the quoted phrase has been coined.
135 Lambrecht, *Administration of Dominion Lands,* 13.
136 For the larger context, see Geoffrey Jones, *Merchants to Multinationals: British Trading Companies in the Nineteenth and Twentieth Centuries* (Oxford: Oxford University Press, 2000).

137 The thesis of Gregory P. Marchildon, *Profits and Politics: Beaverbrook and the Gilded Age of Canadian Finance* (Toronto: University of Toronto Press, 1996).

138 Louis A. Knafla, "Richard 'Bonfire' Bennett: The Legal Practice of a Prairie Corporate Lawyer, 1898 to 1913," in *Beyond the Law: Lawyers and Business in Canada 1830 to 1930,* ed. Carol Wilton (Toronto: Osgoode Society, 1990), 320-76.

139 Friesen, *Canadian Prairies,* 242-47.

140 Martin, *Dominion Lands Policy,* 172-90, 226-30.

141 Lambrecht, *Administration of Dominion Lands,* 3-69; the interpretation is my own.

142 Martin, *Dominion Lands Policy,* 147-50, 190-202. For context, see Christopher McGrory Klyza, *Who Controls Public Lands? Mining, Forestry, and Grazing Policies, 1870-1990* (Chapel Hill: University of North Carolina Press, 1996).

143 The thesis of Klyza, *Who Controls Public Lands?*

144 The thesis of Werner Troesken, *Why Regulate Utilities? The New Institutional Economics and the Chicago Gas Industry, 1849-1924* (Ann Arbor: University of Michigan Press, 1996).

145 Norris Hundley Jr., "The Dark and Bloody Ground of Indian Water Rights: Confusion Elevated to Principle," *Western Historical Quarterly* 9 (1978): 454-82.

146 Donald Worster, *Rivers of Empire: Water, Aridity, and the Growth of the American West* (New York: Pantheon, 1985), placed water as a leading issue in the growth of the American west.

147 John D. Leshy, "The Prior Appropriation Doctrine of Water Law in the West: An Emperor with Few Clothes," *Journal of the West* 3, 29 (1990): 5-13.

148 *North-West Irrigation Act* (1894), S.C., c. 30: the discussion in Tristan M. Goodman, "Assessing the Economic, Legal, and Environmental Factors Affecting Canadian Bulk Water Exports" (PhD dissertation, University of Calgary, 2002), 66-71. For the Australian context, see J.M. Powell, *Watering the Western Third: Water, Land, and Community in Western Australia, 1826-1998* (Melbourne: Oxford University Press, 1998). For the western United States, see Robert G. Dunbar, *Forging New Rights in Western Waters* (Lincoln: University of Nebraska Press, 1983).

149 Frank Quinn, "As Long as the Rivers Run: The Impacts of Corporate Water Development on Native Communities in Canada," *Canadian Journal of Native Studies* 11, 1 (1991): 138-54.

150 James Waldram, *As Long as the Rivers Run: Hydroelectric Development and Native Communities in Western Canada* (Winnipeg: University of Manitoba Press, 1988), 171-72.

151 For the business processes that utility companies developed, see Charles David Jacobson, *Ties That Bind: Economic and Political Dilemmas of Urban Utility Networks, 1800-1990* (Pittsburgh: University of Pittsburgh Press, 2000).

152 Troesken, *Why Regulate Utilities?*

153 R.C. Macleod, "Law and Order on the Western Canadian Frontier," in *Law for the Elephant,* ed. McLaren, Foster, and Orloff, 90-105.

154 Warren M. Elofson, *Cowboys, Gentlemen, and Cattle Thieves: Ranching on the Western Frontier, 1874-1914* (Montreal and Kingston: McGill-Queen's University Press, 2000). I wish to thank Dr. Elofson for a discussion of the ideas, and the cross-border culture of theft, in his most recent study *Frontier Cattle Ranching in the Land and Times of Charlie Russell* (Montreal and Kingston: McGill-Queen's University Press, 2004).

155 Louis A. Knafla, "Violence on the Western Canadian Frontier: A Historical Perspective," in *Violence in Canada: Sociopolitical Perspectives,* ed. Jeffrey Ian Ross (Don Mills: Oxford University Press, 1995; 2nd ed. Somerset, NJ: Transaction Publishers, 2004), 10-39.

156 J.W. McClung, *Law West of the Bay* (Calgary: Legal Archives Society of Alberta, 1998), 90-95, and the discussion at 101-71.

157 William Francis Butler, *The Great Lone Land* (London: Low, Marston, Low and Searle, 1873; reprint 1968), the report at 355-86.

158 Robert Waite, "Violent Crime on the Western Frontier: The Experience of the Idaho Territory, 1863-1890," in *Violent Crime in North America,* ed. Louis A. Knafla (Westport: Praeger, 2003), 53-74; Jonathan Swainger, "Creating the Peace: Crimes and Community Identity in Northeastern British Columbia, 1930-1950," in *Violent Crime in North America,* 131-54; and Warren Elofson, "Law and Disorder on the Ranching Frontier of Montana and Alberta/Assiniboia, 1870-1914," *Journal of the West* 42, 1 (2003): 40-52.

159 Lesley Erickson, "Murdered Women and Mythic Villains: The Criminal Case and the Imaginary Criminal in the Canadian West, 1886-1930," in *People and Place: Historical Influences on Legal Culture,* ed. Jonathan Swainger and Constance Backhouse (Vancouver: UBC Press, 2003), 95-119.

160 Robin Fisher, "Indian Warfare and Two Frontiers: A Comparison of British Columbia and Washington Territory during the Early Years of Settlement," *Pacific Historical Review* 50, 1 (1981): 31-51.

161 Wilbur F. Bowker, *A Consolidation of Fifty Years of Legal Writings, 1938-1988,* ed. Marjorie Bowker (Edmonton: University of Alberta Press, 1989), 448-59, 691-734, the quotation at 448.

162 R.C. Macleod, "Law and Order on the Western Canadian Frontier," in *Law for the Elephant,* ed. McLaren, Foster, and Orloff, 90-105.

163 Knafla, "Violence on the Western Canadian Frontier."

164 John Phillip Reid, *Policing the Elephant: Crime, Punishment, and Social Behavior on the Overland Trail* (San Marino: Huntington Library, 1997), 1. Reid does not hold that violence has been as endemic as previous writers have postulated.

165 Richard Maxwell Brown, "Law and Order on the American Frontier: The Western Civil War of Incorporation," in *Law for the Elephant,* ed. McLaren, Foster, and Orloff, 74-89.

166 Bob Beal and Rod Macleod, *Prairie Fire: The 1885 Northwest Rebellion* (Edmonton: Hurtig, 1984).

167 D'Arcy Jenish, *Indian Fall: The Last Great Days of the Plains Cree and the Blackfoot Confederacy* (Harmondsworth: Penguin, 1999).

168 Jonathan Swainger, *The Canadian Department of Justice and the Completion of Confederation, 1867-78* (Vancouver: UBC Press, 2000), 53-55.

169 R.C. Macleod, *The North-West Mounted Police and Law Enforcement, 1873-1905* (Toronto: University of Toronto Press, 1976), remains the classic study.

170 William R. Morrison, *Showing the Flag: The Mounted Police and Canadian Sovereignty in the North 1894-1925* (Vancouver: UBC Press, 1985).

171 Greg Marquis, "Towards a Canadian Police Historiography," in *Law, Society, and the State,* ed. Louis A. Knafla and Susan W.S. Binnie (Toronto: Law Society of Upper Canada, 1995), 477-95.

172 Most ably, Beal and Macleod, *Prairie Fire.*

173 Harring, *White Man's Law,* 239-50, where problems of translation and misunderstanding plagued the evidence presented in the North-West Rebellion trials of 1885.

174 For the background of this problem, see *The Language Encounter in the Americas, 1492-1800,* ed. Edward C. Gray and Norman Fiering (New York: Berghahn Books, 2000).

175 Thomas Thorner and Neil B. Watson, "Patterns of Prairie Crime: Calgary, 1875-1939," in *Crime and Justice in Europe and Canada,* ed. Louis Knafla (Waterloo: Wilfrid Laurier University Press, 1985), 219-55, the tables at 248-53. For the larger context, see David Bright, *The Limits of Labour: Class Formation and the Labour Movement in Calgary, 1883-1929* (Vancouver: UBC Press, 1998).

176 Provincial Archives of Alberta, Fonds 79.126.

177 David Bright, "Sexual Assaults in Calgary, Alberta, between the Wars," in *Violent Crime in North America,* ed. Knafla, 105-30. Similar conclusions on the role of gender, race, and ethnicity have been documented for Saskatchewan across the twentieth century. See Louis A. Knafla, "Law and Justice," in *The Encyclopedia of Saskatchewan* (Regina: Canadian Plains Research Centre, 2005).

178 Marc G. Stevenson, *Inuit, Whalers, and Cultural Persistence* (Don Mills: Oxford University Press, 1997), 100-1, 130-31, 288-97.

179 Richard A. Willie, *"These Legal Gentlemen": Lawyers in Manitoba: 1839-1900* (Winnipeg: Legal Research Institute, 1994), 284-87.

180 McClung, *Law West of the Bay,* 189-228.

181 Knafla, "Richard 'Bonfire' Bennett," 353-54.

182 Henry C. Klassen, "Lawyers, Finance, and Economic Development in Southwestern Alberta, 1884 to 1920," in *Beyond the Law,* ed. Wilton, 298-319.

183 Louis A. Knafla, "Goodall and Cairns: Commercial, Corporate, and Energy Law in Alberta, 1920-1942," in *Inside the Law: Canadian Law Firms in Historical Perspective,* ed. Carol Wilton (Toronto: Osgoode Society, 1996), 320-56.

184 The results from my statistical study (unpublished) of lawyers admitted to the North-West Territories and their successor provinces.
185 C.C. McCaul, "Precursors of the Bench and Bar in the Western Provinces," *Canadian Bar Review Annual* 3, 1 (1925): 25-40.
186 Wilton, *Inside the Law,* 11-17.
187 Willie, *"These Legal Gentlemen,"* 248-49.
188 Richard A. Willie, "'It Is Every Man for Himself': Winnipeg Lawyers and the Law Business, 1870 to 1903," in *Beyond the Law,* ed. Wilton, 263-97 at 285.
189 Jonathan S. Swainger, "Ideology, Social Capital, and Entrepreneurship," in *Beyond the Law,* ed. Wilton, 377-402.
190 Klassen, "Lawyers, Finance, and Economic Development," 298-319.
191 Knafla, "Goodall and Cairns."
192 A theme of W.H. McConnell, *Prairie Justice* (Calgary: Burroughs, 1980).
193 Louis A. Knafla and Richard Klumpenhouwer, *Lords of the Western Bench: A Biographical History of the Judges of Alberta* (Calgary: Legal Archives Society of Alberta, 1997), 189-90.
194 McConnell, *Prairie Justice,* 16-20, quotation at 19.
195 Louis A. Knafla, "Charles Pringle Conybeare," *Dictionary of Canadian Biography,* vol. 15, *1921-1930* (Toronto: University of Toronto Press, 2005 forthcoming). For their wider colonial context, see Wes Pue, "Planting Legal Culture in Colonial Soil: Legal Professionalism in the Lands of the Beaver and Kangaroo," in *Shaping Nations: Constitutionalism and Society in Australia and Canada,* ed. Linda Cardinal and David Headon (Ottawa: University of Ottawa Press, 2002), 91-115.
196 *R. v. Trainor* [1917], 1 W.W.R. 415.
197 *Schenck v. United States* [1919], 249 US 47.
198 Jonathan Swainger, "Wagging Tongues and Empty Heads: Seditious Utterances and the Patriotism of Wartime in Central Alberta, 1914-1918," in *Law, Society, and the State,* ed. Knafla and Binnie, 263-89.
199 Azimsa Suleman, *"In the Name of Justice": Portrait of a "Cowboy" Judge* (Calgary: Legal Archives Society of Alberta, 1998).
200 J.E. Cote, "The Reception of English Law," *Alberta Law Review* 15 (1977): 29-92.
201 For example, the discussion of medieval statutes by Dubuc J. in *Re Tait* (1890), 9 M.L.R. 617.
202 Knafla and Klumpenhouwer, *Lords of the Western Bench.*
203 Willie, *"These Legal Gentlemen,"* 281-83.
204 Reid, *Law for the Elephant: Property and Social Behavior on the Overland Trial* (San Marino: Huntington Library, 1997), 3-11.
205 *Territories Real Property Act* (1886), R.S.C. 1886, chap. 51, ss. 16-17.
206 William C. Niblack, *The Torrens System* (Chicago: Callaghan, 1903); Blair C. Shick and Irving H. Plotkin, *Torrens in the United States* (Lexington: University of Kentucky Press, 1978), a legal and economic history.
207 Bowker, *Fifty Years of Legal Writings,* 196-98. For his discussion of the *Homestead Acts,* see 595-615.
208 *Proceedings of the Canadian Bar Association* (1920), 358, through (1925), 364.
209 *Re McLeod* [1929], 2 W.W.R. 252, Harvey C.J.
210 Bowker, *Legal Writings,* 248-59, 203-4, 207-8, respectively.
211 Allison Rankin, "Rescinding the Vow: Divorce in Alberta and Prairie Canada, 1905-1930" (master's thesis, University of Calgary, 1998).
212 Paula Petrik, "If She Be Content: The Development of Montana Divorce Laws, 1865-1907," *Western Historical Quarterly* 18, 3 (1987): 261-91, quotation at 282.
213 Robert L. Griswold, *Family and Divorce in California, 1850-1890: Victorian Illusions and Everyday Realities* (Albany: State University of New York Press, 1982), 3-16, 170-72.
214 Norma Basch, *Framing American Divorce: From the Revolutionary Generation to the Victorians* (Berkeley: University of California Press, 1999).
215 Richard Grossberg, *Governing the Hearth: Law and the Family in Nineteenth-Century America* (Chapel Hill: University of North Carolina Press, 1985), 289-307.
216 Griswold, *Family and Divorce,* 175-79.

217 Lawrence Friedman, "Rights of Passage: Divorce Law in Historical Perspective," *Oregon Law Review* 63 (1984): 649-69.

218 Blackstone, *Commentaries,* vol. 1, 104-5, 120.

219 Knafla, "From Oral to Written Memory," 61-64.

220 Martin Daunton and Rick Halpern, eds., *Empire and Others: British Encounters with Indigenous Peoples, 1600-1850* (Philadelphia: University of Pennsylvania Press, 1999).

221 Girard and Phillips, *Essays in Canadian Legal History: Nova Scotia,* 5.

222 Ibid. at 7.

223 Knafla and Binnie, "Beyond the State," 13-18. For a recent example, see "Forum: Constitutions on Edge: Empire, State, and Legal Culture in Eighteenth-Century New York," *Law and History Review* 16, 2 (1998): 257-401.

224 John Phillip Reid, "Some Lessons of Western Legal History," *Western Legal History* 1 (1988): 3-21. For the concept of a moving borderland, see Lawrence M. Friedman, "The Law between the States: Some Thoughts on Southern Legal History," in *Ambivalent Legacy: A Legal History of the South,* ed. David J. Bodenhamer and James W. Ely Jr. (Jackson: University Press of Mississippi, 1984), 30.

225 John William Bennett and Seena B. Kohl, *Settling the Canadian-American West, 1890-1915* (Lincoln: University of Nebraska Press, 1995).

226 Donald J. Pisani, *Water, Land, and Law in the West: The Limits of Public Policy, 1850-1920* (Lawrence: University Press of Kansas, 1996).

227 Gordon Morris Bakken, *Rocky Mountain Constitution Making, 1850-1912* (Westport: Greenwood Press, 1987), 101-3.

228 Sidney L. Harring, *Crow Dog's Case: American Indian Sovereignty, Tribal Law, and United States Law in the Nineteenth Century* (Cambridge, UK: Cambridge University Press, 1994), where he argues that we should ignore the border as the Natives did themselves, whether the Six Nations of the Northeast or the Copper Inuit of the Arctic.

229 The distinctiveness of the region is amply demonstrated in *North America: The Historical Geography of a Changing Continent,* 2nd ed., ed. Thomas F. McIlwraith and Edward K. Muller (Lanham, MD: Rowman and Littlefield, 2001).

230 See Duane A. Smith, *Rocky Mountain West: Colorado, Wyoming, and Montana, 1859-1915* (Albuquerque: University of New Mexico Press, 1992); and Carlos A. Schwantes, *The Pacific Northwest: An Interpretive History* (Lincoln: University of Nebraska Press, 1989).

231 Foster, in the introduction of his keynote address given at the Glenbow-Alberta Institute for the conference on which this collection is based.

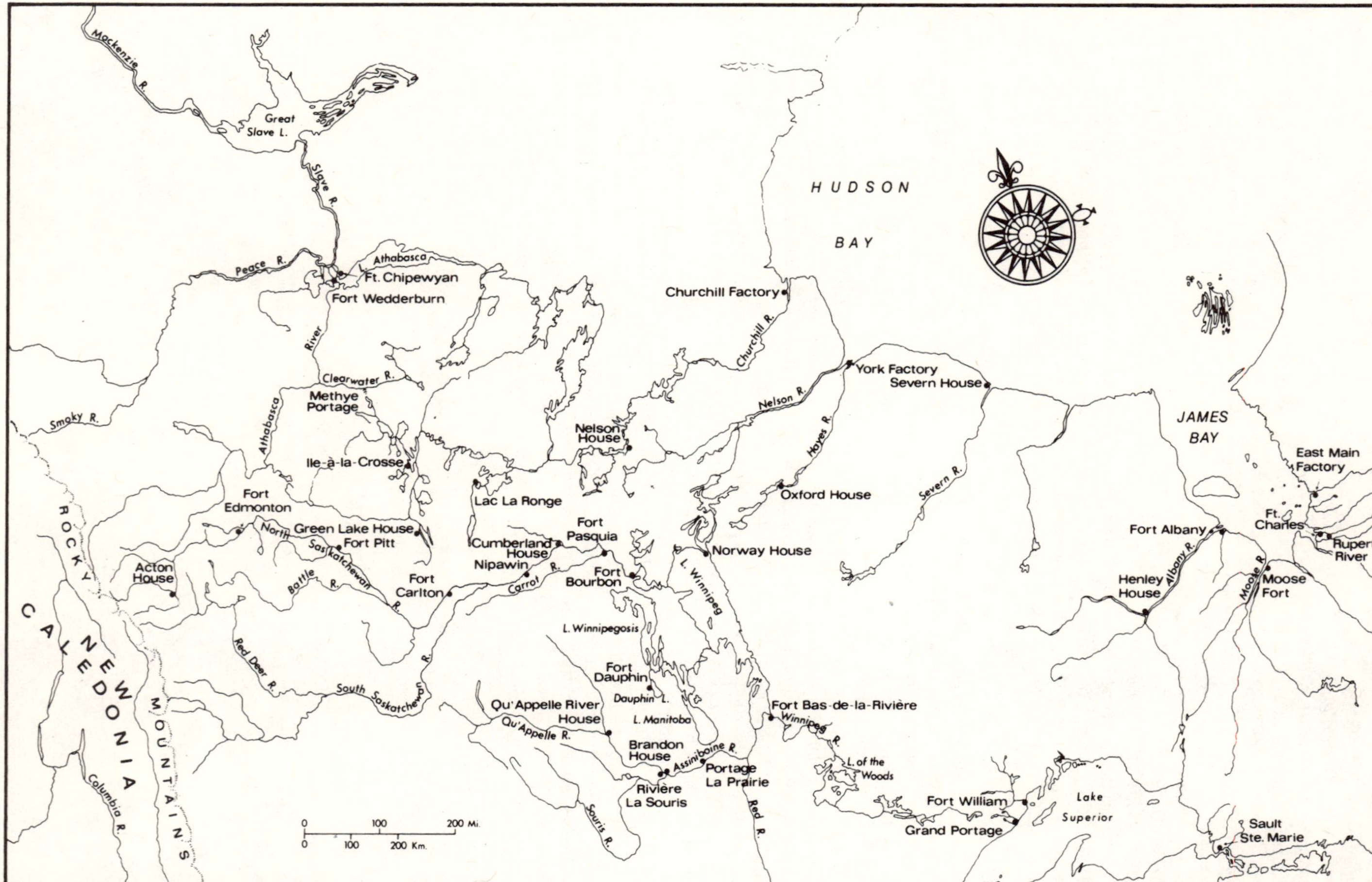

1.1 Fur trade posts

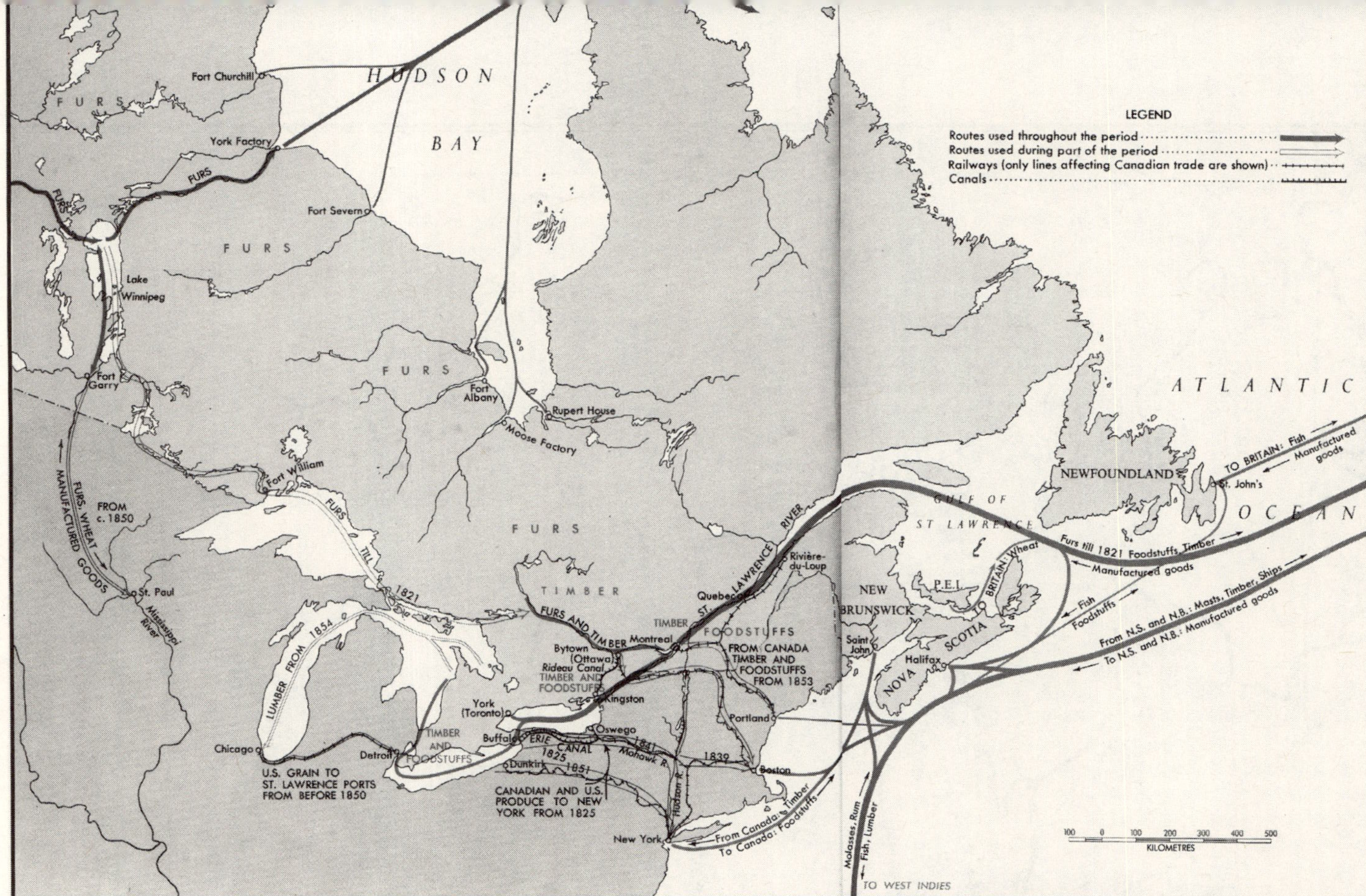

1.2 British North America

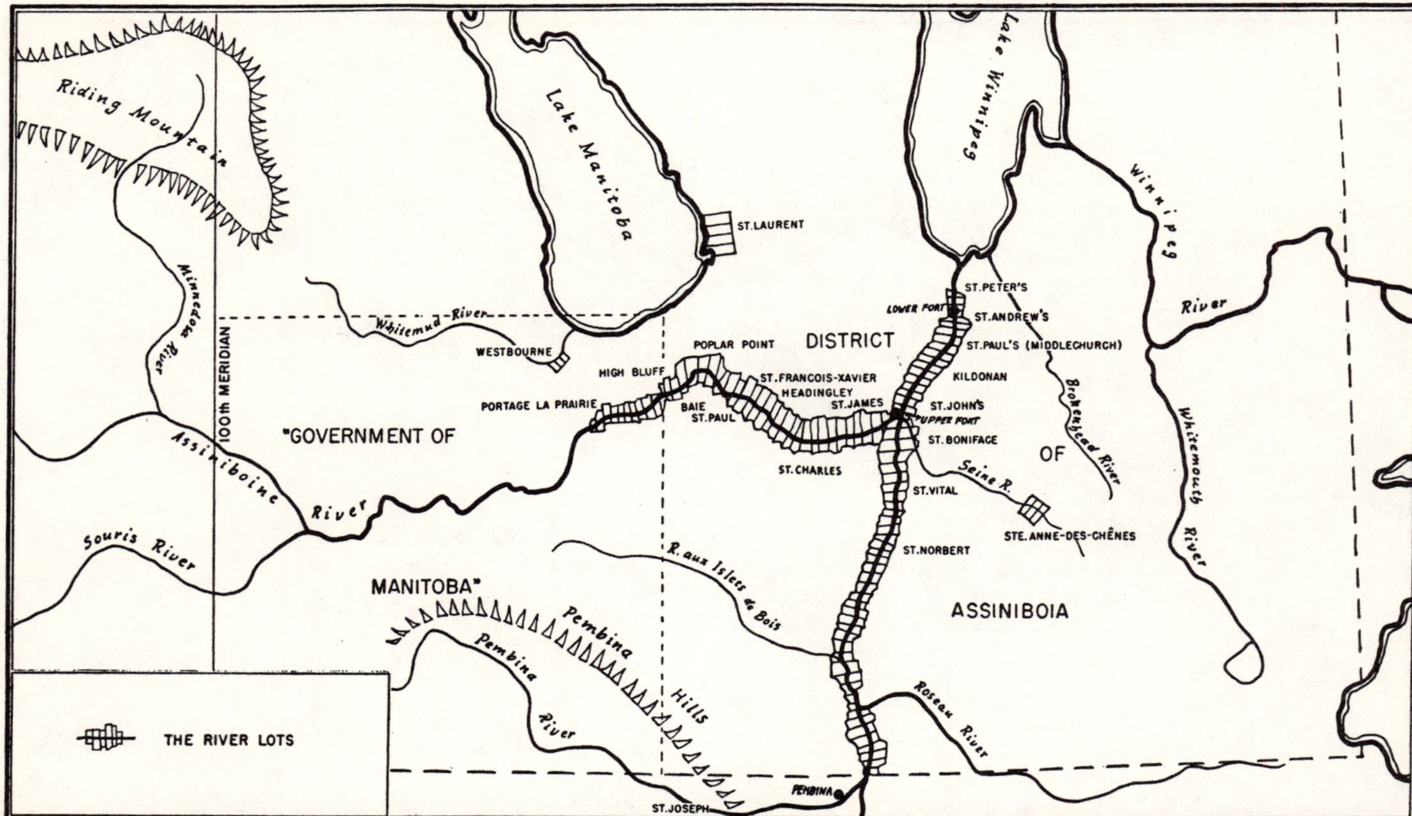

1.3 Prairie settlements, 1811-69

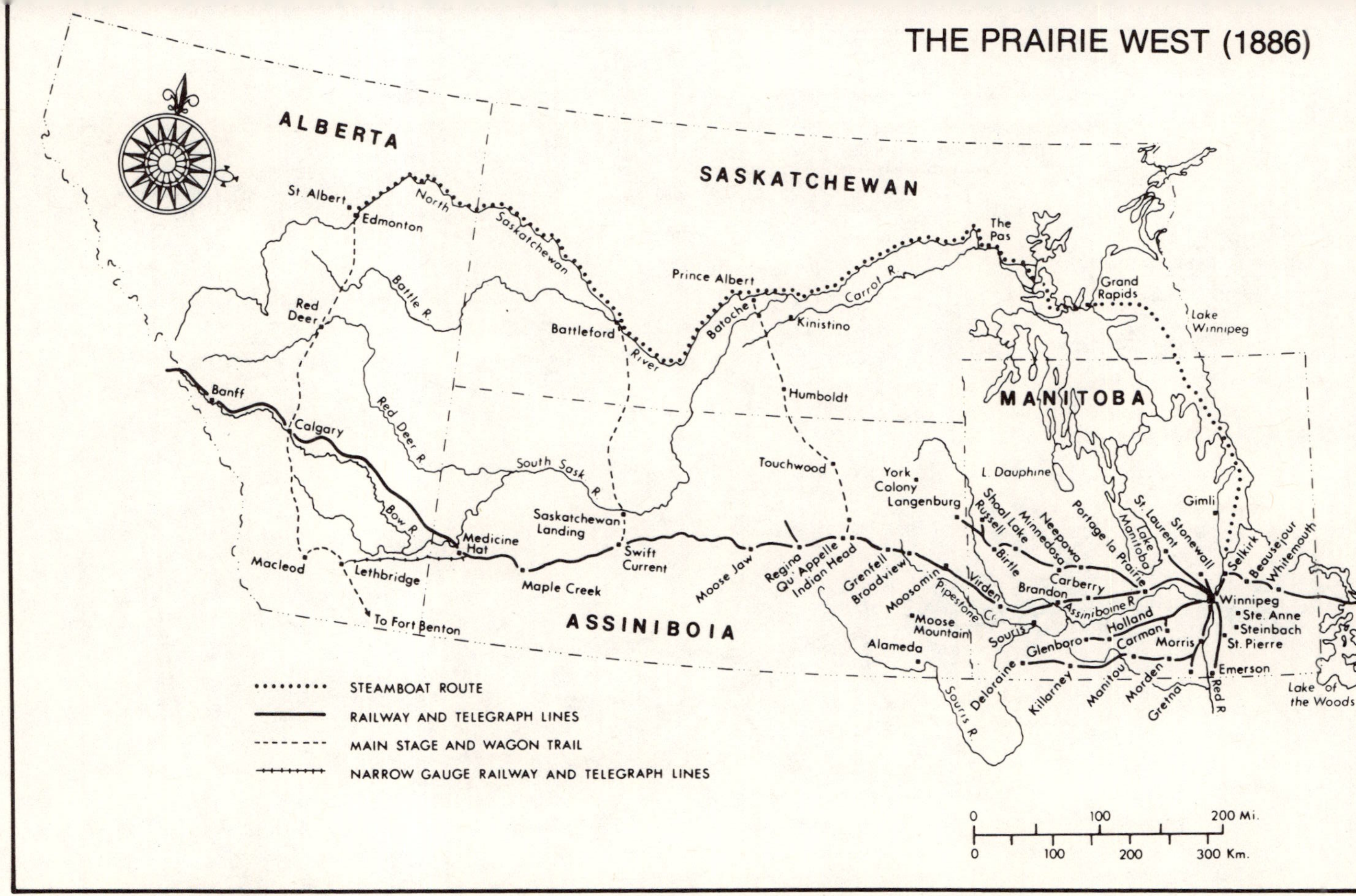

1.4 Western Canada, 1886

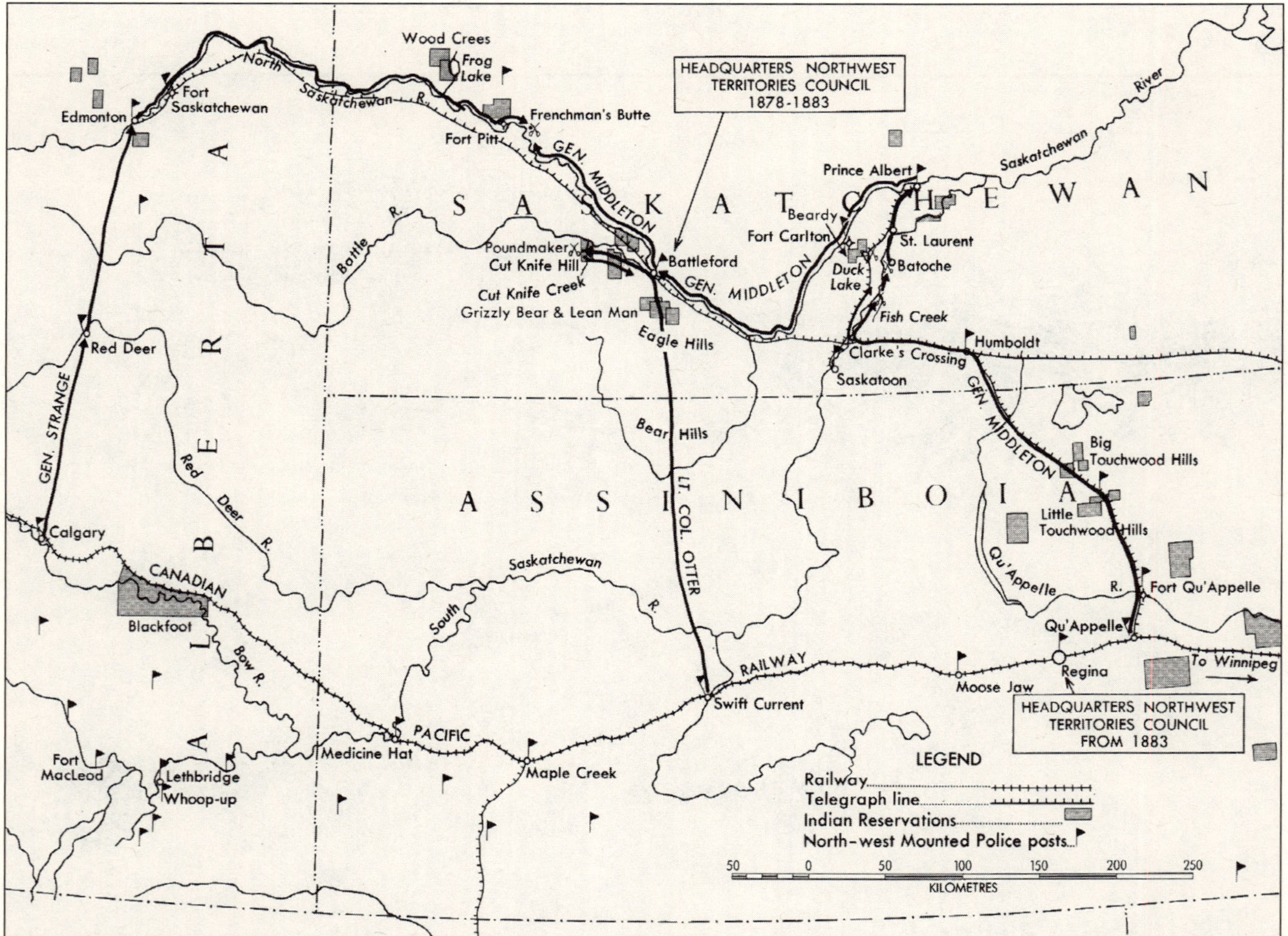

1.5 North-West Territories posts, transport routes, and communications

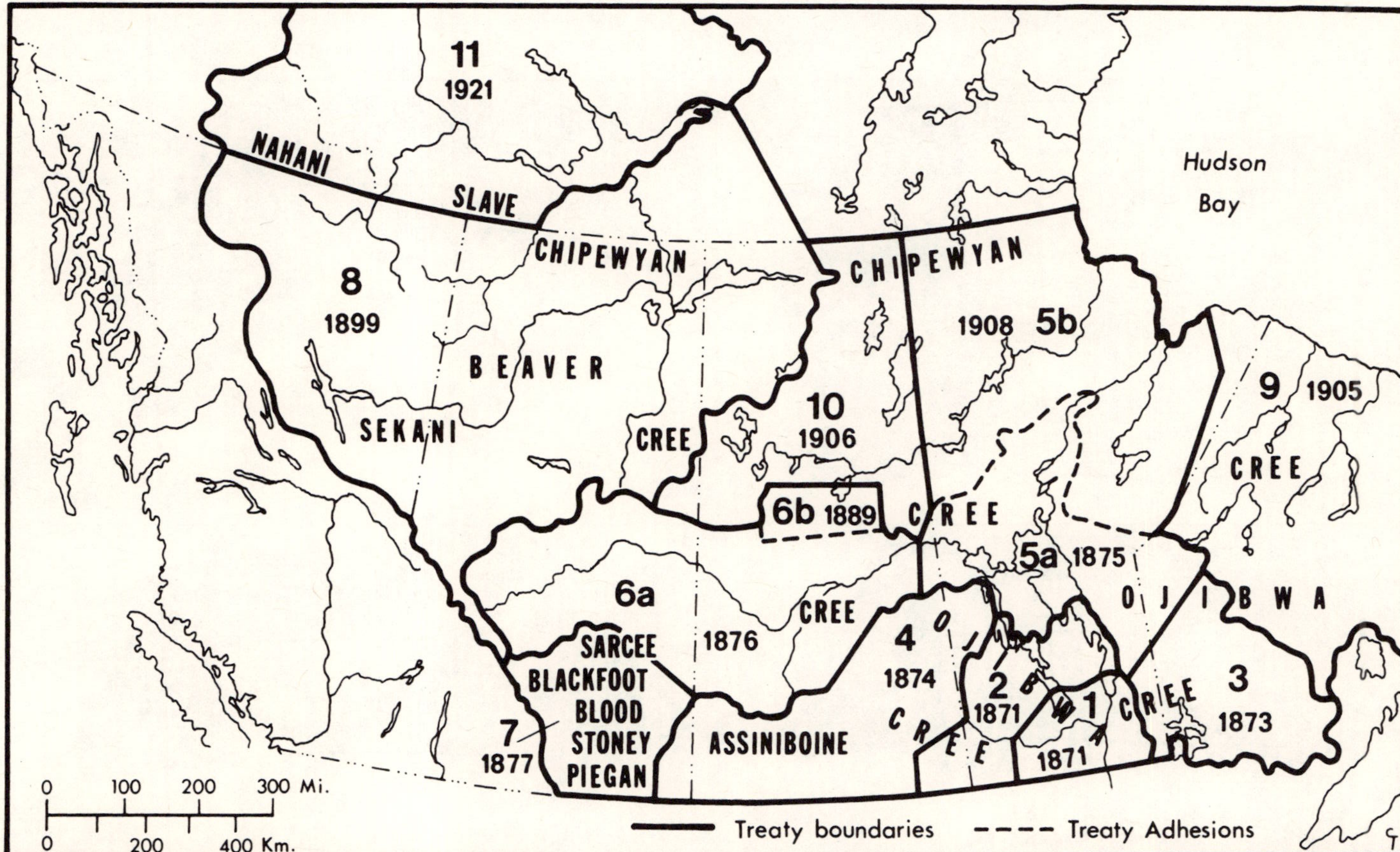

1.6 Numbered Indian treaties

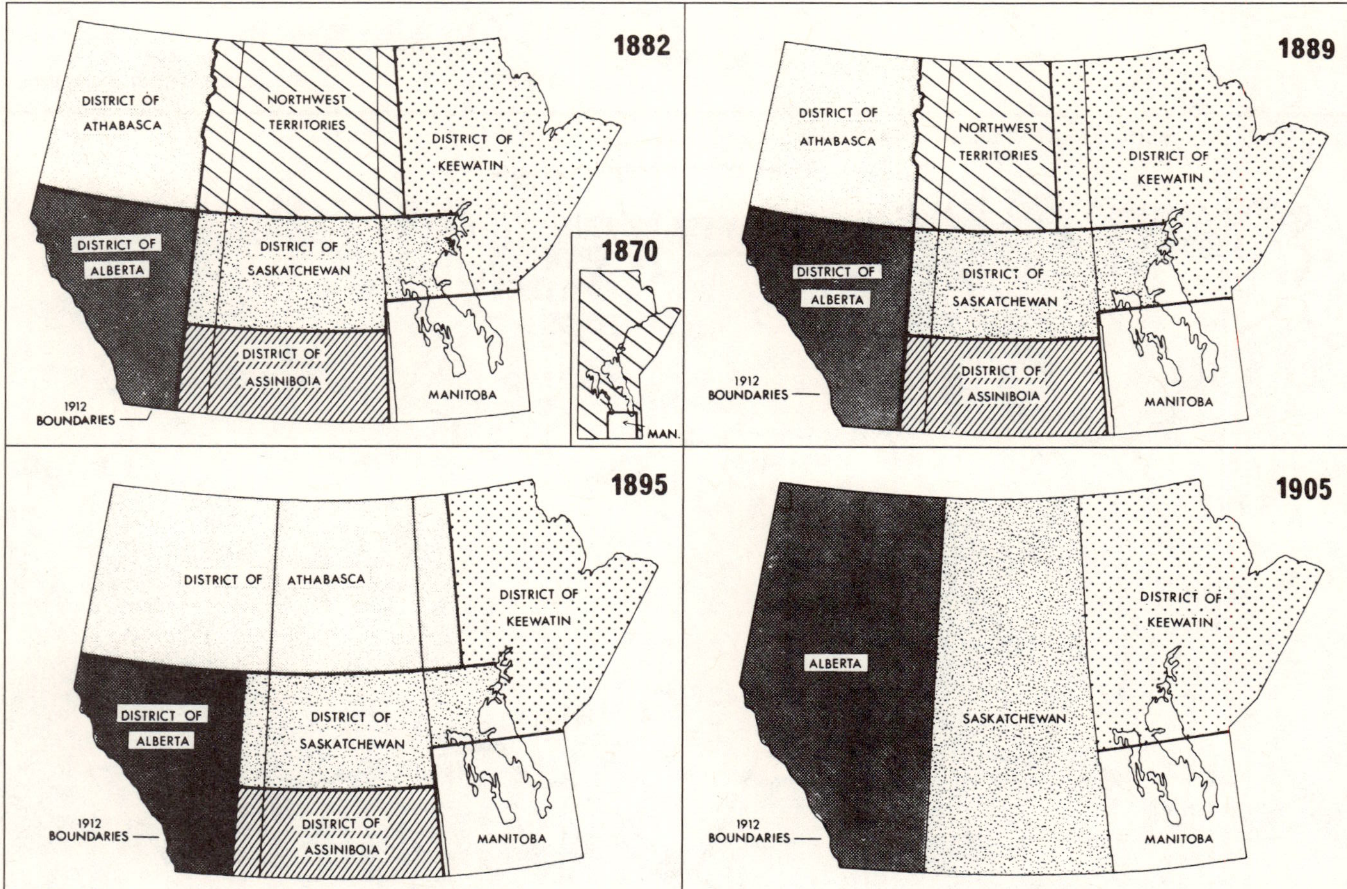

1.7 Prairie political boundaries, 1870-1940

Part 1
First Nations and First Peoples

2
Law and Necessity in Western Rupert's Land and Beyond, 1670-1870

Hamar Foster

Introduction

Although it is customary to say that one is honoured to have been asked to give the "keynote" address for a conference, it can be dangerous. As with judicial appointments, one can never be quite sure how many others turned down the job before they got to you. I was, however, delighted to have been asked, no matter how daunting the initial prospect. Not only did the organizers put together a rich and intellectually stimulating program, but there were also the usual opportunities to make new acquaintances and renew old friendships. Best of all, I was able to do most of my work at the outset and then sit back and enjoy the toil of others.

I was also pleased because I was born in Calgary, so there was a sense, not inappropriate for a history conference, of returning to origins, and of course I had taken part when John McLaren and Lou Knafla hosted what was probably the first western Canadian legal history conference here in 1984. It is gratifying to reflect upon how much has been done since then and challenging to consider how much remains to be done.

There is another reason I had a sense of returning. The organizing committee's invitation to speak summoned up an image from childhood that I had not thought of in years, an image that, appropriately, was related to the conference's theme. Such triggering of memory is known among students of the law of evidence as "present recollection revived," and an American judge once said the following about it: "The creaking of a hinge, the whistling of a tune, the smell of seaweed, the sight of an old photograph, the taste of nutmeg, the touch of a piece of canvas, may bring vividly to the foreground of consciousness the recollection of events that happened years ago."[1] Clearly, e-mailed invitations from Lou Knafla and Jonathan Swainger can have the same effect. The memory that came to the foreground of my consciousness was of being wrapped in a bearskin and my father's enormous buffalo greatcoat, which was standard police issue in the north at the time. I was then taken out of the RCMP (Royal Canadian

Mounted Police) detachment at Fort Vermilion and bundled into a horse-drawn sleigh with my mother. My father did not get on until we negotiated the steep southerly bank of the frozen Peace River, but once he had we headed out onto the ice, crossing over to a point on the other bank. I was not yet two years old. I am told that the occasion was New Year's Eve 1949, or perhaps 1950, and that we were on our way to a party at the Hudson's Bay post. It must have been the sound of the runners on the ice, the sharp, clear, cold air, and the brilliance of the snow in the bright moonlight that impressed these images upon my consciousness, because I remember little else.

As I reflected on this, it occurred to me that I had got hold of at least a piece of the end of an era. My father was the RCMP constable at Fort Vermilion. When he leased a dog team or packhorses to go on patrol with – to use the contemporary terminology – Slavey or Beaver interpreters, when he went on the fall hunt, and when he paid treaty money or carried out a number of other, routine duties, he was doing what others before him had been doing since William McLeod of the North-West Mounted Police, the first constable stationed at Fort Vermilion.[2] I think my father carried out his duties with more respect for Aboriginal people and their cultures than many did, because that was how he spoke about his experiences in later years. And certainly there was more community involvement in law enforcement then than there is now, in Fort Vermilion and just about everywhere else.[3] Nonetheless, he was an important part of a legal system that in the 1940s was alien and new to many of the Aboriginal people of the region and that had largely been imposed, not chosen. The impact of this legal system was addressed in a number of contexts during the conference.[4]

I say my memory was of the end of an era because by 1949 the Mackenzie highway had reached Hay River, and a few years later the last riverboat, no longer able to compete with the airplane, was taken out of service.[5] Soon horses and dogs would be replaced by patrol cars, and paid employees would do the work that my mother, and scores of other RCMP wives in so-called one-man detachments, did. This work included, among other things, cleaning the jail cell (which was just behind the house), cooking for the prisoners (who sometimes ate at our kitchen table), doing clerical work, and often acting as unofficial medical examiner (the makeshift morgue was also out back). The women who did all these things received no wages, and many received no pensions when their husbands died. Some who are alive today are in straitened circumstances, yet their story is largely untold.[6] It is also an example of one sort of law and necessity, which brings me perilously close to having to explain the title of this essay.

First, however, it is important to acknowledge the contributions of two previous conferences on western legal history and in particular to refer to the introductory or keynote address for each conference.[7] The first I have mentioned already. Organized in 1984 by Lou Knafla and John McLaren, it resulted in the publication of *Law and Justice in a New Land: Essays in Western Canadian Legal History*.[8] In that collection, Lou Knafla and the late Graham Parker urged legal historians of the Canadian west to pay attention to culture, not only to culture in a general sense but also to legal culture: those habits of thought and behaviour that might often be more important than written rules and orders and that people might carry with them in canoes and on the trail as well as in their communities.[9] Referring to the work of anthropologist Clifford Geertz, Parker placed particular emphasis upon local knowledge and upon Geertz's view that the analysis of culture is "not an experimental science in search of law but an interpretive one in search of meaning." Legal "sensibility," therefore, is not concerned solely with statutes and cases but also with "stories about events cast in imagery about principles."[10] However, it does involve cases and statutes, and Parker was clear that legal history should be *legal* history and not something else.[11]

In this connection, one could also quote no less an authority than Sir Francis Bacon, who grumbled that "it is a misfortune even of the best historians, that they do not dwell sufficiently upon the laws and judicial acts; or if by chance they use some diligence therein, yet they differ greatly from the authentic reports." One can almost hear him sniffing in disdain. Bacon's advice, incidentally, appears at the beginning of Roy St. George Stubbs' pathbreaking *Four Recorders of Rupert's Land,* an early and fact-filled contribution to the legal history of the Canadian west.[12]

The theme of legal culture as a focus of research was developed in more detail by the plenary speaker at the next conference, which was organized primarily by John McLaren and held at the University of Victoria in February of 1991. This gathering also produced a book, *Law for the Elephant, Law for the Beaver: Essays in the Legal History of the North American West,* a title that, for a while, looked as though it might stand the test of time. (The name of the conference that spawned this volume was "Law for the Buffalo, Law for the Musk Ox.")[13] The emphasis in Victoria was upon comparative Canadian and American legal history and upon transboundary influences and comparisons in the western and northern regions of the continent.

In his plenary address, John Phillip Reid began by noting that "western legal history" was a phrase that, only a few decades earlier, would have conjured up images of the *Corpus Juris Civilis* and the Napoleonic Code rather than gold rushes and homestead acts. He added that general historians "have neglected the history of law in the West even more than ... legal historians have neglected the West in the history of law." Reid then posed the question whether, even now, western legal history is "anything more than the history of developments in law that occurred somewhere west of somewhere else."[14] His answer was that, although the substantive law applied by judges in both east and west was much the same, important differences remain. Not only are there topics peculiar to the North American west – the law of the great fur companies, for example – but also evidence in the nineteenth-century west is richer and more extensive in some fields of historical investigation than it is in other times and places.[15] According to Reid, this is especially true if one is investigating the question "whether – and to what extent – a legal culture determines the personal behaviour and social conduct of ordinary people not trained in the law."[16] Given that there were no courts with legally trained personnel in the land of the buffalo and the musk ox until the second quarter of the nineteenth century, and then only in Assiniboia, this question is an important one for legal historians of Rupert's Land and the Indian Territories.[17]

Law and Necessity

All of which brings me, at last, to my title. The relationship between law and necessity seems to me to be a defining characteristic of legal culture and rhetoric. Most people, whether they have practised law or not, would readily assent to Justice Oliver Wendell Holmes' well-known aphorism that "the life of the law has not been logic: it has been experience" and that not only doctrine but also the "felt necessities of the time" determine results.[18] But what are these "felt necessities," and whose feelings count most? This is a question that resonates in all times and places, from the trial of Socrates in the fifth century BC to the prosecution of suspected al Qaeda operatives in the twenty-first century AD. And for present purposes it can be broken down, made more specific. For example, what happens when there is no mutually acceptable or comprehensible system of law enforcement to tell us whose "feelings" count the most? Or when people's rights on paper are more extensive than they can enforce and others will accept? Or when the "authorities" know that their power is effectively unreviewable? Or, finally, when it appears that the law requires, if not the impossible, at least the highly inconvenient? Such situations do occur, particularly in places such as Rupert's Land and the Indian Territories before 1870.

Obviously, in this sort of colonial or precolonial setting, where different legal cultures co-exist and compete, the fur trader, the Cree middleman, and the recorder of Rupert's Land are often likely to have very different notions of what is "necessary." But in situations where necessity, which is supposed to "know no law," is said to control and dictate behaviour, is there really no law? And to what extent does legal doctrine constrain the range of responses to Holmes' "felt necessities"? In a purely customary system, this last question may not be the right one.

Take as an example the feudal lord in early-twelfth-century England. On the death of one of his tenants, he may have been obliged by custom to admit the heir as his new tenant. Custom may also have provided that the heir is the eldest son. But the canons of inheritance in such a setting are "not rules of law conferring an abstract right on the heir, but customs about whom the lord's court should choose."[19] What if the eldest son were for some reason incapable of doing the military service attached to the fee? The answer appears to be that the lord's court, composed of the lord and his other tenants, could admit a younger son instead. There was no "law" external to this court, so the essentially administrative or managerial decision to pass over the eldest son was both practical and final. Law and necessity, as conceived by the lord and his tenants, were not in opposition. There is good reason to believe that the customary law of most Aboriginal peoples operated much like this.

By the end of the twelfth century, however, military service had degenerated into scutage, a mere money payment, and the king's courts were enforcing the canons of inheritance. Whether by design or by accident, the royal judges were turning these canons into rules.[20] Now the lord's decision of long ago might be undone, because the tenancy of the eldest son, which used to be an expectation governed by the custom of the group, had become a right protected by the law of the land.[21] As Professor Milsom has put it, "the canons of inheritance are unchanged. They can be stated in the same words at the end of this development as they could have been at the beginning. But their operation has been transformed."[22] In other words, positive law had displaced local custom, and the decision that it was necessary to deny the claim of the eldest son now looks illegal, against the rules. The law, instead of accommodating a perceived necessity, opposes it. This is often the case during periods of social change, when there is tension between traditional and emerging ideas about law and justice.

Legal rules may lag conspicuously behind public opinion, or they may lead, in unusual or novel cases, to a result that appears to pit legal doctrine against a particular manifestation of economic or political power. In systems with formal rules backed by state sanctions, it is often judges who decide how these kinds of conflict are resolved. Sometimes they are content with the outcome that a particular rule or policy appears to require; sometimes they strive to avoid it. And, sometimes, judges navigate what they conceive to be a middle path.[23]

To illustrate this point, I invoke a well-known example from the eighteenth century. When Lord Mansfield delivered his judgment in 1772 in *Sommersett's Case,* the issue was whether masters lost their property in their slaves when they brought them to England.[24] It was an issue that Mansfield did not really want to decide. In fact, he had remarked in an earlier case that he hoped the question would never be resolved, because if masters continued to worry that their slaves might be free, and if slaves continued to worry that they were not, "they would both behave better."[25]

Mansfield was also reluctant because in *Sommersett* he was faced with a conflict between the common law, according to which slavery was almost certainly unlawful, and England's legislation and colonial practice, which supported the right of Sommersett's owner to confine him in irons and sell him as property. There was, in addition, a conflict between public opinion, which favoured Sommersett, and the economic interests represented by slave owners. In the end, Mansfield did not rule, as is sometimes thought, that the moment a slave set foot in England he was free. Nor did he say that "the air of England was too pure for a slave to breathe." He ruled only that *habeas corpus* was available to prevent the man from being forcibly removed from England.[26]

Mansfield has come to represent what the upright judge should be: someone prepared to do justice according to law, whatever the cost. As he himself put it, his ruling might ultimately result in a loss to proprietors "of some seven hundred thousand pounds, but *fiat iustitia, ruat coelum*."[27] Let justice be done, though the heavens fall. But the heavens did not fall, and afterward Mansfield continued to nonsuit slaves who brought actions for wages on the ground that, as slaves, they could have no such claim.[28] Nonetheless, for many people, the Latin maxim that he invoked in *Sommersett's Case* represents the principle that, when law and "necessity" – in this case the financial interests of slave owners – conflict, the law must prevail, whatever the cost.

For others, the idea of doing justice, come what may, can mean something rather different. What if, for example, the judges or lawmakers are perceived as unable, or unwilling, to act? One option is self-help. So, eighty years after Lord Mansfield proclaimed that even the prospect of economic calamity for a significant group of property owners would not prevent justice from being done according to law in England, the San Francisco Vigilance Committee made *fiat iusticia, ruat coelum* the motto of American vigilantism.[29] Let justice be done, though the heavens fall was now the banner under which offenders were dealt with, not according to law, but according to something that was crude and dangerous, if not entirely arbitrary.

Doing what is seen to be "necessary" is therefore a powerful motivation to do what may, or may not, accord with existing legal rules. But first these rules must be determined, not only – as in *Sommersett's Case* – at the centre of empire, but also at its outposts: on the fur brigades and in remote settlements, for example. And this is where legal culture comes in.

Here in Canada we are somewhat behind our American counterparts in tackling the legal history of the Prairie west. But in writing about the Prairies and the North-West, we do have one advantage over the Americans, who have wondered aloud whether their Great Plains "as a region is legally distinctive."[30] In Canada, at least insofar as non-Aboriginal law is concerned, there is less room for doubt. The reason is the remarkable grant of Rupert's Land to the Hudson's Bay Company (HBC) in 1670 and the extension of that company's authority west and north into the Indian Territories in 1821.

East of the Rocky Mountains, this authority was not removed until 1870, and until then there definitely was a distinctive legal regime north of the forty-ninth parallel and west of the Canadas.[31] In what follows, I focus upon five selected features of what I have called law and necessity in this region during the 200-year period between the granting of the charter to the HBC in 1670 and the conveyance of the company's lands to Britain and then Canada in 1869-70.

The first is the law of what the Royal Proclamation of 1763 referred to as the "Indian tribes or nations" of North America, including the relationship between those legal systems and the law brought by the fur traders. In Rupert's Land and in the Indian Territories to the north and west of Rupert's Land, these nations were, and are, members of the Athapaskan, Algonkian, Eskimoan, and, in one case, Siouan language families, and they vastly outnumbered the fur traders. Yet the "classic" text on the history of Manitoba, published forty-five years ago, says "nothing of consequence about the era of native dominance in the region."[32] This is changing.

The second is the legal status of the Hudson's Bay Company and what might be called its "proprietary" jurisdiction in Rupert's Land: that is, the nature and extent of the legal rights with respect to competitors and others that were conferred upon the company by the charter of 1670.

The third is related to the second and is often referred to as the private justice system of the company: that is, the body of rules and practices that governed its officers and servants.[33] This might also be referred to as the company's "disciplinary" jurisdiction.[34]

The fourth is what I have called, not very imaginatively, "long-distance justice." By that I mean the legal regime laid down by the imperial Parliament for dealing with serious crime and, at least in theory, expensive civil suits arising in the lands west of the Canadas.[35] The relationship between these statutes and the jurisdiction of the company under its charter was a source of controversy from the passage of the first statute in 1803 to the termination of HBC authority in 1870. For legal historians, it still is.

The fifth is the legal system established at Red River around 1811 that, in 1839, attracted the appointment of the first legally trained official in what is now western Canada, Adam Thom.[36] This was the most concentrated point of European legal authority, and it has received the most scholarly attention. Geographically, however, it affected a relatively small part of Rupert's Land and the Indian Territories, whereas the first feature – Aboriginal law – operated throughout the whole region. To this I now turn.

Law in the Fur Trade

In addressing the laws of the various Indian tribes or nations, the researcher is faced at the outset with a considerable problem: the extent to which the details of these laws, as they operated prior to and immediately after contact, are knowable. Not only are these details part of an oral tradition, but also they are part of many, diverse oral traditions, and they are embedded in social, cultural, and other practices in ways that make them difficult for European eyes to see. There is also a limit to what can be recovered from between the lines of documentary accounts and from contemporary oral history fieldwork. As James Youngblood Henderson has said, "First Nations laws have received only ephemeral attention and documentary evidence remains fragmentary."[37] One is therefore tempted to stray into hyperbole and say that the subject resembles Mark Twain's provocative description of the weather: everyone talks about the importance of Aboriginal customary law in understanding our common past, but no one does anything about it.

But of course that *is* hyperbole. Some progress has been made. For example, we no longer assume that there was no such law, or that it was uniformly harsh and bloody, and recent work by Henderson and others in this area constitutes a significant advance, especially with respect to Iroquoian and Algonkian law.[38] However, although some interesting and encouraging historical and anthropological work has recently been published, Canada lacks the sort of studies done in the United States by Llewellyn and Hoebel or by Rennard Strickland.[39] On the whole, what is known here is more general than particular and consists largely of statements emphasizing the importance of (i) restoring and maintaining social harmony rather than imposing order, (ii) compensation over punishment, and (iii) collective decision making over adjudication. These putative differences between Aboriginal and non-Aboriginal law should of course be acknowledged and understood, but they should not be overemphasized.[40]

Perhaps most is known about customary family law. There is ample evidence, for example, that fur traders formed country marriages with Aboriginal women that were governed by the law of the wife's nation, not the husband's.[41] On occasion, the status of these marriages was determined by non-Aboriginal courts, notably in the well-known case of *Connolly v. Woolrich*.[42] But even here details are sparse, and the extent to which the husband was incorporated into existing kinship systems remains uncertain.[43]

Yet the task is far from hopeless. Oral history continues to be an underutilized resource, and there are many tantalizing clues to be found in fur trade records, not only about Aboriginal law but also about fur trade law and how the two interacted. Most valuable of all are the surviving accounts about such interactions that reveal, as well as any account written only by one side can, both the Aboriginal and the fur trader reactions to the same transaction – as when traders refused offers of compensation in furs for a transgression that, in their legal culture, required punishment. Or when they insisted upon executing everyone involved in a killing, even though only one victim had died.[44] Or the reverse: on one occasion, Alexander Henry the younger refused to demand blood for what was clearly the accidental killing of one of his men. Under Chippewa law, satisfaction would have been mandatory, and the Chippewa man who was responsible was both astonished and relieved; in Henry's legal culture, however, there was no criminal liability for accidents.[45]

Recently, two fairly distinct views have developed with respect to the role of law in the behaviour of fur traders toward the Indian tribes and nations with whom they came into contact. The first sees fur trader retaliation purely in terms of power; the other sees room for the operation of legal culture and legal norms. One way to approach this debate is to provide a text for each side to interpret, and for this purpose I suggest the words of a man whose reputation for violence in the Athabaska country was such that he was initially excluded from the Hudson's Bay Company when the North-Westers merged with the HBC in 1821.

Peter Skene Ogden, whose father was a superior court judge in Lower Canada, is supposed to have said that, because the king's writ did not run in Indian country, "many acts must be committed that would not stand ... strict investigation in the *Banco Regis*." "My legal primer," he allegedly claimed, "says that necessity has no law; and in this place where the custom of the country, or as the lawyers say, the *Lex Non Scripta* is our only guide, we must, in our acts of summary legislation, perform the parts of judge, jury, sheriff, hangman, gallows and all."[46] This statement is intriguingly ambiguous. On one reading, it has a distinct smell of blood about it: of self-help and "payback," of retaliation unconstrained by due process or humanity. In short, necessity knows no law. But we need to be careful that we do not unwittingly adopt the sort of positivism that defines the meaning of "law" very narrowly.[47] Ogden's language in this excerpt can also be construed as describing not necessarily the absence of law but the absence of state mechanisms to enforce it. Moreover, Ogden invokes a "guide" for fur trade behaviour: the custom of the country and what "the lawyers" call the unwritten law. Should we take this seriously?

Most historians tend not to, emphasizing the element of raw power in remarks such as Ogden's, and there is plenty of material to back them up.[48] Beatings, trade sanctions, punitive expeditions to render blood for blood, and even incidents in which blood was rendered merely for theft could be marshalled in support. In the Saskatchewan district, the chief factor at Edmonton House appears to have approved the killing of six members of the Stoney Nation for stealing HBC horses.[49] And, after American trappers had endured a series of thefts and killings, Ogden himself said that he would be content to see the entire Snake Nation, other than the women and children, exterminated.[50] But it would be dangerous to conclude that, because some people spoke or acted in this way, it was the norm or was regarded as acceptable. It may have been, but we need more evidence before we can safely distinguish policy from bravado and the routine from the exceptional. Near Fort Vermilion in 1809, for example, North-West and Hudson's Bay Company traders disagreed about whether a Cree should be killed or merely beaten for stealing horses.[51] If some acts of blood vengeance met with general approval, and others did not, this suggests that something more than blind retaliation was going on.

It is hardly surprising that critics of the Hudson's Bay Company – many of whom had their own individual axes to grind – saw nothing that smacked of law in the company's treatment of Aboriginal people. Thus, James E. Fitzgerald, an HBC rival whose bid to colonize Vancouver Island had been rejected, wrote that the company's "right of exclusive trade is ... a right of exclusive property in the labour, life and destinies of the Indian race. It is an absolute and unqualified dominion over their bodies and their souls – a dominion irresponsible to any legal authority ... It knows but one limit, and obeys but one law, – 'Put money in thy purse.'"[52] This passage, from a lengthy pamphlet written when the company's role in Red River and its proposal to colonize Vancouver Island were the subject of strenuous public debate, is good stuff. And it contains an element of truth. But it reads more like a description of the Spanish missions in California than the trading posts of New Caledonia or Athabaska. In fact, Fitzgerald had never been to the fur country, and it seems likely that, if his informants had, they must have stayed close to the forts. I say this because, although it is true that the Hudson's Bay Company was pretty much immune from any sort of legislative or judicial review, Aboriginal people were generally not the helpless pawns depicted in this passage. Fitzgerald's views should therefore be treated with caution.[53]

But Fitzgerald was not alone. Far from it. Disgruntled former employees and missionaries were also highly critical of the company.[54] Although there were those who saw the HBC as a buffer against what they regarded as a more serious threat to the well-being of Aboriginal people (the Americans), others roundly condemned its record in this area. Not untypical is the view of Adrien-Gabriel Morice, an Oblate priest and missionary who wrote extensively about the history and anthropology of western Canada.[55] But Father Morice's complaint was not Fitzgerald's: the good father thought that it was not the Indians but the traders who had been co-opted. And he included lax marriage customs, dancing, face painting, and, significantly, "rendering murder for murder" in a long list of practices that he charged "were not only countenanced, but actually practiced by the Company's officers and servants." Morice lamented that, instead of "lifting the lower race up to the standard of Christianized Europeans," the Hudson's Bay Company had "stooped to the level of the savages."[56] In short, he appears to have regretted very much that, where culture and perhaps even law are concerned, influence can be a two-way street.

Because Morice regarded the policy of blood for blood as an Aboriginal custom adopted by the Hudson's Bay Company, his remarks provide a convenient introduction to the other approach to the role of law in fur trade interactions. Proponents of this view tend to see legal culture where others see only power. They concede that Aboriginal law generally stressed harmonious relations within the kin group or other communities, but they argue that, when wrongs were committed against group members by others, rather different principles applied. Here the emphasis was upon vengeance or satisfaction for the wrong done, and liability – which appears to have been based on causation rather than guilt – attached not to individuals but to the offender's group as a whole.[57] This was particularly true of homicides between different nations, and fur traders were definitely a different nation (or, indeed, nations).

It is therefore important to examine not only the behaviour but also the language of fur trade retaliation to see whether, consciously or otherwise, HBC men who rendered blood for blood were being influenced by, say, Cree or Inuit law or at least by an emergent fur trade culture that was a mixture of both legal traditions. If marriage was *à la façon du pays,* why not other things as well? Or, as John Phillip Reid has put it, if fur trader retaliation was not based upon English or French law, on whose law was it based?[58]

As we have seen, most historians and critics of the Hudson's Bay Company have answered "no law at all." Because I tend to disagree, it seems only fair to give some space to the most recent exponent of what still seems to be the majority view, historical geographer Cole Harris. After noting the work of Reid and other legal historians, Harris concludes, "I suspect ... that [the practice of violent retribution without trial] has little to do with any system of law, and is better thought of as a particular strategy for the seizure and, if necessary, the killing of people, that has derived from European systems of episodic, destructive power and recontextualized in the particular geography of the fur trade."[59] Perhaps Harris is correct. Legal historians look for law, and I suppose no one should be surprised if we sometimes find it when it isn't there. (In that respect, we may be a little like the fisherman in the old story who concluded that there was nothing in the sea smaller than two inches, forgetting that this just happened to be the size of the mesh in his net.) But fur traders often used a mixture of Aboriginal and European terms to describe acts of retaliation by both sides. Even if they saw these terms as describing behaviour rather than the requirements of custom, does not their use of them at least suggest that a legal culture of some kind was at work?[60] Here I take comfort in the wisdom of British labour historian E.P. Thompson, who conceded that, if law "is no more than the mystifying and pompous way in which ... power is registered and executed, then we must not waste our labour studying its history."[61] But Thompson did study it, with spectacular results. And it is more than statutes and courts.

The Charter of 1670

My second topic is the legal status of the Hudson's Bay Company, and here one quickly discovers that in Canada "charter arguments" are not a recent development. Indeed, when E.E. Rich distinguished four periods of the company's history before 1870,[62] he concluded that all four were "marked by a distinct challenge to the Charter."[63] The 200 years of the HBC regime (1670-1870) therefore provide an almost textbook case study for those who are interested in exploring the relationship between the paper world of legal rights and privileges and the more earthly realm where nations and corporations strive against one another, trade is conducted, and consequences actually happen.

On its face, the charter granted by King Charles II conferred rights of both property and government on the newly formed Hudson's Bay Company. Granted when "the prerogative was high," the charter made the company "the true and absolute Lordes and Proprietors" of the land, guaranteed them the sole right of trade, and bestowed legislative authority upon the governor and committee in London and judicial authority upon the governor and council at each fort or establishment.[64] The language of the grant spoke of all the lands drained by rivers flowing into Hudson Bay. As geographical knowledge gradually increased, this led the company to claim title to a vast territory that not only included lands adjacent to the bay but also stretched all the way from Labrador to the Rocky Mountains, at least in the southwest. Insofar as territorial reach was concerned, it was a proprietary government that made other proprietary governments in seventeenth-century America look like pipsqueaks. On the other hand, except for the colony established at Red River in 1811, the company's domain was never much more than a network of trading posts and canoe routes, and this prompted a series of attacks – legal, commercial, and military – on both the company and its founding document.

The first of the four periods identified by Rich runs from 1670 to 1713, when the French in Canada took understandable exception to the English Crown having granted land in a region to which they laid claim. The company endured repeated attacks on its posts "even in times of peace," and these often resulted in capture.[65] The attacks ended in 1713 when the Treaty of Utrecht – which was oblivious to Aboriginal territorial rights – assigned possession of the bay to the British.

In the second period, from 1713 to 1763, the company no longer had to fear military assaults by the French and did much better financially, but French traders out of Montreal were operating in Rupert's Land, and in England Arthur Dobbs mounted the first serious domestic challenge to the charter. Dobbs, a wealthy Ulsterman, asserted that the charter was void for uncertainty and that it constituted an illegal monopoly; he also accused the company of failing to fulfill the obligations of this monopoly, which were to promote trade and colonization and to search for a northwest passage. When he petitioned the Privy Council in 1748, the petition was referred to the law officers of the Crown: Attorney General Dudley Ryder and Solicitor General William Murray. Reluctant to interfere with an established commerce in furs, these officials advised that the king should not declare against the validity of the charter "till there has been some judgment of a court of justice to warrant it."[66] There never was such a judgment, then or subsequently. But Solicitor General Murray did get an opportunity years later to rule on another form of commerce when, as Lord Mansfield, he decided *Sommersett's Case*. He was reluctant to interfere unduly with an established trade then, too.[67]

The third period runs from the fall of New France in 1763 to 1821, years in which the company was seriously and nearly successfully challenged by British traders operating out of Montreal. This competition so affected the HBC's trade that it was at last obliged to leave the shores of the bay and establish posts in the interior, where "pedlars" from Montreal were intercepting furs that would otherwise have been theirs.[68] The pedlars also competed among themselves, but after the amalgamation of the major players with the partnership known as the North-West Company in 1804 the struggle, often bloody, was solely with the Hudson's Bay Company. Throughout this period, legal opinions were sought and obtained by both sides on a host of problems, most of which were directly related to the legal validity and proper interpretation of the HBC charter.

The importance of this issue can be seen in the roll call of lawyers consulted, beginning with another opinion of the law officers of the Crown in 1777.[69] All were prominent members of the profession, and most went on to hold judicial office.[70] Their opinions and the "statements of case" upon which they were based, especially a joint opinion prepared for the company when Montreal traders attempted to establish a post in James Bay in 1803, provide a rich source of legal-historical material. Ranging over free trade, the Crown prerogative, legislative competence, rights of property, legal remedies, and the proper legal strategy for parties engaged in a fierce commercial struggle, these documents are lectures on law and necessity, at least as conceived by owners of British capital and their legal advisors.

The third period ends with the coalition of the rival trading concerns in 1821. But this did not end challenges to the charter. In the fourth period (1821-70), such "country-born" men as William Kennedy, Alexander Isbister, and John McLoughlin led a sustained attack on the company's monopoly rule in the fur trade and at Red River, and the result in 1849 was yet a third opinion by the law officers of the Crown.[71] On this occasion, the attorney general and the solicitor general concluded that there was no doubt that the company had the territorial rights and governmental powers that it claimed. However, like Murray and Ryder a hundred years earlier, they added that it might be a good idea to refer such matters "to a competent tribunal for ... decision."[72] Because the government of the day took the position that the expense of such a proceeding would have to be borne by the petitioners, this suggestion went nowhere. In 1857, however, a committee of Parliament inquired into the company's affairs and made a number of recommendations. One was that the government and the company should agree to cede Red River and the Saskatchewan country to Canada. Another was that, whatever the validity of the charter, the HBC's right of exclusive trade should be continued in unsettled areas.[73]

I think that this brief overview reveals what a fertile source the charter is for those interested in British and colonial politics, the fur trade, free trade, popular protests, and even the dynamics of closely held corporations. More generally, its history also suggests something important about the relationship between law and business. Most students of the company – for example, Rich, Glyndwr Williams, Gerald Friesen – have concluded that the HBC's success was due more to its business efficiency than its charter rights.[74] Yet the company's secure corporate structure gave it a distinct advantage over the shifting partnership arrangements of the North-Westers, and its exclusive right to the much more efficient trade route through Hudson Bay made its operating expenses that much less. These advantages were conferred by the charter and, arguably, were critically important when the two trading concerns were fighting their war of attrition between 1804 and 1821. The North-Westers tried, without success, to get the HBC to share its trade route, but they could never quite bring themselves to challenge the charter in court.[75] This suited the Hudson's Bay Company because, as the law officers of the Crown said in 1748 and again in 1849, the charter was valid until a court said otherwise. The lawyerly language of this document therefore did shape events in the world; it was not merely words on paper.

All Who Live under Them

In moving on to the third topic, what I have called the "disciplinary" jurisdiction of the HBC, recall that the charter conferred legislative authority on the governor and committee in London to make laws for the good government of the company and its establishments, so long as these laws were "reasonable and not contrary or repugnant ... to the Lawes, Statutes or Customes of this our Realme." It also conferred authority upon the governor and council at each establishment "to judge all persons belonging to the ... Company or that shall live under them according to the Lawes of this Kingdome."[76] Two consequences flowed from this. The first is that persons who were subject to company rule were also subject to company law, so long as it was not contrary to the law of England – a standard formula that produced many political and judicial stand-offs throughout British colonial history. The second is that courts established by the company had jurisdiction to apply these laws not only to their officers and servants but also to "all persons ... that shall live under them," wording that might be construed as including persons who were not employees of some kind. This is the source of the company's civil and criminal jurisdiction over the colonists at Red River.[77]

Whether it was also wide enough to include the original inhabitants of Rupert's Land depends of course upon the canons of interpretation and upon fundamental questions about sovereignty and whose law governs when different legal systems lead to different answers.[78] It also, in my view, depends as a practical matter upon whether the company was engaged in trading furs or in establishing permanent settlements, complete with non-Aboriginal wives, children, and other attributes of the culture and society of the mother country. I have suggested above that in the fur trade period a unique legal regime that was predominantly but not exclusively Aboriginal governed international relations. But when the point of the exercise is not the fur trade but settlement, the situation changes. Colonists generally knew little about the laws of the tribes among whom they had come to live and were likely to feel insecure if they did not extend their own laws, geographically, as far as resources would permit – which in the early years of most colonial projects was not much farther than the immediate vicinity of the settlement. Eventually, and usually without Aboriginal consent, this extension would include not only offences by Aboriginal people against settlers but also – where a threat to the security of the colony was perceived – offences by Aboriginals against other Aboriginals.[79]

In any event, the company clearly had legislative and judicial authority over its employees, and the regime that developed was a patchwork quilt of criminal law, labour law, property, contract, and tort (or delict).[80] In some respects, its rule was a form of "government by debt" because the company also tried to control Aboriginal trappers and freemen (who in some districts were often Iroquois from the east) by advancing traps and supplies that were then paid for with furs sold at rates well below what the company would get for them.[81] This arrangement was in turn enforced by the company's legal monopoly: employees and freemen were not permitted to conduct any trade on their own. Needless to say, such conditions could induce men to desert. When they did, the company sometimes seems to have regarded their recapture as an assertion of corporate property rights over supplies, title to which had not passed. Alternatively, it can be seen as asserting some sort of "wilderness version of a creditor's lien, [by] seizing the property of the men to secure payment of [their] debts."[82] The evidence for these practices comes primarily from the Pacific west, but throughout the fur country the company's employees had a rough ride. Indeed, even in the mid-eighteenth century, the hard work and harsh discipline led some Indians in Rupert's Land to regard "all the Company's servants, except the governor," as "slaves."[83]

The concept of desertion points to another defining characteristic of company rule: its quasi-military flavour. "Mutiny" was one of the "leading" offences listed in the *Code of Penal Laws* published at Moose Factory in 1815, and, while most infractions were punishable by fines, loss of pay, confinement in irons, and flogging, mutiny and desertion were ominously stated to be subject to "the same Punishment ... as in the Army and Navy."[84] This was largely talk; as Smandych and Linden have shown, the eighteenth century had already seen a gradual transition from what they call "coercive" paternalism toward a system in which "post councils were used as juries and the accused was able to exercise some legal rights."[85] But even the beatings and irons of the first phase – which in the Pacific west lasted until well into the 1850s – must be put in context. Floggings and keelhaulings were common in the eighteenth-century army and navy, and the physical penalties imposed in British public schools even in the nineteenth century were harsh by today's standards.[86]

To the commissioned officers of the Hudson's Bay Company, discipline was no less essential at a trading post or on brigade than it was aboard a man-of-war or a ship of the merchant navy, and a lack of clear direction from the London committee only exacerbated the uncertain state of the law. As early as 1682, Governor John Nixon complained that confusion about whether civil or military law was in force had contributed to the disciplinary problems that he faced. He also grumbled about the quality of the men whom the committee had sent out – a lament that echoes down the ages in the records of the honourable company, from Nixon's day to the days when more recruiting was done out of Montreal than Britain.[87]

Directions that were clear but that subordinates suspected were meant to be taken with a grain of salt were no better. Such appears to have been often the case with orders forbidding the summary infliction of corporal punishment.[88] And of course the isolation of many of the posts meant that the severe measures adopted by men such as Joseph Isbister at Fort Albany in the 1740s, and Donald Manson and Donald McLean in New Caledonia a century later, were rarely subject to any form of effective oversight.[89] Other officers were better, but the amount of discretion was such that, to some employees, it seemed that there was "no stated punishment in the Hudson's Bay Company's service."[90]

Yet, technically, there was. The *Standing Rules and Regulations* of the company were regularly revised and promulgated, and they laid down standards of behaviour for most facets of company life.[91] What is less clear is how they were interpreted. It seems likely – and there is considerable evidence of this – that many problems and infractions were handled without careful reference to formal rules, at least when these occurred away from the main depots.[92] There is also, of course, the matter of the HBC's standard form contracts, which were usually "entire" contracts: that is, wages were not due under them until the employee had worked the entire term of the agreement. This meant that, if he quit or was discharged before his term was completed, he was owed nothing.[93] The English law of master and servant was equally one-sided: employees had to sue for their wages, whereas employers could have defaulting servants brought before a justice of the peace and fined or even jailed.[94] The only real limitation upon the company's authority was therefore employees' ability to combine and resist that authority or to complain loudly enough to attract attention in England. The company occasionally had to give in to bad publicity "at home" and was constantly, almost obsessively, on guard against the potential for "mutiny" that it saw in every "combination." In other words, the rhetoric of necessity characterized this aspect of the company's operations as well.

Long-Distance Justice

When the HBC became concerned enough about competition from Canadians trading out of Montreal to end its "sleep by the bay" and establish inland posts, it sought advice as to whether legal action could be taken against the Canadians for violating the HBC monopoly. However, when the Colonial Office passed on this request to the law officers of the Crown in 1777, it did not ask whether the offending traders could be tried in Rupert's Land.[95] The question posed to the law officers was simply whether, "there being no court of justice in Hudson's Bay," the company could seize the Canadians' posts and lay waste their goods. Establishing a court in Rupert's Land was not considered, possibly because the HBC would be both plaintiff and judge – a problem that would cause difficulties later on at Red River.

The law officers of the Crown produced a divided opinion. The solicitor general advised that the company could do nothing of the sort, adding that the charter contained "many extravagant and illegal clauses." The attorney general, however, said that the grant of the soil was valid and that, although the company could not seize goods, it could "enter upon any who attempt to occupy" its territories.[96] Because Canadian traders in this period were more concerned with feuding among themselves than directly attacking the HBC, this rather ambivalent advice was not tested in court.

However, when the old North-West Company took possession of Charlton Island in James Bay in 1803, and a merger between that organization and the XY Company appeared imminent, the HBC took to its lawyers again. This time it wanted to know whether it could take legal action in England. Its charter did in fact contemplate a kind of long-distance justice, providing that, if there were no governor or council in the place where an offence occurred, the chief factor of the region could send the case to "such [place] where justice may be executed or into this Kingdome of England as shall be thought most convenient."[97] But the company wanted to know about civil, not criminal, proceedings and in particular whether there was an appropriate cause of action.

The opinion was taken jointly from a number of private counsel, and the gist of the advice received was that, although the trade monopoly was probably void, the grant of the soil – again no mention of Aboriginal title – was good. But counsel advised against a suit in either trespass or case; the procedural obstacles were such, they said, that the company might be better off applying to Parliament to remedy this "defect of jurisdiction" – something the HBC was loath to do.[98] Insofar as prosecutions are concerned, the Canadian authorities had already reached a similar conclusion.

In August of 1803, the imperial Parliament passed the *Canada Jurisdiction Act* authorizing the trial of fur trade offences in the courts of Upper and Lower Canada, notwithstanding that they had been committed far beyond the indistinct boundaries of these two colonies.[99] The statute was the result of a campaign by Lower Canadian judges and fur trading interests and was supported by the grand jury in a case that had collapsed for want of jurisdiction. Needless to say, these people did not see trials in England as a viable option, nor were they concerned with enabling the Hudson's Bay Company to sue its competitors. Instead, the act that their petition produced was a criminal statute, prompted by increasing levels of violence among fur traders employed by the various British concerns working out of Montreal.[100] But history played a trick: only months after this statute was enacted, the Montreal concerns combined under the name of the North-West Company, and from that point on the *Canada Jurisdiction Act* became a weapon in the developing trade war between the Nor'Westers and the London-based HBC.[101]

But the sharpness of this weapon was not its provision for trials. It was rather what might be called its mesne process: *anyone* could apprehend and convey to Lower Canada persons accused of crimes in the Indian Territories, and the governor of Lower Canada could appoint justices of the peace for that purpose as well. An attractive new option for Nor'Westers eager to remove their bay-side competitors from the fur country, this prospect was much less appealing to the HBC, which had no office or representative in Lower Canada.[102] But even when Lord Selkirk, to whom the HBC had granted Assiniboia, finally managed to have some of his people appointed justices of the peace and to have cases tried in the upper rather than the lower province, not a single Nor'Wester was convicted. In the end, the violent struggle between the North-West Company and the HBC ended only when the two enterprises merged in 1821.

Still, for legal historians the cases sent east pursuant to the *Canada Jurisdiction Act* before the merger of 1821, most of which arose out of the struggle between Lord Selkirk and the North-West Company, are a rich resource. Lord Selkirk's argument was essentially that his people had been killed at Seven Oaks in 1816 for asserting their charter rights of property and jurisdiction. The North-West Company argument was that Selkirk's settlers had no such rights and that the Montreal traders could trace their own possession back to a time when the HBC "slept by the bay." Seeking to impress the settlers with their authority, the Nor'Westers took advantage of the fact that many of their traders were justices of the peace for the Indian Territories and issued War of 1812 uniforms for them to wear when executing warrants against Selkirk's people. Duncan Cameron even invoked the "law of our blessed constitution" when he urged these settlers not to resist his attempts to arrest Selkirk's governor at Red River, Miles Macdonell. Eventually, some of Selkirk's people did begin to fear that "they had not the law on their side."[103] But the North-West Company did not really want to test the charter in court lest it "risk a substance in pursuit of a shadow."[104]

The charges laid as a result of the encounter at Seven Oaks and its aftermath may in fact be unique, because both companies employed a court reporter to transcribe the proceedings. These transcripts run for hundreds of pages and include legal argument as well as testimony.[105] They even reproduce what may well be the most remarkable submission ever made to a Canadian court. Citing Hale and Blackstone in support, lawyers for the men accused of killing Governor Robert Semple at Seven Oaks argued that a state of "private war" existed in the Indian country that was analogous to the baronial wars of fourteenth-century England. They told Chief Justice William Dummer Powell and his colleagues that, in such circumstances, acts that would otherwise be murder were misdemeanours at best. Law and necessity once again. Attorney General John Beverly Robinson described this argument as preposterous, and it seems unlikely that it had much effect. On the other hand, the men were acquitted, and jurors do not give reasons for their decisions.[106]

Although the Seven Oaks incident looms large in the history of western Canada, its legal history has not.[107] And recently Lyle Dick has argued that generations of writers have constructed a historical tradition about Seven Oaks by ignoring, or at least avoiding, oral tradition and legal sources.[108] As a result, Dick argues, these historians transformed a confused and probably accidental encounter into a planned "massacre." They also converted older, more balanced accounts of the incident into a romantic discourse reflecting "the self-image of prairie Anglo Canadian society."[109] If he is right – and a perusal of the trial records suggests that he may well be – one is tempted to conclude that, while necessity may know no law, it certainly has had its share of spin doctors.

After 1821, long-distance justice became an even scarcer commodity than before. Competition between the Hudson's Bay Company and the

Nor'Westers ended with the merger of that year, and the imperial Parliament authorized the Crown to grant the new concern a licensed monopoly over the fur trade of British North America.[110] This statute confirmed that the *Canada Jurisdiction Act* applied to Rupert's Land as well as to the Territories farther west and north and provided for an elaborate system of justice – including a power in the Crown to appoint trial courts west of the Canadas – that was never implemented.

Perversely, these two aspects of the act brought uncertainty rather than clarity, at least for lawyers and anyone trying to figure it all out 180 years later.[111] The reason is that the act went on to deny the projected trial courts jurisdiction over capital cases, which had to be sent to Upper Canada, and to preserve all the jurisdiction that the Hudson's Bay Company was "entitled to claim ... under their Charter."[112] So, did the charter entitle the HBC to try capital cases in Rupert's Land? It seems odd that persons appointed by a private company would enjoy such authority when justices appointed by the Crown would not, and perhaps it was for this reason that the London committee recommended in 1822 against trying capital crimes at Red River.[113] In other British colonies, judges were deciding capital cases and applying English law to both the settlers and the indigenous peoples of those colonies – in Canada, for example, and in Australia, New Zealand, and British Columbia.[114] But even though these colonial judges had been appointed by the Crown and were acting pursuant to statutory authority, questions still arose as to whether Aboriginal law applied in cases that did not involve Europeans.[115]

Half a century after the London committee counselled caution, the company's lawyers remained nervous about capital cases, as the governor of Assiniboia discovered in 1867 when he inquired whether an Indian referred to as "the Wolverine" could be tried for the murder of an American at Portage la Prairie. Citing doubts about whether the accused was a person "living under" the company as contemplated by the charter, the legal opinion advised that, although Portage la Prairie was well within the boundaries of Rupert's Land, "the Wolverine" should be sent to Canada for trial. "This course," the lawyers concluded, "will avoid the discussion of questions as to the jurisdiction of the Company under the Charter" and in particular whether the charter was subject to the statute of 1821.[116] No mention was made of the fact that the company had been trying both Aboriginal persons and capital cases at Red River since Adam Thom's appointment in 1839 and had in fact hanged a Saulteaux named Capinesseweet in 1845.[117] At the conference upon which the present volume is based, Neil Watson made a detailed case for the proposition that Capinesseweet's prosecution and subsequent execution were lawful.[118] I think it more likely, however, that perceived necessities, and the somewhat aggressive approach of Adam Thom, carried the day, not law.

In the Indian Territories beyond Rupert's Land, the law was somewhat clearer: criminal cases had to be sent to Canada. Thom disagreed, stating that the distances involved made "the jurisdiction of Canada, even if valid in point of law ... utterly repugnant to justice and humanity."[119] He therefore ruled that the General Quarterly Court at Red River had jurisdiction over a homicide committed at Peace River, which was not in Rupert's Land.[120] The practice of the Hudson's Bay Company in the Indian Territories reflected this sense of justice – or, rather, necessity – because only the most serious matters were considered for judicial export.

The remainder were dealt with either in the manner of the company's private justice system or by means of summary trials, conducted by commissioned officers of the company, which sometimes displayed the distinct influence of Scots law.[121] So much for the "frontier" thesis that the pioneers invented everything anew.[122] And in some districts – as long as no one important was watching – most transgressions did not qualify even for this treatment; instead, offenders were subjected to an informal sort of "club law": that is, summary corporal punishment.[123] It is of course the more formal type of proceeding that Russ Smandych and Rick Linden have written about and that Paul Nigol addressed in his contribution to the conference.[124] But even in capital cases the company was reluctant to comply with a procedure as expensive and uncertain as trial in Canada. So reluctant, in fact, that it did so only once.

In 1838, an engagé named Baptiste Cadien was tried at Trois Rivières for his part in the massacre of eleven North Slavey (Hare) people, primarily women and children, near Fort Norman. Cadien was a Dogrib, culturally and on his mother's side, and his story is an epic of law and necessity, or at least law and geography, gone wild. The death sentence pronounced in Lower Canada for crimes committed near Great Bear Lake was commuted to transportation to Van Dieman's Land (Tasmania), but Cadien got only as far as England. Too ill to be transported, he died in 1844 aboard the prison hulk *Leviathan* in Portsmouth harbour.[125]

It is noteworthy that, at Cadien's trial, the presiding judge instructed the jury that if they found he was "a mere Indian, attached to no place of residence [meaning a trading post]," he was someone "over whom no jurisdiction could be maintained."[126] Only connection with the Hudson's Bay Company would bring Cadien within the four corners of the *Canada Jurisdiction Act*. This was a view that, in simpler terms, was expressed by the prosecution's only witness, one of Cadien's accomplices. "I never heard," said Baptiste Jourdain, himself at least half Cree, "of an Indian having been made prisoner for killing another."[127] These sentiments reflected HBC policy in the Indian Territories beyond Rupert's Land throughout this period.[128] On what may have been the last occasion when the company considered sending a capital case from the Territories to Canada, the option was predictably dismissed as a "useless expense." So a steersman implicated in the killing of four Inuit by a group of Gwichin (Kutchin) north of Fort Good Hope in 1850 escaped prosecution.[129]

Red River

My fifth and final topic is the legal regime established at Red River. It was a regime British in conception and execution, with Scots overtones, not only in terminology but also in an occasional verdict of "not proven."[130] This should not surprise: the carriers of the so-called birthright of the English settler, which is to say the common law of Blackstone's *Commentaries,* were predominantly Scots. And not only in Rupert's Land. One student of the subject has argued that "everything in New Zealand's legal history confirms that the Scots ... had very little if any commitment to English law and custom." He concludes that the "last thing any Scots settler would think of bringing with him, even if he were able, would be the English common law."[131] The company had a similar attitude toward French law: an early request by Bishop Provencher to have the seigneurial system applied to grants by the Roman Catholic Church was promptly denied. Governor Andrew Bulger told the church that such a system "is not recognized, and, I may say, will never be permitted."[132]

The settlement at Red River was small enough that its history could probably be told solely through a narrative of the lawsuits and prosecutions that took place between what may have been the first criminal case – the alleged theft of a silver teaspoon in 1813 – and the trial sixty years later of Ambroise Lepine, Louis Riel's adjutant general, for the murder of Thomas Scott.[133] Apart from Lepine's prosecution and the Seven Oaks trials in Upper and Lower Canada in 1818, all these cases were tried either by the system instituted by Lord Selkirk in 1811 or by the more formal judicature established when the Selkirk Estate reconveyed Assiniboia to the Hudson's Bay Company in 1835. At that point, the settlement was divided into four judicial districts, each with a magistrate or justice of the peace who held "petty sessions" every three months in each district. A General Quarterly Court was established for more serious cases and for appeals from the magistrates.[134]

Perhaps the best-known Red River case is *The Honourable Hudson's Bay Company v. Pierre Julleaum Sayer,* a prosecution in 1849 for trading furs in violation of the company's monopoly. The jury convicted, but violence was avoided because the court decided, under pressure of circumstance, to impose no penalty. When one of the jurors emerged to give the well-known shout "le commerce est libre!" one of these circumstances – the volatile crowd that had gathered outside the courthouse – dispersed to celebrate. Technically, the conviction upheld the company's rights, but the sentence and the crowd's reaction clearly showed that the days when the monopoly could be enforced were truly over. Law and necessity once again.

The social mores and tensions of the settlement, as opposed to its economic concerns, may be explored through a contextual analysis of cases such as *Foss v. Pelly,* a libel action arising out of an accusation of adultery. The lawsuit split the community's elite, and Thom's role in it effectively ended his career as a judge.[135] Helen Rothney's suit against Thom for back wages is another example. Not only does it shed light upon contracts of service and civil procedure in the settlement, but Rothney was a pregnant former employee of Thom's. This raises somewhat darker questions, not only about how the law was used in this case, but also about the position of women, especially young serving girls, at Red River generally.[136] Twenty years later, what Erica Smith has called a nine-day "melodrama of chaste and fallen womanhood" unfolded in the General Quarterly Court of Assiniboia that raised these questions even more directly.[137]

The Reverend Griffith Owen Corbett was an Anglican minister with some medical training who had testified against the company's rule in the settlement before the parliamentary investigation held in 1857. He was charged in 1863 with attempting on a number of occasions to perform an abortion on Maria Thomas, a sixteen-year-old girl of mixed descent who was a servant in his household and whose mother testified at the trial in Cree. According to Maria's testimony, she was pregnant because Corbett had forced himself upon her repeatedly. According to the defence, she was a "common prostitute." The newspaper reports of the trial and the evidence given by no fewer than sixty-one witnesses are a textbook illustration of what Smith calls the "prevailing racial discourse," wherein "Indian women were agents of men's ruin and white women agents of men's salvation."[138] Letitia Hargrave, the wife of retired chief factor James Hargrave, remarked that it was considered surprising that the *Nor'-Wester* survived as a "family newspaper" after what it had printed about the trial.[139]

Corbett was convicted by a jury and sentenced by a court presided over by Recorder John Black to six months in prison. He agitated for his release, and soon afterward a mob of his friends broke him out of jail. When the leader of this party was arrested in turn, his friends then broke him out too. Wanting "to avoid bloodshed," the authorities left them both at large. But the governor was also motivated by consideration of "the dangerous consequences to the whole community that would have arisen from the Indian tribes witnessing the spectacle of open warfare between different sections of the people."[140]

When Corbett returned to England, he tried, unsuccessfully, to sue for false imprisonment. An ally of Alexander Kennedy Isbister in his opposition to company rule, Corbett and his supporters professed to believe that the charges against him were politically motivated. He seems to have ended his days in England, writing pamphlets against the Hudson's Bay Company and advocating that its lands become a Crown colony.[141]

These politically charged examples can be multiplied, and the records of the General Quarterly Court contain many other, more routine, cases.[142] All told, they provide a remarkable body of evidence concerning an equally remarkable fact: that until 1870 a closely held corporation was the government of a vast territory in the heart of North America. Not only was it the government, but it was also a seventeenth-century proprietary government that included judges who were not appointed by the Crown but who claimed and exercised jurisdiction in capital cases. In short, if this was a state government, it was a highly unusual sort of state.[143] A modified version of this kind of regime was proposed for Vancouver Island in 1848, a suggestion that prompted one well-known Colonial Office official to comment that it could be maintained there only so long as the colonists were "too few and feeble to shake it off."[144] But Selkirk's settlement was established much earlier, and this was the regime that necessity, as perceived by the British government at the time, had ordained. Until 1870, no one in England or Canada was willing to spend the money required to have either the Canadian or the British state replace it with something better. So long as it was worth it to the Hudson's Bay Company to administer its private brand of justice, and so long as public opinion was prepared to tolerate this, the British government was content to go along as well. It is also just possible that in many respects it wasn't as bad a system as some critics of the Hudson's Bay Company, both then and now, would have us believe.[145]

Law, Necessity, and Riel's Adjutant General

I have talked about five aspects of law and necessity in Rupert's Land and the Indian Territories before 1870 in which the law was as flexible and uncertain as Justice Holmes suggested in his 1881 essay *The Common Law*.[146] And in those cases where it would not yield, some other solution could usually be found. Necessity, in effect, created new law.

This also appears to be what happened in the final case that I propose to discuss, a case that arose out of what is sometimes called the first Riel Rebellion. Although the trial was held four years after Rupert's Land ceased to exist, it concerns an event that took place in 1870 and that had roots reaching back much further than that. It is the prosecution of Ambroise Lepine, Louis Riel's adjutant general, for the murder of Thomas Scott.[147]

Lepine's arrest seems to have come as something of a surprise: there had been little outward sign that any charges were imminent, and Lepine, who was working his farm, made no attempt to elude capture. Francis Cornish, a local lawyer and politician who had "aligned himself early with Dr. John Schultz and other anti-French elements in the community," initiated the prosecution.[148] When Lepine was brought before the police magistrate at Fort Garry, his counsel raised an issue as to the jurisdiction of the courts of the new province of Manitoba to try him. The details of this argument in the police magistrate's court and its resolution in the Queen's Bench go on for thirty pages, and they deserve much more attention than I can give them here. But the gist of the submissions made by Lepine's counsel, one of whom stressed that he was less at home in English than French, was that the courts at Red River never had jurisdiction over capital cases; that jurisdiction over such cases throughout Red River's history was, by virtue of the imperial statutes of 1803 and 1821, in Canada; that these statutes had never been repealed; that, for a number of reasons, the combined effect of the relevant statutes and orders in council passed in Westminster and Ottawa between 1868 and 1871 was insufficient to confer jurisdiction upon the new Manitoba Court of Queen's Bench over felonies committed during the time period when Scott was killed; and therefore that only the courts of Ontario or Quebec, as successors to the courts of Upper and Lower Canada in the imperial legislation, could try Lepine.[149] Argument in the police court was heard on 29 September and 9 October 1873, but Justice Betournay was of the view that he needed to decide only if there was sufficient evidence to commit Lepine for trial, and he ruled there was. So in November submissions on the point were repeated at greater length in front of Justice McKeagney in the Queen's Bench.

In support of his jurisdictional argument, counsel for Lepine cited a work by Justice John Hamilton Gray of the Supreme Court of British Columbia to which Attorney General H.J. Clarke repeatedly objected. It was written during Gray's political career, he pointed out, and "few, indeed, are the judges on the bench who would like to accept or admit as sound law, all or even a small portion of what was written or spoken by them as politicians, or to advance the interests of their own party ... while they were in active political life." The attorney general went on to charge that the work was really a pamphlet that was being promoted by a "semi-legal-political newspaper" – an interesting phrase for a lawyer to use – that had "been trying for a long time to convince its readers, not that Louis Riel and others are not murderers, but only that there is no law in Manitoba to try them."[150] At the close of argument, Justice McKeagney announced that he would reserve his decision.

In December, Lepine was granted bail, and in February of 1874 the prosecution and the defence presented themselves to learn the judgment of the court. When Justice McKeagney appeared, he informed those present that he did not think himself "competent or justified in deciding a question of such great importance without a full Bench" and that "one judge is not enough to decide a matter of such grave importance." He would wait until next term, by which time Ottawa was expected to have appointed a chief justice.[151] Such deference might have been appropriate in England prior to the seventeenth century, when the last thing judges wanted to do was decide a point of law; it was somewhat surprising in 1874.

The attorney general was furious, noting that the court had had more than three months to make a decision and pointing out to Justice McKeagney that there had been "absolutely no other business before you during all that time." When he reminded the court that one judge had full authority to decide the issue and accused McKeagney of shirking his duty and acting out of fear, the judge asked whether he could not do as he pleased in the matter. The attorney general said, "most certainly not." It went downhill from there. "If your Lordship wishes to play into the hands of any political party, let us understand it at once, and we will then know that your object is to gain time, so that efforts may be made in another quarter for a pardon – but do not let it go to the world that you do not know your own power and jurisdiction." Justice McKeagney, "much excited," asked the attorney general what he meant by that and, not really waiting for a reply, adjourned the proceedings to June.[152]

By then, Chief Justice E.B. Wood had arrived in Manitoba, and the arguments were duly repeated before him. When counsel had finished, the chief justice proclaimed that he did not have to reserve his decision because he had no doubt that the court had jurisdiction over Lepine and his crime. He then proceeded to deliver a lengthy and detailed judgment that was as technical as the arguments of counsel and that presumably had been prepared beforehand. In the course of it, he reviewed the history of the General Quarterly Court at Red River, stating that, not only had it tried capital cases, but it had even executed a man "without its basis or jurisdiction ever having been formally or authoritatively questioned by the Imperial Government." He then noted that the *Rupert's Land Act,* 1868, also recognized the "validity of this Court and the legality of its jurisdiction."[153]

But of course the jurisdiction of the General Quarterly Court to try capital cases *had* been questioned repeatedly – albeit not "authoritatively." And although the imperial Parliament did recognize the court's jurisdiction in the *Rupert's Land Act,* it did so in the same way that it had always recognized Hudson's Bay Company's authority: without defining it.[154] The truth is that, in 1874, one "felt necessity of the time" was that the prosecution of Lepine, once commenced, could not be allowed to derail and certainly not on such a point as this.[155] So Chief Justice Wood confirmed that, as late as the 1860s, a private company could impose the death penalty at Red River. It was safe to say so now because the court in question, and that company's authority, no longer existed.

When the trial resumed, Lepine relied, in part, upon the defence that he had acted as an officer of a government in *de facto* control of the settlement. The jury convicted but recommended mercy. When it was all over, Lepine's death penalty was commuted to two years' imprisonment.[156] As the reluctant Justice McKeagney had obviously known, the felt necessities in Lepine's case, as with so many others in the middle kingdom in this period, clearly pulled in more than one direction. They still do.

Author's Note

This essay is a slightly revised version of the keynote address for the conference that spawned the papers for this collection. Although it has been updated here and there, particularly with references to some of the work that has been published since then, it is basically the same version that was readied for publication in 1997.

Notes

1 J. Frank, in *Fanelli v. U.S. Gypsum,* 141 F.2d 216 at 217 (2nd Circuit, 1944), cited in Ronald Joseph Delisle, *Evidence: Principles and Problems,* 4th ed. (Scarborough, ON: Carswell, 1996), 323.

2 Pearl Newman, "Community Developments and Prospects: Fort Vermilion," in *Proceedings of the Fort Chipewyan and Fort Vermilion Bicentennial Conference,* ed. Patricia A. McCormack and R. Geoffrey Ironside (Edmonton: Boreal Institute for Northern Studies, 1990), 272-74 at 273.

3 Eugene Dextrasse, "The Changing Roles of Government: Community Cooperation in Development," in *Proceedings of the Fort Chipewyan and Fort Vermilion Bicentennial Conference,* ed. McCormack and Ironside, 155-58 at 157.

4 See, for example, the other essays in Part 1 of this volume and the following conference papers presented to the 1997 conference titled "Law for the Buffalo, Law for the Musk Ox," at the University of Calgary: Constance Backhouse, "The Legal Prohibition of Aboriginal Dance on the Canadian Prairies: The 1902 Trial of Wanduta, Oak River Dakota 'Heyoka'"; Anne McGillvray and Russell Smandych, "Governing Aboriginal Childhood: Canadian Indian Affairs Policy and the Aboriginal Child in Western Canada, 1870-1930"; Anthony Gulig, "Hunting, Fishing, and Bombing: Natural Resources, Land, and the Struggle for Northern Saskatchewan in the Twentieth Century"; and R. Scott Sheffield and Hamar Foster, "Fighting the King's Wars: Harris Smallfence, Verbal Treaty Promises, and the Conscription of Indian Men, 1944." The last paper has since been published in *UBC Law Review* 33 (1999): 53-74.

5 Newman, "Community Developments and Prospects," 273.

6 A start has been made, however: see Joy Duncan, ed., *Red Serge Wives* (Edmonton: Centennial Book Committee, 1974). There are also memoirs such as L. Munday, *A Mounty's Wife: Being the Life Story of One Attached to the Force but Not of It* (London: Sheldon Press, 1930). Since the conference, A. Harold Clark's *The Unpaid Second Man: A Salute to the Wives and Widows of the Now Retired Members of the Royal Canadian Mounted Police* (Altona: Crocus Creative Publishing, 2002), which deals with the fact that many of these widows have no pensions, has also appeared.

7 There was also a workshop at the University of Manitoba in 1991 entitled "Conversations across Disciplines: Women, Law, and Prairie History."

8 Louis A. Knafla, ed., *Law and Justice in a New Land: Essays in Western Canadian Legal History* (Toronto: Carswell, 1986).

9 Louis A. Knafla, "From Oral to Written Memory: The Common Law Tradition in Western Canada," in *Law and Justice in a New Land,* ed. Knafla, 31-77; Graham Parker, "Canadian Legal Culture," in *Law and Justice in a New Land,* ed. Knafla, 3-29.

10 Parker, "Canadian Legal Culture," 5, 7, quoting from Clifford Geertz, *The Interpretation of Cultures* (New York: Basic Books, 1973), 4-5.

11 Parker, "Canadian Legal Culture," 8, 28.

12 Roy St. George Stubbs, *Four Recorders of Rupert's Land* (Winnipeg: Peguis Publishers, 1967). Bacon is quoted on the page immediately following the title page.

13 For the 1991 conference, see John McLaren, Hamar Foster, and Chet Orloff, eds., *Law for the Elephant, Law for the Beaver: Essays in the Legal History of the North American West* (Regina: Canadian Plains Research Center; Pasadena: Ninth Judicial Circuit Historical Society, 1992).

14 John Phillip Reid, "The Layers of Western Legal History," in *Law for the Elephant,* ed. McLaren, Foster, and Orloff, 23-73 at 24-26.

15 And because of the prodigious record keeping of the Hudson's Bay Company, in Canada this may also be true of the eighteenth-century west. Other topics singled out by Reid include mining law, the law of the borderlands in the southwest, the law of the Mormons, the law of cattle drives and the open range, and the law of the Indian Territory properly so called (i.e., present-day Oklahoma).

16 Reid, "Layers," 39. A similar prescription is offered in Sally Merry, "Law and Colonialism," *Law and Society Review* 25 (1991): 889-922, who stresses the importance of learning who brought new conceptions of law to the colonies and what those conceptions were.

17 The classic example of this approach is Reid's own *Law for the Elephant: Property and Social Behaviour on the Overland Trail* (San Marino: Huntington Library, 1980), but he discusses a number of others in "Some Lessons of Western Legal History," *Western Legal History* 1 (1988): 3-21.

18 Oliver Wendell Holmes Jr., *The Common Law and Other Writings* (Birmingham: Legal Classics Library, 1982), 1.

19 S.F.C. Milsom, *The Legal Framework of English Feudalism* (Cambridge, UK: Cambridge University Press, 1976), 180.

20 J.H. Baker, *An Introduction to English Legal History,* 3rd ed. (London: Butterworths, 1990), 261. The traditional view is that this development was intentional but that interpretation was challenged in the 1960s by Milsom. For a brief description of the debate, see G.R. Elton, *F.W. Maitland* (New Haven: Yale University Press, 1985), 45-48.

21 S.F.C. Milsom, *Historical Foundations of the Common Law,* 2nd ed. (London: Butterworths, 1981), 107; see also the example that Milsom provides in *Legal Framework,* 181-82.

22 Milsom, *Legal Framework,* 182. Milsom's view of how the early common law developed is not uncontroversial: see, for example, Paul Brand, *The Making of the Common Law* (London: Hambledon Press, 1992), chapter 9; and John Hudson, *The Formation of the English Common Law: Law and Society in England from the Norman Conquest to Magna Carta* (London and New York: Longman, 1996), 19-21. Milsom has recently summed up his work and replied to his critics in *A Natural History of the Common Law* (New York: Columbia University Press, 2003).

23 As the Supreme Court of Canada appears to have done with respect to Aboriginal fishing rights in such cases as *Regina v. Van der Peet,* [1996] 4 C.N.L.R. 177. Now see *Delgamuukw v. British Columbia,* [1997] 3 S.C.R. 1010, decided in eight months after the conference, in December 1997.

24 *R. v. Knowles, ex parte Sommersett* (1772), 27 State Tr. 1, 98 E.R. 499.

25 Quoted in Edward Fiddes, "Lord Mansfield and the Sommersett Case," *Law Quarterly Review* 50 (1934): 499-511 at 504.

26 Ibid. at 499.

27 Ibid. at 505.

28 Ibid. at 506. Benjamin Franklin wrote to the newspapers about *Sommersett's Case,* commenting on what he saw as "the hypocrisy of [a] country which encourages a detestable commerce by laws for promoting the Guinea trade while it piques itself on its virtue, love of liberty and the equity of its Courts in setting free a single negro"; quoted in ibid., 500n.

29 There were two Vigilance Committees in San Francisco, in 1851 and 1856. Philosopher Josiah Royce described the latter as "a Business man's Revolution" because it was essentially an attempt to apply "private enterprise to the administration of justice"; quoted in Walton Bean, *California: An Interpretive History* (New York: McGraw-Hill, 1978), 130. *Fiat iusticia, ruat coelum* is also the motto of the Faculty of Law at the University of British Columbia, but I suspect that they were thinking of Lord Mansfield.

30 John R. Wunder, "Toward a Legal History of the Great Plains," in *Law and the Great Plains: Essays on the Legal History of the Heartland,* ed. John R. Wunder (Westport: Greenwood Press, 1996), 3-8 at 6.

31 West of the Rockies, Vancouver Island and British Columbia effectively ceased to be part of the "Indian Territories" when colonial governments were established there in 1849 and 1858, respectively.

32 This point is made by Gerald Friesen in *The Canadian Prairies: A History* (Toronto: University of Toronto Press, 1984), 10, referring to W.L. Morton, *Manitoba: A History* (Toronto: University of Toronto Press, 1957).

33 See, for example, Michael Payne, *The Most Respectable Place in the Territory: Everyday Life in Hudson's Bay Company Service York Factory, 1788 to 1870* (Ottawa: Minister of Supply and Services Canada, 1989); and, more recently, Russell Smandych and Rick Linden, "Administering Justice without the State: A Study of the Private Justice System of the Hudson's Bay Company Prior to 1800," *Canadian Journal of Law and Society* 11 (1996): 21-61.

34 I have borrowed the terms "proprietary" and "disciplinary" from Milsom's *Legal Framework,* though not in a way that would necessarily be pleasing to him! H. Robert Baker, in an essay published two years after the conference, uses the term "conciliar" justice to refer to the former aspect of the HBC's jurisdiction, and it may well be a happier choice: see "Creating Order in the Wilderness: Transplanting the English Law to Rupert's Land, 1835-51," *Law and History Review* 17 (1999): 209-46.

35 See Hamar Foster, "Long-Distance Justice: The Criminal Jurisdiction of Canadian Courts West of the Canadas, 1763-1859," *American Journal of Legal History* 34 (1990): 1-48.

36 On Thom and the legal system at Red River, see Stubbs, *Four Recorders of Rupert's Land;* Dale Gibson and Lee Gibson, *Substantial Justice: Law and Lawyers in Manitoba 1670-1870* (Winnipeg: Peguis Publishers, 1972); Kathyrn M. Bindon, "Adam Thom and the Institution of Order in Rupert's Land 1839-1854," in *Essays in the History of Canadian Law,* vol. 1, ed. David H. Flaherty (Toronto: Osgoode Society, 1981), 43-87; Dale Gibson, "Company Justice: Origins of Legal Institutions in Pre-Confederation Manitoba," *Manitoba Law Journal* 23 (1995-96): 247-92; Russell Smandych and Karina Sacca, "The Development of Criminal Law Courts in Pre-1870 Manitoba," *Manitoba Law Journal* 24 (1996): 201-57; and, most recently, Baker, "Creating Order in the Wilderness."

37 James Youngblood Henderson, "First Nations Legal Inheritances in Canada: The Mikmaq Model," *Manitoba Law Journal* 23 (1995-96): 1-31 at 9, since republished as Chapter 1 in *Canada's Legal Inheritances,* ed. DeLloyd J. Guth and W. Wesley Pue (Winnipeg: Canadian Legal History Project, 2001), 1-31.

38 The earlier stereotype lives on, however. As an example, see the judgment of McEachern C.J.B.C. in *Delgamuukw et al. v. The Queen* (1991), 79 D.L.R. (4th) 185 (B.C.S.C.), reversed in part at [1993] 5 W.W.R. 97 (B.C.C.A.), new trial ordered at [1997] 3 S.C.R. 1010 (S.C.C.) (emphasizing the importance of oral history).

39 Karl N. Llewellyn and E. Adamson Hoebel, *The Cheyenne Way: Conflict and Caselaw in Primitive Jurisprudence* (Norman: University of Oklahoma Press, 1941); Rennard Strickland, *Fire and the Spirits: Cherokee Law from Clan to Court* (Norman: University of Oklahoma Press, 1975). Recent Canadian work includes Jo-Anne Fiske, "From Customary Law to Oral Traditions: Discursive Formation of Plural Legalisms in Northern British Columbia, 1857-1993," *BC Studies* 115-16 (1997-98): 267-88; and "The Supreme Law and the Grand Law: Changing Significance of Customary Law for Aboriginal Women of British Columbia," *BC Studies* 105-6 (1995): 183-99.

40 Not today at least: see Bruce G. Miller, *The Problem of Justice: Tradition and Law in the Coast Salish World* (Lincoln: University of Nebraska Press, 2000).

41 See Jennifer S.H. Brown, *Strangers in Blood: Fur Trade Families in Indian Country* (Vancouver: UBC Press, 1980); and Sylvia Van Kirk, *"Many Tender Ties": Women in Fur-Trade Society, 1670-1870* (Winnipeg: Watson and Dwyer, 1980). See as well Jay Nelson, "'A Strange Revolution in the Manners of the Country': Aboriginal-Settler Intermarriage in Nineteenth Century British Columbia," in *Regulating Lives: Historical Essays on the State, Society, the Individual, and the Law,* ed. John McLaren, Robert Menzies, and Dorothy E. Chunn (Vancouver: UBC Press, 2002), 23-62.

42 *Connolly v. Woolrich* (1867), 17 R.J.R.Q. (Qc. S.C.), aff'd. (1869), 17 R.J.R.Q. 266 (Qc. Q.B.).

43 John Phillip Reid, "Certainty of Vengeance: The Hudson's Bay Company and Retaliation in Kind against Indian Offenders in New Caledonia," *Montana: The Magazine of Western History* 5 (1993): 4-17 at 16n, 17. An example of a trader-Aboriginal marriage that may have complicated a homicide case may be found in Hamar Foster, "'The Queen's Law Is Better than Yours': International Homicide in Early British Columbia," in *Essays in the History of*

Canadian Law, vol. 5, *Crime and Criminal Justice,* ed. Jim Phillips, Tina Loo, and Susan Lewthwaite (Toronto: Osgoode Society, 1994), 41 at 41-45. See also notes 45 and 57 below.

44 As late as 1898 in the Yukon, three young Tagish men who had been charged with murdering a miner expected that one of them would have to pay with his life, but they could not understand why the verdict of the Territorial court was that all three of them had to hang. To them, such disproportionate reparation was proof that white men were "maliciously unjust." See Alan Grove, "'Where Is the Justice, Mr. Mills?': A Case Study of *R. v. Nantuck,*" in *Essays in the History of Canadian Law,* vol. 6, *British Columbia and the Yukon,* ed. Hamar Foster and John McLaren (Toronto: Osgoode Society, 1995), 87-127 at 100, quoting from the *Klondike Nugget* of 5 November 1898.

45 I am indebted to John Phillip Reid for this example, which is from Henry's journal, the entry for 30 October 1805. For a case in which a European was killed because he did not observe Gitksan law respecting accidental homicides, see *Regina v. Haatq als Aht* in note 57 below.

46 Quoted in Ross Cox, *Adventures on the Columbia River,* 2 vols. (London: H. Colburn and R. Bentley, 1831), 2: 242-45.

47 Reid, "The Layers of Western Legal History," 43-44, criticizing what he sees as the Austinian view that miners' law was anarchy because there was no federal or state "law" in the camps.

48 See, for example, the incidents described in Foster, "'The Queen's Law,'" 49-60; and John Phillip Reid, "Principles of Vengeance: Fur Trappers, Indians, and Retaliation for Homicide in the Transboundary North American West," *Western Historical Quarterly* 24 (1993): 41-23 at 21.

49 See J.G. MacGregor, *John Rowand: Czar of the Prairies* (Saskatoon: Western Producer Prairie Books, 1978), 101.

50 See Reid, "Principles of Vengeance," 29.

51 See Reid, "The Hudson's Bay Company," 8. Eventually, those favouring execution prevailed.

52 James E. Fitzgerald, *An Examination of the Charter and Proceedings of the Hudson's Bay Company* (London: T. Saunders, 1849), 135-36, cited in Smandych and Linden, "Administering Justice without the State," 28-29. On Fitzgerald's attempt to secure the right to colonize Vancouver Island, see Paul Knaplund, "Letters from James Edward Fitzgerald to W.E. Gladstone concerning Vancouver Island and the Hudson's Bay Company, 1848-1850," *British Columbia Historical Quarterly* 13 (1949): 1-21; and John S. Galbraith, "James Edward Fitzgerald versus the Hudson's Bay Company: The Founding of Vancouver Island," *British Columbia Historical Quarterly* 16 (1952): 191-207.

53 Fitzgerald's pamphlet was part of a propaganda war between the HBC and its opponents. Fitzgerald gave up on North America after he lost his bid to colonize Vancouver Island and emigrated to New Zealand, where for three months in 1865 he was the minister for Maori affairs. On his role there, see Alan Ward, *A Show of Justice: Racial 'Amalgamation' in Nineteenth Century New Zealand* (Auckland: Auckland University Press, 1974), 183-93.

54 See, for example, W.S. Wallace, ed., *John McLean's Notes of a Twenty-Five Year's Service in the Hudson's Bay Territory* (Toronto: Champlain Society, 1932).

55 See David Mulhall, *Will to Power: The Missionary Career of Father Morice* (Vancouver: UBC Press, 1986).

56 A.G. Morice, *The History of the Northern Interior of British Columbia* (Smithers: Interior Stationery, 1978 reprint), 115. Missionaries and reformers made similar complaints about East India Company employees in India.

57 Thus, a life taken in satisfaction need not be, and often was not, the life of the actual offender, and blood debts could usually be compromised, especially if the death were accidental. Europeans with experience on the ground knew this. As a prosecution witness at the trial of a Gitksan man in 1884 told defence counsel, "a person could always pay enough to save their neck. That is one good thing about Indians." In that case, a young Gitksan boy had died accidentally while in the employ of a trader. Custom required that he explain this to the family and offer compensation. He did not, so the boy's father killed him. See *Regina v. Haatq als Aht,* 1884, Library and Archives Canada (LAC), RG 13, vol. 1421, file 190. This is the case referred to in notes 43 and 45 above.

58 Reid, "Principles of Vengeance," 43. Reid's work in this area has since been published as *Patterns of Vengeance: Cross-Cultural Homicide in the North American Fur Trade* (Pasadena: 9th Circuit Historical Society, 1999).

59 Cole Harris, "Towards a Geography of White Power in the Cordilleran Fur Trade," *Canadian Geographer* 39 (1990): 131-40 at 135. See also the same author's *The Resettlement of British Columbia: Essays on Colonialism and Geographical Change* (Vancouver: UBC Press, 1997), 55-56.

60 Reid, "Principles of Vengeance," 41.

61 E.P. Thompson, *Whigs and Hunters: The Origin of the Black Act* (Harmondsworth: Penguin, 1977), 264.

62 Here I add parenthetically that the history of the Canadian west will have come of age when we have a major work that divides the subject into periods that reflect Aboriginal rather than European interests. See the framework suggested by Friesen, *The Canadian Prairies,* 23. Works dealing with Aboriginal-European relations – for example, J.R. Miller's *Skyscrapers Hide the Heavens* (Toronto: University of Toronto Press, 1989); and The Royal Commission, *Report of the Royal Commission on Aboriginal Peoples* (Ottawa: Minister of Supply and Services Canada, 1996) – have now moved in this direction.

63 E.E. Rich, *The History of the Hudson's Bay Company 1670-1870,* 2 vols. (London: Hudson's Bay Record Society, 1958), 1: 58-60.

64 Ibid. at 57; see also Hudson's Bay Company, *Charters, Statutes, Orders in Council, Etc. Relating to the Hudson's Bay Company* (London: Hudson's Bay Company, 1931).

65 Ibid. at 58.

66 *Report from the Select Committee on the Hudson's Bay Company* (London: House of Commons, 1857), Appendix 1, 359-61.

67 See text accompanying notes 24-28 above.

68 The first inland post was Cumberland House, established by Samuel Hearne in 1774.

69 See opinions of Solicitor General Wedderburn and Attorney General Thurlow, dated 9 April and 5 August 1777, respectively, in Hudson's Bay Company Archives (HBCA), A.39/1-2. For a discussion of the dates of these opinions, see Foster, "Long-Distance Justice," 12n.

70 The list includes Alexander Wedderburn, Edward Thurlow, Thomas Erskine, Vicary Gibbs, Samuel Romilly, Francis Hargrave, Joseph Berens, John Gurney, George Bell, George Holroyd, William Cruise, John Scarlett, and Stephen Lushington.

71 See Barry Cooper, *Alexander Kennedy Isbister: A Respectable Critic of the Honourable Company* (Ottawa: Carleton University Press, 1988), especially chapters 7-10. Unfortunately, this otherwise useful book lacks an index.

72 Quoted in James Dodds, *The Hudson's Bay Company: Its Position and Prospects* (London: Edward Stanford, 1866), 23-24.

73 The select committee also recommended that the company's "connexion" with Vancouver Island should be terminated "as soon as it can conveniently be done." *Report from the Select Committee,* iv.

74 See, for example, Friesen, *The Canadian Prairies,* 87, citing the others.

75 Nor, after 1690, did the HBC ever seek parliamentary confirmation: see Foster, "Long-Distance Justice," 13n, 14.

76 Hudson's Bay Company, *Charters, Statutes, Orders in Council, Etc.*

77 The most recent discussion of this aspect of Rupert's Land's legal history is Baker, "Creating Order in the Wilderness."

78 On the theoretical issues posed, see Brian Slattery, "Aboriginal Sovereignty and Imperial Claims," in *Aboriginal Self-Determination,* ed. Frank Cassidy (Lantzville, BC: Oolichan Books, 1991), 197-217.

79 See, for example, Foster, "'The Queen's Law,'" 60-91, 82, and 109n; and, more generally, also Foster, "Measures Essentially Unjust: English 'Law' and Native 'Custom' in New Zealand, Vancouver Island, and British Columbia, 1769-1871" (master's thesis, University of Auckland, 1988).

80 For a comprehensive overview of social life in the largest of the HBC posts, see Payne, *The Most Respectable Place.*

81 John Phillip Reid, "The Beaver's Law in the Elephant's Country: An Excursion into Transboundary Western Legal History," *Western Legal History* 4 (1991): 149-201 at 154-58.
82 Ibid. at 165.
83 Smandych and Linden, "Administering Justice without the State," 35, citing from Joseph Robson, *An Account of Six Years Residence in Hudson's Bay from 1733 to 1736, and 1744 to 1747* (London: J. Payne, 1752), 49.
84 Hamar Foster, "Mutiny on the *Beaver:* Law and Authority in the Fur Trade Navy, 1835-1840," in *Glimpses of Canadian Legal History,* ed. Dale Gibson and W. Wesley Pue (Winnipeg: Legal Research Institute, 1991), 15-46 at 19. This essay was originally published in volume 20 of the *Manitoba Law Journal* (1991).
85 Smandych and Linden, "Administering Justice without the State," 33.
86 Rich, *The History of the Hudson's Bay Company,* 607-8.
87 Smandych and Linden, "Administering Justice without the State," 37-38. This raises the question of ethnic relations in the fur trade, the records of which are replete with generalizations and stereotypes about the relative abilities of Orkneymen, Irishmen, Iroquois, Canadians, and so on. See, for example, Payne, *The Most Respectable Place;* and Carol M. Judd, "'Mixt Bands of Many Nations': 1821-1870," in *Old Trails and New Directions: Papers of the Third North American Fur Trade Conference,* ed. Carol M. Judd and Arthur J. Ray (Toronto: University of Toronto Press, 1980), 127-46.
88 See Foster, "Mutiny on the *Beaver,*" 37; and "Killing Mr. John: Law and Jurisdiction at Fort Stikine, 1842-1846," in *Law for the Elephant,* ed. McLaren, Foster, and Orloff, 176-77.
89 For Isbister, see Smandych and Linden, "Administering Justice without the State," 52-59; and Paul C. Nigol's conference paper, "The Hudson's Bay Company's Private Justice System in the Eighteenth Century: Deference, Autonomy, and Governors James Isham and Joseph Isbister," presented to the 1997 conference "Law for the Buffalo, Law for the Musk Ox" at the University of Calgary. For Manson and McLean, see Morice, *The History of the Northern Interior,* especially chapters 16 and 18.
90 Charles Beardmore, 23 July 1851, British Columbia Archives and Records Services, GR 322, vol. 1, 348. Beardmore said that "no man in his right senses" would work for the HBC. "'Twas worse than transportation."
91 See, for example, *Standing Rules and Regulations* (1835), HBCA, B.229/k/2.
92 See, for example, Foster, "Mutiny on the *Beaver,*" 37-38.
93 Ibid. at 41.
94 See Hamar Foster, "British Columbia: Legal Institutions in the Far West, from Contact to 1871," *Manitoba Law Journal* 23 (1995-96): 293-340 at 312, 312n, since republished in *Canada's Legal Inheritances,* ed. Guth and Pue, 293-340.
95 Possibly because such persons did not, in the words of the charter, "live under them:" see text accompanying notes 76-79 above.
96 See Foster, "Long-Distance Justice," 12.
97 Ibid. at 3.
98 Ibid. at 14. By the eighteenth century, the courts had come to the curious conclusion that trespass was the appropriate action for direct harm, whereas trespass upon the special case (or "case") was for indirect harm. See, for example, *Reynolds v. Clarke* (1725), 1 Strange 634; and *Scott v. Shepherd* (1773), 2 Wm Bla. 892.
99 (1803), 43 Geo. III, c. 138 (U.K.).
100 Foster, "Long-Distance Justice," 6-11.
101 There was, of course, a time lag, and some cases were dealt with in ignorance of the new imperial law: see, for example, the case of *Oiseaux du Plan* discussed in ibid. at 17-19 and that of *John M'Donald* discussed in Hamar Foster, "Conflict Resolution during the Fur Trade in the Canadian North West, 1803-1859," *Transactions of the Jean Bodin Society for Comparative Institutional History* 63 (Bruxelles: De Boeck University, 1996), 207-15 at 207-9.
102 Compare, for example, the *Mowat* and *de Reinhard* cases, discussed in Foster, "Long-Distance Justice," 19-23 and 27-29. See this essay as well in connection with suggested answers to the questions posed by Baker, "Creating Order in the Wilderness," 216n.
103 J.M. Gray, *Lord Selkirk of Red River* (Toronto: Macmillan, 1963), 110.

104 Chester Martin, *Lord Selkirk's Work in Canada* (Toronto: Oxford University Press, 1916), 49, 91.

105 See A. Amos, *Report of Trials in the Courts of Canada, Relative to the Destruction of the Earl of Selkirk's Settlement on the Red River: With Observations* (London: J. Murray, 1820); W.S. Simpson, *Report at Large of the Trial of Charles De Reinhard* (Montreal: J. Lane, 1819); and the Northwest Company's *Report of the Proceedings Connected with the Disputes between the Earl of Selkirk and the North-West Company at the Assizes, Held at York, in Upper Canada, October 1818* (London: n.p., 1819).

106 See Hamar Foster, "Forgotten Arguments: Aboriginal Title and Sovereignty in *Canada Jurisdiction Act* Cases," *Manitoba Law Journal* 21 (1992): 343-89 at 377.

107 But see G.M. Gressley, "Lord Selkirk and the Canadian Courts," in *Canadian History before Confederation: Essays and Interpretations,* 2nd ed., ed. J.M. Bumsted (Georgetown: Irwin Dorsey, 1979), 277-93; and Gray, *Lord Selkirk of Red River,* chapter 12.

108 Such as the trials and the report of the commissioners appointed to investigate the incident. The trials are considered in Foster, "Forgotten Arguments," 375-77.

109 Lyle Dick, "The Seven Oaks Incident and the Construction of a Historical Tradition, 1816 to 1970," in *Making Western Canada: Essays on European Colonization and Settlement,* ed. Catherine Cavanaugh and Jeremy Mouat (Toronto: Garamond Press, 1996), 1-30 at 24.

110 (1821), 1 & 2 Geo. IV, c. 66 (U.K.).

111 See, generally, Desmond Brown, "Unpredictable and Uncertain: Criminal Law in the Canadian Northwest before 1888," *Alberta Law Review* 17 (1979): 497-512. Baker, "Creating Order in the Wilderness," 245n, criticizes Brown for describing the law this way without having looked at the case record. I agree that one should do this, but Brown's point, I think, was more theoretical.

112 Foster, "Forgotten Arguments," ss. 12, 14. Civil cases involving claims of more than £200 were also excluded.

113 J.H. Pelly, Thomas Langley, A. Colville, and N. Garry to Andrew Bulger, 1 June 1822, in *The Canadian North-West: Its Early Development and Legislative Records,* vol. 1, ed. E.H. Oliver (Ottawa: Government Printing Bureau, 1915), 222. When the colony of Vancouver Island was established in 1849, the provisions of the statutes of 1803 and 1821 were specifically repealed in order that the new colonial courts could try capital cases locally.

114 This point is made by Smandych and Sacca, "The Development of Criminal Law Courts," 242, and is a theme of Smandych's contribution to the current volume. See also Foster, *Measures Essentially Unjust,* chapters 3 and 5.

115 In Canada, see the despatches concerning the *Shawanakiskie* case in the 1820s, where the issue was whether a treaty might prevent the application of criminal law to the Ottawas: A.G. Doughty and N. Story, eds., *Documents Relating to the Constitutional History of Canada 1819-1828* (Ottawa: J.O. Patenaude, 1935), 175-78. The case is discussed in Foster, "Forgotten Arguments," 377-79; and more recently in Mark D. Walters, "The Extension of Colonial Criminal Jurisdiction over the Aboriginal Peoples of Upper Canada: Reconsidering the *Shawanakiskie* Case (1822-26)," *University of Toronto Law Journal* 46 (1996): 273-310; and Smandych and Sacca, "The Development of Criminal Law Courts," 5-6 (manuscript version).

In Australia, the courts of Victoria and South Australia ruled in the 1830s and 1840s that English criminal law did not apply to crimes committed by Aborigines against other Aborigines; in *R. v. Jack Congo Murrell* (1836), Legge 72, the Supreme Court of New South Wales disagreed. These cases are considered in Sidney L. Harring, "The Killing Time: A History of Aboriginal Resistance in Colonial Australia," *Ottawa Law Review* 26 (1994): 385-423.

In New Zealand, the Treaty of Waitangi appeared to subject Maori to the criminal law, but a question arose as to whether this was true of *hapu* (subtribes) who had not signed the treaty. The attorney general advised that the criminal law did not apply to them, but he was overruled by the Colonial Office, which cited statute and other authority in support. See Peter Adams, *Fatal Necessity: British Intervention in New Zealand 1830-1847* (Auckland: Auckland University Press, 1977), 161-64.

116 HBCA, A.39/7, fos. 340-343d (opinion of Montague Bere, 3 May 1867).

117 See Neil Watson, "'Tried in the Regular Way': *The Public Interest v. Capinesseweet,*" presented to the 1997 conference "Law for the Buffalo, Law for the Musk Ox" at the University of Calgary; and Smandych and Sacca, "The Development of Criminal Law Courts," 18 (manuscript copy).

One has to be careful when assessing the overseas impact of the British legal system in the nineteenth century. While it is true, for example, that obstacles were placed in the way of Aboriginal people testifying as ordinary witnesses in many colonies, removing these obstacles did not permit them to testify in their own defence: in Canada, accused persons, whether Aboriginal or not, were generally barred from giving sworn evidence at trial until 1893.

Although it may also be true (the figures are not exact) that between 1860 and 1869 twenty-five of the twenty-seven people hanged in British Columbia were Aboriginal, one needs to know whether the judge in such cases recommended against commuting the sentence before one can conclude with confidence that he was an "Indian-hanging Judge" (Tina Loo, "Savage Mercy: Native Culture and the Modification of Capital Punishment in Nineteenth Century British Columbia," in *Qualities of Mercy: Justice, Punishment, and Discretion,* ed. Carolyn Strange [Vancouver: UBC Press, 1996], 104-29 at 106, citing a newspaper review of a biography of BC judge Matthew Baillie Begbie). He may have been. But juries, not judges, decided guilt or innocence in capital cases, and if the verdict was guilty the death penalty was mandatory. The judge was required by law to pronounce it.

118 See Watson, "'Tried in the Regular Way.'" This was also, presumably, the view of Chief Justice Wood in the *Lepine* case, discussed below.

119 Quoted in Stubbs, *Four Recorders of Rupert's Land,* 14.

120 *In the Case of James Calder* (1848), 2 *Western Law Times and Reports* 1, 10 (1891). This case stands in contrast to that of the "Wolverine" (see note 116 above), in which the company's lawyers doubted that the company had capital jurisdiction even within Rupert's Land.

121 See, for example, the case that Governor George Simpson decided on a stopover at McLeod's Fort on his second transcontinental tour of inspection in 1828, reported in Malcolm McLeod's edition of Archibald McDonald, *Peace River: A Canoe Voyage from Hudson's Bay to the Pacific, by the Late Sir George Simpson, in 1828* (Ottawa: J. Durie and Son, 1872), 21.

122 Reid, "Some Lessons," 7-8.

123 The phrase is a contemporary one.

124 Smandych and Linden, "Administering Justice without the State"; Nigol, "The Hudson's Bay Company's Private Justice System."

125 For an account of this remarkable case, see Hamar Foster, "Sins against the Great Spirit: The Law, the Hudson's Bay Company, and the Mackenzie's River Murders, 1835-1839," *Criminal Justice History: An International Annual* 10 (1989): 23-76.

126 Report of Chief Justice James Reid in LAC, MG 11 ("Q" Series), Lower Canada no. 245, part 1, vol. 6, 55-56.

127 *Case of Baptiste Cadien for Murder* (Three Rivers: G. Stobbs, 1838), LAC, MG 11, CO 42, vol. 281, 50-61.

128 As opposed to what appears to have been the policy within Rupert's Land or at least at Red River: see text accompanying notes 76-79 and 113-17 above.

129 HBCA, B.157/z/1, fos. 1-6; see also the account in Sir John Richardson, *Arctic Searching Expedition,* vol. 1 (London: Longman, Brown, Green and Longmans, 1851), 216-17.

130 Stubbs, *Four Recorders of Rupert's Land,* 119.

131 N.J. Jamieson, "English Law but British Justice," *Otago Law Review* 4 (1980): 488-502.

132 Quoted in Gibson, "Company Justice," 269.

133 For the teaspoon case, see ibid. at 258-59; and Smandych and Sacca, "The Development of Criminal Law Courts," 232-33. For Lepine's, see Elliott and Brokovski, *Preliminary Investigation and Trial of Ambroise D. Lepine for the Murder of Thomas Scott* (Montreal: n.p., 1875); and, much more recently, J.M. Bumsted, "The Trial of Ambroise Lépine," *Beaver* 77 (1997): 9-19; and Baker, "Creating Order in the Wilderness." Bumsted's latest contribution to the history of the Red River Colony is *Thomas Scott's Body and Other Essays on Early Manitoba History* (Winnipeg: University of Manitoba Press, 2000), and it deals with a number of the incidents that I have touched on in this chapter.

134 Gibson, "Company Justice," 271. In 1837, the districts were reduced to three, each with two magistrates, and petty sessions were required to be held before three magistrates, one of whom had to come from outside the district.

135 The case is described in a number of sources, including ibid. at 277-78; Stubbs, *Four Recorders of Rupert's Land,* 36 ff.; and Frits Pannekoek, *A Snug Little Flock: The Social Origins of the Riel Resistance 1869-70* (Winnipeg: Watson and Dwyer, 1991), 124-40.

136 See Dale Gibson, "A Scandal at Red River," *Beaver* 70, 5 (1990): 30-38.

137 Erica Smith, "'Gentlemen, This Is No Ordinary Trial': Sexual Narratives in the Trial of Reverend Corbett, Red River, 1863," in *Reading beyond Words: Contexts for Native History,* ed. Jennifer S.H. Brown and Elizabeth Vibert (Peterborough: Broadview Press, 1996), 364-402.

138 Ibid. at 375. Smith says that there were about "100" witnesses, but Stubbs, *Four Recorders of Rupert's Land,* 149, says 61, and I bet he counted.

139 Stubbs, *Four Recorders of Rupert's Land.*

140 Ibid. at 154, quoting from an official document.

141 See, for example, *Notes on Rupert's America* (1868), published in facsimile by the Bibliographical Society of Canada in 1967.

142 See Stubbs, *Four Recorders of Rupert's Land;* Smandych and Sacca, "The Development of Criminal Law Courts"; and Baker, "Creating Order in the Wilderness."

143 Smandych and Sacca, "The Development of Criminal Law Courts," 211, 247, equate formal justice systems with state systems and trace Red River's "state" system to before 1835.

144 James Stephen, quoted in Knaplund, "James Edward Fitzgerald," 269.

145 On this point, see Baker, "Creating Order in the Wilderness."

146 Holmes, *The Common Law.*

147 Riel had also been charged, but only Lepine returned to Red River from the United States. Most of what follows is taken from the report of the proceedings published in 1875 by Elliott and Brokovski, *Preliminary Investigation.*

148 Gibson and Gibson, *Substantial Justice,* 97, 115. Schultz, who controlled the *Nor'-Wester* newspaper, figures prominently in the political and legal history of Red River. At one point, Recorder John Black forbade him from suing in his court until he purged his contempt – a remedy that counsel in England quickly pronounced illegal. Defending his action, Recorder Black asserted that, "during the whole of my own eighteen years experience in the Settlement there has not ... occurred a single instance in which a contempt of Court has been punished in the strictly legal way, although I suspect ... offences of that class have been neither few nor small"; "Further Opinion of Montague Bere on the Black and Schultz Case," 1 February 1867, HBCA, A.39/7, fos. 323-9. See also Stubbs, *Four Recorders of Rupert's Land,* 163-71.

149 For a somewhat similar case in the Yukon, in terms of both the French-English context and the jurisdictional arguments, see *R. v. Nantuck,* in *British Columbia and the Yukon,* ed. Foster and McLaren, a prosecution of three Tagish Indians for murder.

150 Elliott and Brokovski, *Preliminary Investigation,* 14. The newspaper in question was published in Quebec.

151 Ibid. at 19.

152 Ibid. at 20-21.

153 Ibid. at 27. That singular person was, of course, Aboriginal: Capinesseweet.

154 See, for example, s. 14 of (1821), 1 & 2 Geo. IV, c. 66 (U.K.), and accompanying text to note 108 above.

155 In *R. v. Nantuck,* the execution of two Tagish Indians proceeded in spite of the trial judge's opinion and the opinion of independent counsel that the trial was a jurisdictional nullity.

156 Gibson and Gibson, *Substantial Justice,* 117. The Gibsons also point out that in 1875 the Court of Queen's Bench pronounced a sentence of "outlawry" against Riel.

3

"There Seemed to Be No Recognized Law": Canadian Law and the Prairie First Nations

Sidney L. Harring

Since the settlement of the Prairies occurred after Confederation, a "Canadian" Indian policy was implemented in the region as opposed to the various colonial policies of Ontario, Quebec, the Maritimes, and British Columbia. The dominion Indian policy applied, however, was Ontarian: the tribes were to sell their lands through treaties, be settled on small reserves, and find a place in the broader Canadian society as small farmers.[1] This Indian policy, a political decision, was to be implemented within a legal framework. Canadian law was to precede settlement, and Mounties, led by officers (generally, but not always, nonlawyers) who were also appointed as stipendiary magistrates, were central to this process.[2] Lieutenant Governor Alexander Morris of Manitoba, formerly chief justice, was sent to negotiate these treaties – legal documents in which the Indian nations sold their lands to the Canadian government.

While this history is also central to the mythology of Canadian history and politics, it degenerated into oppression, land theft, and starvation, culminating in a Métis and Indian rebellion in 1885. The Indians who joined in that rebellion bore the brunt of the repression that followed. Dozens of warriors and a handful of Métis were tried on various charges, including Cree chief One Arrow on a charge of treason. As his indictment was read in a Regina courtroom, the chief listened as the charge was translated into Cree. In English, it read that he, "together with divers and other evil disposed persons ... armed and arrayed in a warlike manner, that is to say with guns, rifles, pistols, bayonets and other weapons, being then wickedly and feloniously assembled and gathered together against our said Lady the Queen, most wickedly and felonious did levy and make war against our said Lady the Queen ... and against the peace of our said Lady the Queen, her Crown and dignity." One Arrow heard the indictment translated into Cree as an accusation that he had "knocked off the Queen's bonnet" and "stabbed her in the behind with his sword." First confused, then enraged, he demanded to know if the interpreter was drunk. He had never even met the queen.[3]

This literal translation of the indictments was evidently the practice in all of the Riel Rebellion trials. Big Bear, another Cree chief, was confused by the reading of his indictment and denied its charges: "These people all lie. They are saying that I tried to steal the Great Mother's hat, how could I do that? She lives very far across the Great Water, and how could I go there to steal her hat? I didn't want her hat, and didn't know that she had one."[4]

These incidents describe as well as any other both the comedy and the tragedy of the imposition of British and Canadian law on Prairie Indian nations. The Canadian law of treason had no meaning at all for speakers of the Cree language and could not be translated. A crown, after all, really is only a hat. Why does a hat need land? How can a hat own the land? And why would a powerful Cree chief stab a lady whom he had never met in the behind with a bayonet? Moreover, even if all of this made sense to Indians held in irons, the English law of treason governs only those who owe allegiance to the English Crown and then intentionally turn against it.

The "sale" of Hudson's Bay Company (HBC) rights in western Canada to the dominion in 1869 for £300,000 brought two fully functioning legal systems together on the Canadian Prairies, Anglo-Canadian and Native. Unlike the Six Nations in 1780s Ontario, who were unable to understand their inferior legal status because nothing in their experience or history had prepared them for it, Native people on the Prairies were alert to the history of Canadians' dishonesty and avariciousness in their dealings with Indians. The "sale" of company lands to Canada infuriated the Native people living there: it was they, not the HBC, who owned those lands.[5] Native people were explicit about their ownership. The immediate impetus for a hurried signing of Treaty 6 was Chief Poundmaker's blocking of progress on telegraph lines near Battleford: lines could not be strung across Cree lands without a treaty.[6]

This aspect of the treaty process – the treaties' recognition of Aboriginal rights – is central to any modern Canadian understanding of Indian law. It is important to recognize that Indians had clear reasons for negotiating treaties with the Crown and brought their own agendas to the negotiations. Not all of these reasons were legal ones, but many were. Poundmaker's insistence that the telegraph not cross Cree lands without a treaty involved, for example, an insistence that the Crown acknowledge both Cree ownership of the land and their sovereignty as a nation by paying for crossing it with telegraph wires. The ceremonial and political functions of the treaty-making process were as important to Native people as the recognition of their legal rights.

The NWMP and the Myth of the Legally Structured Frontier

Before the making of Treaties 3 through 7 and their implicit recognition of tribal law, the North-West Mounted Police (NWMP) were created in 1873, central to the dominion government's strategy to settle the frontier in an orderly way. While the contribution of the NWMP to the Canadian national culture is enormous, with the familiar red uniform of the "Mounties" recognized around the world, it is important to dissect the legal portions of the NWMP mythology: the myth that the Canadian frontier was peaceably settled because the NWMP were there, providing law and order.[7]

Any legal history considering the NWMP needs to begin with a recognition that the force was far more than a national police force; it was directed from Ottawa expressly so that it was not responsive to local pressures from either settlers or Indians. It was a self-contained legal institution organized on a quasi-military model: Mounties arrested, prosecuted, judged, and jailed offenders under their jurisdiction. The commissioner and assistant commissioners were appointed stipendiary magistrates with full judicial powers extending even to capital crimes. Inspectors and captains were appointed justices of the peace (JPs) with authority to summarily try minor crimes.[8] This legal function was not incidental to the force but was conceptualized at its core. From the beginning, a portion of NWMP officers was legally trained, balancing military with legal training in the officer corps. James F. Macleod, assistant commissioner in the early 1870s and its second commissioner from 1876 to 1880, articled in the law offices of Alexander Campbell, a member of Sir John A. Macdonald's cabinet and former law partner of the prime minister.[9]

This extraordinary delegation of judicial power over a civilian population in peacetime reflects the clear determination of the Macdonald government to control and settle the frontier on its own terms. A popular explanation for such a drastic measure is that it reflects a Canadian determination to avoid the American experience of Indian trouble caused by settlers; there is even a parallel US-centred explanation – that the NWMP was created to push American hunters, trappers, and whisky traders back across the border, stopping a continued American threat to Canadian sovereignty in the west. A Canadian-centred explanation, however, reflects what actually occurred on the frontier. The dominion government, aware of the resistance of western Ontario Indians to settlement (and familiar with US Indian wars), both feared and perhaps even expected that the Prairie Indians would resist settlement. Thus, it created the NWMP to both protect settlers and implement the dominion's Ontarian Indian policy of settling Indians as farmers on small reserves.[10] Any kind of military force could have asserted Canadian sovereignty in the west, as had already been proved in the suppression of the Red River Rebellion of 1869-70. But only a federal police force could bring Indians and Métis within the reach of Canadian law.[11] In any case, the question of the origins of the force is irrelevant: the issue is the legal impact of the NWMP on Indian nations.

The most salient single fact in NWMP history is the story of its immediately favourable reception by western tribes. This occurred because the tribes, each for its own reason and weary of the chaotic state of social relations on the frontier, grasped a conception of the NWMP as the immediate representatives of the queen. They were led by highly visible officers who were "in charge," able to make decisions and take limited but appropriate actions consistent with those decisions. These officers led their own parties of armed, red-coated "warriors" who roamed the prairie, carrying out the queen's business. This structure was familiar to the tribes, consistent with their traditional forms of meeting and face-to-face negotiation.[12] The model, moreover, saw the political function of the NWMP as inseparable from its legal one, a structure also true in Native society.

The HBC operated a substantial legal system by the nineteenth century. It recognized tribal law and applied its legal order only to employees, other settlers, or Indians within the sphere of company operations – especially their small communities around trading posts or those engaged in trading activity.[13] The First Nations law had been recognized by Hudson's Bay authorities for several hundred years.[14]

Native society in the west had been destabilized by both the fur trade and the beginnings of settlement. The largest First Nation in Canada, the Cree, had been primary beneficiaries of the fur trade. Initially woodland Indians occupying the northern forests, the Cree lived around the southern shores of Hudson Bay. This put them in an immediate position to serve both as fur trappers and as middlemen in the fur trade. This trade enriched them, giving access to trade goods and guns. A rapid expansion of their population brought thousands west and south, out on the prairie. There they clashed with the Blackfoot Confederacy, traditional occupants of much of the southern Canadian plains. The Saulteaux Ojibwa, allies of the Cree in the fur trade, also moved west to the Prairies from the woodlands around Lake of the Woods. And the American Sioux, involved in repeated wars with the United States, moved north from the Great Plains in large numbers beginning with the Sioux Uprising of 1863. These shifting Native populations destabilized the existing indigenous social order in the Prairies. The use of weapons in tribal warfare transformed Indian warfare from quasi-legal and highly symbolic international exchanges with few casualties to highly destructive, destabilizing enterprises that decimated tribes. The whisky trade further decimated some bands, undermining the traditional authority of the chiefs.

The introduction of the NWMP was useful to the tribes in offering the potential to stabilize the Prairies. In the Plains Indian worldview, the Mounties were representatives of another powerful nation, long embodied in the west by the HBC. The NWMP cultivated the goodwill that it found among Indian nations. Officials were deferential to the chiefs and worked through traditional tribal structures. Narrow law enforcement concerns gave way to policy considerations favouring good relations between the Mounties and the tribes. For example, cattlemen in southern Alberta in the 1870s were told that it was impossible to patrol their herds to protect against occasional Indian cattle stealing. Obviously, this reflected the policy choice that it was not worth incurring the hostilities of the tribes by using limited NWMP resources against them. Intra-Indian offences were punished only when some member of the band complained and then only when the chiefs yielded up the offenders.[15] Annual Indian arrests, even in the late 1870s, were measured by the fingers on one hand.[16]

The North-West Rebellion was a watershed in NWMP-Indian relations. The rebellion exposed the weaknesses in the dominion's Prairie Indian policy. The Indian Department had determined that its policy was too expensive and that it created Indian dependency. Thus, it cut rations to starvation levels to force Indians to work as small farmers. The policy was cruel and unworkable. In legal terms, it put a law enforcement burden on the NWMP that they could not bear: they had to effectively police starving Indians. As levels of resentment rose, altercations between reserve Indians and department officials increased. Grown Indian men were forced to beg petty department officials for extra food for starving and sick children. Their refusal met not infrequently with violence as individual Indians took the law into their own hands, striking officials or stealing food. Yayakootyawapos, the father-in-law of Big Bear, served two months in the guardhouse at Fort Battleford for striking a distribution officer at Fort Pitt, an arrest that helped to drive Big Bear into rebellion.[17] This was no way to treat Cree elders, and the injury must have run deep.

By the early 1880s, the arrest and punishment of Indian offenders rose to far higher levels than in the 1870s, reaching arrests of forty to fifty a year. This was still a low level given the size of the population but high compared to the small statistics of the earlier decade. Policing cattle theft, impossible in the 1870s, became standard police procedure in the 1880s, leading to an arrest of eighteen Blood warriors in one sweep.[18] The significance of this large increase in arrests and imprisonments of Indians is not measured in simple numbers: imprisonment was an enormously powerful symbol of the meaning of police authority. Imprisonment destroyed the spirits of Plains Indians who were culturally accustomed to the openness of prairie and sky.

Throughout the nineteenth century, the evidence is that tribal law enforcement was predominant in "intra"-Indian affairs. Within the band of Cree chief Foremost Man, only two nineteenth-century intra-Indian offences were reported to the NWMP for settlement, both assaults.[19] In two famous incidents, Indians who had killed NWMP officers were protected by their tribes for lengthy periods of time. Almighty Voice, a Cree warrior in the

Mannechinas Hills north of the Saskatchewan River, shot a settler's cow in 1895. Evidently, a Mountie told him that they were going to hang him, and he escaped from custody. NWMP sergeant Colebrook was sent to arrest Almighty Voice. Warned to keep back, he was shot to death at a distance of fifteen feet.

There was an extensive NWMP effort to capture Almighty Voice. The thick police file on the search contains many false leads, including a report of his suicide. These false leads appear to have come from Cree helping him avoid capture. He stayed at large a year and a half before being surrounded. Almighty Voice held off the police for several days, killing another Mountie. He was finally killed in a barrage of cannon fire but only after keeping the police awake singing his death song.[20]

Almighty Voice was the grandson of One Arrow, arrested in 1880, also for shooting cattle. His father, John Sounding Sky, had served six months in jail for stealing a coat and money.[21] The activity of this family, coupled with evidence of both material support and actual assistance in evading the police, makes it clear that the Cree warrior culture used means of survival that were illegal under Canadian law. It is impossible to say either how extensive this form of adaptation was or why it was not more extensive. Clearly, there must have been some significance in shooting cattle as well as in Almighty Voice's carrying out an act that led to his father's imprisonment.

A Blood warrior, Charcoal, engaged in a series of killings in southern Alberta in the early 1890s. His actions were more individualistic and less tribally supported than Almighty Voice's. His killings were for a religious purpose: to secure a spirit to guide him through the spirit world in an effort to commit suicide because his young wife had run off with a rival. Although his actions divided the tribe, Charcoal had substantial support and evaded capture for months. Ultimately, he killed a Mountie and was later betrayed by his own brother. He was captured, tried, and hanged for murder at Fort Macleod.[22]

Almighty Voice and Charcoal were famous cases that left lengthy archival records because they were so rare. The NWMP put massive resources into such manhunts to make the point that individual Indians should expect the full force of the Crown if they chose to kill settlers or defy Canadian law. The new wing built at Stony Mountain Penitentiary after the imprisonment of several dozen Indians involved in the 1885 rebellion was kept filled with Indians after the early 1890s, most on charges of cattle theft. Sentences were mostly short, generally a year or two, but the warriors who returned from Stony Mountain were sick and rarely resisted again.[23]

The North-West Rebellion Trials

The North-West Rebellion looms large in western Canadian history as the most important Indian war in a country largely without them. Wars are not ordinarily the subject of legal history, but Canada insisted on treating the rebellion as an internal act of treason, trying dozens of Indians for criminal offences in order to impose the legal framework of its Prairie Indian policy on the aftermath of the uprising. Ultimately, eight were hanged for murder and more than forty sentenced to Stony Mountain Penitentiary in Manitoba, causing the new wing to be built there. While the rebellion is seen primarily as a Métis matter, few were tried, although Louis Riel, the rebellion's leader, was executed for treason.[24]

The largely Métis rebellion spawned an almost unrelated, and limited, Indian uprising fed by distinct grievances against the dominion government but stemming from settler occupation of Native lands, impoverishment, and starvation.[25] A small number of Indians were in the Métis trenches at the Battle of Batoche, the most important military engagement of the rebellion. But most of the casualties occurred in an Indian uprising in northwest Saskatchewan that centred on the siege of Battleford. The killings of nine settlers at Frog Lake by Cree warriors were a central event in the Indian uprising, stemming from Cree resentment at their mistreatment by Indian Department employees on that reserve.[26]

The most famous Indian criminal trials in Canada – still legendary among Native people – were those of Poundmaker and Big Bear for treason. The very definition of treason, and the reason that it is such an infamous crime at common law, requires the specific intent to betray one's own country.[27] Not only was the entire conception of the offence unknowable to the Cree, Sioux, and Assiniboine warriors who rose against the Canadian state, but also the whole question of how and when Indian nations were incorporated into Canada was not raised and left unanswered. The failure of the Cree language to permit a translation of the offence rendered it impossible for the Indians charged to defend themselves. Even the Crown recognized this issue, choosing to charge them with the reduced offence of "treason-felony" instead of high treason (the charge against Riel) "because the Indians have an indefinite notion of the allegiance which they owe to their Sovereign."[28]

F.B. Robertson, a Winnipeg attorney, was retained by the government to defend all of the Indians in custody.[29] He did not raise either of these defences, focusing narrowly on challenging the Crown's evidence in a cross-examination as rigorous as any ordinary criminal case. The substantive law of treason was part of his defence in another, more minor, way: he argued the evidentiary point that the *mens rea,* the specific intent to commit treason, could not be proven by inference from mere presence. But this argument was consistently overruled by the judge.[30] Obviously, such an evidentiary ruling permitted an all-white jury to find Indians physically present near a battle guilty of treason by inference.

The rebellion trials occurred in two stages. Riel and the leaders of the rebellion, including Poundmaker, Big Bear, and One Arrow, were tried for treason at Regina. Only Riel was charged with high treason, carrying the death penalty. All of the other defendants were charged with treason-felony, a lesser charge. Later a larger number of Indians were tried at Battleford for ordinary criminal offences occurring at Frog Lake and Battleford during the rebellion, although additional Indians were tried for treason in the second set of trials as well. Only two Métis, Riel and Magnus Burston, were tried for treason, along with two whites.[31] Nearly a hundred Indians were in custody and charged with individual criminal offences, with sixty ultimately convicted. Indians drew the brunt of the legal repression of the North-West Rebellion.

These trials can be analyzed on several levels. The political decision to try Indians and not Métis for the rebellion showed that the Crown intended to stage these trials with the intent of breaking the back of the Indian resistance that had characterized the reserve situation in the early 1880s. The trials were "show" trials, designed to convince the Indians of the futility of further resistance and to remove dozens of Indian leaders, almost all Cree, to prison until they were no longer a threat to Canadian officials. Prison sentences were death sentences for many Indians: One Arrow, Poundmaker, and Big Bear were sick and dying old men after serving only parts of three-year sentences.[32]

In legal terms, the quality of justice rendered was a travesty. The evidence against most of the Indians – usually dubious eyewitness testimony of victims observing a number of Indians in a violent attack of some kind – was weak. It is clear that the interpreters did not do an adequate job. Appointed lawyers did not conduct vigorous defences, and judges conducted the trials in a partisan way. Judge Charles-Borromée Rouleau of Battleford had his own house looted and burned in the rebellion as he sat in judgment of Indians accused of looting and burning the town. Judge Hugh Richardson, who presided in Regina, insisted on a definition of treason that included merely being present among persons engaged in the rebellion at some identifiable point.[33] Juries, all white and all male in the 1880s' west, seeking revenge for settlers killed in the rebellion and anxious to open up Saskatchewan to settlement by repressing the Indian threat, returned "guilty" verdicts by rote no matter what the evidence.[34]

Cultural factors influenced individual members of Indian tribes in ways incomprehensible to either Canadian juries or Canadian law. Even at that time, for example, it was recognized that Big Bear, a Cree chief, had opposed the war. But his band had engaged in killing settlers and burning Frog Lake, and Big Bear had remained with his band. Robertson, in his summation to the jury, sought to educate them in the role of an Indian chief: "The Indian looks to his own little band; apart from them he can do nothing; apart from them he cannot live; he must remain with his band; he cannot get away from them; he is not free if he sees mischief being done, he is not free to say, I will move away from here, I will go among other people who won't do these things; he cannot do that, and what else has my learned friend, Mr. Scott, to rest upon here in making a case against Big Bear, except that he was with his band?"[35] While Robertson was overstating the control that a band had over an ordinary Indian warrior who was free to leave, he understated the responsibility of a chief. A chief was responsible for his band and obligated to stay with them, even when they refused to follow his leadership. Big Bear remained with his people to offer them what guidance he could.[36] One Arrow was convicted on even less evidence than Big Bear. One person saw him at Batoche, carrying a rifle and speaking to Riel. Robertson pointed out that all Indians routinely carried rifles and that no one had any idea of what he had said to Riel.[37]

The Sioux chief White Cap was acquitted on treason-felony charges with evidence not much different than that of One Arrow. White Cap had left his reserve near Saskatoon for Batoche, where one witness, a messenger, swore that he had seen him manning a gun in the rifle pits. Defence attorney Robertson viewed that testimony as incredible, vigorously attacking the witness for his positive identification of White Cap "out of one hundred and fifty other Indians in the excitement of the moment." Another witness put White Cap in a meeting of Riel's Métis Council. Robertson pointed out that he spoke only Sioux, while the council meetings were held in French and Cree. More importantly, Robertson angrily sparred with Judge Richardson over his jury instructions on the law of treason, raising the standard from mere presence to "aiding and abetting or encouraging rebellion or the prosecution of the unlawful design." Perhaps upset (and at the end of his cases), Robertson insulted the jury for convicting his clients quickly in all the previous cases. This time the jury acquitted White Cap in fifteen minutes.[38]

Given that the testimony in this case put White Cap in a rifle pit where his "aiding and abetting" were clear, it seems that the key to acquittal was not the judge's instruction. White Cap did have the testimony of a witness, Dr. Gerald Willoughby, who testified to his honesty and peaceful behaviour. By the time of the Battle of Batoche, White Cap claimed to have fled to Saskatoon, where he complained to Willoughby that he had been forced to join the Métis Council. This added something of a defence of duress to White Cap's story. The two stories are inconsistent, but the jury did not believe that the Crown's witnesses were telling the truth when they placed White Cap in the trenches at the Battle of Batoche.[39]

Besides One Arrow, Poundmaker, Big Bear, and White Cap, two groups of Indians were tried for treason-felony at Regina, resulting in convictions. Nine Cree were charged with offences from Frog Lake, Fort Pitt, and Frenchman's Butte. These cases were all based on the testimony of witnesses to the events, often with the same kind of identification problems attending the White Cap case. But the juries convicted. The next day Robertson defended four Sioux and one Cree charged with treason-felony for participating in events at Duck Lake and Batoche. The cases were so weak that Robertson did not even bother a summation argument. Again convictions were returned.[40] In all, eighteen Indians were tried for treason-felony, leading to seventeen convictions with prison sentences of two or three years.

All of these cases tried at Regina were overshadowed by the trials and hangings at Battleford. According to one observer, Father Alexis André, Judge Rouleau was "a vindictive man and a servile instrument in the hands of the government."[41] Underlying these mass trials was a clear motive on the part of the Crown to hang a large number of Indians before Indian witnesses, impressing upon them the seriousness of Canadian justice and putting an end to the large-scale resistance disrupting the reserves. As Assistant Commissioner of Indian Affairs Hayter Reed put it, "I am desirous of having the Indians witness it – No sound threshing having been given them I think a sight of this sort will cause them to meditate for many a day."[42]

Among the Crees at Frog Lake who were sentenced to death, only Wandering Spirit pleaded guilty. Bad Arrow, Miserable Man, Walking the Sky, Little Bear, and Iron Body were convicted individually of the various killings. Itka and Man without Blood, Assiniboines, pleaded guilty to two unrelated killings in the Battleford area. Louison Mongrain, a Frog Lake Cree, was sentenced to death for killing an NWMP corporal at Fort Pitt. Charlebois and Dressy Man were sentenced to death for killing a wendigo (supernatural creature) in an unrelated event in the Cree camp after the Frog Lake killings. Bright Eyes was convicted of manslaughter in the same killing and received a twenty-year sentence.[43] Unlike for the trials at Regina, no defence lawyer was assigned at Battleford. This meant much more perfunctory process with a number of murder trials occurring in one day.

Mongrain, Charlebois, and Dressy Man had their sentences commuted, but the first eight were hanged at Battleford on 26 November. Hundreds of witnesses were admitted to the fort, and more waited outside. The warriors sang their death chants and then were led to a gallows outfitted with eight ropes. The condemned were given ten minutes for final statements. Except for Wandering Spirit, they were defiant. They smiled, sang, and shouted sharp war cries. Little Bear told the Indians to remember how the whites had treated him and urged his companions to have contempt for the punishment that the government was about to inflict on them. Black caps were drawn over their faces, and the execution was quickly carried out. The men were buried on the fort grounds.[44]

The rest of Rouleau's sentences for ordinary theft were more severe than those received for treason in Regina, averaging six years for horse theft. Two Indians who pleaded guilty to arson at Frog Lake received ten-year sentences. Another received a fourteen-year sentence for burning the Frog Lake church. In all, Rouleau tried more than thirty Indians for these property offences in addition to the twelve murder cases.[45]

Cree Law and the Canadian Law of Treaty 6

The immediate context of Cree participation in the North-West Rebellion was massive Native dissatisfaction with Treaty 6. The "numbered treaties," 1 through 7, negotiated with western Indians beginning in Manitoba in 1871 were intended to open up the west for settlement.[46] They continued an Ontarian Indian policy: Indian lands were to be purchased with the tribes moving to small reserves to take up the life of small farmers.[47] The tribes, however, had a different understanding of the treaties. Since a treaty is an international agreement, somewhat analogous to a contract, the very validity of the agreement turns on both parties having an identical understanding of the nature and substance of the agreement.[48]

The opening of the North-West Territories to settlement followed its 1869 "sale" to the Crown in Canada by the HBC for £300,000. The Native nations knew of this sale and resented it. In their view, the company did not own the land and had no right to sell it: it was Indian land.[49] The scale of the land cessions was unprecedented in Canadian treaty history. In 1871, the Crown in Treaties 1 and 2 purchased land needed for immediate settlement in southern Manitoba.[50] But Treaties 3 through 7 involved huge tracts of land, not yet settled, where Native people carried on in their traditional ways, modified by changing economic and environmental realities – especially the decline of the fur trade and the great buffalo herds.[51]

There are substantial oral histories of Native understanding of these treaties. Most of them can be corroborated by the logic of the time. It must be clear, for example, that, having shared the Prairies with Euro-Canadian fur traders for two hundred years, Native people must have seen the treaties as recognizing that pre-existing relationship. The concept of the sale of land and its permanent alienation cannot have been known to Indians who never held private property. The idea of permanently settling on reserves was similarly impossible to Indians who covered hundreds of miles each season searching for buffalo or returning to winter shelter. There is a complexity to Indian views of agriculture, although such economic activity did not originally exist on the Prairies west of Winnipeg (outside of some limited farming around HBC posts). Prairie Indians were aware of farming as the basis of the Canadian economy and saw it as one solution to their impoverishment.[52]

The First Nations understood the treaties as peace and friendship agreements, with specific cessions on some land use rights in return for payments in cash and goods from the Crown. Treaties 3, 4, and 6, for example, secured railway, road, and telegraph routes across the Prairies. Treaty 6 elders invariably remember that the Crown bought the rights to the top six inches of soil for farming, promising that the nations could continue to use all of the land not suitable for farming. It was assumed in 1876 that very little of the prairie could be successfully farmed. The First Nations expected the land to serve a number of different users for different purposes. These usages were regulated through First Nations law and ordinarily did not produce any conflict. For example, the family and clan trapping, hunting, and fishing territories in the north had existed for generations.

The immediate context of the treaties – the treaty-making meetings – reinforced this view. Treaty commissioners, high-ranking politicians, were preceded by parties of Mounties. The tribes were called together from across the region and had been meeting among themselves for days. The negotiations were delayed in Treaty 6 while the tribes engaged in a sacred peace-pipe ceremony, purifying the words exchanged in the treaty-making process. These words, of course, were translated from English to Native languages and back. It is still not clear how these words, representing complex legal terms, were translated, but it is clear that they were not translated well. Land in Cree, for example, takes on a number of meanings using different words depending on the context. A belief of modern Cree that the nation sold only the top six inches of their land at Treaty 6 may stem from a mistranslation of the kind of "land" that they were negotiating for.[53]

One famous mistranslation from Treaty 6 became important following Big Bear's trial for treason in 1885. Big Bear had apparently expressed a fear of being hanged at the time of the negotiation of Treaty 6 in 1876. This was also expressed as a desire on his part to exempt Indians from Canadian law by providing that they could not be hanged for their violations. Rather, it seems that Big Bear spoke of "having a rope around his neck" like a wild horse, captured and no longer free. The interpreter confused *ay-saka-pay-kinit* (lead by the neck) with *ay-hah-kotit* (hang by the neck).[54] This point, if properly understood, would have put directly on the table one of the major unresolved issues of Treaty 6. The Indians did not realize that they would be confined to their reservations but believed that they would be allowed to continue their traditional hunting patterns, with the reserves serving as a base. It seems impossible to conclude any other interpretation than that the Crown's negotiators were deliberately vague because they wanted to keep the Indians negotiating and induce them to sign the treaty.

This view is reinforced by two famous clauses in Treaty 6 – one providing for a "medicine chest" to be kept by the agents, and another providing that the Crown "render assistance in time of need." Both of these clauses originated with the Indians. This is important when it is recognized that the British Colonial Office, as well as Canadian authorities, had boilerplate treaty language and that all of the numbered treaties are similar in provisions. This means that the final language of the treaties does not reflect a negotiated agreement between the Crown and the Indian nations but the efforts of Crown negotiators to induce Indians to sign a prepared text. The price of these provisions was negotiable: Indians in Treaty 3 had held out for higher payments, a fact known to the signers of later treaties.

But in Treaty 6, the tribes had specific concerns not addressed by money alone. Disease and starvation were too common and beyond the existing resources of the tribes. They sought specific provisions to alleviate these hardships caused by settlement, dislocation, and the scarcity of buffalo. What resulted was the "medicine chest" and "assistance in time of famine" clauses.[55] Their meaning is still at issue. The Crown reads these terms literally and narrowly; the tribes read them broadly and in the context of 1879. In this view, for example, a "medicine chest" in 1876 terms can refer only to adequate medical assistance in modern terms. The complete destruction of tribal economies created a permanent famine, requiring permanent "assistance in time of famine." Much of the underlying tension leading to the North-West Rebellion reflected the government's refusal to provide adequate relief from starvation, in violation of the treaty.

Explicit references to Canadian law were made in several places in the treaties. For example, Indians agreed to be subject to Canadian law and to assist Canadian law enforcement officials by yielding up offenders. Liquor was outlawed in Native communities, and the Crown pledged to enforce those prohibition laws. The right of Indians to hunt and fish was recognized but subject to "such regulations as may from time to time be made by her Majesty's Government of the Dominion of Canada."[56] Other laws were proposed and discussed in the various councils but not included in the treaties. The Crees at Fort Carlton, for example, proposed a "strong law, prohibiting the free use of poison (strychnine). It has almost exterminated the animals of our country, and often makes us bad friends with our white neighbors. We further request, that a law be made, equally applicable to the Half-breed and Indian, punishing all parties who set fire to our forest and plain."[57]

The legal status of the treaties was not an issue in nineteenth-century courts outside of the *St. Catherine's Milling* case. Yet there is no question that the Indian nations saw the treaties as legal documents. The sacred pipe ceremony bound the participants to speak the truth and carry out their agreements. The tribes ceded up certain rights to their lands in return for payments, in cash and goods, from the government. Alexander Morris, chief negotiator for the Crown, was a lawyer, former chief justice of Manitoba, and lieutenant governor of Manitoba.[58] British courts and American courts had held treaties to be legal documents, with their terms enforceable in court.[59]

It is impossible to fully articulate the Indian understanding of these treaties. Part of the evidence is contradictory. For example, the Indians at Fort Carlton, according to official documents, discussed leasing their lands to the whites for four years rather than selling the land. This discussion itself would indicate that the tribes understood that they were selling the land. But that assumes Indians knew what a lease was. Other Indians counselled against selling the land, again indicating that the tribes knew they were discussing a land sale. The final language – the Indians "hereby cede, release, surrender and yield up to the Government ... forever, all their rights, titles and privileges whatsoever, to the lands" – seems unambiguous. But it is boilerplate language, inserted in all the treaties, and it is not clear how it was translated.[60]

Since the political process occurring at treaty was constructed by dominion authorities, an unknown number of bands refused to participate in the process. Big Bear's band is the best known of these, but it is still not clear what proportion of the tribes actually signed treaties. It was in the interests of the Crown to exaggerate the representation of the bands. Various bands had been fragmented for any number of reasons, and it is not clear whether they were represented at treaty. It is also not clear that people signing for some bands had authority to do so or to make the kinds of cessions allegedly made. The Crown's fiction that Indian land was being voluntarily ceded inherently recognized the opposite: that the tribes were free to not participate in the treaty process and decline to cede their lands. Big Bear's opposition is the most thoroughly documented.

Big Bear and his followers objected to both the process and the substance of treaty making. As a young man, he had a dream about being trapped by the queen's presents, offered to Prairie Indians with the promise that the government would treat them justly. But the presents obligated the Indians to participate in a formal relationship with the Crown. "When we set a fox trap we scatter pieces of meat all around but when the fox gets into the trap we knock him on the head. We want no baits! Let your Chiefs come like men and talk to us."[61] Yellow Sky, an Ojibwa, allied with Big Bear and refused to take treaty as well, explaining his reasons to Indian Agent M.G. Dickieson. As Dickieson wrote, "after some time a spokesman rose and said they desired to be independent ... that they did not wish to take anything from the Government, or to come under the law. He said I was not to think it was because they were unfriendly to the Government or to the white man that they do not join with the other Indians but they wished to remain as they were. They had likewise been told that by holding out, 'better terms' would be granted to them."[62] This account diminishes the idea of tribal independence as an option. Local officials appear to have regarded all Indian objections to treaty as negotiating ploys, merely designed to get more money. It is hard to believe that Big Bear's underlying motives were merely to secure money.[63] Rather, the evidence consistently supports the view that Big Bear and his people believed that they had a choice to take or not take treaty. Ultimately, his band took treaty four years later. They were starving, and signing the treaty gave them a right to government relief.[64] In retrospect, it has to be clear that Indians did not have the choice to remain independent and outside of the treaty-making process.

It seems clear now that the motivation of tribes in initiating the process was to implement a political and legal framework for the protection of their rights. Beginning with Treaty 1 in 1871, seven treaties were signed in seven years. These treaties were interrelated for both Canadians and Indians: in each treaty, the treaty commissioners followed similar instructions from Ottawa, and the Indians present knew of the terms of previous treaties. Alexander Morris led the commissioners at Treaties 3, 4, 5, and 6, thus providing continuity in the negotiations.[65]

The treaty documents are remarkable because they reveal a detailed negotiating process with a clear Native agenda. They also reveal two distinct sets of negotiations and understandings: while the formal, written treaties outline a broad understanding, they also include some specific rights guaranteed to Indians. At the same time, the negotiations reveal a number of verbal promises and understandings that were clearly perceived by the Indians to be part of the broad treaty agreement. In retrospect, there can be no question that the Indian nations, unschooled in European international law and accustomed to a tradition in which agreements between Indian nations were verbal, took these verbal agreements as part of the treaty. Within six months of the signing of Treaty 1, Governor Archibald wrote to Ottawa that "it is impossible to be too particular in carrying out the terms of the agreements made with these people. They recollect with astonishing accuracy every stipulation made at the Treaty, and if we expect our relations with them to be of the kind which is desirable to maintain we must fulfill our obligations with scrupulous fidelity."[66] Indian complaints about Crown violations of treaty provisions were continuous, with angry words from within a few months of their signing. These involved both promises written into the treaties and "outside" or verbal promises made in the treaty context. If the dispute about the meaning of "maintaining a school on each reserve,"[67] a measure both favoured by the tribes and consistent with the government's own Indian policy, is any indication, the Crown's actions show bad faith and fraud from the outset.

In 1873, Treaty Commissioner J. Provencher requested from Ottawa an appropriation to build a school at Brokenhead Reserve. Deputy Superintendent General of Indian Affairs VanKoughnet responded: "According to the terms of Treaty 1 a school is to be maintained on each Reserve thereby made – of which there is one – whenever the Indians on the Reserve should desire it ... Mr. Provencher states that the Indians of Brokenhead desire an appropriation towards the erection of a school house. No stipulation is made in the Treaty that an appropriation shall be provided for such effect."[68] In VanKoughnet's view, the phrase "maintaining a school" meant an annual appropriation of $300 for the operation of each school. While Provencher, a good bureaucrat, did not want to challenge directly his superior's legal interpretation of the meaning of this treaty provision, he dutifully pointed out the problem raised. This request was "just one more instance of the misunderstanding that took place at the time of the making of the Treaty. By the obligation of 'maintaining a school' assumed by the government, the Indians misunderstood that all the expenses connected with the school would be supported by the Government."[69] This exchange is revealing on a number of levels. In terms of simple legal interpretation, it seems obvious that the Crown's narrow interpretation of the plain meaning of the phrase "maintain a school" is both dishonest and intended to injure the Indians, not only in a 2005 context reading backward, but also in the context of 1873. If the Crown refused to build the schools referred to by treaty, who would build them?

But more important, the exchange occurred in early 1873, more than six months before Treaty 3 – containing the same language – was signed on 3 October. The treaty commissioners at Treaty 3, aware that the phrase "maintaining a school" was being interpreted by the Crown and the tribes in an inconsistent way, used it anyway, knowing that it would mislead the Indians. The Treaty 3 Indians were deliberately misled on this provision, and the deceit was incorporated repeatedly into all of the succeeding Prairie treaties.

This basic illegality goes to the heart of the treaty-making process. What was the Crown's ultimate "policy" toward the Indians as revealed by this fraud? Stealing even a basic education from children cuts against any serious policy of assimilation, even in the terms of 1870s Canadian policy. Rather, it seems to indicate that the Crown's policy was to buy Indian land as cheaply as possible without regard to the social costs that fell on tribes forced onto reserves with no source of income. This attitude was communicated to the treaty commissioners, who understood their role as simply getting the tribes to sign treaties no matter what had to be promised in order to accomplish this end.

If promises directly written into the treaties in plain language fared this poorly, then the "outside" promises made at the time must have been calculated to mislead the Indians about the extent of their benefits under the treaties and to induce them to sign. The treaty reports, prepared for publication by Alexander Morris himself, show extensive outside promises and the intentional use of ambivalent language.[70] These accounts, in English and self-serving, are only one side of a complex and disputed negotiation process and do not reveal the full extent of those promises.[71]

The precise substance of these miscommunications is less important than understanding that this misunderstanding was recognized at the time, was intentional, and was at the heart of the treaty process. The range of issues misunderstood goes well beyond the narrow technical interpretation of a simple concept such as maintaining schools. There seems to be no question, for example, that the difficult and complex issues of Native self-government, the recognition of Indian law, the nature of the title to land that was ceded, the function and ownership of the reserves, and the promised level of Crown economic support for impoverished Aboriginal communities were all understood in different ways by the Crown and Indian tribes.[72] To call this "misunderstanding" is to put a neutral cast on the process. The Crown, as drafter of the treaties, and the imposer of its legal order on Prairie Indians who lacked any experience with that order, was responsible for their clarity of meaning: it deliberately structured that miscommunication in order to make it easier to get Indians to sign the treaties.

Treaties, Buffalo, and the Loss of the Commons

The signing of the Prairie treaties occurred in the context of social and ecological changes on the frontier that would permanently change Native economies and social orders. Unrestricted organized buffalo hunts by American and Métis hunters had reduced both the size and the distribution of the herds. As a result, traditional hunting cycles of the Prairie Indians were no longer possible: tribes had to range farther and farther in search of buffalo. Not only did this change existing land use patterns, but it also may have exacerbated tribal conflict between the Cree and their traditional enemies in the Blackfoot Confederacy since the Cree were forced to hunt farther south and west of their traditional ranges. Even with increased hunting ranges, hunger and starvation became serious matters for the Prairie Indians.[73] This was beyond the collective memory of cultures accustomed to the wealth of large buffalo herds.[74]

White and Métis hunting on the plains was beyond the control of the tribes. The Sioux had attempted to stop the well-organized Métis hunting parties but had been defeated in the 1851 Battle of Grand Couteau, a victory that marks one "beginning" of the Métis Nation.[75] Plains Indians had taken a number of steps to control access to their lands and to regulate hunting practices. As early as 1858, the Plains Cree, in council, "determined that in consequence of promises often made and broken by the white men and half-breeds, and the rapid destruction by them of the buffalo they fed on, they would not permit either white men or half-breeds to hunt in their country or travel through it, except for the purpose of trading for their dried meat, pemmican, skins and robes."[76]

This tragedy of the loss of the commons did much to force the Plains Indians to treaty. Chief Sweet Grass of the Plains Cree put it simplest: "Our country is no longer able to support us."[77] Just as the direct pressure of white settlement had forced many (but not all) of the eastern Indians to treaty, it was obvious to the Indians that a negotiated agreement with the Crown might stabilize some set of existing relations on the frontier. Some idea of the state of Indian society on the Prairies soon after Canada negotiated its agreement with the Hudson's Bay Company, and what this new order might be from the Cree perspective, follows from the full context of the chief's words.

Sweet Grass, on his own volition, went to the HBC post at Edmonton House on 13 April 1871 accompanied by a few warriors. He met with W.J. Christie, the chief factor. Sweet Grass was moved by poverty and uncertainty to go to the post – the only white institution in his country – to ask both if his land had already been sold and what the intention of the Canadian government was toward his people. He had heard about negotiations in Treaty 3 (which, at this point, had failed because the Saulteaux had angrily refused the commissioner's terms) more than 1,000 miles to the east and wanted to know when he would be offered a treaty. Sweet Grass referred to an epidemic that had raged through the country in the past summer, the starvation and poverty of Indians, and the diminution of the buffalo. He asked for presents at once.[78]

Christie had no governmental authority to act but promised that Canada would deal "liberally" with the Indians as it had in previous Indian treaties. Then, on his own volition, he gave presents to Sweet Grass and "otherwise satisfied them," convinced that "they would have proceeded to acts of violence, and once that had commenced, there would have been the beginning of an Indian war, which it is difficult to say when it would have ended."[79] Finally, he agreed to take a message from Sweet Grass to the lieutenant governor of Manitoba.

The message was simple in its terms. Beginning with a strong statement that the Cree "don't want to sell our lands; it is our property, and no one has a right to sell them," Sweet Grass went on:

> Our country is getting ruined of fur-bearing animals, hitherto our sole support, and now we are poor and want help – we want you to pity us. We want cattle, tools, agricultural implements, and assistance in everything when we come to settle – our country is no longer able to support us.
>
> Make provision for us against years of starvation. We had great starvation the past winter, and the small-pox took away many of our people, the old, young, and children.
>
> We want you to stop the Americans from coming to trade on our lands, and giving firewater, ammunition and arms to our enemies the Blackfeet.
>
> We made a peace this winter with the Blackfeet. Our young men are foolish, it may not last long.
>
> We invite you to come and see us and to speak with us.[80]

While it is doubtful that most of the Cree took this position as early as 1871, it is clear that some did, a view that partially coincided with dominion policy at the time. The end of the Plains economy supported by the buffalo commons fit two dominion objectives: farmers could not occupy plains ranged by buffalo, and Indians could not carry out their nomadic hunting activities on a prairie devoid of game.

It is difficult in an age of environmental consciousness to assess what conservation options the dominion may have held after 1870. It is clear that one of those considered was a legal option: legislation to severely limit the buffalo hunt in order to preserve the buffalo and the deployment of the NWMP to enforce such conservation laws. Given the extent of the hunt and the depth to which the hunting culture and economy permeated Plains life, the idea of a law enforcement effort to save the buffalo may have been unrealistic. But this was also a Canadian government committed to the idea of a policed transition to an orderly frontier.

In any case, by 1874 the government was aware of the depth of the problem: the buffalo were fast disappearing, and the Plains Indians were dependent on them for food and shelter. The loss of the buffalo would leave many thousands of Indians with no means of sustenance.[81] The dominion government recognized that it had a choice here, with some Liberal and Conservative members of Parliament believing that the dominion had a treaty obligation to preserve the buffalo.[82] This view in itself presumes a liberal policy of interpreting treaties in favour of Indians, since no treaty had any express provision regarding the preservation of game.

The Department of Justice, in charge of all government legislation, prepared an extensive report on the protection of buffalo. Because the matter was of local rather than national concern, the report was referred to the North-West Territorial Council. A subcommittee of that council did its own investigation of the problem, taking evidence from witnesses. There was no shortage of ideas, nor was there disagreement about the seriousness of the problem. Witnesses suggested the introduction of a hunting season for Métis and whites (but not for Indians) as well as severe punishment for those who killed buffalo without using at least half of the meat – another measure aimed at white and Métis hunting practices that took skins and tongues but left the meat to rot. In addition, an export duty on hides and pemmican was directed at the Americans who worked at the heart of the trade.[83]

Ottawa deferred the whole matter to the North-West Territorial Council, which ultimately passed a watered-down ordinance in November of 1877. The act forbade the use of "buffalo pounds" and the running of buffalo off cliffs. Slaughter for amusement or to "secure their tongues, choice cuts or peltries" was prohibited. A closed season on cows ran from 15 November through 14 August, and no calves under two years old were to be killed.

Indians were subject to the law but granted certain concessions during winter months. Severe penalties were provided, with half of the fine going to the informer.[84]

The ordinance was repealed a year later, a monument to the ineffective North-West Territorial Council, Ottawa's lack of interest, and Native distrust of Canadian law.[85] Indians, especially at the making of Treaty 4 and Treaty 6, urged a law to protect the buffalo. Yet other Indians did not accept any legal regulation of their hunts. Sitting Bull, then in exile in Canada, asked rhetorically, "when ... did the Almighty give the Canadian government the right to keep the Indians from killing the buffalo?"[86] It should not be surprising that internal differences on such matters existed within Indian tribes. The idea of relying on Canadian law to regulate age-old hunting activities was foreign to their culture.

The underlying issue was probably not the potential effectiveness of such laws in preserving buffalo. Rather, it was a vision of a social order under the control of Canadian police. NWMP commissioner George A. French had testified before the subcommission, urging the adoption of sweeping laws to protect the buffalo. He never indicated any sense that the NWMP could not carry out this law enforcement task.[87] If the NWMP were effective enough to police western settlement, the policing of the buffalo hunt should have been no problem. As the commissioners at Treaty 4 reported, "many of the bands have no desire to settle and commence farming, and will not turn their attention to agriculture until they are forced to do so on account of the failure of their present means of subsistence by the extermination of the buffalo."[88] Unsettling within this whole context is the idea that the dominion government deliberately failed to take action because it was understood that the buffalo hunt was central to the social orders of Plains tribes; the government knew that destroying the buffalo would force the Indians to reserves. There is no question that American authorities deliberately failed to protect the buffalo for these reasons.[89] Ottawa's two-year hesitation was critical in the defeat of the effectiveness of the bill. Similarly, Ottawa's deference to the new North-West Territorial Council, because "it could probably devise a cheaper and better plan than this parliament," was as disingenuous as the Territorial Council's abandonment of a duty on pemmican and hides because the matter properly belonged to the dominion government.[90] The council was directly appointed from Ottawa and worked under dominion authority. Yet, as in so many critical matters in Indian policy, there is no direct evidence that the dominion intended to wait idly while the buffalo were exterminated. However, there can be no question, in an era when American Sioux were an international problem on the border between the Dakotas and Canada, that Canadian authorities were unaware of American policy on exterminating the buffalo.

Indian problems on the American border also turned on the migration of the buffalo herds as tribes moved back and forth across a border that was meaningless to their traditional hunting patterns. While a tribe was on either side of the border, it engaged in all kinds of political relationships with the respective governments of Canada and the United States. This included accepting "presents" and other forms of aid from both sides, a practice that American and Canadian authorities found both dishonest and evident of the bad character of Indian people even though it was completely consistent with the tribes' own view of themselves as in nation-to-nation relationships with both countries. This international problem would also disappear with the end of the buffalo.

The preservation of the buffalo, on the other hand, would have kept the Indians eating well for a number of years while a gradual policy of settling the reserves was implemented. Feeding the Indians was an expensive proposition, far more costly than the police efforts that might have prolonged the great buffalo herds. Whatever the reasoning process, it must be clear that a corollary of the same logic that created the NWMP and the idea of the lawful and peaceful frontier would have protected the buffalo and prolonged the life of the herds. Therefore, there is a clear reflection of official choice in choosing which laws to implement and enforce and which ones to ignore.

The *Indian Act*

The *Indian Act* does not loom large in Canadian legal history, yet it consigned Indian nations and Indian people to a legal never-never-land. Parliament's passage of the acts of 1869 and 1876 institutionalized Ontario Indian policy in all of Canada but was aimed primarily at the Prairie Indians. At the core, it was inconsistent with the ongoing treaty-making process. If Indians were legally children in the eyes of the law, dependants without the capacity to negotiate contracts, then they could not sell their land to anyone, not even the Crown. If the Crown was their legal guardian, then it was a conflict of interest to sell Indian lands to itself at any price. To sell Indian lands to itself at very low prices was not only a violation of fiduciary duty but also fraud. The Crown's legal view denied any actual Indian ownership of the land, recognizing the treaties as merely political documents.

It seems unlikely that any of the Indians in the numbered treaties had any knowledge of the *Indian Act,* much less of their inferior status under it, during any of the negotiations. Indeed, the act did not even exist until just before the time of the negotiations for Treaty 6.[91] While there is no evidence that the Indians of Treaty 6 were aware of either the *Indian Act* or any legal meanings it might have had, the same cannot be said of the Crown. Deputy Superintendent General of Indian Affairs VanKoughnet acknowledged in a memorandum on 22 August, the day before Treaty 6 was signed, that "the legal status of the Indians of Canada is that of minors, with the Government as their guardians."[92]

Minors, of course, cannot sign either political or legal documents, so the resulting treaties, whether political or legal documents, were invalid according to this logic: the Crown wanted to have it both ways. The illegality and illogic of this position, simultaneous to the treaty-making process, raise a number of issues. The most demeaning is that the Crown policy behind treaty negotiations was simply to pacify children, a treacherous and hypocritical betrayal of principle. It is impossible to believe that VanKoughnet's official statement of policy was new or unknown to the treaty commissioners. Even if the statement, made only one day before the signing of Treaty 6, was unknown to the commissioners at that time, the same treaty-making process continued through Treaties 7 and 8, when the commissioners would have been aware that they were conducting a solemn political and legal negotiation with "children." The point here is obvious: the *Indian Act* was facially inconsistent with both the political and the legal elements of the treaty process. Politically, the tribes would never accept the status of children. Legally, children could not negotiate anything at all.

Few provisions of either the 1869 or the 1876 *Indian Act* were new. The acts' origins were in Upper Canada in the 1830s, with individual laws protecting Indians from the depredations of whites. The first of these forbade whites to purchase, lease, or otherwise contract to buy Indian lands. Later acts prohibited whites from making any contracts at all with Indians or foreclosing on Indian property.[93] While these acts only forbade whites from engaging in legal transactions with Indians, the effect was to make it impossible for them to engage in many forms of commerce. An Indian farmer, for example, could not mortgage his buildings to borrow money to make improvements. He could not sell the hay or produce of his farm without the approval of the Indian agent, a law that interfered with the operation of the government's policy of promoting Indian self-sufficiency.[94]

This paternalism worked in two opposing ways. On the one hand, the *Indian Act*s criminalized a good deal of the routine actions of rural whites living in the area of Indian reserves. Purchasing or leasing Indian lands, or buying hay, firewood, lumber, or produce from individual Indians, was against the law, punishable by either imprisonment or fine. Not only was this substantive law broad and general, but it also carried with it summary procedures before a special court: the Indian agent was designated a magistrate for offences under the act. Local whites regularly violated these laws.

On the other hand, the *Indian Act* made Indians a special class of persons – legal dependants of the Crown or children in the eyes of the law. They could not vote, buy or use alcohol, sell the produce from their own farms, enter into contracts for any purpose, mortgage their property, or sell or lease their lands. Although they were subject to the penal provisions of the act in the same way as all residents of Canada, these social disabilities were more often civil in nature. Agreements made contrary to the *Indian Act* were unenforceable in court.

The acts, then, not only consisted of civil disabilities and criminal penalties but also created a top-down and autocratic legal order on the reserves. This organization of the rule of law into what amounted to an administrative order on the reserves paralleled the function of the NWMP as both a law enforcement and judicial agency. It prompted an Anglican missionary in the North-West to comment on the peculiar quality of this law: "There seemed to be no recognized law except the decision of a Magistrate, and no one could tell what this would be or the code that might rule him. There was, in fact, no law, although there was supposed to be a Government. We were not in Ontario, or Quebec, or Manitoba. We were in an undefined territory, subject to the man who happened to be in office, and he was a great distance from his superiors and found no difficulty in shielding himself behind his own reports."[95]

The scope of the *Indian Act* was enormous. Thousands of adult Indians, with strong cultural ideals of autonomy and freedom within their tribal social order, were put under this legal order, with many of the details of their daily lives under the control of Indian agents, lower-level reserve officials, or police. It is impossible to document the precise level of resistance. Starving Indians resisted in a number of ways. There are many documented assaults on Indian agents and employees of the Indian Department. Big Bear's father-in-law, Yayakootyawapos, had returned in 1884 empty-handed from a long hunt in the dead of winter. He went to the reserve farmer, Delaney, to beg food for his family. Delaney brusquely turned him down and ordered him out of the ration house. Yayakootyawapos refused, and Delaney grabbed him by the arm. Yayakootyawapos produced a knife. Delaney ran out of the building, locking it after him, with Yayakootyawapos locked inside. The NWMP came shortly, arrested him, and had him sentenced to two years in the guardhouse at Battleford.[96] Yayakootyawapos' trial would have consisted of a hearing of a few minutes, with Delaney probably serving as the only witness. This harsh sentence represents the use of criminal law to defend the agent-dominated social order on the reserves. Evidently, this was not the limit of such prosecutions. When the Sarcee Crow Collar broke the scales in the ration house in a dispute over the distribution of food, he was defended by his chief, Bull's Head. NWMP assistant superintendent John McIllree threatened to arrest Bull's Head on the theory that the chief was responsible for disorder on his reserve.[97]

Compulsory school attendance was required under the *Indian Act* in 1895, with criminal penalties for parents who refused to send their children to boarding schools. But even this new use of law to coerce assimilation was balanced against the reality of tribal power on the Plains: the passage of the law had been delayed because officials were fearful that it would "irritate the Indians."[98] Thus, it was not only the NWMP who were selective in deciding when to use formal legal mechanisms in controlling Indians. "Benevolent despotism" performed important functions in making the legal order flexible and able to adapt to circumstances that made law enforcement a poor policy.

The Pass System

The *Indian Act,* in the end, did not offer Canadian authorities sufficient control over Prairie Indians. Thus, a pass system was introduced after the 1885 rebellion, confining Indians to reserves unless they procured a "pass" from the Indian agent stating their place of travel, reason, and duration of visit. This pass system was completely extralegal and recognized as such by all Crown officials. The universal adoption of the pass system on the Prairies was the product of Ministry of Interior policy but without resort to the necessary legislation that would have extended the *Indian Act.* The fact that it was not even necessary to get legislation to cover such a wholesale and widespread illegality reflects the extralegal nature of "Indian Act" law on the Prairies. NWMP policy was to enforce the system insofar as it was possible, given that it had no validity in law.[99]

While the intent of dominion authorities was to force Plains Indians onto reserves, nothing in the texts of the treaties bound them to live there. The language of the treaty negotiations, in fact, expresses the opposite intent: Indians were determined to carry on their traditional ways as much as possible and would have refused to sign any agreement, in effect imprisoning themselves on reserves. It was the Riel Rebellion of 1885, however, that gave Canadian authorities their immediate pretext to force Indians back to reserves as a matter of military necessity. General F. Middleton wrote to Edgar Dewdney early in the war, requesting that he issue an order for Indians and Métis to return to their reserves or be treated as rebels. Dewdney did so.[100] Immediately after the war, Dewdney reminded an Indian agent that the order was due only to the exigencies of war and that there "exists no law by which Indians can be punished for being off their Reserves."[101]

The Indian Department, however, took matters into its own hands. On 16 August 1885, Hayter Reed, assistant Indian commissioner for the North-West Territories, issued an order that Indians in the Battleford area not be allowed to leave their reserves without passes: "I am adopting a system of keeping the Indians on their respective Reserves and not allowing any leave [for] them without passes – I know this is hardly supported by any legal enactment but we must do many things which can only be supported by common sense and by what may be for the general good. I get the Police to send out daily and send any Indians without passes back to their reserves."[102] The policy was soon general throughout the Prairies. The Indian Department ordered pass forms commercially printed. Reed sent three books of printed passes to the Indian agent at Peace Hills in October, with instructions that he distribute the forms to his agency farmers. These printed pass forms were in general use until at least 1918.[103] The pass system was unique to the Prairie reserves.

Sam Steele, NWMP commander of the Macleod District, reported on the difficulties of enforcing the pass system:

> I have the honour to report for your information that as usual immediately after treaty payment there are a great many Indians moving about visiting other reserves, etc., and probably with the view to keeping them on their Reserves, the Agent at the Blood Reserve has refused them passes, the Piegans who have been met off their Reserve have all been provided with passes.
>
> I doubt the possibility of keeping the Indians at home by such coercive measures as stopping their rations or refusing a pass, they will go in spite of all their Agent can do and if they have to start on a long journey without any rations the chances of their killing cattle is very greatly increased. There is an order throughout the district to turn back any Indians without a pass but a difficulty arises in the fact that few of our men can speak sufficient Blackfoot to make themselves understood and the Indians when it suits their purpose can be very obtuse: they are aware too that we have no legal right to turn them back.[104]

Reed's response was to caution Indian agents not to allow Indians to leave their reserves.[105]

Steele's choice of language is significant. An Indian's assertion of his treaty right to travel amounts to acting "very obtuse." It does not require much to imagine hundreds of confrontations between Indians travelling off their reserves and NWMP, or local functionaries of all sorts, insisting that they return. The language of treaty rights and knowledge of the law must have informed individual Indian's discussions with the Mounties. Treaty negotiations make it clear that the tribes were concerned about carrying on their traditional ways of life and did not want to be forced to live on the reserves. They were assured that the lands were "reserved" for their exclusive use but that they did not have to live there. The traditional right to "pursue their hunting and fishing" avocations, which required extensive travel "throughout the lands surrendered," was specifically reserved by treaty.[106]

The enforcement of extralegal "laws" was evidently no ethical problem for the NWMP as a legal institution, but it was clearly troublesome to its officers. Indians off the reserve without passes could either be ordered or escorted back or, if they were in local towns, charged with vagrancy – the criminal offence of living without lawful means of support.[107] No record exists of the numbers of Indians either charged with vagrancy in western towns or run back to the reserves under threat of prosecution and jail. There was no offence of vagrancy in the *Indian Acts*. Such a provision would have been redundant: Indians, subject to the civil and criminal laws of Canada, were subject to the laws of vagrancy on the same terms as whites. Most likely, the threat of imprisonment for vagrancy was used to get Indians to move out of town, since few western towns wanted to fill their jails with visiting Indians.

Nor are there any records of the internal administrative process of granting or denying passes. Magnus Begg, agent at the Blackfoot Reserve, reported that "some Indians have asked me lately for passes to Red Deer to pick berries, but I would not grant them. If I hear of any number going North I will notify the Police to look after them."[108] Agents were warned, by circular from the Indian Department headquarters in Regina, to monitor "the arrival of any strange Indians, even though from other agencies under pass ... and their business ascertained." Another circular limited passes to one every three months. Still another warned of the problem of Indians visiting the industrial schools without passes. Indian children were isolated in these schools, and it is significant that the efforts of family and friends to visit them were seen as an administrative problem.[109]

These circulars indicate the extent to which this official lawlessness was structured and institutionalized. The administration of the *Indian Act* in the North-West must be understood in the context of the structured illegality of the administration of the pass system by both Indian agents and the NWMP. These officials were law enforcement officers and magistrates, undeterred by the administration of illegal rules confining Indians to small reserves. Such confinement amounts to imprisonment, falling easily within the common law tort of false imprisonment. More than that, this demonstration of official lawlessness symbolizes the nature of the rule of law in Indian reserves on the Prairies.

The Legal Assault on Tribal Culture

Perhaps the most infamous provisions of the *Indian Act* were those that prohibited Indian dancing.[110] Indian Department officials were only partially aware of the place of ceremony in Native life, but they did understand that it was at the heart of tribal culture. This culture was to be broken. It not only symbolized values primitive and un-Christian – considered inappropriate in a modern, white, Eurocentric Canada – but also directly threatened white domination of Indian tribes. Big Bear had begun the North-West Rebellion by calling the tribes together for a thirst dance. The Indian agents could never understand the complexity of what went on at that ceremony, but it bound the tribes together in an unknown world.[111]

Two distinct amendments to the *Indian Act* were aimed at the repression of Indian ceremonies. The first, passed on 19 April 1884, was aimed at the potlatches of the Northwest Coast tribes:

> Every Indian or other person who engages in or assists in celebrating the Indian festival known as the Potlatch or in the Indian dance known as the Tamanawas is guilty of a misdemeanour, and shall be liable to imprisonment for the term of not more than six nor less than two months in any gaol or other place of confinement; and any Indian or other person who encourages, either directly or indirectly an Indian or Indians to get up such a festival or dance, or to celebrate the same, or who shall assist in the celebration of same is guilty of a like offense, and shall be liable to the same punishment.[112]

This act was not specifically aimed at Plains Indians, but, when read in the context of both the pass system and the overbroad scope of the act, it should not be surprising that Indian agents on the Prairies attempted to use it. The NWMP had serious questions about the legality of the act, as did Judge Matthew Begbie of the British Columbia Supreme Court. Begbie struck down the law in the first case to come before the courts.[113]

Eleven years later, a time span indicating that the government was in no hurry, a revision was passed narrowing the scope of the law to two specific kinds of ceremonies:

> Every Indian or other person who engages in, or assists in celebrating or encourages either directly or indirectly another to celebrate, any Indian festival, dance or other ceremony of which the giving away or paying or giving back of money, goods, or articles of any sort forms a part, or is a feature, whether such gift of money, goods or articles takes place before, at, or after the celebration of the same, and every Indian or other person who engages or assists in any celebration or dance of which the wounding or mutilation of the dead or living body of any human being or animal forms a part or is a feature, is guilty of an indictable offense.[114]

Once again the act was aimed at Northwest Coast Indians and was meant to satisfy difficulties with the ambiguity of the 1885 act. The two targets referred to were the potlatch and Hamat'sa rituals. But the language would also have included two common Plains rituals: the sun dance, which involved the piercing of human flesh, and several ceremonies in which dog flesh was consumed.[115]

It is difficult to determine the impact of these laws on the daily religious and ceremonial life of Plains Indians. The Cree chief Piapot was arrested twice, once in the late 1890s and again in 1901. Piapot agreed to include a traditional piercing ritual in his annual rain dance, a version of the sun dance. The Indian agent heard of the event and had Piapot arrested and imprisoned in Regina. Through a visitor, the chief learned that a sign on his cell indicated that he was imprisoned for being drunk. The chief, who did not drink, became enraged.[116] In 1901, he was arrested for participating in a give-away dance along with five other band members. The others were released, but Piapot, who had allegedly incited the others to resist arrest, was given two months in jail. This imprisonment of an old chief was intended to have a repressive impact on the tribe.[117]

Within the context of the Indian Department's assault on tribal life, these laws were probably not very significant on the Plains in terms of the actual use of the criminal sanction. Only a handful of Indians actually went to jail on such charges, either real or fictitious. But these laws were important as part of the machinery of repression. Children were removed to schools, tribes were broken up as families were scattered on small plots of land, language was repressed as children were forced to speak only English in school, and church services on the Christian sabbath became major social events on reserves.

The more important function of the laws regulating these ceremonies was symbolic. The ceremonies indicated how distinct Plains Indian culture was from Euro-Canadian culture. Since government policy was based first on repression, then on forced assimilation, the rich ceremonial life of the tribes was a serious threat to both policies. Large gatherings of warriors for sun dances left the Indians there free to engage in any kind of discussions and actions.

There is no assessment of the effectiveness of these laws in repressing Prairie Indian culture. Most Native ceremonial activity went underground: some to the far corners of reserves in secret and some out in the open in disguised form. Traditional ceremonies took over official holidays, even Christian ones. Moreover, many Indian agents simply ignored the laws, either because they came to believe that Indians had a right to their own cultural and religious activities, or because the difficulty of their positions made it politic to do so. The NWMP never enthusiastically investigated such offences because they did not see them as criminal. For the Mounties, the greater problem was Indian defiance of official authority: Piapot was punished more for resisting authority than for holding a sun dance.

While the attack on tribal culture through outlawing Native ceremonies has received most of the scholarly attention because of its legal absurdity, it is important to note that it was compulsory residential schooling that represented the major thrust of the government's assimilationist policy. Adult Indians would always harbour their cultural traditions. Children, however, could be resocialized. The policy of compulsory residential school, also a legal policy provided for in the *Indian Act,* was at the centre of this plan. Employing a resistance similar to that launched against the legal repression of tribal customs, Indians found a number of ways to oppose the residential school movement – from keeping their children at home to the children's own resistance to the overbearing school regimes.[118]

Conclusion: Law on the Canadian Prairie, 1870-1900

The Dominion of Canada imposed an undemocratic and authoritarian legal order in the North-West Territories in the 1870s. The objects of that legal order were two groups without voices in Canadian society: Americans and Indians. Both groups, with no relationship to each other, stood in the way of the peaceful settlement of farmers on the Canadian Prairies and the expansion of the Canadian state to the Pacific.

The NWMP still carry two images in the west. At best, they constituted a liberal, authoritarian, and paternalistic legal institution, officered by eastern Canadian and British gentlemen under strict orders to protect the interests of the queen's Indian "children" from avaricious settlers and Americans in order to secure an orderly frontier. At worst, the NWMP were a racist and paramilitary organization charged with the task of quieting the Indians with the most judicious use of violence possible under the circumstances. In either model, they served as police, prosecutor, judge, jury, and executioner, imposing a form of Canadian law unrecognizable in Ontario or Quebec on the Indians and Métis of the Prairies. Native accommodation of the NWMP stemmed more from their political than their legal role: it was easy to meet with them and negotiate small solutions to immediate problems. The force had a quasi-military structure apparent to the tribes, one much more familiar than the faceless bureaucrats of the Indian Department.

Governor Dewdney and the North-West Territorial Council, appointed by the dominion government in Ottawa, had extensive legal powers but exercised those powers in a disreputable manner, reckless of Native interests and life. Two examples clearly establish this. Legislation to protect the buffalo was within their range of authority and was requested by the tribes. There is no question that such legislation would have involved some difficult enforcement issues. But that was equally true of legislation against American whisky traders or Indian cattle thieves, enforcement activities that the NWMP were clearly able to carry out. The council made no effort to present such legislation even in attenuated form. Treaty 6 guaranteed the Indians Crown assistance in time of starvation. But local Indian Affairs authorities were given direct orders to starve able-bodied Indian men and issued inadequate rations for Indian women and children. This forced adult Indian warriors to stand by idly and watch their families starve. Indians used a number of adaptive strategies to circumvent this abuse of authority, including forms of overt resistance that led to the 1885 Riel Rebellion.

But the Indian nations also made use of law in their negotiations with the Canadian government. Cree, Saulteaux, Blood, Blackfoot, and Dakota social order survived tenaciously through the early reserve process. The traditional legal authority of the chiefs kept order among the tribes but was tested by the hardships imposed by reserve life. The traditional divisions between peace chiefs and war chiefs gave way to different kinds of social divisions, with traditionals and young men testing existing authority structures. Many of the chiefs, including Poundmaker, Big Bear, and Piapot, exercised great leadership ability in keeping the diverse elements of their bands together. The 1885 North-West Rebellion divided a number of bands, although a number also held together either in joining the rebellion or remaining outside it. The Indian nations brought their own legal cultures to the treaty-making process and did everything they could to negotiate treaties according to Indian legal traditions.

The process that emerged, however, reflects more Canadian than First Nations law. The illegality of the treaty process still pervades the legal culture of the Plains tribes. The sense of dishonesty and betrayal was immediate, brought out in the open in the discussions at treaty, then repeated over the succeeding months and years as it became increasingly obvious that the Crown would not keep its treaty agreements with impoverished Indian nations. This was not an option open to Indians, who approached treaty with pure hearts after purification rituals obligating them to speak true words. There was no tradition of dishonesty and the manipulation of the meanings of words in Aboriginal law. There were no Indian bureaucrats or courts to decide the legal meaning of plain words such as "maintain a school" or "provide a medicine chest." This left the First Nations with a deeply held belief both that they were cheated by Canadian law and that the law itself was dishonest and could not be trusted to protect their treaty rights. Over a century later, these two contrasting legal histories of the extension of Canadian power over the Plains Indians are still in sharp contention.

Notes

1 Helen Buckley, *From Wooden Ploughs to Welfare: Why Indian Policy Failed in the Prairie Provinces* (Montreal: McGill-Queen's University Press, 1992); Gerald Friesen, *The Canadian Prairies: A History* (Toronto: University of Toronto Press, 1984), 129-61.

2 R.C. Macleod, *The North-West Mounted Police and Law Enforcement, 1873-1905* (Toronto: University of Toronto Press, 1976).

3 Tache Papers, Cochin to Tache, 14 August 1885, Saskatchewan Archives Board. Quoted in Bob Beal and Rod Macleod, *Prairie Fire: The 1885 Northwest Rebellion* (Edmonton: Hurtig Publishers, 1984). A similar mistranslation may have occurred during Big Bear's trial. See also the account in Blair Stonechild and Bill Waiser, *Loyal till Death: Indians and the North-West Rebellion* (Saskatoon: Fifth House Publishers, 1997).

4 F.W. Spicer, in *Story of Saskatchewan and Its People,* 3 vols., ed. John Hawkes (Regina: S.J. Clarke, 1924), 1: 143. Quoted in Hugh Dempsey, *Big Bear: The End of Freedom* (Lincoln: University of Nebraska Press, 1984), 185. Although the trial is unreported, its details are found in "The Queen v. Big Bear," *Sessional Papers, 1886,* 221.

5 *The Spirit of the Alberta Treaties,* ed. Richard Price (Edmonton: University of Alberta Press, 1987), 168.
6 The Cree undoubtedly knew that the Saulteaux had forced the Crown to Treaty 3 by blocking the Dawson Route across northwestern Ontario: George F. Stanley, *The Birth of Western Canada: A History of the Riel Rebellions* (Toronto: University of Toronto Press, 1936; reprint 1992), 210-13; John L. Taylor, "Two Views on the Meanings of Treaties Six and Seven," in *The Spirit of the Alberta Treaties,* ed. Price, 9-45; Jean Friesen, "Magnificent Gifts: The Treaties of Canada with the Indians of the Northwest, 1869-76," *Transactions of the Royal Society of Canada,* series 5, 1 (1986): 41-51.
7 There is a substantial literature on the origins of the RCMP: Macleod, *North-West Mounted Police;* Desmond Morton, "Cavalry or Police: Keeping the Peace on Two Adjacent Frontiers, 1870-1900," *Journal of Canadian Studies* 12 (1977): 27-37; Hugh Dempsey, *Men in Scarlet* (Calgary: McClelland and Stewart West, 1974).
8 Macleod, *North-West Mounted Police,* 35-36.
9 Ibid. at 40.
10 John N. Jennings, "The Northwest Mounted Police and Indian Policy, 1874-1896" (PhD dissertation, University of Toronto, 1979), 7-11.
11 Macleod, *North-West Mounted Police,* 19-20.
12 Barbara J. Mayfield, "The Northwest Mounted Police and Blackfoot Peoples, 1874-1884" (master's thesis, University of Victoria, 1979).
13 Jennings, "Northwest Mounted Police," 51.
14 Hamar Foster, "Sins against the Great Spirit: The Law, the Hudson's Bay Company, and the Mackenzie's River Murders, 1835-1839," *Criminal Justice History: An International Annual* 10 (1989): 23-76; John Phillip Reid, "Certainty of Vengeance: The Hudson's Bay Company and Retaliation in Kind against Indian Offenders in New Caledonia," *Montana: The Magazine of Western History* 43 (1993): 4-17.
15 Jennings, "Northwest Mounted Police," 303.
16 Ibid. at 182-85.
17 Dempsey, *Big Bear,* 123. On Big Bear generally, see also W.B. Fraser, "Big Bear, Indian Patriot," *Alberta Historical Review* 14, 2 (1966): 1-13.
18 Jennings, "Northwest Mounted Police," 303-5.
19 David Lee, "Foremost Man, and His Band," *Saskatchewan History* 36, 3 (1983): 94-101 at 98.
20 Jennings, "Northwest Mounted Police," 329-44.
21 Ibid. at 337-38.
22 Hugh Dempsey, *Charcoal's World* (Saskatoon: Western Producer Prairie Books, 1978).
23 Jennings, "Northwest Mounted Police," 304-5.
24 Stanley, *Birth of Western Canada;* Beal and Macleod, *Prairie Fire;* Stonechild and Waiser, *Loyal till Death*. Stonechild and Waiser list by name and offence fifty-five Indians convicted of crimes occurring during the rebellion; see Appendix Five, 261-63.
25 Stonechild and Waiser, *Loyal till Death,* argue that the Indians had a distinct agenda in the rebellion and were not allies of the Métis. Beal and Macleod, *Prairie Fire,* analyze the nature of the Métis-Indian alliance in detail. While neither side fully trusted each other (116), they did recognize common interests – chiefly in their land rights. Riel calculated that, if there were 1.1 billion acres of land in the North-West, each Indian and Métis "owned" 11,000 acres. Unimproved Indian lands were, in his calculation, worth 12.5¢ per acre, while "improved" Métis lands were worth 25¢. Exactly how the Métis came to own as much land as the Indians in his analysis is unclear, revealing the weakness of the alliance: Riel had created an artificial equality of interests (123). Only a few Indians served under Métis in the actual rebellion.
26 William Bleasdell Cameron, *Blood Red the Sun* (Calgary: Kenways, 1950); Stuart Hughes, *The Frog Lake "Massacre": Personal Perspectives on Ethnic Conflict* (Toronto: McClelland and Stewart, 1996), collects the major primary sources on the killings.
27 D.H. Brown, "The Meaning of Treason in 1885," *Saskatchewan History* 28, 2 (1975): 65-73.
28 Beal and Macleod, *Prairie Fire,* 310.
29 Sandra Estlin Bingaman, "The Trials of Poundmaker and Big Bear, 1885," *Saskatchewan History* 28, 3 (1975): 81-102.

30 Beal and Macleod, *Prairie Fire,* 310-33. It seems clear, even by the standards of 1880s common law, that Robertson was right on this point and the judge's ruling in error. Presence itself at a treasonous event was an evidentiary fact that the jury could have properly considered. But it did not prove treason by itself without additional evidence. Beal and Macleod believe that Robertson was ignorant of the law of treason (329).

31 Eighteen Métis, the most prominent members of the council, accepted a plea bargain on treason-felony charges and pled guilty in return for short sentences. Eleven were sentenced to seven years in jail, three to three years, and four to one year. Ibid. at 309.

32 Bingaman, "Trials of Poundmaker and Big Bear"; Stonechild and Waiser, *Loyal till Death.* All were sentenced to three years in prison in August 1885. Poundmaker was released on 4 March 1886, sick with tuberculosis, and he died four months later at the age of forty-six. Big Bear, convicted at the same time, was released on 27 January 1887 because he, like Poundmaker, was sick and the government did not want him to die in prison. He lived another year. One Arrow, also sentenced in August, was released in April 1886, too sick to travel home, and he died in Winnipeg before the month was over.

33 Beal and Macleod, *Prairie Fire,* 311-12, 329-30. The precise legal issue is that treason clearly requires a narrow *mens rea:* as a specific intent offence, it requires proof beyond a reasonable doubt of an intent to make war on the Crown. Defence attorney Robertson repeatedly pointed out that the Crown had to show that a defendant "participated in it, or at least knew it was happening" (311). The Crown took the view that, once a rebellion appeared, the onus was on the defendant to show that he was present innocently. Although the judge apparently understood the issue, his jury instructions never clarified it, allowing racially prejudiced juries to draw an inference of treason from mere presence among Indians in the region of the rebellion. This interpretation of the law would have made every Indian and Métis in northern Saskatchewan guilty of treason by mere physical presence in the region.

34 Ibid. at 328, 331. Only one Indian won an acquittal in all of the trials.

35 Ibid. at 323.

36 Ibid. David Manelbaum, *The Plains Cree: An Ethnographic, Historical, and Comparative Study* (Regina: Great Plains Research Centre, 1940; reprint 1979), 106-10.

37 Beal and Macleod, *Prairie Fire,* 309-12.

38 Ibid. at 327-30.

39 Gontran Laviolette, *The Dakota Sioux in Canada* (Winnipeg: DLM Publications, 1991), 252-55.

40 Beal and Macleod, *Prairie Fire,* 325-27.

41 Quoted ibid. at 331. André was an Oblate priest from the Batoche area: Stonechild and Waiser, *Loyal till Death,* 110.

42 Assistant Commissioner Hayter Reed to Lieutenant Governor Dewdney, quoted ibid. at 331.

43 Ibid. at 332.

44 Cameron, *Blood Red the Sun,* 146-48.

45 Beal and Macleod, *Prairie Fire,* 331-32.

46 Taylor, "Two Views on Treaties Six and Seven," 9-45.

47 John Leonard Taylor, "Canada's Northwest Indian Policy in the 1870s: Traditional Premises and Necessary Innovations," in *The Spirit of the Alberta Treaties,* ed. Price, 3-7.

48 John L. Tobias, "The Origins of the Treaty Rights Movement in Saskatchewan," in *1885 and After: Native Society in Transition,* ed. F. Laurie Barron and James Waldram (Regina: Canadian Plains Research Center, 1986), 241-52. A number of Indian elders give views of these treaties that have been handed down through oral history. See "Interviews with Elders," in *The Spirit of the Alberta Treaties,* ed. Price, 113-60.

49 J.E. Foster, "The Saulteaux and the Numbered Treaties: An Aboriginal Rights Position," in *The Spirit of the Alberta Treaties,* ed. Price, 161-80 at 168.

50 D.J. Hall, "A Serene Atmosphere? Treaty 1 Revisited," *Canadian Journal of Native Studies* 4 (1985): 321-58.

51 Arthur J. Ray, *Indians in the Fur Trade: Their Role as Hunters, Trappers, and Middlemen in the Lands Southwest of Hudson Bay, 1660-1870* (Toronto: University of Toronto Press, 1974), 195-230.

52 Sarah Carter, *Lost Harvests: Prairie Indian Reserve Farmers and Government Policy* (Montreal and Kingston: McGill-Queen's University Press, 1990), 15-49.
53 *The Spirit of the Alberta Treaties,* ed. Price, 42-43, 113-27.
54 Dempsey, *Big Bear,* 75. The exchange is reported in Alexander Morris, *The Treaties of Canada with the Indians of Manitoba and the North-West Territories,* 2 vols. (1880; reprint Saskatoon: Fifth House Publishers, 1991), 1: 240.
55 "Treaty Number Six," in Morris, *Treaties of Canada,* 1: 354.
56 Ibid. at 353.
57 "Report," G. McDougall to Lieutenant Governor Morris, 23 October 1875, ibid. at 174-75.
58 Jean Friesen, "Alexander Morris," *Dictionary of Canadian Biography,* vol. 11, *1881 to 1890* (Toronto: University of Toronto Press, 1982), 608-14.
59 There is a substantial nineteenth-century British literature on treaties. The leading case up to the time of the numbered treaties was *The Mohegan Indians v. Connecticut,* (1770), in Joseph Henry Smith, *Appeals to the Privy Council from the American Plantations* (New York: Octagon Books, 1965). The case went to the Privy Council before the American Revolution, representing the first determination of the legal rights of an Indian tribe under British law. In the United States, the Marshall Court constructed the legal meaning of British Indian treaties in *Cherokee Nation* (1832) and *Worcester v. Georgia* (1833), holding them legally binding. Canadian courts did not directly construe Indian treaties as legal documents until *St. Catherine's Milling Company* (1885), where they were held documents of "political expediency" and not of legal force.
60 Morris, *Treaties of Canada,* 352.
61 Dempsey, *Big Bear,* 63.
62 Ibid. at 79.
63 The belief that Treaty 3 Indians tricked Crown negotiators into paying a far higher price than the lands were worth was at the core of Ontario's litigation with the dominion in *Province of Ontario v. The Dominion of Canada* (1898). The idea that Indian negotiating tactics were "tricks," and that their oratorical statements were "dishonest," permeated contemporary Canadian views of the treaty process.
64 Dempsey, *Big Bear,* 120.
65 The process has been described in detail in individual treaty reports.
66 Quoted in Hall, "A Serene Atmosphere?" 321.
67 "And further, Her Majesty agrees to maintain a school on each reserve hereby made, when ever the Indians of the reserve should desire it": Treaty 1, in Morris, *Treaties of Canada,* 315. Each of the numbered treaties contains some version of this clause in approximately the same language.
68 VanKoughnet to Provencher, 12 March 1873, RG 10, quoted in Vic Savino and Erica Schumacher, "'Whenever the Indians of the Reserve Should Desire It': An Analysis of the First Nation Treaty Right to Education," *Manitoba Law Journal* 19 (1992): 476-97.
69 Ibid. at 490.
70 Morris, *Treaties of Canada.*
71 *The Spirit of the Alberta Treaties,* ed. Price, contains a number of essays that illustrate the complexity of Native understanding of the substance of the treaties.
72 "Interviews with Elders," in ibid. at 113-43; Taylor, "Two Views on Treaties Six and Seven," 9-45; John L. Tobias, "Canada's Subjugation of the Plains Cree, 1879-1885," *Canadian Historical Review* 64, 4 (1983): 519-48.
73 Irene Spry, "The Tragedy of the Loss of the Commons in Western Canada," in *As Long as the Sun Shines and Water Flows,* ed. A. Getty and A. Lussier (Vancouver: UBC Press, 1984), 203-28.
74 Plains Indians faced periodic game shortages, particularly in winter. The ordinary ranges of buffalo were always irregular, so some years hunts were sparse. The Cree, inhabitants of the mixed forest and plain parkland south of the boreal forest, had access to the resources of the forests as well and did not face such seasonal shortages. Spry, "The Tragedy," 205-6.
75 Beal and Macleod, *Prairie Fire,* 38.
76 Henry Youle Hind, *Northwest Territory: Report of the Assiniboine and Saskatchewan Exploring Expedition* (Toronto: J. Lovell, 1859), quoted in Spry, "The Tragedy," 210.

77 Morris, *Treaties of Canada,* 171.
78 Ibid. at 168-69; Ray, *Indians in the Fur Trade,* 227.
79 Morris, *Treaties of Canada,* 170. This warning of an Indian war is probably exaggerated or may have been influenced by the wars in the United States. Christie's next paragraph points out that these Indians would come to the HBC for relief from starvation and that there was no force in the North-West sufficient to stop them from simply taking what relief they wanted.
80 Ibid. at 171.
81 Deputy of the Interior Merideth to Minister, undated (probably spring 1874), RG 10, 3229 (black series), quoted in Noel E. Dyck, "The Administration of Federal Indian Aid in the Northwest Territories, 1879-1885" (master's thesis, University of Saskatchewan, 1970), 21.
82 DHC, 26 March 1877, vol. 3, 990-93, quoted in Dyck, "The Administration of Federal Indian Aid," 22.
83 Dyck, "The Administration of Federal Indian Aid," 23-24.
84 Stanley, *Birth of Western Canada,* 222-23.
85 Ibid. at 223.
86 Ibid. Sitting Bull's presence in Saskatchewan was viewed as a kind of "wild card" by all participants in the treaty process. The Sioux, an American tribe, did not take treaty. At the same time, their presence in Canada stemmed directly from their role in two American wars, the Minnesota Sioux Uprising of 1863 and the Sioux War of 1876, leading to victory over General Custer. Therefore, the spectre of Indian wars was not simply US history in the Canadian Prairies.
87 Dyck, "The Administration of Federal Indian Aid," 23.
88 Christie and Dickieson to the Minister of the Interior, 7 October 1875, CSP, 1876, vol. 7, no. 9, quoted in Stanley, *Birth of Western Canada,* 218.
89 J.R. Miller, *Skyscrapers Hide the Heavens: A History of Indian-White Relations in Canada* (Toronto: University of Toronto Press, 1989), 171-72, attributes the decline of the buffalo to a number of factors, including an American policy of eliminating the buffalo hunt in an effort to starve the tribes into submission, particularly in the context of the Sioux War of 1876.
90 Stanley, *Birth of Western Canada,* 222; Noel Dyck, "An Opportunity Lost: The Initiation of the Reserve Agricultural Programme in the Prairie West," in *1885 and After,* ed. Barron and Waldram, 24-25.
91 Treaty 6 was signed on 23 August 1876. The *Indian Act* had been passed on 12 April 1876. It consolidated and expanded the 1869 *Indian Act,* which had consolidated the Ontario and Quebec acts. There was no systematic effort to post the act in the North-West, and no one has argued that Indians there were aware of its provisions. As the existence and meaning of the act were not part of treaty negotiations, the Crown must have chosen not to use the opportunity of a large assembly of Indians to make its provisions known. Obviously, it would have angered them and made the signing less likely.
92 L. VanKoughnet, memorandum to Indian Branch, Department of the Interior, 22 August 1876, RG 10 (red series), vol. 1995, file 6886.
93 John Leslie and Ron Maguire, *The Historical Development of the Indian Act,* 2nd ed. (Ottawa: Department of Indian and Northern Affairs, 1978).
94 Peter Douglas Elias, *The Dakota of the Canadian Northwest: Lessons for Survival* (Winnipeg: University of Manitoba Press, 1988), 88.
95 Don McLean, *1885: Metis Rebellion or Government Conspiracy?* (Winnipeg: University of Manitoba Press, 1985), 58.
96 Dempsey, *Big Bear,* 123.
97 Jennings, "Northwest Mounted Police," 217.
98 J.R. Miller, *Shingwauk's Vision: A History of Native Residential Schools* (Toronto: University of Toronto Press, 1996), 129.
99 Ibid. at 219-20.
100 B. Bennett, "Study of Passes for Indians to Leave Their Reserves" (Ottawa: Department of Indian and Northern Affairs, Treaties and Historical Research Centre, 1974), 1-2.
101 Ibid. at 2. Dewdney to J.M. Rae, Indian Agent, Treaty 6, 23 June 1885, Dewdney Papers, NW Rebellion, MG 27, vol. 5, 1948-49; quoted in Bennett, "Study of Passes," 2-3.

102 Reed to Dewdney, 16 August 1885, Dewdney Papers, NW Rebellion, MG 27, 2076-87; quoted in Bennett, "Study of Passes," 3.
103 Bennett, "Study of Passes," 3, 8.
104 Steele to Commissioner, NWMP, undated 1891, RG 10, 3863; quoted in ibid. at 4.
105 Reed to Superintendent General of Indian Affairs, 10 December 1891, RG 10, 3863; quoted in Bennett, "Study of Passes," 5.
106 For Treaty 6, for example, see Morris, *Treaties of Canada,* 215, 218, 353. The other treaties carry parallel language.
107 Jennings, "Northwest Mounted Police," 219-20.
108 Begg to Indian Commissioner, Regina, 26 July 1894; quoted in Bennett, "Study of Passes," 5.
109 A.E. Forget, Indian Commissioner, Regina, confidential circular to Indian Agents, 30 July 1894, RG 10, 1137; Forget to Indian Agents, 8 April 1889; Forget, circular, 29 March 1889, RG 10, 1142; quoted in Bennett, "Study of Passes," 5-6.
110 Katherine Pettipas, *Severing the Ties That Bind: Government Repression of Indigenous Religious Ceremonies on the Prairies* (Winnipeg: University of Manitoba Press, 1994); Douglas Cole and Ira Chaikin, *An Iron Hand upon the People: The Law against the Potlatch on the Northwest Coast* (Vancouver: UBC Press, 1990).
111 Dempsey, *Big Bear,* 123-30. This dance was also known as the sun dance.
112 47 Victoria (1884), cap. 27.
113 Begbie held that the statute was so overbroad that it was not clear what specific conduct was prohibited by it. A fundamental principle of British common law is that a penal statute has to indicate clearly the kind of conduct prohibited.
114 Leslie and Maguire, *The Historical Development of the Indian Act,* 95.
115 Pettipas, *Severing the Ties That Bind,* 96.
116 Ibid. at 116. The Department of Indian Affairs believed that Piapot held the only sun dance in Canada in 1895. His reserve was a centre of Native religion, listed as 85 percent "pagan" in 1896. David Lee, "Piapot: Man and Myth," *Prairie Forum* 17, 2 (1992): 251-62 at 258.
117 Pettipas, *Severing the Ties That Bind,* 118-19. Thus, Piapot, although arrested twice for holding religious ceremonies, was arrested once on charges of drinking, and once for resisting arrest, indicating the reluctance of the police to directly charge him with holding religious ceremonies under the *Indian Act.*
118 Miller, *Shingwauk's Vision,* 129, 343-74.

4

The Exclusionary Effect of Colonial Law: Indigenous Peoples and English Law in Western Canada, 1670-1870

Russell C. Smandych

On 4 August 1845, a Saulteaux Indian by the name of Capinesseweet was placed on trial at Red River for the murder of a Sioux by the name of Pa-tunga-o'kay-snay and the accidental killing of another Saulteaux. At the trial, it was disclosed that Capinesseweet killed Pa-tunga-o'kay-snay as an act of revenge for the killing of his father, who had died at the hands of the Sioux a year earlier. It was also disclosed that, shortly after the murder took place, Capinesseweet's elder brother offered "to pay for the Soiu [sic]" who was killed by giving up "two oxen, a cow and a colt."[1] Despite this attempt at offering compensation to the offended Sioux, Capinesseweet was convicted by the twelve jurors of the General Quarterly Court of Assiniboia and sentenced to hang by Adam Thom, the first recorder of Rupert's Land. In his book on the history of the Red River settlement, written a decade later, Alexander Ross, who in 1845 was sheriff at Red River and one of the witnesses who testified, wrote the following about the trial and execution:

> However justifiable the conduct of the Indian might be, according to his idea of things and the laws of his country, few acts more daring in its nature, or more insulting to the whites, had ever been committed in this quarter, and the universal voice called aloud for justice. The fourth day after the murder was committed, he was tried in the regular way by a jury, found guilty, and condemned to be hung – the first instance of the kind in Rupert's Land. Being one of the Catholic converts, he was regularly attended in his last moments by the Reverend Mr. Belcourt, a Catholic priest. A gallows was erected over the prison gate, and there he was executed on the 6th September 1845.[2]

The trial and execution of Capinesseweet have been mentioned in the accounts of many legal historians of western Canada.[3] However, none of these authors has addressed the question of why he was placed on trial instead of being left alone, with his people and the visiting Sioux, to settle the matter as they would have done before the arrival of Europeans. This gap in the written legal history of western Canada is especially curious in view of the statements that several historians have made about the way in which the Europeans who arrived in western Canada adopted the practice of not interfering with "crimes committed by Indians against other Indians"[4] as well as the practice of sometimes accepting the use of traditional – often "blood-for-blood" – Aboriginal methods of dispute settlement themselves.[5] While twentieth-century legal historians of the Canadian west have overlooked the significance of criminal cases such as the one involving Capinesseweet, it is interesting to note that in 1856 Ross wrote what he viewed to be the reason that Capinesseweet was executed before "more than a thousand spectators" at Red River:

> Long before this affair took place, the Indians had become insolent and overbearing; the peace and safety of the whites loudly called for some check on their growing audacity, and a fairer opportunity than now offered could never occur. Had we through a false sympathy overlooked this insult, our leniency would have been attributed to nothing but fear; and thus would have increased their assurance, and our danger. The propriety of the decisive course adopted has been proved by its salutary influence on the conduct of the Indians generally, demonstrating that they were amenable to the laws, and that crime, either by the whites or Indians, would not be tolerated within the colony.[6]

This chapter addresses the question of how the trial of Capinesseweet was made possible. It does this by placing his trial and execution, on the orders of Adam Thom, within a wider study of law and colonialism. The first part explains in some detail why it is important to move toward adopting a more sociologically informed comparative-historical approach to the study of the application of English law to indigenous peoples. The second part demonstrates how applying this approach to the study of English law and indigenous peoples in western Canada can produce a better understanding of how "Aboriginal offenders" such as Capinesseweet came to be subjected to the rigours of English law.

Toward a Comparative Study of Colonial Law: Looking for Contemporaries of Adam Thom

A recent study of the development of criminal law courts in the Red River Settlement after 1812 has examined the transition of the Hudson's Bay Company from a "private justice" system run by employees, who had little or no legal training, to a more formal system of English-based criminal courts, which were later presided over by colonial judges such as Adam Thom.[7] The study also included an analysis of criminal cases heard before the General

Quarterly Court of Assiniboia from 1844 to 1872, with particular attention given to cases in which Aboriginal people were involved as witnesses, accomplices, or accused. While providing new insights into the operation of criminal courts in pre-1870 Manitoba, this study, like those completed by earlier historians, did not fully address the question of why Thom believed he had the authority to order Capinesseweet to be hanged at Red River in 1845. To answer this question, we must look at both Thom's views of English criminal law and the manner in which it should be applied in the Canadian west and the extent to which his thinking about the application of English criminal law to indigenous peoples was consistent with the thinking of colonial judges in other parts of colonial North America and elsewhere in the expanding British Empire.

Thom was appointed "Councillor and Recorder of Rupert's Land" and councillor of the District of Assiniboia in March 1839, offices that made him "the active head of legal affairs" in the district.[8] Legal historians have written a great deal about the role that he played as the first recorder of Rupert's Land. In general, previous investigators have portrayed him as the single most important person who affected the development of the settlement's legal system after 1839. In his pioneering study, Roy St. George Stubbs notes that, "as the first Recorder of Rupert's Land, Adam Thom must be accorded the distinction of being 'the father of the Bench and Bar of Western Canada.'"[9] Thom played an important role in revising and consolidating the laws of Assiniboia.[10] Soon after he arrived at Red River, he also took the initiative to draft his own *Proposed Penal and Civil Code for Rupertsland*[11] and write a long treatise entitled *Observations on the Law and Judicature of Rupertsland*.[12]

In his *Observations,* Thom provided a detailed rationale for his view on why the Indians of western Canada should be subject to English law. Significantly, one of his major concerns in writing this document was to justify the fur trade monopoly of the Hudson's Bay Company in Rupert's Land and the Indian Territories. After reviewing the fate of monopolies granted by the English Crown to trading companies that existed elsewhere, he stated, "but, if one turns from law to policy, the Monopoly of The Hudson's Bay Company stood on peculiarly strong grounds. With respect to India and the Baltic, monopoly was not necessary at home, nor would competition have been mischievous abroad; but with respect to this country, occupied by ignorant savage tribes 'few and far between' and cut off from the rest of the world by almost inaccessible seas and almost impossible wilderness, competition could not have failed to involve England in expense and inconvenience and Rupert's Land in dissension and misery."[13]

In a later section in which he discussed the "legal principles of colonization," which he considered to be a further justification for the company's monopoly, Thom cited William Blackstone's reasoning about the distinction that had to be made between colonies "where the lands are claimed by right of occupancy only, by finding them desert and uncultivated," and others "where, when already cultivated, they have been either gained by conquest or ceded ... by treaties." Thom argued that Blackstone's rule for classifying different types of British colonies "is utterly inapplicable to the hunting-grounds of wandering and dis-united savages, and were the rule perfectly applicable, the exception would effectively neutralize it." However, he reasoned that if one had to decide on which of these classifications more accurately described the situation that existed in Rupert's Land, one would have to conclude that it seemed "rather to resemble the first class."[14] According to his reasoning, while the Aboriginal peoples of western Canada had no legitimate claim to the land that currently fell under the company's monopoly, nevertheless they were fully subject to the penal laws that the company decided to enforce. In a written judgment following a case that Thom presided over in the General Quarterly Court of Assiniboia in 1845, he reiterated the rationale underlying his approach to dealing with Indians suspected of committing serious crimes: "Every community possesses the acknowledged right of avenging the wrongs, which its members may have sustained at the hands of any other community, either by public war or by private reprisals. – a right, by-the-bye, which is expressly vested in the Hudson's Bay Company by its Charter. Now such a right obviously comprises, what is far more consistent both with humanity and with justice, the lesser right of demanding, or, if necessary, of seizing, for the purposes of trial, any Indian, who may have injured us even within the territory of his tribe."[15]

Thom's approach was not restricted only to "serious" crimes involving Aboriginal people, committed either against whites or "within the territory" of their own "tribe." Previous legal historians of the Red River Settlement have made note of this but have largely ignored addressing the question of why he adopted this approach. While offering a generally favourable view of his personal character and legal qualifications, Dale and Lee Gibson raise the question of why Thom began applying "legal sanctions to the conduct of the native population." In the fall of 1839, he summoned the first grand jury in the colony's history to determine whether a charge of murder should be brought against an Indian boy who had killed one of his friends with an arrow. According to the Gibsons, this type of incident "in the past would have been overlooked, or treated very leniently, but Thom insisted on invoking the same legal procedures that would have been applied if members of the white community had been involved."[16] The Gibsons also highlight the fact that Thom brought Indians into the criminal justice system at Red River by urging the Council of Assiniboia to pass a decree ordering the imprisonment of Indians who were found to be intoxicated. While previous laws had been directed solely against those who supplied Indians with liquor, the new law passed in 1845 stipulated "that any Indian found intoxicated should, in default of providing two sureties, be imprisoned until he prosecuted the person who furnished him with liquor."[17] In related work on the operation of the Quarterly Court from 1844 to 1872, Smandych and Sacca provide a quantitative picture of the number of cases involving Indians that came before it. Significantly, this analysis showed that the majority of cases involved charges of "Selling and/or Giving Alcohol to Indians" in which Aboriginal people were convicted as accomplices. The data also reveal that by the mid-1840s the testimony of Aboriginal witnesses was routinely accepted as evidence for decisions made by the court.

While documenting important aspects of Thom's role in pulling Aboriginal people into the legal system that developed in pre-1870 Manitoba, legal historians of the Red River Settlement have failed to adequately contextualize and explain why he acted the way he did. In the following sections of this chapter, I will pursue the argument that a better understanding of Thom's role in bringing colonial criminal law to the Red River Settlement can be gained by examining the extent to which his legal thought and actions were consistent with what was happening elsewhere.

The Colonial Project of Replacing Aboriginal Law: North American and Other Comparisons

Writing in the *Canadian Indian* in March 1891, an author under the pseudonym of "Fair Play" commented on the way in which Europeans undermined traditional Aboriginal law:

> And is it altogether just to treat the Indian in the way we are doing? Is it altogether fair to deprive them of their nationality, to laugh at their old laws and customs and traditions, to force upon them our own laws and customs as though there could be no two questions as to their superiority in every way, and that they must, of course, be just as suitable and applicable to the Indian as they are to ourselves. Is there nothing – nothing whatever – in the past history of this ancient people to merit our esteem, or to call forth our praise? Were their laws in the past all mere childishness?[18]

There is an emerging, although still rather scattered, literature that can enable us to better understand the timing and specific circumstances surrounding the colonial project aimed at replacing Aboriginal law. Specifically, a number of studies have been completed that provide evidence of what happened elsewhere in colonial North America[19] and in other parts of the developing British Empire.[20] An examination of this type of comparative secondary literature, along with related primary historical data, shows that the practices that Adam Thom introduced at Red River in the 1840s were consistent with legal thought and practice that existed elsewhere on how colonial criminal law should be applied to indigenous peoples. In addition, evidence points to the fact that, rather than being haphazardly imposed by colonial judges working with little guidance on how to apply the law, the move toward including indigenous peoples in English-based colonial criminal courts was part of a conscious policy of the British Colonial Office that began to be applied with some consistency in a number of different British colonies by the 1840s.

The trial of Capinesseweet had precedents even in British North America. In the chapter "Natives, Society, and the Law," Brendan O'Brien documents a case that occurred in 1823 setting a precedent that in Upper Canada an Indian could be tried and executed for the murder of another Indian.[21] The case involved an Ottawa Indian by the name of Shawanakiskie, who was convicted of the murder of an Indian woman in the streets of Amherstburg. The case was referred by Lieutenant Governor Peregine Maitland to Lord Bathurst at the Colonial Office for review and later passed on to Sir Robert Peel for a decision.[22] In his report on the case to Bathurst, Maitland enclosed a report from the trial judge, William Campbell, revealing that it was Campbell who originally sought to have the case sent back to England for review on the following grounds: "It having been urged by his Counsel that other Judges had on former occasions expressed an Opinion that the Indians of this Country are in no case amenable to our Laws, being exempted therefrom by Treaty."[23]

In 1826, Peel confirmed the sentence of the trial judge by issuing a warrant giving Governor Dalhousie discretionary power to carry out the death sentence against Shawanakiskie. More specifically, Peel left it to Dalhousie and Maitland to decide whether to carry "the said sentence into full effect" or commute it either to transportation to New South Wales or Van Dieman's Land or imprisonment for life "in some Prison in the said Province."[24]

This Upper Canadian precedent seems to establish clearly that by 1826 the Colonial Office did not object to the principle of placing Indians on trial for crimes committed against other Indians. Although there was clearly some uncertainty among colonial judges (e.g., William Campbell) about whether the courts had the jurisdiction to try such cases, this uncertainty did not last long. In a recent study that extends the work of O'Brien, John Pratt argues that any lingering "uncertainties about the extent of British jurisdiction" over Indians charged with crimes in Upper Canada were entirely set aside in 1839 in a report written by Chief Justice Macauley.[25] According to Macauley, Indians had "always" been subject to British justice. In his report, he stated that "the [Iroquois] Six Nations have, I believe, asserted the highest pretensions to separate nationality, but in the Courts of Justice they have been always held amenable to, and entitled to the protection of the Laws of the land. Instances could be cited in which Indians in different parts of the Province have been arraigned, criminally, for homicides committed on white people and on each other, and also for other indictable offences."[26] Is it simply coincidental that Macauley offered this assessment of how colonial criminal law applied to Aboriginal peoples in the same year that Thom travelled from Montreal to Red River to take up the new post of recorder of Rupert's Land with similar legal thinking in mind? This question can be answered by turning elsewhere to look at other contemporary precedents and parallels.

Thom's approach to dealing with indigenous peoples also paralleled developments in other British colonies, such as Australia. Indeed, colonial judges in Australia faced many of the same issues as Thom did in determining how English criminal law could be applied to the indigenous.[27] Many Australian historians have pointed out that, when the British government first decided to colonize New South Wales, it used the legal doctrine of *terra nullius* to claim that the land was previously unoccupied. Ironically, however, as Jane Samson points out in her recent comparative study of the issue of Aboriginal legal testimony in New South Wales and British Columbia, the instructions given to governors in Australia "acknowledged the Aborigines, and designated them as British subjects."[28] Not surprisingly, as elsewhere, there was also some initial confusion in Australia about how far English criminal law should be applied to Aborigines.

As early as 1805, colonial courts in Australia began to raise the question of whether courts could hear pleas from Aborigines who did not understand either the language or the procedure of British courts.[29] In a legal opinion on the treatment of Natives, written in July 1805, Judge Advocate Atkins addressed this issue in light of reported "outrages committed by the Natives of the Hawkesbury, &c." against white settlers. In his opinion, the fact that "evidence of Persons not bound by any moral or religious Tye can never be considered or construed as legal evidence" made it impossible, under existing law, to bring a Native to trial for a crime committed against a settler. In light of this, Atkins endorsed the practice of settlers carrying out reprisals against Natives by pursuing and inflicting "such punishment as they may merit."[30] The punishments ultimately inflicted on the Aborigines for committing the "outrage" of killing two settlers and two stockmen near Hawkesbury involved the use of both "blood-for-blood" reprisal and less brutal measures, which included both short imprisonment and forced labour. In a letter that he wrote to Earl Camden less than two weeks after receiving Atkins' legal opinion, Governor Philip Gidley King elaborated on how he had dealt with the outrage, specifically noting that he was happy to inform his lordship that "the Natives' late excesses" were terminated "by their voluntary giving up the Agresssors [sic] who are now ... lodged in the Gaol at Parramatta." In addition, he noted that, since "six of the Natives and those the most Guilty were Shot in a pursuit by the Settlers – I have therefore impressed on the Natives that altho' the Delinquents now in Custody ought to suffer, Yet as Two Black Men more than Settlers have been shot, I shall forego any farther retaliation, but as they were so desirous of shewing their Sorrow for what had passed by giving up the Delinquents and requiring them to be punished, I should try the expedient of sending them to another Settlement to labour which has been much approved by the rest."[31]

These types of "blood-for-blood" reprisals and less "coercive measures" were no doubt frequently used. However, these measures were not supported by all colonial officials. In 1824, Saxe Bannister, the attorney general of New South Wales, made the opposite complaint in a letter that he wrote to Colonial Office undersecretary William Horton. Bannister remarked on the continuing "denial of Justice" caused to "Black Natives" by the fact that a law had not yet been enacted to allow them to testify in court without taking an oath.[32] The issue of the capacity of Aborigines to testify in court was finally resolved, at least in parts of Australia, when the British government passed an act in 1843 "permitting" colonial legislatures in their turn to enact such legislation.[33] While Western and South Australia quickly did so, New South Wales did not.[34] When Adam Thom assumed the job of recorder of Rupert's Land in 1839, he did not face this issue, since the Council of Assiniboia had already passed a resolution in 1837 that allowed "the evidence of a Native [to] be considered valid and be admitted as such in all Courts" in the district.[35] Although, unlike at Red River, uncertainty surrounding the acceptance of Aborigines' testimony continued to persist in Australia, in both jurisdictions indigenous people began to appear as accused in criminal cases quite routinely by the mid-1840s.[36]

The Aborigines Protection Society and British Colonial Office Policy

The move toward including indigenous peoples in the colonial justice systems developing in British North America, Australia, and elsewhere in the late 1830s and 1840s must also be examined within the context of British colonial policy regarding treatment of Aborigines. Specifically, we need to look in more detail at what kinds of guidance and instruction were given to colonial judges by the British government and the Colonial Office in the 1830s and 1840s.

Evidence suggests that a close connection existed between the direction taken by British colonial policy on the treatment of Aborigines and the work of the Aborigines Protection Society. Saxe Bannister, attorney general of New South Wales from 1824 to 1826, was one of the founders of the Aborigines Protection Society. According to Jane Samson, it was Bannister's "disgust at the unfairness of the colonial justice system" that "prompted him to help found the Aborigines Protection Society on his return to Britain."[37] In a report prepared by Alpheus Henry Snow for the US State Department in 1918, *The Question of Aborigines in the Law and Practice of Nations,*[38] the (more fully named) British and Foreign Aborigines Protection Society was formed in 1835 by members of the British and Foreign Anti-Slavery Society. According to Snow's account, these two societies kept their separate identities and carried on work along their own lines until 1909, when they were merged again as the British Anti-Slavery and Aborigines Protection Society.[39]

The Aborigines Protection Society drew together a group of MPs and professionals who were motivated by humanitarian and religious (mainly evangelical Protestant) ideals to push the British government and Colonial Office toward changing colonial policy regarding the treatment of Aboriginals. According to Snow, the influence of the society was the main factor in prompting the British House of Commons to establish a select committee in 1835 "to study the question of aborigines in the law and practice of nations." More specifically, the committee was established largely through the influence of Thomas Fowell Buxton, a former antislavery leader, who was a member of the House of Commons and one of the founders of the society. After persuading the commons to appoint him as chair of the committee, Buxton "founded and became chairman of the British and Foreign Aborigines Protection Society to act as a pressure group" on the government.[40] Another member of the committee was William Gladstone, who apparently drafted its final report issued in 1837.[41] Significantly, according to the resolution passed in the House of Commons establishing the committee, it was authorized to consider which measures ought to be adopted with regard to the Native inhabitants of countries where British settlements were made and to the neighbouring tribes, in order to secure for them the due observance of justice and the protection of their rights, to promote the spread of civilization among them, and to lead them to the peaceful and voluntary reception of the Christian religion.[42]

Among the numerous other recommendations made in its lengthy report, the committee suggested that gradual steps be taken to move in the direction of applying English criminal law to Aboriginal peoples.[43] This recommendation stemmed, at least in part, from the sensibility that this measure would help to better protect the rights of Aboriginal peoples from being further encroached on by Europeans. This sensibility is reflected throughout the report in statements about the need "of preventing abuses of power by civilized states and their citizens" against the "uncivilized" indigenous peoples.[44] Thus, the committee noted, "it is not too much to say that the intercourse of Europeans in general, without any exception in favor of the subjects of Great Britain, has been, unless when attended by missionary exertions, a source of many calamities to uncivilized nations. Too often, their territory has been usurped, their property seized; their numbers diminished, their character debased, the spread of civilization impeded. European vices and diseases have been introduced amongst them, and they have been familiarized with the use of our most potent instruments for the subtle or the violent destruction of human life, viz. brandy and gunpowder."[45]

The committee's recommendation on the need to move gradually toward applying colonial criminal law to Aboriginal peoples – which was included as one of the committee's nine suggestions on the future of colonial policy regarding Aboriginal peoples – deserves to be quoted at length, since it lays out the way in which it thought Aboriginal people should be dealt with in colonial legal systems that were developing across the British Empire. As part of its suggestion seven on the "Punishment of Crimes," the committee noted:

> Provision has already been made by law for the punishment of crimes committed by Her Majesty's subjects on the North American continent, beyond the northern and western limits of the Canadas; in Southern Africa, beyond the limits of the Cape of Good Hope; and in the islands of the South Sea, beyond the jurisdiction of the Australian Colonies. But the provision thus made for the redress of wrongs is defective and unsatisfactory. Beyond the frontier justice is feebly administered, and within it ignorant savages are often made amenable to a code of which they are absolutely ignorant, and the whole spirit and principles of which are foreign to their modes of thought and action. It would be vain to expect the establishment of any other than a most imperfect system of justice amongst persons placed in such circumstances; but for the improvement of the present system some suggestions may be offered. Thus, when the British law is violated by the Aborigines within the British dominions, it seems right that the utmost indulgence compatible with a due regard for the lives and property of others should be shown for their ignorance and prejudices. Actions which they have been taught to regard as praiseworthy we consider as meriting the punishment of death. It is of course impossible to adopt or sanction the barbarous notions which have urged the criminal to the commission of the offence, but neither is it just to exclude them from our view in awarding the punishment of his crime.
>
> Again: in the case of offences committed beyond the borders, British subjects are amenable to colonial courts – the Aborigines are not. From this distinction arises, not merely a failure of justice, but, as far as our own people are concerned, an appearance at least of partiality and wrong, of which they are the victims. British subjects exposed to outrages in a country where there is no established form of civil government, and attacked by persons who are not amenable to our own courts, must be expected to resort to other means of self-defence, and not seldom to urge those means beyond the strict bounds of necessity of justice. It would, therefore, on every account, be desirable to induce the tribes in our vicinity to concur in devising some simple and effectual method of bringing to justice such of their own people as might be guilty of offences against the Queen's subjects. For that purpose, treaties might be made with the chiefs of the independent tribes,

> defining, with all practicable simplicity, what acts should be considered as penal, by what penalities they should be visited, and in what form of procedure those penalities should be enforced.[46]

The committee's recommendation on the punishment of crimes committed by Aboriginal peoples was made alongside other suggestions for their "protection" and "civilization." Most significantly, it suggested that steps also be taken by local colonial governments to prevent the sale of "ardent Spirits" to Aboriginal peoples because of the way in which the sale of alcohol worked as a deadly weapon "for the extermination of [indigenous peoples] who are exempt from the restraints of Christianity and civilization" and that the revenue generated in each of the British colonies be "subject to a charge for such sums as may be necessary to provide for the religious instruction and protection of the survivors of the tribes to which lands comprised in that Colony formerly belonged."[47] Evidently, the initial move toward the more uniform application of English criminal law to indigenous peoples was informed by both a humanitarian sensibility about the need for "compassionate protection" and greater observance of the legal rights of Aboriginals and the belief that new settlers in the colonies thought that they were being discriminated against by being made subject to English law while Aborigines were not. Significantly, in his early study titled *British Colonial Policy in the Age of Peel and Russell,* W.P. Morrell notes that "the developments of the thirties in colonial government and colonization were in large measure the work of a small body of men, Colonial Reformers, who were in touch with the spirit of the age; but the imperialism of the Colonial Reformers was not the only new imperialism." In addition, "another equally ardent body of men were chiefly interested in transforming the relations of the Empire with its backward races."[48] According to Morrell, the Select Committee on Aborigines in British Settlements (1835-37) was one of the forums through which both disparate colonial reformers and missionaries "sought to consolidate their influence upon colonial policy."[49]

The Aborigines Protection Society, which embodied more the evangelical views of Protestant missionaries than the systematic colonization ideas of colonial reformers, continued to campaign for the rights of Aborigines after 1837. Among numerous other investigations and reports that it sponsored, in 1840 the society had Standish Motte, a well-known London barrister and member, write an *Outline of a System of Legislation for Securing Protection to the Aboriginal Inhabitants of All Countries Colonized by Great Britain.*[50] In this wide-ranging report, Motte argued the need for "an efficient system of legislation" to better protect Aboriginals from "the reckless and lawless conduct which has hitherto characterized colonization." He alluded to the inhumanity of previous coercive measures:

> [To] teach them to obey our laws, we must convince them of their reasonableness; to induce them to conform to our customs, we must gradually remove their prejudices, and by persuasion rather than by force, bring about such a change, as to make them appreciate the benefits of our religion, the wisdom of our laws and institutions, the utility of our sciences, and the advantage of our manners and customs. Lastly, if we would prevent cruelty – if we would abolish sanguinary vengeance, and feuds between the colonists and the aborigines, or among themselves, of whatever race they may consist, whether of Africa or America, of New Holland or the islands of the Pacific, – peace should be our motto, – the olive branch our weapon, – the wheatsheaf our offering, – and the Bible the code from which to frame our laws.[51]

With regard to the administration of justice, Motte recommended "that in all cases, civil as well as criminal, the evidence of the aborigines shall be admitted in British courts of justice." He argued "that such evidence shall not be invalidated by reason of their customs preventing them from taking an oath, but that the evidence taken in the manner sanctioned by their own customs shall be admissible." To further ensure their fair treatment in court, he argued "that the aborigines shall not only be entitled to trial by jury in all civil and criminal cases, but shall be also entitled to demand a mixed jury of half colonists and half native aborigines."[52] While Motte's recommendation on Native jurors would never be endorsed by a racist such as Thom, his report was consistent for the most part with Thom's legal thinking on the way in which the criminal law should apply to Aboriginals. Motte's views were also consistent with those that would soon come to be expressed by the Colonial Office.

James Stephen, permanent undersecretary of the Colonial Office from 1836 to 1847, had a powerful influence in shaping British colonial policy toward Aboriginals during this period.[53] Stephen was followed by Herman Merivale as assistant undersecretary in 1847 and permanent undersecretary in 1848.[54] Both Stephen and Merivale were critics of Gibbon Wakefield's ideas on systematic colonization that were beginning to be applied in Australia and New Zealand.[55] While coming from different backgrounds, both officials identified themselves closely with the interests of indigenous peoples.

According to Morrell, Stephen was a deeply religious, sensitive, and introspective man with "immense powers of work and untiring devotion to duty." Moreover, Morrell notes that Stephen was "brought up in Wilberforce's 'Clapham Sect,' the son of a barrister of St. Kitts [in the West Indies] who had been stirred to the very depths by the evils of slavery, he sympathized profoundly with the humanitarians: and he had in fact by his influence in the Colonial Office been one of the principal agents of abolition."[56] Stephen was also deeply concerned about the treatment of Aborigines in the British settlements, and he thought that the British government should accept the responsibility of protecting them from settlers and that the Colonial Office should administer the colonies with this responsibility in mind.[57] According to T.J. Barron, "Stephen's attitude to race, like his administrative paternalism, was rooted in a deep concern not for cultural diversity but for the universality in the nature of man. This, in turn, derived from his religious beliefs. He was convinced that men have a common father in God. He therefore accepted that they have common attributes: intellect, understanding, conscience, the social and moral instincts."[58] This Christian humanitarianism permeated many of the reports that Stephen wrote on colonial laws and greatly influenced the approach that he took in dealing with the colonial problems that affected Aborigines.[59]

Stephen was a believer in the need for criminal law reform both at home and in the colonies, and his "Christian conscience," which caused him to revolt "against the barbarities inflicted upon dark-skinned people, gave edge to his insistence upon equality before the law."[60] He condemned the treatment meted out to Australian Aborigines, and his ideas concerning the rights of Natives were embodied in the Treaty of Waitangi (1840), by which the Maoris ceded New Zealand to Britain.[61] Although the treaty introduced a "gradualist policy of assimilation," which granted the Maoris the right to continue dealing with crime in their communities according to traditional custom, even here a great deal of pressure was placed on local authorities by settlers who began demanding that Maori criminal offenders be dealt with in English common law courts.[62] Stephen was also the person who, along with the new colonial secretary, Lord Stanley, prepared the *Colonial Evidence Act* of 1843. Pointing to Stephen's role in this legislation, Jane Samson notes:

> This act is one of the most important and certainly one of the most neglected pieces of legislation on colonial aboriginal issues. Its preamble noted the injustices caused by the inadmissibility of Aboriginal evidence in British colonies of settlement, and called for the usual role of legal compatibility to be overturned to permit unsworn testimony in the colonies. All the Legislative Councils had to do was to pass their own enabling legislation. It is worth noting that Stanley's bill passed completely unopposed in Parliament and caused no visible backlash – indeed, no comment – in the major newspapers or periodicals of the day.[63]

It seems clear that Stephen derived many of his ideas on Native policy from Thomas Fowell Buxton and the Aborigines Protection Society. In the aftermath of the antislavery campaign in 1834, it was Buxton who began to argue that government intervention on behalf of Aborigines in all British colonies was also urgently called for. Buxton also specifically called for the protection of Aborigines through changes in the law, arguing that "it appears to me that we ought to fix and enforce certain regulations and laws, with regard to the natives of all countries where we make settlements." Buxton contended that "those laws must be based on the principles of justice. In order to do justice we must admit 1st. That the natives have a right to their own lands. 2ndly. That as our settlements must be attended with some evils to them, it is our duty to give them compensation for those evils, by imparting the truths of Christianity and the arts of civilised life."[64] In her recent detailed study of Protestant missionaries in the Cape of Good Hope, Elizabeth Elbourne points out that during the period of the height of House of Commons interest in "Aborigines" in British settlements in the mid-1830s – highlighted in the work of Buxton's House of Commons "Aborigines Committee" from 1834 to 1837 – the Colonial Office was "very much under the control of the permanent under-secretary, the evangelical and abolitionist James Stephen."[65] Elbourne also documents the fact that Stephen gave careful attention to reading the minutes of evidence included in the select committee report of 1837 and that it had a profound effect on his views concerning the need to provide better protection for the rights of Aborigines throughout the British Empire.[66]

Herman Merivale came to the Colonial Office from Oxford University, where he had the chair of Drummond professor of political economy. Like Stephen, Merivale was a close observer of the impact of colonization on indigenous peoples. Merivale is most famous, or at least most widely cited, for the series of *Lectures on Colonization and Colonies* that he delivered at Oxford between 1839 and 1841.[67] In his lectures, Merivale pointed out that there were in essence four alternative strategies that could be adopted to deal with Natives in the British colonies. These were, namely, extermination (as was happening in Australia), slavery (as was happening in Africa and elsewhere), insulation (or coercive segregation from white settlers through creating Native reservations), and amalgamation (or the rapid assimilation of Natives into white society). In his lectures, published in 1841, Merivale concluded that amalgamation was the best alternative for dealing with the "Native question" in the British colonies. Specifically, Merivale explained:

> By amalgamation, I mean the union of natives with settlers in the same community, as master and servant, as fellow-labourers, as fellow [equal] citizens, and if possible, as connected by intermarriage. And I mean by it, not that eventual and distant process to which some appear to look, by which a native community, when educated and civilized, is to be, at some

> future period, admitted *en masse* to the full rights of citizenship; but I mean an immediate and an individual process – immediate, if not in act, at least in contemplation. To answer the view which I am anxious to lay before you, each native must be regarded as potentially a citizen, to become such in all respects as soon as possible. To this end, every step in his instruction and management must conduce. It must be the object in framing every law, in making every provision for his support.[68]

In reading this paragraph, one cannot help but think that Merivale was also alluding to the need for Natives to be treated in the same way as their fellow non-Native citizens in colonial legal systems. In fact, he was well aware of, and lectured in detail about, the need for steps to be taken to ensure that Natives who were accused of crimes were not dealt with violently by settlers or unfairly in colonial criminal courts. Drawing on Saxe Bannister's recently published book, *British Colonization and Coloured Tribes* (1838), Merivale noted that "the history of the European settlements in America, Africa, and Australia, presents everywhere the same general features – a wide and sweeping destruction of native races by the uncontrolled violence of individuals, if not of colonial authorities, followed by tardy attempts on the part of governments to repair the acknowledged crime."[69] In turn, he addressed several questions relating to how Natives should be dealt with instead, including "how far, and in what mode, are natives, resident or found within the limits of an English colony, to be brought within the pale of English law?" and "how far ought the natives to be brought at once within the jurisdiction of English criminal law, in respect of their conduct towards one another?"[70]

Merivale took the view that English law and forms of legal procedure should be introduced gradually, since it denied "the moral feeling on which all criminal codes must rest" to apply laws to "persons as incapable of incurring voluntary guilt against them as the lunatic or idiot, who are in all societies exempted from their infliction."[71] He recommended a gradual shift by first introducing a modified system of summary justice that would protect Natives from settler violence while making them subject to English law. The system would require a new office of "Protectors, or Commissioners of the Indians," answerable to the British government (and not colonial legislatures), who would, among other duties, be responsible for "the detection and prosecution of offences" committed by Natives.[72] More specifically, Merivale proposed that:

> So long as the natives remain in their uninstructed state, the first purpose for which they are to be brought within the pale of criminal justice is that of deterring them from attacks on the persons and property of colonists.

> Until this is done, other considerations are premature. And perhaps this result would be better attained by placing them, in the first instance, under a species of martial or summary law, to be administered by the chief police functionaries; with opportunity for defence, or for application in mitigation of punishment, in serious cases, by the protector and his agents. Such a scheme, besides avoiding the extreme inconvenience and striking absurdity of formal process in such affairs, would have the additional advantage of removing the white settlers themselves from any share in judicial proceedings against the natives, with whom they have already too many causes of collision; with which a jury system is inevitable. And it would have this further advantage, – that it would leave opportunity for the admission of the native to full civil rights at a future period, when converted and instructed, and able to satisfy some sufficient test of his fitness for full participation in the rights and duties of civil society.[73]

While arguing the need for the gradual introduction of English law, Merivale did not rule out the need for sometimes taking retaliatory justice against Natives, even to the point of using capital punishment. Responding to the recommendation made by others that "in no case should death or corporal punishment be inflicted upon a native," Merivale noted:

> Although, in most of the regions in which we are brought into contact with savage races, it does appear that the settlers are very rarely exposed to acts of violence from the savages, unless they have themselves given the first provocation, yet it must be remembered that all savages are habitually pilferers; that the difficulty of securing movable property and stock against their depredations is one of the greatest with which colonists in exposed situations have to contend ... But with respect to death, one thing appears plain; that if it must be inflicted at all, it should be confined, as far as possible, to cases in which it may follow immediately upon the act as a consequence; as when the murderer is taken in the manner – that it may strike terror as a retribution, not appear as an act of deliberate justice; a view of capital punishment which no uncivilized mind can possibly entertain.[74]

In discussing the question of how far Natives should "be brought at once within the jurisdiction of English criminal law, in respect of their conduct towards one another," Merivale cited at length Sir George Grey's observations on how he thought the law should work. Merivale noted that, although Grey's observations "were intended to have application to the case of the Australian aborigines," they applied "equally on other instances." He drew specifically on the report that Grey prepared for the Colonial Office covering his first year as governor of South Australia. In Grey's view, the former principle that Natives should be allowed to exercise their own customs among themselves could not be defended any longer, since any nation subject to such "barbarous customs" could never "emerge from the savage state." Moreover, he felt that this was a faulty principle for two related reasons: first, because "savage and traditional customs should not be confounded with a regular code of laws"; and, second, because when Great Britain ensured "to a conquered country the privilege of preserving its own [British] laws, all persons residing in this territory become amenable to those laws, and proper persons are selected by the government to watch over their due and equitable administration."[75] Since nothing of this kind existed with regard to the customs of Natives, the argument that they should be allowed to retain their own laws was inadmissible. In his 1840 report to the Colonial Office, Grey concluded:

> I would submit, therefore, that it is necessary, from the moment the aborigines of this country are declared British subjects, that they should, as far as possible, be taught that the British laws are to supersede their own; so that any native who is suffering under their own customs may have the power to an appeal to the laws of Great Britain; or, to put this in its true light, that all authorised persons should, in all instances, be required to protect a native from the violence of his fellows, even though they be in the execution of their own laws.[76]

Grey wrote these lines four months after Thom wrote his *Observations on the Law and Judicature of Rupertsland* at Red River. While it is doubtful that they had any direct communication with one another, the similarity of their views is remarkable. It is also notable how consistent Grey's views were with Merivale's. It is not surprising that Merivale cited and largely agreed with Grey's view on the need for British laws to supersede Aboriginal custom, since, at least in the early 1840s, both of them believed that "amalgamation" or rapid cultural assimilation was the best way to address the "Native question." During his first term as governor of New Zealand, from 1845 to 1853, and later as governor of Cape Colony in South Africa, Grey followed a strategy of racial amalgamation – or systematic assimilation. In a recent study of the legacy of his governorships of New Zealand and Cape Colony, James Gump notes that "from Grey's perspective the only solution was amalgamation – by exposing societies like the Maori and Xhosa as rapidly as practicable to western justice, education, health care, and agricultural technique, by absorbing them into white employment, and by teaching them Christian morality, these native peoples could compete as equals with European settlers and advance accordingly."[77] Gump concludes that well into the 1860s – even after Grey returned to New Zealand for another term as governor and faced a great deal of Maori resistance – the Colonial Office "remained committed to his amalgamation strategy in principle." As Gump points out, however, this strategy reflected "the contradictory impulses of mid-Victorian imperialism," or "the imperialism of cultural assimilation," in that, "for Grey as well as colonial officialdom in general, 'amalgamation,' despite what the term implied, never meant a genuine sharing of power or an authentic merging of cultures. Instead, amalgamation required indigenous societies such as the Maori and Xhosa to capitulate wholeheartedly to white domination."[78]

The Exclusionary Effect of Colonial Law in the Canadian West

It would be wrong to conclude that Merivale remained a consistent exponent of the policy of rapid assimilation. After joining the Colonial Office in 1847, he began to support policies that departed in significant ways from his former favoured policy of amalgamation. In his study of Merivale's influence on Colonial Office Indian policy in mid-nineteenth-century British North America, David McNab points to the pragmatic approach that he adopted in this context. McNab notes, for instance, that, while Merivale came to favour a "blend of insulation and amalgamation" as the basis for Colonial Office Indian policy in the Canadas,[79] he took a rather different, hands off, approach by allowing Governor James Douglas to develop his own Indian policy for Vancouver Island and the coast of British Columbia. However, according to McNab, the policy that Douglas pursued also consisted of a combined strategy of "insulation for those Indian people who lived close to areas of non-Indian population, and amalgamation for all other areas."[80] In the same way that he came to back the interests of James Douglas and the Hudson's Bay Company west of the Rockies, Merivale also backed the company at Red River. According to McNab, "Merivale believed paradoxically that despite the Company's monopoly, the Company's presence was generally in the economic interests of the native peoples. The future of the native people here would be developed by amalgamation, particularly miscegenation, because of the impact of the fur trade. The presence of the Métis was a sign that his process of amalgamation had already begun. Consequently Merivale always defended the *status quo ante bellum,* and the Hudson's Bay Company."[81] The "hands off" approach that Merivale and his colleagues took when dealing with the Hudson's Bay Company left its governors and judges, such as James Douglas and Adam Thom, with a great deal of discretion to decide how they were going to enforce laws against indigenous peoples. Douglas' long association with and respect for the culture of Aboriginal peoples west of the Rockies led him to adopt the practice of allowing Indians to settle disputes among themselves according to traditional custom.[82] This appears to have remained largely the case on Vancouver

Island until after 1864, when Douglas was replaced as governor.[83] In British Columbia, the famous "Hanging Judge" Matthew Baillie Begbie, unlike Douglas, had already begun to apply the law "equally" to Aboriginal peoples in the early 1860s.[84] By the mid-1860s, indigenous peoples west of the Rockies – on both the mainland and Vancouver Island – began to be brought more frequently before colonial criminal courts. This was, at least in part, facilitated by the passing of local Native evidence bills in the colonies of British Columbia, in 1865,[85] and Vancouver Island, in 1866.[86] As Hamar Foster points out in his study of "international homicide" in early British Columbia, by 1884 the provincial secretary, John Robson, told the Kit-au-max Gitksan people that "it is by the Queen's law that all people, Indians and whites, alike, are now governed ... and those who disobey that law must be punished, no matter what they may have been accustomed to before."[87] Despite the different circumstances and timing, the end result appears much the same. At both Red River and west of the Rockies, as well as in many other parts of the British Empire, indigenous people eventually came to be caught up in colonial criminal justice systems. These systems were intended simultaneously to include them as British subjects amenable to English law and to exclude them from settling their disputes in the ways that they did before the arrival of Europeans.

Notes

1 Provincial Archives of Manitoba (PAM), District of Assiniboia, General Quarterly Court Records, 4 August 1845.

2 Alexander Ross, *The Red River Settlement: Its Rise, Progress, and Present State with Some Account of the Native Races and Its General History to the Present Day* (1856; Edmonton: Hurtig, 1972), 331-32.

3 Kathryn Bindon, "Hudson's Bay Company Law: Adam Thom and the Institution of Order in Rupert's Land 1839-54," in *Essays in the History of Canadian Law,* vol. 1, ed. David H. Flaherty (Toronto: University of Toronto Press, 1981), 43-87; R.C. Macleod, "Law and Order on the Western-Canadian Frontier," in *Law for the Elephant, Law for the Beaver: Essays in the Legal History of the North American West,* ed. John McLaren, Hamar Foster, and Chet Orloff (Regina: Canadian Plains Research Center, 1992), 90-105; Roy St. George Stubbs, *Four Recorders of Rupert's Land: A Brief Survey of the Hudson's Bay Company Courts of Rupert's Land* (Winnipeg: Peguis Publishers, 1967); Dale Gibson and Lee Gibson, *Substantial Justice: Law and Lawyers in Manitoba 1670-1970* (Winnipeg: Peguis Publishers, 1972); Dale Gibson, "Company Justice: Origins of Legal Institutions in Pre-Confederation Manitoba," *Manitoba Law Journal* 23 (1996): 247-92.

4 Gibson and Gibson, *Substantial Justice.*

5 Macleod, "Law and Order," 94-95; Hamar Foster, "Sins against the Great Spirit: The Law, the Hudson's Bay Company, and the Mackenzie's River Murders, 1835-1839," *Criminal Justice History: An International Annual* 10 (1989): 23-76 at 27; Hamar Foster, "Conflict Resolution during the Fur Trade in the Canadian North West, 1803-1859," *Advocate* 51 (1993): 871-77 at 874; Hamar Foster, "British Columbia: Legal Institutions in the Far West, from Contact to 1871," *Manitoba Law Journal* 23 (1996): 293-340 at 302-7; John Phillip Reid, "Principles of Vengeance: Fur Trappers, Indians, and Retaliation for Homicide in the Transboundary North American West," in *Historical Perspectives on Law and Society in Canada,* ed. Tina Loo and Laura McLean (Toronto: Copp Clark, 1994), 14-32.

6 Ross, *Red River,* 332-33.

7 Russell Smandych and Karina Sacca, "The Development of Criminal Law Courts in Pre-1870 Manitoba," *Manitoba Law Journal* 24 (1996): 201-57.

8 E.H. Oliver, *The Canadian Northwest: Early Development and Legislative Records,* vol. 1 (Ottawa: Government Printing Bureau, 1914), 63, 87; Stubbs, *Four Recorders;* Bindon, "Hudson's Bay Company Law."

9 Stubbs, *Four Recorders,* 1.

10 For a recent, more detailed examination of Thom's work as a consolidator of the laws of Assiniboia, see Robert Baker, "Law Transplanted, Justice Invented: Sources of Law for the Hudson's Bay Company, 1670-1870" (master's thesis, University of Manitoba, 1996). These laws were consolidated and codified on three occasions after 1839: in 1841 and 1852, during the period of Adam Thom's term of office, and in 1862. See also Gibson and Gibson, *Substantial Justice,* 30; and council minutes, 1 June 1841, in Oliver, *Canadian Northwest,* 295-306.

11 Hudson's Bay Company Archives (HBCA), E 16/1, fols. 1-78; Council of Assiniboia, *Proposed Penal and Civil Code for Rupertsland* (July 1840).

12 HBCA, E 16/1, fols. 79-141; Adam Thom, *Observations on the Law and Judicature of Rupertsland* (May 1840).

13 Ibid. at fol. 82d.

14 Ibid. at fols. 86d, 87.

15 Adam Thom, *A Charge Delivered to the Grand Jury of Assiniboia, 20th February, 1845; by Adam Thom, Esq., Recorder of Rupert's Land* (London: Couchman, 1845), 22.

16 Gibson and Gibson, *Substantial Justice,* 30. Although the grand jury indicted the accused, he was subsequently acquitted at trial by reason of being under the age of fourteen and therefore immune from criminal liability.

17 Ibid. at 30.

18 Fair Play, "The Future of Our Indians," *Canadian Indian* 1 (1891): 160.

19 On British North America, New France, and Canada before 1900, see Brendan O'Brien, *Speedy Justice: The Tragic Last Voyage of His Majesty's Vessel* Speedy (Toronto: Osgoode Society, 1992); John Pratt, "Aboriginal Justice and the Good Citizen: An Essay on Population Management," in *Legal Pluralism and the Colonial Legacy: Indigenous Experiences of Justice in Canada, Australia, and New Zealand,* ed. Kayleen M. Hazlehurst (Aldershot, UK: Avebury Press, 1995), 39-71; Sidney L. Harring, "'The Liberal Treatment of Indians': Native People in Nineteenth Century Ontario Law," *Saskatchewan Law Review* 56 (1992): 297-371; Sidney L. Harring, "The Wendigo Killings: The Legal Penetration of Canadian Law into the Spirit World of the Ojibwa and Cree Indians," unpublished manuscript; John Dickinson, "Native Sovereignty and French Justice in Early Canada," in *Essays in the History of Canadian Law,* vol. 5, *Crime and Criminal Justice,* ed. J. Phillips, T. Loo, and S. Lewthwaite (Toronto: Osgoode Society, 1994), 17-40; Jan Grabowski, "Crime and Punishment: Sault-St-Louis, Lac-des-Deux-Montagnes, and French Justice, 1662-1735," *European Review of Native American Studies* 7 (1993): 15-21; Hamar Foster, "'The Queen's Law Is Better than Yours': International Homicide in Early British Columbia," in *Crime and Criminal Justice,* ed. Phillips, Loo, and Lewthwaite, 41-111; Foster, "British Columbia"; Tina Loo, "The Road from Bute Island: Crime and Colonial Identity in British Columbia," in *Crime and Criminal Justice,* ed. Phillips, Loo, and Lewthwaite, 112-42; Tina Loo, *Making Law, Order, and Authority in British Columbia, 1821-1871* (Toronto: University of Toronto Press, 1994); Tina Loo, "Savage Mercy: Native Culture and the Modification of Capital Punishment in Nineteenth-Century British Columbia," in *Qualities of Mercy: Justice, Punishment, and Discretion,* ed. Carolyn Strange (Toronto: University of Toronto Press, 1996); R.C. Macleod and H. Rollason, "What Happened to Native Justice? Native People in the Criminal Courts of the North West Territories, 1878-1885," paper presented at the Annual Meeting of the Canadian Law and Society Association, Brock University, 1996.

On colonial American and US developments to 1900, see Yasuhide Kawashima, *Puritan Justice and the Indian: White Man's Law in Massachusetts, 1630-1763* (Middletown, CT: Wesleyan University Press, 1986); Lyle Koehler, "Red-White Power Relations and Justice in the Courts of Seventeenth-Century New England," *American Indian Culture and Research Journal* 3 (1979): 1-31; Sidney L. Harring, *Crow Dog's Case: American Indian Sovereignty, Tribal Law, and United States Law in the Nineteenth Century* (Cambridge, UK: Cambridge University Press, 1994).

20 See, for example, Philip T. Ahire, "Re-Writing the Distorted History of Policing in Colonial Nigeria," *International Journal of the Sociology of Law* 18 (1990): 45-60; Sidney L. Harring, "'Please Send Six Copies of the Penal Code': British Colonial Law in Selangor, 1874-1880," *International Journal of the Sociology of Law* 19 (1991): 193-208; David Neal, *The Rule of Law in a Penal Colony: Law and Power in Early New South Wales* (Cambridge, UK: Cambridge University Press, 1991); John Pratt, "Citizenship, Colonisation, and Criminal Justice," *International Journal of the Sociology of Law* 19 (1991): 293-319; John Pratt, *Punishment in a Perfect Society: The New Zealand Penal System, 1840-1939* (Wellington, NZ: Victoria University Press, 1992); John Pratt, "Penal History in Colonial Societies: New Issues in the Sociology of Punishment," unpublished paper; James Gump, "The Imperialism of Cultural Assimilation: Sir George Grey's Encounter with the Maori and the Xhosa, 1845-1868," paper presented at the joint Neal and Commonwealth Fund Conference, London, England, February 1997.

21 O'Brien, *Speedy Justice,* 39-41.

22 Maitland to Bathurst, 14 February 1823, and 4 November 1825, in *Documents Relating to the Constitutional History of Canada, 1819-1828,* ed. Arthur Doughty and N. Story (Ottawa: King's Printer, 1935), 175, 177.

23 Cited in O'Brien, *Speedy Justice,* 41.

24 "Warrant vesting the Governor or Lieutenant Governor of Upper Canada with the discretionary Power in the case of Shawanakiskie Convicted of Murder," in *Documents,* ed. Doughty and Story, 177-78. Since there was no penitentiary in Upper Canada before 1835, it doesn't seem likely that this last option was pursued. I have found no evidence to confirm whether Shawanakiskie was executed or transported to one of the Australian penal colonies. O'Brien, *Speedy Justice,* 41, mentions only that "there is no evidence that Shawanakiskie received a pardon."

25 Pratt, "Aboriginal Justice," 46.

26 *Report of Chief Justice Macauley* (1839), cited in ibid. at 47. For a more detailed discussion of the legal status of Indians in nineteenth-century Ontario, see Harring, "'The Liberal Treatment of Indians,'" 297-371. His study also points to evidence of the growing view that Aboriginals should be included in the justice system in Upper Canada. In particular, he cites an 1839 report of the Aborigines Protection Society as evidence that supporters of the London-based society believed that "the full extension of law to Indians was necessary to assimilate them into the mainstream of Canadian life" (305).

27 Support for this argument can be found in Susanne Davies, "Aborigines, Murder, and the Criminal Law in Early Port Philip, 1841-1851," *Australian Historical Studies* 22 (1987): 313-35; Barry Bridges, "The Extension of English Law to Aborigines for Offences Inter Se, 1829-1842," *Journal of the Royal Australian Society* 59 (1973): 264-69; Jane Samson, "British Voices and Indigenous Rights: Debating Aboriginal Legal Status in Nineteenth-Century Australia and Canada," *Cultures of the Commonwealth* 2 (1996-97): 5-16.

28 Samson, "British Voices," 8.

29 Ibid. at 9.

30 "Judge-Advocate Atkins' Opinion on the Treatment of Natives," 8 July 1805, in *Historical Records of Australia, Series 1, Governors' Despatches to and from England, volume 5, July, 1804-August, 1806* (Sydney: William Applegate Gullick, Government Printer, 1922), 502-4.

31 Governor King to Earl Camden, 20 July 1805, in *Historical Records of Australia,* 496-97.

32 Bannister to Horton, 16 August 1824, in *Historical Records of Australia, Series 4, Legal Papers, Section A, volume 1, 1786-1827* (Sydney: William Applegate Gullick, Government Printer, 1922), 554-55.

33 *An Act to Authorise the Legislatures of Certain of Her Majesty's Colonies to Pass Laws for the Admission, in Certain Cases, of Unsworn Testimony in Civil and Criminal Proceedings, 1843,* 6 & 7 Vic., c. 22, cited in Samson, "British Voices," 6.

34 A.G.L. Shaw, "British Policy towards the Australian Aborigines, 1830-1850," *Australian Historical Studies* 25 (1992): 278-79. For a more recent detailed analysis of this Australian legislation, see Russell Smandych, "Contemplating the Testimony of 'Others': James Stephen, the Colonial Office, and the Fate of Australian Aboriginal Evidence Acts, circa 1839-1849," *Australian Journal of Legal History* 8 (2004): 237-83.

35 Minutes of the Council of Assiniboia, 16 June 1837, cited in Gibson, "Company Justice," 272.

36 Davies, "Aborigines," 314-18, highlights a case tried in 1841 in Port Philip involving five Aborigines tried for the murder of a white man. Although Aborigines were not allowed to testify either as witnesses or on their own behalf, a full jury trial was conducted. While the three female defendants were found not guilty, the two male Aborigines were convicted, sentenced to hang, and executed. In the five years following the first execution of Aborigines at Port Philip, three more Aborigines were hanged there for killing white men (ibid. at 320). Although Australian legal historians such as Susanne Davies have recently begun to look more closely at the specific circumstances associated with the application of English criminal law to Aborigines, the topic still requires further study. Support for this view can be found in Stephen Garton's recent historiographical essay on Australian criminal justice history, "The Convict Taint: Australia and New Zealand," in *Crime History and Histories of Crime: Studies in the Historiography of Crime and Criminal Justice in Modern History,* ed. Clive Emsley and Louis A. Knafla (Westport, CT: Greenwood Press, 1996), 271-90.

37 Samson, "British Voices," 9.

38 Alpheus Henry Snow, *The Question of Aborigines in the Law and Practice of Nations, Including a Collection of Authorities and Documents* (1918; reprint Northbrook, IL: Metro Books, 1972).

39 Ibid. at 9-10.

40 Ibid. at 10; Shaw, "British Policy," 269.

41 Snow, *The Question of Aborigines,* 10.

42 Great Britain, Parliament, House of Commons, *Report from the Select Committee on Aborigines (British Settlements); with Minutes of Evidence, Appendix, and Index* [26 June 1837] (Shannon: Irish University Press Series of British Parliamentary Papers, 1968).

43 Ibid. at 79-80.

44 Snow, *The Question of Aborigines,* 11.

45 *Report from the Select Committee on Aborigines,* 5.

46 Ibid. at 78.

47 Ibid. at 78, 79.

48 W.P. Morrell, *British Colonial Policy in the Age of Peel and Russell* (Oxford: Clarendon Press, 1930), 21-22.

49 Ibid. at 25-28.

50 Standish Motte, *Outline of a System of Legislation for Securing Protection to the Aboriginal Inhabitants of All Countries Colonized by Great Britain ...* (London: Aborigines Protection Society, 1840).

51 Ibid. at 10.

52 Ibid. at 19-20.

53 Paul Knaplund, *James Stephen and the British Colonial System 1813-1847* (Madison: University of Wisconsin Press, 1953); Paul Knaplund, "James Stephen on Granting Vancouver Island to the Hudson's Bay Company, 1846-1848," *British Columbia Historical Quarterly* 9 (1945): 259-71; T.J. Barron, "James Stephen, the 'Black Race,' and British Colonial Administration, 1813-47," *Journal of Imperial and Commonwealth History* 5 (1977): 131-50.

54 D. McNab, "Herman Merivale and Colonial Office Indian Policy in the Mid-Nineteenth Century," *Canadian Journal of Native Studies* 1 (1981): 207-302 at 280.

55 Morrell, *British Colonial Policy,* 11-13.

56 Ibid. at 40; Barron, "James Stephen," 131; Knaplund, *James Stephen,* 11. Stephen's stepmother was the sister of William Wilberforce. She married Stephen's father when Stephen was eleven years old, thus bringing him into the inner circle of the antislavery movement in England.

57 Morrell, *British Colonial Policy,* 45-46. However, as Barron points out in his study of Stephen's views of the "Black Race" of Africa, this is not to say that Stephen was entirely free of

holding racist views of some indigenous peoples. For a more detailed discussion of Stephen's Evangelical background and role in the antislavery movement, see Russell Smandych, "To Soften the Extreme Rigor of Their Bondage: James Stephen's Attempt to Reform the Criminal Slave Laws of the West Indies, 1813-1833," *Law and History Review* 23, 3 (2005): in press.

58 Barron, "James Stephen," 145-46.

59 Knaplund, *James Stephen,* 15.

60 Ibid. at 20-21.

61 Ibid. at 21-22.

62 See Pratt, "Citizenship"; and Pratt, *Punishment in a Perfect Society.*

63 Samson, "British Voices," 10.

64 Charles Buxton, ed., *Memoirs of Sir Thomas Fowell Buxton,* 2nd ed. (London: John Murray, 1849), 369 ff. Cited in Klaus E. Knorr, *British Colonial Theories, 1570-1850* (Toronto: University of Toronto Press, 1944), 386.

65 Elizabeth Elbourne, *Blood Ground: Colonialism, Missions, and the Contest for Christianity in the Cape Colony and Britain, 1799-1853* (Montreal and Kingston: McGill-Queen's University Press, 2002), 285.

66 T. Buxton to A. Gurney, 24 November 1837, Thomas Fowell Buxton Papers, vol. 2, 81-85, cited in ibid. at 285-86.

67 Herman Merivale, *Lectures on Colonization and Colonies* [delivered at Oxford University in 1839, 1840, and 1841 and reprinted in 1861] (London: Humphrey Milford, 1928).

68 Ibid. at 511.

69 Ibid. at 490.

70 Ibid. at 496, 499.

71 Ibid. at 497.

72 Ibid. at 494-95.

73 Ibid. at 498-99.

74 Ibid. at 499.

75 Ibid. at 500-1.

76 "South Australian Record of November 7, 1840," also printed in *Parliamentary Papers concerning New Zealand* (1841), cited in Merivale, *Lectures,* 501.

77 Gump, "Imperialism," 5.

78 Ibid. at 14.

79 McNab, "Herman Merivale," 285.

80 Ibid. at 278.

81 Ibid. at 288.

82 Robin Fisher, *Contact and Conflict: Indian-European Relations in British Columbia, 1774-1890,* 2nd ed. (Vancouver: UBC Press, 1992), 56-57.

83 Douglas was replaced by Arthur Kennedy, who had previously served as a colonial administrator in Sierra Leone and Western Australia.

84 Loo, "Savage Mercy," 106, notes that from 1860 to 1869 Begbie sentenced fifty people to hang. Twenty-seven of them were hanged, and twenty-five of those (93 percent) were Aboriginal.

85 Legislative Council of British Columbia, Minutes, 26 January 1865, in *Journals of the Colonial Legislatures of the Colonies of Vancouver Island and British Columbia 1851-1871,* vol. 4, ed. J. Hendrickson (Victoria: Provincial Archives of British Columbia, 1980), 272-73.

86 Legislative Council of British Columbia, Minutes, 28 November 1866, in *Journals of the Colonial Legislatures of the Colonies of Vancouver Island and British Columbia 1851-1871,* vol. 1, ed. J. Hendrickson (Victoria: Provincial Archives of British Columbia, 1980), 325, 340.

87 Foster, "The Queen's Law," 44.

5

Discipline and Discretion in the Mid-Eighteenth-Century Hudson's Bay Company Private Justice System

Paul C. Nigol

The legal authority of the Hudson's Bay Company (HBC) was created in Rupert's Land in 1670 with the granting of a royal charter under the great seal of England to the "Governor and Company of Adventurers of England Trading to Hudson's Bay." During this age of mercantile expansion, chartered companies such as the HBC were formed to supply European manufacturers with raw materials for a burgeoning trade in luxury items. Its trading empire was first proposed when Pierre-Esprit Radisson and Médard Chouart Des Groseilliers, formerly engaged by the French in the overland fur trade centred in New France, approached the English in the mid-1660s and persuaded some of the gentlemen of the court of Charles II to finance an expedition to the heart of the fur trade country by sea into Hudson Bay. After gaining the support of Prince Rupert, a Royalist trooper in the English Civil War and the cousin of Charles II, Des Groseilliers returned from the bay in 1669 with a number of furs. The charter of 2 May 1670 granted, under the king's seal, eighteen adventurers, including Prince Rupert, the right to the "sole trade and commerce of all those seas, straits, bays, rivers, lakes, creeks, and sounds, in whatsoever latitude they shall be, that lie within the entrance of the straits commonly called Hudson's Straits, together with all the lands and territories upon the countries, coasts and confines of the seas, bays, lakes, rivers, creeks and sounds aforesaid, that are not already actually possessed by or granted to any of our subjects, or possessed by the subjects of any other Christian Prince or State."[1]

In legal terms, the charter gave the HBC proprietary rights derived from the Crown according to the accepted forms of English law. The company had the right to build fortifications and military establishments and to make peace and war with any non-Christian prince or people. As well, the ultimate sovereignty of the Crown was recognized in the charter where the "land was to be held of the King as of our Manor of East Greenwich, on our County of Kent, in free and common Socage."[2] Finally, the charter gave the governor and committee the right to assemble and make laws and ordinances for the good government of the company and its colonies and forts, and for the advancement of trade, as well as the right to impose penalties and punishments, provided that they were reasonable and not repugnant to the laws of England. The HBC was also given the right to try civil and criminal cases in Rupert's Land and to appoint officers and governors.[3]

Protection of the HBC's monopoly in the fur trade was of utmost importance, and the company developed an intricate set of sanctions to prevent private trading. Aside from the trading aspects of the charter, priority was placed on the colonization potential of the territory since, as E.E. Rich noted, the English fully supported the dictum that "prescription without possession availeth nothing."[4] However, the HBC did little for settlement since colonization was anathema to a staple trade based on the extraction of animal skins that was reliant on Native trappers and middlemen.[5] In 1690, additional legislation was passed by Parliament in the form of an *Act for Confirming to the Governor and Company Trading to Hudson's Bay Their Privileges and Trade*. According to the Act, it was "necessary that such a Company should have sufficient and undoubted powers and liberties to manage, order and carry on the said trade and to make Bye-Laws, orders, rules and constitutions for the due management and regulation as well of the said Company and for the punishment of offenders and recovering forfeitures and penalties which cannot be so effectively done as by authority of Parliament."[6] The act was to remain in effect for seven years, although the company continued to claim its force for almost another 180 years.

It has been suggested by Rich that the antecedents of the legislation were based on the company's need to derive its privileges from something more reliable than the royal prerogative. Since the charter was derived from the prerogative, it was open to attack as the prerogative itself came under fire in succeeding years.[7] The legality of the charter did adhere to the general forms of incorporation similar to those of boroughs and livery companies. But the fact that the HBC's claim was based on the prerogative did not nullify it. Instead, it exhibited continuity of what had been a long-standing practice of assigning authority and defraying costs for the better governance of certain areas of Britain (in this instance, the royal manor of East Greenwich) that were under royal control.[8]

Despite the fact that the charter gave the company an adequate claim to its political and economic powers, the additional legislation of 1690 confirmed the company's legal basis when its governors secured commissions by royal warrant with powers to maintain English sovereignty on the bay. During this period, HBC management had also undergone a number of changes, the most notable of which was that by 1680 the gentry stockholders had relinquished control to a group of London merchants and financiers who placed greater emphasis on making the trade profitable.[9] Although it can be argued that the 1690 act of Parliament was not entirely necessary to support the company's claim and contained some unwanted restrictions, it was nevertheless sought by its management to bolster its charter rights. The defects of the grant were the facts that it lasted only seven years, required the HBC's fur sales to be controlled by felters and furriers in London, and tied its claims to the success of William of Orange.[10]

During this period, and until the Treaty of Utrecht in 1713, French traders under the command of Pierre d'Iberville were making incursions into the James and Hudson Bay areas. By the 1730s, the company had re-established a firm hold on James and Hudson Bays, re-occupied Albany, Eastmain, York, and Churchill Forts, and established Moose Fort. Nevertheless, the French continued to challenge the company's ability to obtain the best furs of the country by trading along the Great Lakes and the river system routes from the west. Although the HBC had the advantage of a much shorter trade route and controlled the bulk of the gun trade in its enterprise, the French, by moving inland, were obtaining better-quality furs for an assortment of light trade items that could be carried more easily.[11]

The structure of the company's management was based on the model of other chartered companies created in the seventeenth century. In London, a governor, deputy governor, and committee of seven (elected from the shareholders) made all of the central business decisions. In turn, they hired resident managers who were known as officers, chiefs, factors, and bay-side governors to manage the company's business at the various posts, factories, and forts. The upper echelon of bay-side employees was comprised of the governors and chiefs and professional men such as surgeons, doctors, and clerks fitting intermediately between the labourers and officers. The remainder of the employees were known as servants,[12] further divided into two categories of skilled labourers and their apprentices and unskilled labourers. Because the posts themselves were visited only once a year by the company's ships, communication between the bay and London took place annually only, and resident managers were left primarily to their own devices to maintain order and discipline as well as foster the fur trade.

Although HBC employees exercised a customary right to trade on their own accounts, following medieval custom as well as the precedent set by other chartered companies, this was forbidden by the charter and orders and instructions sent to the bay.[13] Nevertheless, the company allowed a degree of private trade to ships' captains and bay-side officers. According to Rich, the evidence contained in the minutes of the HBC "makes it clear that both the captains and the crews and the Frenchmen took part in the private trade on their accounts."[14] In 1672, the company's London headquarters ordered that no employees were to trade in beaver, and in 1679 the privilege was completely curtailed. Private trade of any sort by company employees was considered to be one of the greatest breaches of its law in the context of a competitive fur trade.[15] However, the orders and instructions from the company's management had little effect on recalcitrant bay-side governors who regularly ignored unpopular decisions made thousands of miles away. The governors exercised a large amount of individual discretion, often ignoring the company's directives against allowing Natives into the forts, while at the same time striving to establish a strict sense of discipline among its servants.

From an early date, the HBC had become embroiled in an extended rivalry with the French fur trading interests of New France. Already in the 1680s, the French and the Compagnie du Nord were making incursions in the bay. By 1686, an expedition organized by the Marquis de Denonville, governor of New France, captured all English posts at the bottom of the bay, with the exception of the newly established one at Nelson River.[16] With the signing of the Treaty of Ryswick in 1697, the French and English agreed to set up separate spheres of influence on Hudson Bay, the French officially retaining the posts at the bottom of the bay and the HBC holding on to York Factory. However, the opposite resulted as hostilities continued over the next sixteen years until the signing of the Treaty of Utrecht in 1713, which brought an end to French-English rivalry on the bay.[17]

With its title to the area on a relatively more secure footing, the HBC began shifting to a more civilian-based legal system.[18] However, the war with France and the French occupation of the bay remained relatively fresh in its memory. When renewed hostilities began to break out in Europe, the company governors sought to foster discipline in the forts along military lines in case of another attack.[19] By 1744, the English were once again fighting the French and the Spanish in Europe. In a letter to Governor Thomas White and the council at York Fort, the governor and committee wrote:

> 4th The English and French having declared war against each other and the war with Spain still continuing, we do hereby strictly direct you to be always on your Guard and to keep a good watch and that you keep all your men as near home as possible ... 7th We do also direct that you fix your cannon in the most proper place to defend your selves and Annoy an Enemy ... [You] are also to keep small arms loaded and in good order & at hand to be Easily come at and ... you are to exercise your men once a week till they are disciplined and afterwards once a month.[20]

Even the partial shift to a more civilian form of internal discipline lasted for only thirty years and ended with the renewal of continental hostilities.

Legal Pluralism and Company Law

The legal pluralism paradigm best suits the study of the HBC's private justice system for a number of reasons. First, because it was a private system, it fell outside the scope of England's central common law courts. As well, the officials of the Hudson's Bay Company were not trained for the most part in the law, and the system functioned without state-appointed justices. According to Harry Arthurs' definition, legal pluralism consists "primarily of rules by which persons in society order their conduct, and only secondarily of norms of decision developed by the courts and of legislation enacted by the state."[21] Law in this paradigm consists of both statute and unwritten law as well as codes defining normative standards of behaviour. It is the latter codes and the customs that developed in the early decades of the HBC that form the major body of this chapter.

The Hudson's Bay Company governed Rupert's Land under the authority of a royal charter:

> The Governor and Council of the several and respective places where the said Company shall have plantations, forts, factories, colonies or places of trade ... in case any crime or misdemeanour shall be committed in any of the said Company's plantations, forts, factories or places of trade within the limits aforesaid, where judicature cannot be executed for want of a Governor and Council there ... [it] may be lawful for the chief Factor of that place and his Council to transmit the party, together with the offence, to such other plantation, factory or fort where there shall be a Governor and Council, where justice may be executed, or into this kingdom of England, as shall be thought most convenient, there to receive such punishment as the nature of his offence shall deserve.[22]

In reality, however, the bay-side governors had a great deal of latitude in how they managed the everyday functioning of the posts. Governors brought with them backgrounds that were as diverse as their governing styles. While the authority outlined in the charter was permissive on sending accused persons either to a quasi-judicial council presided over by the governor and made up of all the important officers and workers of the post, or to England at the annual sailing presumably to face trial there, it seems that most disciplinary issues were dealt with summarily. In fact, according to Joseph Robson, employed by the HBC as a stone mason and a surveyor during the 1730s and 1740s, "if a servant is guilty of theft, or any act that would be deemed gross felony by the laws of England, and subject him to capital punishment, the governor only whips him, and afterwards sends him home to be prosecuted by the company: but from a mistaken lenity, or for some secret reasons, they proceed no farther than a quiet dismission from their service."[23] Robson's comments, part of a larger attack on the company's charter launched in the 1750s under the guiding hand of Arthur Dobbs, reveal that the company's methods of discipline within the forts closely resembled the disciplinary system at work in the navy. In his diatribe against the company's disciplinary system, Robson described HBC officers as men who "have generally sea-officers principles and exert the same arbitrary command, and except the same slavish obedience here, as is done on board a ship."[24] Because company posts were essentially closed systems, with only occasional communication with the outside world, the social environment of a post was broadly similar to the shipboard environment.

In the case of the HBC, the legal pluralism approach to the study of its private justice system is particularly useful because of the wide discretionary powers of the bay-side governors. The fact that they communicated with the company's headquarters only once a year meant that the private justice system in the first century of the company developed independently from management directives originating in London. This enabled the governors to slide into a form of benevolent despotism that was a hybrid of the type of society that existed in the navy and the master-servant domestic relationship that existed in Britain.[25] As well, internally the criminal and civil jurisdiction of the charter applied to the relationship between all company employees as well as between employees and itself.

With respect to First Nations, the company was granted proprietary rights in Rupert's Land under British law, but in practice nation-to-nation interaction applied. This meant, essentially, that First Nations were not subject to British law. The company was primarily "hugging the bay" for the first century of its existence and was acutely dependent on the local or "Home Guard Indians" for provisions as well as furs. Thus, the officers of the company were directed not to have sexual liaisons with Native women or allow any Natives within the walls of the fort. According to Jennifer Brown, even though the company "demanded both celibacy and chastity from its Bay employees," the documents suggest that the "company was overly optimistic about the degree of regulation that could be imposed from London."[26] Instead, country marriages were not uncommon between the officers of the forts and Native women, marriages that created an entirely new form of customary law in Rupert's Land.

The employment and disciplinary system of the HBC was, with a few exceptions, not unlike the model used to govern employment relationships in England. With respect to unskilled labourers, the employment relationship was flexible where workers signed on for contracts of a year or more. The *Statute of Frauds* (1677) applied to all service contracts of less than a year where a note or memorandum in writing was required and needed to be signed by the servant.[27] The basis of this relationship was the household, which was not only the basic unit of production but also the nucleus of the social order.[28] This relationship, contractual in origin, was an association in which, according to Marc Linder, "the rights and duties involved ... were fixed to a large extent by law and not by the agreement of the parties."[29] Much of the relationship was customary, such as a set hiring day in addition to the duties and obligations of both parties. In England, 90 percent of hiring days were set at Michaelmas in the south, Martinmas in the north, and May Day.[30] Hiring fairs existed to bring servants and masters together.

British husbandry service contracts usually lasted one year and could be distinguished from HBC service based on their degree of mobility. Unskilled workers in England were socially mobile over time and space. While in service, servants were implicitly bound to obey the reasonable, as revealed by their masters, and masters were bound to pay servants even if there was no work to perform or the servant was unable to perform it. According to Ann Kussmaul, there was a degree of strain in this relationship, as revealed by the records of masters who wrote about their servants.[31] In England and in the HBC, reports of good character or ability were used to measure the performance of servants, while skill was rarely mentioned. Physical punishment was a traditional method of dealing with insubordinate servants. What distinguished practice within the company from that in Britain was that in Britain servants could easily leave an abusive master through stealth or settle a dispute at the local petty or quarter sessions. This was not a practical option for a servant of the HBC.

Service as an unskilled labourer was generally transitional, fitting between childhood and marriage. It was primarily a method to save money prior to marriage. Room and board were provided, and wages were paid annually with the possibility of periodic advances.[32] In contrast, skilled labourers functioned under the master-apprentice relationship that existed in seventeenth- and eighteenth-century Britain. Apprenticeship was a statutory relationship that lasted from three to seven years depending on the trade. By its completion, skilled workers were entitled to all the rights accrued from the various trades, including the setting of wages and prices. Nevertheless, there was no rigid dichotomy between skilled and unskilled labourers.[33] It was not unusual for all labourers to combine in protest against the officers and clerks who comprised the bay-side management of the company. True to form with British society across the Atlantic, servants of the company who stepped outside the traditional forms of behaviour faced social censure. Sexual crimes, as well as excessive drunkenness and insubordination, were often dealt with swiftly and severely.

In the context of the HBC, there was a degree of similarity between the household and life at a post. However, because the company factory represented a closed society and a total institution, complete with a surgeon and a command structure, the model of the navy holds more relevance because of the distant locale, the perceived importance of discipline, and the military emphasis on war with non-British nationals.[34] Thus, while both models were present in the company's employment relationships, for the most part its disciplinary regime resembled the navy of the 1740s and 1750s. According to N.A.M. Roger, "the Navy in the middle years of the eighteenth century retained a large degree of informality, even of intimacy ... All of them were united by the shared experience of a dangerous profession, in which teamwork was essential to survival. In their working lives, officers and men lived close together, sharing similar discomforts and lack of privacy. Moreover it was easy for them to transcend the wide social disparities which existed as much in the Navy as in society ashore, for they accepted these divisions without thought."[35]

Indeed, in the case of naval discipline as well as in factory life, it was often more humane to give a quick blow and forget the transgression than to invoke the apparatus of a formal flogging or court martial, as in the navy, or flogging and the summoning of a post council, as in a company fort. Authority in this context was not lax because the officers were unable to act more firmly. Instead, it was a conscious choice of people who believed that it was right and natural for both employers and employees to behave in that manner.[36] As well, in cases where brutality did occur, it tended to destroy discipline, which could be maintained successfully in that environment only when it rested in unstated consent and not force. Thus, power was not exercised systematically, and domination was based more on consent and deference than on authoritarianism.

In cases where class lines were transgressed among the company's officers and servants, social chaos was often the result. As Ferdinand Jacobs, the governor of Fort Prince of Wales from 1751 to 1762, noted in his journal entry on 13 February 1755,

> I mentioned on Sunday Last Mr. Squire's keeping Company & Setting with William Mathews when he had the Watch; Here is Now Gentlemen another Example, Mr. Wills the Surgeon was Drinking most if not all Last Night with Guilford Long who had then the Middle Watch, and with the afore said William Mathews, this Gentlemen is Some out of many Such Examples of Behaviour of these two Officers in Particular, it is also a Common thing with them to be Frequently Drinking with the Tradesmen and at the times of their Watch which Tradesman's behaviour Gives me great Room to think that there is a Combination to Disturb the peace of the Factory, Retard the work & make me Uneasy; for why Should those officers Choose to Drink with these Tradesmen on those Particular Nights that they have Watches, Unless it is that I Should always have Cause to Find Fault & be Continually Chiding them; these Gentlemen are your Second & Surgeon, Officers that are appointed to assist me in the Management of your Honours affairs in the Room of which they are of no Manner of Service to Me, and I find they do all they Can to Disturb the Peace of the Factory.[37]

By ignoring the class implications of their actions, Mr. Wills, the surgeon, and Mr. Squire, the second-in-command, had broken the power relationship between master and servant, as well as that between officers and men, by fraternizing with people below their station in life. Jacobs alluded to the fact that by doing this they were acting in an almost mutinous fashion. What becomes apparent from this discourse is that, when lower-ranking servants neglected their duty or resisted the orders of the governor, their insolence was most often accepted and summarily punished with little mention. However, when HBC officers socialized with the servants, it was tantamount to conspiracy, which once again has a strong similarity to the naval model of social ordering.

Discretion and Authority on the Bay: Internal Legal Relations

Discretion was an important aspect of the HBC's private justice system in the first century of its operation, and company officers played a major role in how internal discipline functioned in Rupert's Land. Through the charter, they were bound by the laws of England. They also had a great deal of discretionary power and in most cases practised little that resembled common law in the eighteenth century. For the most part, disciplinary problems were dealt with on a case-by-case basis, where the backgrounds and motivations of the company officers played a major role in how they exercised personal discretion. Such problems are revealed in the post journals that they were responsible for producing. The journals contained a record of every event that took place at the post, including weather and work, and were written for the eyes of the governor and committee in London. The majority of this research is drawn from these journals.

To contextualize the general themes, in the early period, from 1670 to the 1730s, war and the French takeover of many of the company's posts reinforced a disciplinary regime that emphasized firm control and quasi-military conduct premised on staving off an external threat. In the later period, from the 1730s to 1770, the company's disciplinary emphasis shifted to the internal threat of sloth and drunkenness, punctuated with the threat of mutiny. During that period, the officers of the HBC were not as concerned with a French attack as they were with their men rising up or simply not fulfilling their contractual agreements. Of particular interest in this later period are the careers of Joseph Isbister, James Isham, Ferdinand Jacobs, and Humphrey Marten, who governed Albany Fort, York Fort, Fort Prince of Wales, and Eastmain Fort from the 1730s to the 1770s. For the most part, these officers were chosen because they conveyed enthusiastic attitudes about discipline and their powers to correct. The reason for this, it would seem, was to show the company's London management that they were actually dealing with the issue of discipline.

The governing styles of these HBC governors were various and for the most part dissimilar. One generalization is that Isbister was the most vigorous disciplinarian of the group. Whether this was grounded in reality is another question, since recording the events of the post for the scrutiny of the company's management may have resulted simply in an expansion of the records. Because Isbister was undoubtedly the most vocal of these governors, he will serve as the point of reference with which to compare the whole group.

Isbister made a reputation for himself as a harsh disciplinarian who was handy with his fists. Compared to other governors, he tended to mete out the most summary punishment. He was verbose about his correction and generally beat anyone who stood in his way. An example took place at Eastmain Fort in 1738, when William Fosset and William Maclean refused to follow orders and Isbister reacted with violence. According to his account, "I Called for the Water but Nobody had obeyed My orders Nor Gone for Water; then I Down To Know the Meaning of it & Whose Turn, & found it to be William Fossets Turn & William Maclean cleans: I Gave Each of Them two or three Cuffs with My hand as for a Small fault Not according to their Deserving."[38] After these men began shoving Isbister and continued their "Sasey" language, he finally managed to convince them to do what he ordered. Cuffing, for Isbister, was an acceptable form of summary punishment. However, he stated that "there ought to be Gentle Correction allowed When Men Won't Do their Duty: as for My part I shall Not punish No Man Without a fault & if there be No Straightness of Command you honours interest Must be Neglected or Else a Master must Do the Work him Self."[39]

Another example of such discipline took place in the same year, when Isbister, through his own initiative and with the aid of some of the "Home Indians," apprehended a company servant who apparently had deserted the Eastmain post. According to Isbister's journal,

> No sooner Had I Got Down but Saw the Canoe a Coming I Laid wait in order to take him when he Landed But the Indians Had tied him hand & foot & Landed So I Went to Him Cast the Lashing of his feet & Made Him Walk to the Boat, he also began to Berate Me & told Me that all this Should Not hinder his Design, as yet also the Indians told Me that he had been Enquiring how far it was to the french & that He would Go to them No Sooner had we Come to the House but I put him in Irons & turned him on board the Sloop.[40]

Desertion, as well as labour discipline, were seen by Isbister as warranting summary punishment by his fists or in irons. He seemed to believe that constant correction was necessary to the proper functioning of a fort. Comparatively, the other governors shied away from the use of irons and beatings. Clearly, Isbister's naval background affected the frequency of his use of manual correction and irons. However, the question of whether this was anathema to the laws of England deserves some scrutiny. It seems that this was acceptable in the master-servant relationship. In contrast to labourers in Britain, a servant could not leave the post or take his employer to court until the next sailing out of the bay, which could take considerable time.

At Eastmain, Isbister managed to make a name for himself as a master capable of bringing order to disorderly posts. On one occasion in 1737, Ralph White, a company carpenter, returned to the post half drunk and threatened not to obey Isbister's orders. This was a common disciplinary problem in all of the posts. Isbister dealt with White by first threatening to make sure his wages would not be paid, but in the end he simply threatened to beat him and place him in irons. Again, according to Isbister, White

> began to Give Me abundance of Sauce Language & Saying that he Would Not be Under My Command No More ... Then He told Me he would Not Strike or Speak More about it Very Well I Said your Wages shall Suffer No Work No pay he Still Continued his ill Language & had the Assurance to Damn My blood & Very Sauce Language So I took him by the Neck & Turned him out of My Room then he Said he Would fight Me & Lick Me to, but I Threatened to beat him & putt him in Irons.[41]

While Isbister was allowed to correct company employees, it seems that he could not unilaterally deny a servant's wages. Thus, he resorted to the threat of irons.

The career of Isbister was advanced in 1740 when he was appointed by the council to command Albany Fort upon the death of Roland Waggoner.[42] Isbister's advancement was based largely upon his ability to check abuses and rule sternly. Upon becoming chief at Albany, Isbister continued his firm disciplinary regime to end private trading, drunkenness, and liaisons with Aboriginal women that had become a concern to the governor and committee in London.[43] Then in 1743 he established Henley House, 120 miles upriver from Albany, the first company post to be opened away from the shores of the bay. It was hoped that this fort would circumvent the French, who had established themselves in the region and had been intercepting the Natives on their way to Albany. Unfortunately, Henley was later attacked and destroyed by Natives in 1754. Isbister returned to England in 1744 but was re-engaged by the HBC for five years as chief factor of Albany. However, his health was poor, and the company paid him to convalesce in Bath prior to his return to the bay. He was again allowed to break his contract for health reasons in 1747 but was engaged by the company in 1748 at Fort Prince of Wales on the Churchill River. He remained there until 1752, when he returned to England again and was subsequently re-appointed to Albany, where he remained until 1756.[44]

Another governor who served in the middle of the eighteenth century was James Isham. Born in London in 1716, he was employed as a writer and bookkeeper for York Fort in 1732. Described as a "very Sober, honest and

Diligent, young man" by Thomas White, chief factor at York, Isham was appointed to the care of the fort in 1737 with the assistance of two other officers.[45] By 1741, he had proven his abilities to the governor and committee in London, who named him chief factor of Prince of Wales Fort on the Churchill River. He remained there for four years, where he suffered from ill health and petitioned the governor and committee to be allowed leave, which was granted in 1745. In the following year, he was appointed chief factor at York but was recalled to London in 1748 to help the company fend off an attack on its charter by Arthur Dobbs.[46]

During the winter of 1741, two ships under the subscription of Dobbs and his associates unsuccessfully attempted to find the North-West Passage and wintered, against Isham's wishes, in the vicinity of Fort Prince of Wales. The company's committee was already apprised of the plan when they sent Thomas White to assume command of York Factory so that Isham could assume command of Fort Prince of Wales. When the ships arrived, Isham tried to make the explorers as comfortable as possible, giving them James Knight's old fort, about six miles upstream from the new fort, where they drew the ships out of the water and settled in for the winter.[47] According to Rich, this expedition created a particularly difficult disciplinary problem on the bay: "Even the Company's own ships' captains and crews provoked comparisons as to terms of service and wages, standards of food and drink and conduct. They often provoked crises of discipline, challenged and defied the Governor and his authority, introduced excessive alcohol to the posts, and facilitated private trade. If the Company's own ships could produce such problems, how much more were Middleton and his independent command to be dreaded!"[48]

Captain Middleton's abuse of alcohol was at the root of most of the problems and his differences with Isham. According to Rich, "[it] prostrated his men, it provoked difficult comparisons with the Company's rules and practices, and it provided Middleton with a means of making good his losses at the Company's expense."[49] Over the course of the winter, the problems mounted as Isham endeavoured to keep the fort under control by resorting to the use of irons and lashes when his men got drunk and tried to desert. In the end, the fort lost five men to Middleton when they forfeited their wages from the company to sign on as sailors.[50]

The most common breach of discipline within the ranks of the company servants invariably was drunkenness, documented in great detail during the tenure of Isbister at Albany Fort. This offence was almost always met with being confined to the servants' cabin or being placed in irons until sober. As well, Isbister did not hesitate to administer a certain amount of physical punishment by way of a cuffing or beating. In the post journals, alcohol and the disciplinary problems attached to excessive drinking were a far more prevalent concern at Albany than they were at York Fort. The irony of this was that the company supplied the alcohol that created its most common disciplinary problem.

With characteristic detail, Isbister recorded an incident that took place in 1748 related to drunkenness, mutiny, and his rule. On 2 October, he was informed of a conspiracy against his life by the Fort Prince of Wales armourer, John Watson. He stated that

> John Watson having formed a design to Stab me had prepared a weapon for that purpose any first intelligence of this was brought me by our Surgean & Mr. Jacobs declaring ... that it was not Safe for me to let him go Unconfined for that he disturbed the Whole People on friday Night, Seemingly mad Saying that the Governor was there with guns & Pistols to Shoot him ... and more openly began to declare his designs, on Me which the people in this Factory Vouches for Truth and this without any & all cause for so doing. Mr. Morton our Surgeon informed that he had Seen this John Watson sharpen the point of a Tile and asked the Said John Watson what he intended that for but was Answered with these words to defend my Self (and swore he would have the hearts Blood of Somebody this Night, also Several of our Men told me they had heard him Say so & had seen the weapon with which he intended to so the deed ... I thought this Sufficient to Convince me of the danger I was in so Consulted with Mr. Jacobs & Mr. Morton & Concluded that the best way to prevent Matters of [?] Consequence would be to [?] into Irons.[51]

After placing Watson in irons, Isbister interrogated him, asking why he planned on murdering his governor, to which Watson replied that he was only defending himself. Searching him, Ferdinand Jacobs discovered that he was indeed preparing to assault his governor, whereupon Isbister wrote that

> At this Mr. Jacobs discovered Something in his bosom Concealed upon which [he] Seized hold of him & take it from him and found it to be a long half round Tile pointed being 7 inches long from the half. I must observe that his acting the mad man is only to Cloak his Evil design to take away my life for he Spoke reasonable till I began to say that I must put him into irons to prevent his doing any Mischief, so hand cuffed him and sent him to his Cabin, there in his Mad fits would Swore I was there at his Cabin with Pistols to Shoot him, this Morning I had his head Shaved, bled him and Laid a plaster on his back but he continued Very obstinate.[52]

In his account, Isbister noted that Watson was "most-intolerably addicted to liquor" and that he was constantly given to drunkenness and neglect of duty. On the day following his punishment, Isbister stated:

> John Watson our Armourer being brought to a True Sum of his Errors acknowledged that he had Committed a Great Crime against me in his [criminal] intentions on my life, he Seemed earnestly to beg pardon for the offences given upon which and to let him See that I am not of so [criminal] a disposition as he (I let him out of Irons for which Gentleness & lienience toward him he promised good behavour for the future, and that if he are got drunk whilst in this factory he would [?] to the greatest punishment I Should think proper to inflict, and fell down to his Knees and thanked me for this Gentle treatment).[53]

Isbister's entry in his journal was written to create an impression on the people who would read it: the governor and committee of the HBC in London. For this reason, he was fulfilling his mandate of bringing his men under control with a harsh form of naval discipline while concurrently ignoring the criminal jurisdiction of the company's charter. Instead, his discipline was usually a summary beating at his own hands, followed by an apology and Isbister's forgiveness. There was no similarity to this at common law.

In Isham's case, the connection between alcohol and disciplinary problems is surprisingly absent in the post journals of York Factory while Isham served as chief and governor. The only mention of alcohol involved giving it to the "Home Indians" and of servants defrauding the HBC of a couple of quarts of brandy. In the instance of the company servants, the case involved the sale of stolen brandy from Richard Satchfield to John Wood for ten shillings, one sixpence. As a punishment, Isham ordered that both men were to be deprived of any liquor for the remainder of the year and lashed in the presence of the entire complement of men:

> The Said Richard Satchfield some time Last Summer or fall, Sold to Thomas Lushington a Bell for two shilling Knowing the same to be the property of Humphry Martins, which he Clandestinely Stole by his frivolous Excuses also in Searching Last fall Several Knives were found upon the said Richard Satchfield not being his own property ... for which Misdemenours I do order for an Example that the said Richard Satchfield be Lashed to the press and receive 39 Lashes upon his bare back. Accordingly had him brought too but Excused him with 32 Lashes, he promising to be honest in future.[54]

It seems that the tranquility of York Factory, at least regarding alcohol and discipline, was maintained with excessive punishments meted out infrequently. This assessment is based on the post journals and therefore fraught with the inaccuracies that they may contain. However, it must be remembered that it was in the best interest of the post's chief to include an account of all the disciplinary problems that did occur, since it was a record of what happened that would back up a governor's actions if a servant decided to sue the HBC in England. As well, it seems that the London management of the company was content to see the governor occasionally chastise the servants as proof of their governance. This was, in fact, the motivation behind Isbister's promotion.

Inevitably, insubordination, often exacerbated by excessive drinking, occupied the second most common category of disciplinary breakdown. It becomes obvious when examining the evidence concerning insubordination that the governors were fairly autonomous. For the sake of general deterrence, Isham was paternalistic in his treatment of servants and refrained from administering harsh punishment unless it served as an example to all the servants. Isbister, on the other hand, was more than happy to correct unco-operative workers with a cuffing and then place them in irons on a regular basis.

Such was the case at Albany Fort in 1741, when, according to Isbister, Thomas Nelthorpe "had the boldness absolutely to Deny his Duty the first Step to a Mutiny an Example & Precedent to all others in the factory to Go by & for this ... given him a few Cuffs with my hand."[55] This insubordination continued until the next ship's sailing, when Isbister sent Nelthorpe back to England. On another occasion, Isbister issued a similar punishment to Peter Isbister for not following his orders and giving him foul language, which was corrected with a reprimand and a "Green willow."[56] Isbister's method of correction in many ways reflected his experience as a sailor and master in the sense that a quick blow was often more useful in cases of simple and drunken insubordination than a proper flogging.

Mutiny, as most insubordination was called, was dealt with by Isham at York Fort through confinement rather than physical punishment. In addition to threatening to send servants home, Isham used irons to bring them under control. Just prior to the yearly sailing in August 1753, Isham wrote that "at noon James Jarvis Behaved in a most Sad manner Refused working put him in Irons broke the Lock no Irons would hold him, Thomas Smith has been these two Days Cursing Swearing and abusing in a most Sad manner, Benjamin Picard who is a wicked man Combined together Before for to Cause Disturbance in a mutinous manner Dangerous to Keep Such men in a fort, Sent a 6 oared boat for the Captain to Come and take them on board."[57] In another case, in which the York Factory doctor began acting irrationally, Isham again resorted to the use of irons on one of his officers in order to protect him from himself. In his journal entry of 6 April 1753, Isham wrote that "at 12 Last night was Disturbed by a gun fired of, upon Examining found it to be the mad Doctor, who over night threatened to Shoot himself, – he fired the gun out of his window but first took the Lock of his Door that persons the Sooner might Come to his Relief, he Did this to make us Imagine he had Shot himself, but afterwards Said he Did it to Alarm us. I Called old Ferd up, put the Doctor in Irons till 5 morning, then Released him upon his promising better Behaviour."[58] Indeed, rather than holding a formal trial in the form of a post council, Isham preferred to have unruly servants and officers placed in irons and forgive them when they came to their senses. In essence, he exhibited a great deal of leniency, acting as a father rather than a captain. He governed moderately and paternally rather than tyrannically and austerely.

In other cases of more serious crime involving sexual impropriety, Isham exhibited his usual restraint while at the same time employing ritualistic punishment to create an example for the men under his charge. Cases of sexual impropriety in the first century of the company's history in Rupert's Land have traditionally focused on sexual liaisons between company employees and Native women.[59] Sexual relations between the employees themselves have not received any attention. This is undoubtedly because there is very little evidence to suggest that such relations were common at HBC posts. Nevertheless, a few incidents at least warranted references in the post journals. Isham, in one year, reported several cases of sodomy taking place in York Factory. However, it can be gleaned from the sources that post governors and factors generally exercised a great deal of discretion in reporting such incidents. There was no need for a chief to report incidents of sexual impropriety unless he was intent on infamously marking the perpetrators. It was left to the company's initiative to prosecute these crimes in England, which would have subjected the HBC to questions of venue as well as potentially bad press. It can be assumed that many of these incidents were dealt with informally, which would have made reporting unnecessary.

York Factory was the foreign headquarters of the company in the middle of the eighteenth century. It was also its largest and most lucrative post and the home of the bay-side governor. The social relationships that existed in the factory could be seen as a microcosm of British society, distinguished by forced military service if required. Discipline in this society was an aspect of power where individuals functioned as objects in what Michel Foucault called a "calculated but permanent economy."[60] Not unlike a carceral institution in the nineteenth century, the fort had much in common with the penitentiary in practice if not in philosophy. Forts were total institutions that restricted freedom by employing enclosure, rank, functional sites, and surveillance.[61] At York Factory, enclosure was by far the most ominous category of distribution. The only Europeans within thousands of miles were either the British at other HBC posts, which were generally weeks of sailing or walking away, or French pedlars, who were considered enemies of the company as well as of the British in general. Desertion was a mortally dangerous option. Therefore, resistance was invariably met with an exercise of power, whether at the end of a cat-o'-nine-tails, the fist of an officer, or a more ritualized form of punishment.

An incident of sodomy – a capital offence in common law as well as naval law – was discovered at York Factory in 1754. The incident involved Peter Isbister, who seems to have come from Albany and been punished by Isham earlier while assigned there. Isham's journal entry reads, "at noon Brought Peter Vincent to have him Rammed, that is Every man a Slap on his back side with a Barrel stave, for making a disturbance Last night, and attempting that abominable sin of Sodomy on George Dorell."[62] Three days later, on 30 December 1754, Isham wrote, "at noon Brought Peter Isbister too, Every Man two Lashes, this old Rogue upon enquiry [was] found to be the person who seduced the above Peter Vincent to that wicked and sinful act of Sodomy, by his own Confession was twice in the young man's bed, and offered several sent him home to your Honours to being in my power to bring him to any further punishment than what I have done which is much too favourable for such notorious crimes."[63] Instead of dealing with this incident through the use of a formal post council, Isham chose summarily to mete out less severe punishments. That is, he ordered the men to be "rammed, that is Every man a Slap on his back side with a Barrel stave."[64] This form of ritualized punishment was not, however, the type of penalty that would have been meted out by a court martial of the same period.

At a court martial, sodomy required the death penalty if the charge was proved in full. According to N.A.M. Roger, during the Seven Years War of 1757-63, there were eleven courts martial for sodomy, which led to four acquittals and seven convictions on indecency and uncleanliness.[65] In most cases, courts were reluctant to impose the death penalty in even fully proven instances and instead preferred accepting a partial proof and imposing a sentence of several hundred lashes.[66] This was a crime that was officially detested and difficult to conceal. As well, according to Roger, during the Seven Years War at least, "it is difficult to believe that there can have been any serious problems with a crime so much detested, but so seldom mentioned."[67] In the navy, the crime simply was not prosecuted in most cases because the officers had no collective interest in pursuing a charge.

At common law, the crime of sodomy was also relatively rare according to extant records. In England, there were not many prosecutions, as Table 5.1 indicates. At Hudson Bay, these men were not subject to any form of punishment that even came close to those prescribed in common law or the Articles of War. The relationship between Isbister and Vincent included one more occurrence just prior to the ship's arrival, when Isham wrote, "when I was Going to Bed at 8 Martin Came up with Peter Vincent who Complained of Peter Isbister's offering again that sin of Sodomy, I directly had him Lashed up and Every man 3 strokes with a good Young Willow and Separated them from being in the same Cabin."[68]

For what Isham called "such notorious crimes," the men were sent back to England the following summer, where they both escaped any documen-

Table 5.1

Capital convictions for sodomy in England, 1755-1818

Criminal courts	Convictions	Executions	Executions as % of convictions
London and Middlesex			
1756-1804	9	5	55.5%
1812-18	4	4	100%
Home Circuit			
1755-1814	14	12	85.7%
Norfolk Circuit			
1768-1818	4	3	75%
Western Circuit			
1770-1818	7	4	57%

Source: Clive Emsley, *Crime and Society in England 1750-1900* (London: Longman, 1987), 214.

tary record. Notwithstanding, it can be safely assumed that the company did not prosecute these men since it was already experiencing a public relations disaster with the parliamentary inquiry of 1749 that threatened its charter.[69]

Sodomy, considered a moral crime by Isham, created the spectacle of punishment in the context of social relationships among the company's servants at York Factory. As Isham described it in the post journal, sodomy was "wicked and sinful," an "abominable sin," and a "Heinous Sin."[70] Vincent, younger than Isbister, seemed to be a willing participant in the act, because they were detected through the mechanism of surveillance as well as Isbister's confession. Isham's judgment on the incidents was based on patriarchalism and Christian morality. Punishment in this context was spectacle. The servants were called together as a group to administer beatings to Vincent and Isbister in order to signify their collective disgust over their behaviour. As was common with English practice during the same period, punishment was not a hidden aspect of penal practice but was corporal; it had a direct effect on the bodies of Vincent and Isbister. Both men were of the lower rank of the post's hierarchy, guilty of a capital crime, and therefore subject to public torture and being branded with infamy. In these cases of torture, pain was used to produce truth as well as punishment for the sin of sodomy. The spectacle had to be limited so as not to demoralize the recipients, who were vital to the functioning of the factory. The punishment was also intended to prevent further acts of sodomy but not be too excessive so as to eventually diminish Isham's exercise of power. Cognitively linking the punishment to the crime in an unambiguous way, the ritual of paddling the rear ends of the culprits was maintained in successive punishments.[71]

Eighteenth-century concepts of a social contract serve to explain Isham's use of torture as punishment in the context of the factory. Accepting such practices as part and parcel of society, whether in England or at Hudson Bay, Isbister and Vincent were viewed as enemies of their societies and participated in their own punishments in a more generalized sense.[72] The bodies of the accused men were linked to their crime and were punished accordingly. Thus, the invisibility of disciplinary power was exercised in a visible manner through the spectacle of the public paddling. After returning to Britain, Vincent and Isbister were not mentioned again in the York Factory post journal.

An instance of sexual impropriety involving animals occurred in 1744 at Henley House. At the time, William Isbister, the brother of Joseph Isbister, was the chief of the satellite post. The purpose of Henley House was to display the company's goods in order to entice local Aboriginal people to travel to the bay-side posts, where they could be incorporated into the company's trading scheme. In September 1743, there was one journal entry related to the behaviour of a boy named Dingley. He had run off from the post and faked his watch with a desire to conspire with the French against the company.[73] Dingley was one of a number of teenage apprentices employed by the HBC in the eighteenth century. These apprentices, many of whom came from London charity schools, were partially trained in mathematics, navigation, and surveying, which made them desirable as apprentices to the company. They usually came to the bay at the age of fourteen or fifteen for a period of about seven years.[74] Dingley was undoubtedly a member of this class of employees who came from the metropolis in a school system that was designed to solve the problems of irreligion and pauperism but that exposed them to the vices of the city. He was not mentioned in the journal again until 10 April 1744, when William Isbister wrote, "last night about Eleven o'clock I got out of bed and found the boy Dingley fast with the bitch, he was as fast with her as Ever I seed a Dog with a bitch, for he had not power to part from her until I came and Drove him away – he is guilty of all bad properties that I can mention."[75] There is, however, no mention of punishment for this act. Dingley was eventually transferred back to the bay, where, it can be conjectured, he was subject to closer supervision. Nevertheless, Isbister did little to mete out punishments in the frontier post, which was symptomatic of his tenuous position. Without a full complement of loyal officers, post chiefs had to be careful not to invite mutiny through gratuitous punishments.

Another case that involved sexual impropriety with animals occurred under the charge of Humphrey Marten at York Factory in 1761. Marten began his service in the HBC in 1750 as a writer, clerk, and steward. In 1758, he was selected to replace James Isham when he returned to England and was later named second at York and master at Severn House when Isham returned to York the following year. Under the guidance of Isham, Marten developed a similar style of governance. He was named chief at York on the occasion of Isham's death on 13 April 1761 and was recalled to England the following year. Marten inherited a fort that was rife with disciplinary infractions. It seems that on the company timeline the first year of a post command was invariably a period of adjustment. A new chief had a very short time in which to assert and exercise power over employees, who constantly tested his patience and discretion. During Marten's first six months as chief of York Factory, he encountered a serious case of sexual impropriety perpetrated by one of his officers.

The incident involved James Bloxham, the surgeon of York Fort, and took place on 21 October 1761. The journal entry was as follows:[76]

> This day at 11 O'clock, I missed William Brown from his Works, I asked where he was gone, and was informed he was sent for by the Surgeon, on which I went to the Surgeons Cabin, the Doors of which was shut, I called for William Brown, no answer being made I pushed hard against the Door, the Lock being none of the Best it flew open, when I discovered not William Brown but the Surgeon in the Following posture his Breeches were down, a part of his waistcoat open, and the great Bitch that was sent from Churchill some time since almost in his embraces, I can't say I actually saw him Copulating, for he Stood in the utmost Flavour of Countenance that I ever saw: for some time we were both Silent, I was ready to Sink into the Earth, at last he spoke the Words following, (A, Sir, you cant find her I have hid her) by this time I was a little recovered from the Shock I had read: I went into the Cabin I looked into all the Places I thought a Woman could probably hide herself in his Cabin but Alas I found none, all the same time he had not the Power to put up his Breeches, or to turn the Bitch out of his Cabin, but [?] crying out, you can't find her Sir, I have hid her, at last I replied, I wish you had Doctor, I went down to the Bank ... I neither can, or will speak to you at present, he went down, when I sat down to write as Follows,
>
> Sir You have Offended God / not (it certainly an offence against all men, but I was for much Conceived to write better) me / make your peace with the Almighty, emplore God humbly and sincerely for Pardon, if you are sincerely sorry for / O' Heavens! / your crime, you will thank me for this advice, I can't go on I tremble so, I am your Afflicted Country Man. H. Marten
>
> PS. I you should think fit to sent an Answer, do it in writing, as I am not in a Condition fit to see you at Present!
>
> October the 21, 1761
>
> To Mr. James Bloxham Doctor

In reply to this, Bloxham responded in writing:

> Sir, By the Behaviour of you to me it seems that I was guilty of a most Monstrous indecent Action, The way that you found me was certainly Indecent, but the reason was / in Truth / to made Water, to be thought of being guilty of any Familiarity with a Brute Beast would be enough to Vex a Saint Far was it from me I had just before been reading [F.] Turner of the Veinercate Diseases concerning the fallopian Tubes, in the Womb, he recommends it in his Works to be tried on a Bitch and as I was willing to try it, I did put my fingers into the [Pudenda] of the Animal, but if it was any intention in the Mind of [?], At him never Know happiness in this life, or in any other.
>
> As I am thought to be so great a Monster (as you believe me to be and certainly deserved had I been guilty) I will if you please refrain from your Table until you think I am not so great a Villain.
>
> I am Sir your most humble Servant James Bloxham
>
> PS. I read your letter and am sorry that you think so.

Because Bloxham's services to the post were indispensable, Marten was left with no recourse but to keep his secret as a bond for future good behaviour. Marten, using the informal apparatus of his position, manipulated this incident to compel the doctor to behave himself. As it turned out, Bloxham continued to cause disciplinary problems in the fort all year, leading Marten to confront him with loaded pistols in December 1761. After Bloxham had sobered up, Marten again used the issue of his liaison with a dog to try to compel him to behave himself. He wrote, "I sent word down, I could keep my Own Secrets but was Stanch to my Word."

Marten's position in the fort was precarious. He did not have a commission and was made master of York Factory because he was the second at the time of Isham's death. As a result, rank began to play an important role in his use of the company's private justice system governing relations between its employees. Because Bloxham was a peer according to company custom, and a member of the post council, Marten was forced to let his defiance go unpunished. In fact, the only disciplinary action taken on the surgeon came at a time when, in a fit of drunkenness, the surgeon apparently went mad.[77] In his response to this, Marten violated the rules of class and rank when he confined the doctor to his cabin and kept him under guard. The following week Marten fixed an order on the wall in the factory's guard room. His journal entry stated:

> A Caution to the Honourable Hudson's Bay Companys Servants not to admit James Bloxham Surgeon of York Fort into their Cabins, on any account without the Consent of the Chief of the said Fort nor are they to give lend

> or sell the said Bloxham any Spiritous Liquors as they will answer it at their Peril if the said Bloxham should ask for any Liquors as aforesaid, and no being refused should [?] the Person so refusing* is directly to acquaint the Chief of the same who will take proper care in [?] them too.
> Signed, Humphrey Marten
> *George Richardson informed me that the Doctor used to ask the men for Liquor and which they were afraid to refuse him, when an Officer will drink with the Common Men, it is all over with him.[78]

Particularly telling is the asterisked section regarding class and rank. Here Marten reveals why he did not discipline Bloxham in the same manner as other men.

Rank shielded Bloxham from the punishments commonly delivered to company servants. Indeed, the incident of sexual impropriety involving Bloxham shows the way in which rank functioned in the total institution of the factory. Bloxham, in this case, was immune to the private justice system of the HBC, although his crimes were as great as those committed by Peter Isbister and Peter Vincent. The reason was class. Bloxham was educated, a gentleman expected to set an example for other company servants. When the system of rank broke down, so did discipline in the factory itself. An example of this took place in the spring of 1762, when Marten entered in the journal a letter written by Hugh Jones, a company labourer who had threatened another servant with a pistol and spoken insolently to Marten:

> These Letters would never have appeared had not his very bad behaviour since forced me to enter them: one Morning when I sent to order the Men to their work he was standing by the Fire and though not spoke to, made the following expression
> NEW LORDS, NEW LAWS
> NEW DEVILS, NEW CLAWS
> my having no Commission from your Honours to act as Chief of York Fort, but on the Contrary it being well known that I was ordered home, long before the Packet was opened, seem to be the reason for this strange Behaviour however let the cases be how it will, I will behave my self suitable to the Station Providence has so remarkably placed me in, and this in Justice I must declare that Christopher Atkinsen has behaved in the best manner, his whole study as well as Anthony Hendey being to keep the peace below [?] your Honours will [be] pleased to remember I have not one of the Council at this place fit to consult with.[79]

With this level of disciplinary breakdown, the only instrument available to Marten to restore order at York was to summon a post council to discipline Jones.

Mutinous words and a letter sent to Humphrey Marten led to summoning the company's highest private court on 2 April 1762. As a disciplinary instrument, the post council was established in the 1680s as an active component in the private justice system of the company to deal with refractory employees. It was probably modelled on its central management, which utilized a governor and committee to make major decisions.[80] However, in other ways, the council was similar to a court martial and the petty sessions of a magistrate. The punishments handed out by councils were in most ways similar to those of the military, and they were conducted with a quorum of post officers. They were differentiated from a court martial in the law that they followed and the flexibility of the instrument. Unlike a court martial, a council could be summoned at any time. Depositions might be taken, or a person accused of a disciplinary infraction might just be interrogated by the post's officers. All the proceedings, however, were recorded in the post journals for a permanent record.

The post council convened by Marten was based on the evidence of a letter written by Hugh Jones on 2 April 1762. In it Jones stated:

> I Beg to acquaint you that as you some to thereto and have told me that you have been informed that I have been plotting Cabals and [?] to raise a mutiny ... and to clear your suspicion in this I made be a Leave to quit the factory, some score miles, for I would not nor cannot stay Here or any place else where my Master has such an opinion of me on any account whatever ... as it can be of no manner of Service to their honours of my staying Here I humbly beg that you would please to let me go away either with these North river Indians now come down while the rest comes ... Otherwise I must leave this place by my self and trust to Providence for I am resolved not to stay here.[81]

Upon receiving this letter, Marten resolved that the only way he could prevent Jones' desertion was to hold a post council. However, as he stated in the months prior to this incident, he did not have adequate officers to properly use the instrument. Fortunately for Marten, the company's private justice system allowed a certain amount of flexibility and discretion on the part of its chief officers, since the matter would be resolved before Marten's London employers had a chance to scrutinize his actions. For this reason, detailed records were kept, complete with dates and signatures. The post council held on 2 April 1762 was attended by Hugh Jones, the accused, and Humphrey Marten, Christopher Atkinson, Anthony Henday, and George Richardson, who, except Marten, were all tradesmen and labourers. The transcript reads as follows:

Question the 1: Pray Sir what is your Reason for wanting to leave the Fort
His Answer: Because I don't like to stay at it,
Question the 2: What make's you dislike it? did I ever use you ill? If so, speak in Gods Name and tell me in what.
His Answer: No Sir you never did, but somebody else has,
Question the 3: Pray who is the Person,
His Answer: I Know who very well, Mr. Atkinson
4th Question: In what Pray as you are both now face to face, speak and Justice shall be done you.
Jones Answer: No Sir I shall not say anything now, but if I meet him in England: I will let him know, This answer made [Marten] most angry, when I expressed my self in the Following Terms You deserve Sir to be horse whipped for declaring you would leave the Fort, as you have not given one Substantial Reason / and indeed I know none can be given / for so doing: so far Sir am I from giving you leave to quit the Fort: that You must immediately sign this piece of Paper or be confined in Irons until shiptime, so take your Choice, Jones hesitated some time, but at last signed the Following Paper which was Sealed with your Honours Seal
York Fort April the 2nd 1762
I Hugh Jones do declare I will not leave the Factory at which I now at without the leave of Humphrey Marten Chief of the Fort, witness my Hand, Hugh Jones
Present as Witnesses: George Richardson, Anthony Hendey

We whose Names are under-written do testify and are ready to make Oath / if so required / that Hugh Jones Servant to the Hudson's Bay Company at York Fort did Voluntarily declare in our hearing that Mr. Humphrey Marten Chief of the said Fort had not in the past used him ill,
Witness our Hands this second of April, 1762: George Richardson, Anthony Hendey
I Humbly hope your Honours will pardon my Prolixity in this Affair, as I would willingly have my Character appear as clear as noon day.[82]

Regardless of this, Marten's tenuous control over his charge was compromised again on 18 April 1762, with Jones once again penning letters although no longer signing them. As Marten commented, "he laughed full in my face and gave me such Language that I could not bear it: he has frequently called all in this house without distinction Blackguards, Irishmen and Taylors, which was repeated to my face this day on which provocation I gave him Manual Corrections had I been Born in Ireland I should not have been ashamed of my Country, but I can glory in being an Englishman Born in Somersetshire, neither to my knowledge is there an Hibernian in the

Fort."[83] Jones' actions were representative of the plebeian culture of England as much as they represented the company's internal discipline. The idea of class conflict and resistance abounds in these records. In addition, it is apparent that ethnicity played an important role in the social ordering of the fort. The company hired English and Orcadian employees who, among the ranks of the officers, often had a background in the navy. In this example, the aspersions cast against Irishmen are in many ways no different from those cast against Orkneymen. Joseph Isbister was from the Orkney Islands and ruled with an iron hand, while Isham, Marten, and Jacobs, all English-born officers, tended to a softer rule.

Discretion and Authority on the Bay: External Legal Relations

Discretionary punishment was administered in varying degrees by the company officers and depended on their personal beliefs. Internally, the metaphor of a ship served well in the case of factory discipline. Externally, a completely different legal system functioned with respect to First Peoples. What began as diplomatic cross-fusing developed into cultural cross-fusing where custom and ritual were adapted on both sides in order to foster a relationship between nations.[84] What resulted was an elaborate set of tributes and ceremonies that took place on trading days. The thread that seemed to weave through the first hundred years of the charter was a legal system based on nation-to-nation interaction in which the bay-side governors either ignored imposing the HBC's private justice system on First Peoples or adopted the "custom of the country" to legitimate company law.

A new form of social organization emerged in Rupert's Land with the fur trade. Within Aboriginal society, the establishment of a "trading captain" from the ranks of the primarily Cree "Home Guard" meant that company officers had to develop an understanding of that position as well as an appreciation of what motivated an Aboriginal man to seek that role. They had to realize that in the egalitarian Aboriginal society the role of the "trading captain" was precarious. Thus, bay-side governors extended many courtesies such as extra tobacco and clothing to develop the status of the captain among his own people.[85] In this way, the governors often co-opted the prestige of local leaders to curry favour with the locals. However, the attempt to impose an English form of dispute resolution on First Peoples was not discussed in the company's orders to the bay-side posts.

The discretion of its officers toward Aboriginal people was largely influenced by their dependent position in regard to provisions and fur trading. A good example of this attitude was expressed in the orders to John Bridgar, the governor of Port Nelson, in 1682. The governor and committee stated that "there is another thing which we think of great Moment and therefore recommend to your particular care that is that you Endeavour to make such Contracts with the Natives for the River in & above Port Nelson as may in future times ascertain to us a right & property therein and the Sole Liberty to trade & peaceable Cohabitation with such Ceremonies as you shall find to be most Sacred and Obligatory amongst them."[86] This directive was made when the company was just beginning to establish a post on the bay and when French aggression against the HBC was at its height. Rich wrote,

> If ... it could be argued that the Muscovy Company's long neglect of the north-west left the area open to other adventurers, then did not the same argument hold good in respect of the immense unoccupied territory of which even the fringes were not so much as prospected by the Company in 1682, the date of the first open challenge? That the Hudson's Bay Committee feared that this might be so clearly shown by their nervous anxiety to get forts erected at Port Nelson and New Severn and by their attempts to secure their title by making with the Indians, covenants purporting to be transfers of blocks of territory.[87]

Bridgar himself was captured by the French in 1683. After his release, he returned to the bay, where he was captured again in 1686.

With respect to external discipline in the mid-eighteenth century, the journal entries of Isbister and Isham are illustrative. Isham, in contrast to Isbister, tended to be more paternalistic and generous with First Peoples and was the father of a "country-born" son.[88] Curiously, one of his specific orders was not to entertain Native women in the fort in order to set an example of sobriety for the other men. He was also responsible for sending expeditions inland.[89] While both men served as chiefs for the HBC during the same period, it is impossible to see any uniformity in their governing styles. Isbister, with a background in the navy, seems to have administered a harsh form of discipline. Isham, a company veteran, did not. As well, their respective opinions of the "Home Indians" also seem to suggest a certain lack of uniformity in their governing styles as well as the high level of discretion in their daily decision making. It seems that some of the servants preferred Isham over Isbister. According to Isbister, James Walker, after calling Ferdinand Jacobs, who was Isbister's second at Fort Prince of Wales, "Pimp & Tale bearer with many other unbecoming expressions," said that he wished it could have been his "fortune to have been under Mr. Isham & that he would rather Serve at York Fort for £30 per year then here for £40."[90] Apparently, Walker wanted to entertain Native women in his cabin but found that Isbister was not very receptive to his aspiration.

An example of Isham's attitude toward Aboriginal people can be found in one of his final journal entries. By 1756, Isham, who had been suffering from a prolonged fit of gout, requested to be allowed to return to England but was not given permission until 1758. In his dispatch to London, he stated that he was "surprized of the Constant Complaint of those Gentlemen of

Enticing the Natives from their Forts, in particular Churchill," and added "I want them not; and a Strange thing they cannot keep their Indians. The truth is they are a free people, and will go where they find best usage & not for the Interest of Honours."[91]

Isham, contrary to the charter and the established practice of conquest on the continent of North America, did not believe that the HBC had any legal jurisdiction in Native-European relations. Indeed, as the orders to John Bridgar of 1682 intimate, even the London headquarters of the company realized early that the right of conquest was not possible in Rupert's Land and directed company officials to make treaties with First Peoples.[92] This was repeated in the following year in orders to Henry Sergeant. They stated that he was to take over the governorship of the bay and "that in the several places where we are already settled or shall hereafter make new Discoveries you contrive to make compacts and Agreements with the Captains and chiefs of the Rivers & Territories that our right & propriety therein may be always understood & owned by them and the sole freedom of Trade there and let such Leagues of Friendship as they are capable of making be with them by such Ceremonies as you shall find to be most sacred and obligatory to them."[93]

Externally, both Isham and Isbister operated rather different legal mechanisms for dealing with First Peoples. The worldview of each man was quite different. Isham favoured the idea of country marriages if they benefited trade. As he wrote concerning Anthony Henday on his return from a year-long voyage inland, "I Can but own if I had been in Captain Hendays place when the King of the Earchithinues offered him his Daughter in Marriage/ and I a single Man as he was/would have Embraced that proposal which would have Created a firm friendship and would have been a great help in Engaging them to trade."[94] Isbister, for his part, operated his post according to the rules prescribed in London and made every attempt to stamp out any liaisons that his men had with Aboriginal women.

While it seems that Isham tacitly agreed with the concept of Aboriginal nationhood, Isbister sought to impose legal sanctions and capital punishment on Natives. Two cases provide examples of the differing governing styles of these two chief factors. Isham, upon learning of the death of Samuel Skrimsher, found out that his injuries had been inflicted by a Native before Skrimsher left for his goose-hunting trip. When Isham examined the deceased, he "found the Right side of his face had Received a Blow, the Right Eye very Red, Surled & Closed, and is our opinion the blow Get by the Indian and the cause of his death."[95] He ignored the criminal jurisdiction of the company's charter as well as the restitutive aspects of the custom of the country, and the incident was not spoken of again.

Isbister, when faced with a similar occurrence at Henley House, invoked the full retributive power of the company's charter. He passed a death sentence on the three Natives whom he and his council found guilty. How much Isbister recognized the law of blood feud when he retaliated cannot be known. Nevertheless, on 4 March 1755, news reached Albany that the inhabitants of Henley House, namely William Lamb, Robert Ash, Daniel Bowland, James Short, and George Gun, had been murdered. Isbister instructed the local "Home Guard" to trade in the perpetrators of the crime. Upon learning that the perpetrators were Wouldbee, his two sons Sheanapp and Young Snuff the Blanket, as well as his son-in-law and another, Isbister forced confessions from Wouldbee and his sons, who were visiting the fort, by using a degree of coercion. By coercion, I refer to the method by which Isbister extracted his confessions. As he wrote, "so soon as I had Separated and Confined these Villains and fired 2 pistols in the Yard in order to know the sentiment of the Indians, making believe I had killed two of them and that one only was left alive, and likwise that each of the three prisoners would think that he only was Spared."[96] After this, Isbister, along with two of his officers and twenty-one men belonging to the factory, examined the accused. Then a council of the chief officers and men was called together and passed judgment unanimously. The three were hanged at Albany on 21 June 1755. In the post journal entry for 21 June, Isbister wrote, "they hung 30 minutes until they were dead, after which we let them down And put them all three into an old Sawpitt which is some distance below this Fort and Covered them with Earth, a Gentle punishment for so heinous a Crime, at the Same time to let the Indians Know that the English will not put up with Such Villainous Treatment from Indians, although we are a people Strangers to all Savage brutality."[97]

Particularly striking about this incident is that it set a precedent in regard to the company's private justice system. This was the first time that the English in Rupert's Land attempted to establish criminal jurisdiction over First Peoples. Although it was described as a trial by Isbister, it seems that this trial and execution were closer to retaliation.[98] He unilaterally used the rights contained in the charter that applied to HBC employees as well as all other Europeans to prosecute First Peoples. Even prior to the hanging of the suspected murderers, he summoned the formal post council, made up of all the "Chief Officers and Men at Albany Fort" to "pronounce them to outlawry and Condemn them to be hanged or shot when they are ever Caught. And wee the Said Council, do in behalf and in the Name of the Governor and Hudson's Bay Company (And in justice to our unfortunate Country men, pronounce the Sentence of death upon Wappisiss Alia Wouldbe the Land Pirate, and his two Sons, Sheanapp, and Young Snuff the Blanket, to be hanged until they are dead, dead, dead for a terror to all the Savage Natives from ever being guilty of the like barbarity in future."[99] It can be discerned from this that Isbister was motivated by retaliation and the purpose of setting an example, even though the proceedings leave an impression of formal legality and collective decision making.

Isbister was recalled to London in 1756, and he subsequently retired from the service. It appears that he went to the new colony of Quebec by 1770 and died between November 1770 and August 1771, leaving behind his wife, Judith.[100] In his penultimate entry in the Albany Fort journal that accompanied him to the London committee in 1756, he stated "that all the Indians highly Condemned the behaviour of Woodbee & that he was but rightly Served for behaving so barbarously to ye English at Henley House."[101]

Isham and Isbister developed rather different techniques for dispute resolution. In the closed system of the individual fort, discretion defined the type of society that existed. In Isham's case, benevolence and the discriminant exercise of power seemed to be the rule. When dealing with Aboriginal people, he seemed more willing to overlook or ignore the company's directives concerning nonfraternization. It also seems that he was unwilling to impose the English standard of criminal justice when dealing with Natives.

In Isbister's case, the full range of legal alternatives available was administered to the men under his charge as well as to the local Natives. In most instances, discipline within the fort followed the model of naval discipline, in which Isbister would administer summary punishments personally. In addition, it can be argued that Isbister, whether he realized it or not, partially followed the example of the custom of the country when dealing with the Henley House murders by retaliating in the face of aggression. Alternatively, it can be argued that, because he chose to invoke the legal apparatus sanctioned by the charter with regard to criminal law, he was actually imposing the English criminal justice system on the perpetrators.

Conclusion

James Isham returned to York Fort in 1759 after recovering in England, and he died on 13 April 1761 after suffering from gout and other ailments for almost twenty years. In his will dated 16 February 1760, he bequeathed all his property to Charles Isham, his country-born son.[102] After being recalled in 1762, Marten was replaced by Ferdinand Jacobs, and stability was restored to the fort after a year of adjustment. Marten returned to the bay in the following year as second to Robert Temple at Albany Fort. In 1765, he was appointed chief at Albany and Henley House, which he re-established in 1765.[103] He remained chief at Henley until 1768, when he returned to England due to illness. He returned to his post in 1769 to face once again a series of disciplinary transgressions. The London committee sent a letter to Thomas Hopkins, and the council at Albany, expressing their disapproval of an altercation between Marten and John Richards, the master. The committee's letter detailed the chain of command to the council, stating that the chief at Albany was always to be obeyed by the master of Henley and any other subordinate servants. Marten's career in the HBC continued for another two decades.[104] Ferdinand Jacobs' career with the company also continued well into the 1760s. While Jacobs was portrayed by the chiefs of Fort Prince of Wales as a sober and honest man, he began to diverge from the example of the governors under whom he served and their predecessors.[105]

Autonomous decision making was an important characteristic of the private justice system of the HBC. Governors, because of their lack of proximity to London and the obvious communication problems that accompanied this, were given a great deal of latitude in their dealings with insubordinate company servants as well as First Peoples. Although the charter, legislation, and company orders and instructions laid out rather rigid remedies for behaviour that could be regarded as illegal, the personalities of the officers influenced the private justice system to a greater degree. Therefore, what is referred to as a private justice system can also be considered a personal justice system in the context of justice at the various posts, factories, and forts of the HBC.

There has been a general lack of research in the field of the HBC's private justice system. Aside from the work of Edith Burley, Hamar Foster, Dale Gibson, Louis Knafla, Kathryn Bindon, Rick Linden, Karina Sacca, and Russell Smandych, who deal primarily with the nineteenth century, there is no modern work on the early formative period.[106] Indeed, it is only in the work of Smandych and Burley that the company's private justice system in Rupert's Land in the seventeenth and eighteenth centuries is addressed with any significant detail. This present work is part of a larger one that will explore topics of the company's private justice system thematically. It will investigate the issues of international law and the right of conquest, the management structure, class and ethnicity within the company's ranks, the role of women in its trading system, the role of First Peoples and their response to the company's intrusion into the West, the internal ordering of factory life, discipline, and resistance within the fort, and discipline and resistance to the HBC among First Peoples.

Acknowledgments

I am grateful to Louis Knafla, who undertook the organization of the legal history conference from which this chapter originates, for his helpful commentary on earlier drafts. As well, thanks are due to Russell Smandych and the staff of the Hudson's Bay Company Archives for assisting me in gathering much of the primary documentary evidence.

Notes

1 "The Royal Charter Incorporating the Hudson's Bay Company, 1670," in *The Canadian Northwest: Its Early Development and Legislative Records,* vol. 1, ed. E.H. Oliver (Ottawa: King's Printer, 1914), 135-54.

2 M.F. Lindley, *The Acquisition and Government of Backward Territory in International Law* (New York: Negro Universities Press, 1969), 5-96.

3 Oliver, *The Canadian Northwest,* 22.

4 E.E. Rich, *The Fur Trade and the Northwest to 1857* (Toronto: McClelland and Stewart, 1967), 31.

5 See, generally, Daniel Francis and Toby Morantz, *Partners in Furs: A History of the Fur Trade in Eastern James Bay, 1600-1870* (Montreal and Kingston: McGill-Queen's University Press, 1983); Arthur J. Ray, *Indians in the Fur Trade,* 2nd ed. (Toronto: University of Toronto Press,

1998); "The Royal Charter Incorporating the Hudson's Bay Company, 1670," in *The Canadian Northwest: Its Early Development and Trade: Their Role as Trappers, Hunters, and Middlemen in the Lands Southwest of Hudson Bay, 1660-1870,* vol. 1, ed. E.H. Oliver (Toronto: University of Toronto Press, 1974), 135-53; and Arthur J. Ray and Donald B. Freeman, *"Give Us Good Measure": An Economic Analysis of Relations between the Indians and the Hudson's Bay Company before 1763* (Toronto: University of Toronto Press, 1978).

6 *Act for Confirming to the Governor and Company Trading to Hudson's Bay Their Privileges and Trade,* 2 William & Mary (1690), c. 23.

7 E.E. Rich, *The Hudson's Bay Company,* vol. 1 (New York: Macmillan, 1960), 57. The most important contention that Rich makes with regard to the royal prerogative is that it was granted at a time when the prerogative was an accepted method of granting prescriptive rights over the course of time. See also H. Robert Baker, "Law Transplanted, Justice Invented: Sources of Law for the Hudson's Bay Company in Rupert's Land, 1670-1870" (master's thesis, University of Manitoba, 1996), 11. Baker takes exception to Rich's idea that the HBC's charter came under attack as the royal prerogative itself was becoming discredited and seen as being opposed to the common law.

8 Baker, "Law Transplanted," 41.

9 Edith Burley, *Servants of the Honourable Company: Work, Discipline, and Conflict in the Hudson's Bay Company, 1770-1870* (Toronto: Oxford University Press, 1997), 24-25.

10 Rich, *The Fur Trade,* 60.

11 Rich, *The Hudson's Bay Company.* The most notable trade item that the French brought inland was French brandy, which was superior to English brandy and generally afforded them the best furs.

12 Burley, *Servants of the Honourable Company,* 1.

13 Ibid. at 24n15.

14 E.E. Rich, ed., *Minutes of the Hudson's Bay Company, 1671-1674* (Toronto: Champlain Society, 1942), 5n3; and Burley, *Servants of the Honourable Company,* 24n15.

15 Burley, *Servants of the Honourable Company,* 24-25; Gerhard Ens, "The Political Economy of the 'Private Trade' on the Hudson Bay: The Example of Moose Factory, 1741-1744," in *Le Castor Fait Tout: Selected Papers of the 5th North American Fur Trade Conference, 1985,* ed. Bruce G. Trigger et al. (Montreal: University of Montreal Press, 1987), 382-410.

16 Rich, *The Fur Trade,* 55.

17 Rich, *The Hudson's Bay Company,* 61-426.

18 Russell Smandych and Rick Linden, "Administering Justice without the State: A Study of the Private Justice System of the Hudson's Bay Company to 1800," *Canadian Journal of Law and Society* 11 (1996): 21-61 at 44.

19 HBCA, B.239/a/29, York Factory Journal, 26 August 1746.

20 HBCA, A.6/7, fols. 39-40, York Factory Extracts, Governor and Committee to Thomas White and Council at York Fort, 10 May 1744.

21 H.W. Arthurs, *"Without the Law": Administrative Justice and Legal Pluralism in Nineteenth Century England* (Toronto: University of Toronto Press, 1985), 2.

22 Oliver, *The Canadian Northwest,* 50.

23 Russell Smandych, "Company Discipline in the Hudson's Bay Company, 1660-1770," paper presented to the Canadian Law and Society Association and the Canadian Historical Association at the Learned Societies Conference, Calgary, 1994; Joseph Robson, *An Account of Six Years Residence in Hudson Bay* (London: T. Jeffreys, 1752), 17.

24 Smandych, "Company Discipline," 37; Robson, *An Account,* 38.

25 Smandych and Linden, "Administering Justice," 41.

26 Jennifer S.H. Brown, *Strangers in Blood: Fur Trade Company Families in Indian Country* (Vancouver: UBC Press, 1980), 12-13.

27 Francis Raleigh Batt, *The Law of Master and Servant,* 4th ed. (London: Pitman, 1950), 43.

28 Burley, *Servants of the Honourable Company,* 20-21.

29 Marc Linder, "The Employment Relationship in Anglo-American Law: A Historical Perspective," *Contributions in Legal Studies* 54 (1989): 46-47.

30 Ann Kussmaul, *Servants in Husbandry in Early Modern England* (Cambridge, UK: Cambridge University Press, 1981), 50-51.

31 Ibid. at 45-46.
32 Ibid. at 31-32, 38-39, 45-46.
33 Linder, "The Employment Relationship," 6.
34 Smandych and Linden, "Administering Justice," 33.
35 N.A.M. Roger, *The Wooden World: An Anatomy of the Georgian Navy* (London: Longman, 1986), 237.
36 Smandych and Linden, "Administering Justice," 41.
37 HBCA, B.42/a/44, Churchill Post Journal, 13 February 1755.
38 HBCA, B.59/a/2, Eastmain Post Journal, 7 January 1738.
39 Ibid.
40 HBCA, B.59/a/1, Eastmain Post Journal, 3 June 1738.
41 HBCA, B.59/a/4, Eastmain Post Journal, 6 October 1739.
42 HBCA, search file, biography section, Joseph Isbister.
43 See, generally, Brown, *Strangers in Blood;* and Sylvia Van Kirk, *Many Tender Ties: Women in Fur-Trade Society, 1670-1870* (Norman: University of Oklahoma Press, 1983).
44 HBCA, search file, biography section, Joseph Isbister.
45 HBCA, A.11/114, fol. 79, York Factory Correspondence Out, 27 August 1736. See also K.G. Davies, ed., *Letters from Hudson's Bay 1703-40* (London: Hudson's Bay Company Record Society, 1965), 219-22.
46 HBCA, search file, biography section, James Isham.
47 Rich, *The Hudson's Bay Company,* 566.
48 Ibid. at 567.
49 Ibid. at 569.
50 Ibid.
51 HBCA, B.42/a/32, Fort Churchill Post Journal, 2 October 1748.
52 Ibid.
53 Ibid.
54 HBCA, B.239/a/36, York Factory Journal, 17 February 1753.
55 HBCA, B.3/a/30, Albany Post Journal, 10 August 1741.
56 HBCA, B.3/a/33, Albany Post Journal, 6 June 1742.
57 HBCA, B.239/a/36, York Factory Journal, 29 August 1753.
58 HBCA, B.239/a/36, York Factory Journal, 6 April 1753.
59 Brown, *Strangers in Blood;* and Van Kirk, *Many Tender Ties.*
60 Michel Foucault, *Discipline and Punish: The Birth of the Prison* (New York: Vintage Press, 1979), 141.
61 Ibid. at 170.
62 HBCA, B.239/a/37, York Factory Journal, 27 December 1754.
63 HBCA, B.239/a/37, York Factory Journal, 30 December 1754.
64 HBCA, B.239/a/39, York Factory Journal, 27 December 1754.
65 Roger, *The Wooden World,* 80.
66 Arthur N. Gilbert, "Buggery and the British Navy, 1700-1861," *Journal of Social History* 10 (1976): 72-98.
67 Roger, *The Wooden World,* 81.
68 HBCA, B.239/a/39, York Factory Journal, 16 July 1755.
69 See HBCA, search file, biography section, James Isham; Arthur S. Morton, *The History of the Canadian West to 1870-71* (London: Thomas Nelson and Sons, 1939), 217-25. Isham was involved in providing information to a parliamentary select committee when he was recalled from the bay in 1748. His help was required in London on account of attacks being made by Arthur Dobbs of London in conjunction with a group of Liverpool and Bristol merchants on the company's charter privileges.
70 HBCA, B.239/a/37, York Factory Journal, 27 and 30 December 1754.
71 Foucault, *Discipline and Punish,* 105.
72 Ibid. at 90.
73 HBCA, B.86/a/1, Henley House Journal, 11 September 1743.
74 Richard Ruggles, "Hospital Boys of the Bay," *Beaver* (Autumn 1977): 4-11.
75 HBCA, B.86/a/1, Henley House Journal, 10 April 1744.

76 HBCA, B.239/a/49, York Factory Journal, 3 December 1761, for the quotes here and below.
77 HBCA, B.239/a/49, York Factory Journal, 7 January 1762.
78 HBCA, B.239/a/49, York Factory Journal, 16 January 1762.
79 HBCA, B.239/a/49, York Factory Journal, 2 March 1762.
80 Smandych and Linden, "Administering Justice," 39. In this study, the authors draw a conclusion that military law was in effect in the company between 1680 and 1713, even though the idea of collective decision making was encouraged by the London management.
81 HBCA, B.239/a/49, York Factory Journal, 2 April 1762.
82 Ibid.
83 HBCA, B.239/a/49, York Factory Journal, 18 April 1762.
84 For a discussion of the anthropological and historical antecedents of colonialism and European–First Peoples contact, the metaphor of the middle ground is useful since it can be described as a place where cultural adaptation flows from cultural similarities and forms bridges between societies with truly different cosmologies. For a more comprehensive examination of this concept, see Richard White, *The Middle Ground: Indians, Empires, and Republics in the Great Lakes Region, 1650-1815* (Cambridge, UK: Cambridge University Press, 1991).
85 See, generally, Ray and Freeman, *"Give Us Good Measure."*
86 "Instructions for Mr. John Bridgar Governor of Port Nelson the 15th of May 1682," in *Copy-Book of Letters Outward &c Begins 29th May, 1680 Ends 5 July, 1687,* ed. E.E. Rich (Toronto: Champlain Society, 1948), 34-37 at 36.
87 E.E. Rich, "Introduction," in *Copy-Book of Letters Outward &c Begins 29th May, 1680 Ends 5 July, 1687,* ed. E.E. Rich (Toronto: Champlain Society, 1948), xiii.
88 E.E. Rich, ed., *James Isham's Observations on Hudson's Bay, 1743* (Toronto: Champlain Society, 1949), 318-25.
89 HBCA, A.6/8, fols. 118d-19, Correspondence In; HBCA, A.6/7, fol. 170, Correspondence In.
90 HBCA, B.42/a/38, Fort Churchill Post Journal, 8 February 1751.
91 HBCA, A.11/115, fol. 9, York Factory Correspondence Out, 18 August 1757.
92 Sharon Korman, *The Right of Conquest: The Forcible Acquisition of Territory in International Law and Practice* (New York: Oxford University Press, 1996), 8-9.
93 Rich, *Copy-Book of Letters Outward,* 79.
94 HBCA, B.239/a/40, "Anthony Henday's Account of a Journey and Isham's Notes of That Journey," 23 June 1755.
95 HBCA, B.239/a/38, York Factory Journal, 24 May 1755.
96 HBCA, B.3/a/47, Albany Post Journal, 7 June 1755.
97 HBCA, B.3/a/47, Albany Post Journal, 3, 7, 21 June 1755.
98 Baker, "Law Transplanted," 64-65.
99 HBCA, B.3/a/47, Albany Post Journals, 12 June 1755.
100 HBCA, search file, biography section, Joseph Isbister.
101 HBCA, B.3/a/48, Albany Post Journal, 8 September 1756.
102 HBCA, A.11/114, fol. 196v, York Factory Correspondence Out, 16 February 1760.
103 HBCA, search file, biography section, Humphrey Marten (LC 17253, 18 October 1933, to J.B. Tyrell).
104 Ibid.
105 Rich, *The Hudson's Bay Company,* 626.
106 Burley, *Servants of the Company;* Hamar Foster, "Long-Distance Justice: The Criminal Jurisdiction of Canadian Courts West of the Canadas, 1763-1859," *American Journal of Legal History* 34 (1990): 1-48; Hamar Foster, "Mutiny on the Beaver: Law and Authority in the Fur Trade Navy, 1835-1840," *Manitoba Law Journal* 20 (1991): 15-45; Louis Knafla, "From Oral to Written Memory: The Common Law Tradition in Western Canada," in *Law and Justice in a New Land,* ed. Louis Knafla (Toronto: Carswell, 1986), 31-77; Kathryn Bindon, "Hudson's Bay Company Law: Adam Thom and the Institution of Order in Rupert's Land 1839-54," in *Essays in the History of Canadian Law,* vol. 1, ed. David H. Flaherty (Toronto: Osgoode Society, 1981), 43-87; Smandych and Linden, "Administering Justice"; Russell Smandych and Karina Sacca, "The Development of Criminal Law Courts in Pre-1870 Manitoba," *Manitoba Law Journal* 24 (1996): 201-57; and Smandych, "Company Discipline."

Part 2
Adaptations to Modernity

6
Policing Two Imperial Frontiers: The Royal Irish Constabulary and the North-West Mounted Police

Greg Marquis

> Buy a six-penny map of Ireland, nail it to a tree, and then, standing twenty-five yards from it ... fire ... a gun loaded with snipe-shot.[1]

> The whole vast country is covered like a network by a most efficient system of patrolling. A map of the North-West indicating the posts, outposts and patrols of the North-West Mounted Police, looks as if the country were covered with a series of cobwebs, the larger ones representing the divisional posts and their patrols, the smaller the outposts or detachments and theirs.[2]

The two organizations were among the best-known constabularies in the late-nineteenth-century British Empire if not the world. They also were important experiments in state authority. The North-West Mounted Police (NWMP) was formed in 1873 and survived a change of government in 1896 and the creation of the provinces of Saskatchewan and Alberta in 1905. Awarded the prefix "Royal" in 1904, the regional force merged with the Dominion Police in 1920 to produce a constabulary more national in character, the Royal Canadian Mounted Police (RCMP), whose duties included security and intelligence. The scarlet tunics of the riders of the plains figured prominently in popular fiction, radio, and film. The force has also been an irresistible topic for producers and consumers of popular history; witness the recent tome on how the Mounties "conquered the West."[3]

The Irish Constabulary had its antecedents in Napoleonic-era police reforms. The British government restructured Irish policing in 1836 by joining the constabulary, organized in 1822, with the Peace Preservation Force set up by Peel in 1814. More than one commentator argued that the Irish Constabulary was the prototype of the NWMP and other imperial forces.[4] According to travel writer Sir Francis Bond Head, governor of Upper Canada in 1837, a map depicting constabulary post locations in 1852 resembled a target peppered with shotgun pellets. The force, which became the Royal Irish Constabulary (RIC) in 1867 in recognition of service against the Fenians, was dismantled in 1922 with the termination of the Anglo-Irish War. The Free State formed an unarmed civic guard, the *Garda Siochana*. Ulster, which remained under British control, retained a successor of the RIC known as the Royal Ulster Constabulary (RUC), which to this day polices the Six Counties. In 2001, as a result of the Good Friday Agreement, the RUC's name was changed to the Police Service of Northern Ireland.[5]

This chapter compares and contrasts the RIC and the NWMP, in terms of recruitment, training, conditions of service, and relations with the public, from 1867 to 1922. Both were paramilitary forces imposed by colonial regimes to deal with the legal, security, and bureaucratic administration of territories that can be considered frontiers of the British Empire. Both met resistance, but both also performed useful service functions for the local population. Changing political circumstances spelled the demise of the RIC in 1922, whereas in 1920 the NWMP, in becoming the RCMP, began its transformation from a regional rural constabulary to a truly national police force.

The bulk of writing on the Mounties has been filiopietistic, creating a powerful symbol for a nation in need of unifying mythology.[6] Since the 1960s, journalists and academics investigating security and intelligence policy, labour history, and minority relations have tarnished the institution's armour. A greater sensitivity to First Nations history and culture in particular challenges the more benign image of the Mounties in the west and north. As Morrison explains in the case of the Yukon, the Mounted Police was an institution of Canadian imperialism. But the overall reputation of the NWMP remained sufficiently positive to be commodified for several years in the late twentieth century through Disney Corporation marketing. This image is in part the result of a skilful public relations campaign by the Mounties.[7]

Within Great Britain and the white settler dominions, the RIC circa 1900 was generally regarded as disciplined and professional, the ideal model for dealing with problem rural populations, especially in colonial or frontier situations.[8] Because of the organization's role in maintaining Protestant dominance, landlordism, and the British connection, its historiography, at least in Ireland, has traditionally been one-sided. In contrast to the Mounted Police, the Irish Constabulary has fulfilled a negative role in national historical myth. Historians in the Irish Republic until recently failed to examine the RIC in any detailed or balanced fashion. Perhaps its heavily Catholic nature embarrassed nationalist sensibilities by suggesting too complex a version of the past. Whatever the reason, much of the interesting work on Irish policing is being done by American and British historians.[9] Canadian police studies can benefit from a comparative approach. The excellent volume *Policing the Empire,* edited by Anderson and Killingray (see note 4), did not really do full justice to the Canadian dimensions of imperial policing. The following examines the NWMP and the RIC in terms of recruitment, training, promotion, conditions of service, and relations with the public. The last area, which could generate an extensive study in its own right, will be an overview. The evidence is taken from contemporary published accounts, the annual reports of the NWMP/RNWMP (Royal North-West Mounted Police), Canadian parliamentary debates, and four detailed inquiries into the pay and working conditions of the RIC between 1872 and 1914.[10]

Recruitment

The RIC, which prided itself on a high standard of recruiting, hired over 16,000 men from 1872 to 1890. According to Brady, it was "a native force, raised from the sturdier elements of the peasantry and rigorously drilled, trained and officered by Englishmen."[11] As with the Dublin Metropolitan Police and many English constabularies, the Irish Constabulary preferred sons of the soil. In 1909, Commissioner C.W. Leatham, who joined in 1866, wrote that recruits tended to be "the sons of farmers, and the sons of members of the force, or of RIC pensioners." From 1895 to 1901, roughly 10 percent of recruits were sons of policemen.[12] Inspector General Neville Chamberlain testified in 1914 that the "labouring classes" did not meet RIC standards and that he preferred not to recruit British army veterans into the police rank and file, largely because of their lack of respectability.[13]

Some commentators have disputed the reported professionalism of the force. Townshend, commenting on the militaristic qualities of the RIC, its emphasis on physical size, and promotion by seniority, notes that the "amiable slow-wittedness" of RIC constables "was legendary."[14] Leatham, in an assessment reminiscent of a colonialist in Africa or India, depicted the RIC as "essentially an Irish force, with all the distinctive qualities of national character." Fortunately, as with Irish soldiers, the faults of the rank and file could be "refined by discipline and the virtues trained and elevated for a worthy purpose."[15] An English police official agreed in 1914 that both the Welsh and the Irish excelled at drill. In the words of an inquiry commissioner, this was part of the "Celtic instinct."[16]

Certain areas of Ireland, as Lowe notes, produced larger percentages of recruits. This pattern was inherited by the twentieth-century *Garda,* which developed a tradition of enlistment "from along the west and southwest coast."[17] The poorer and more isolated areas, such as the west, seem to have produced more recruits. According to Head Constable John Chalke, testifying in 1882, few joined from Belfast, whose industrial economy provided alternative employment opportunities.[18] Recruits generally were not posted to home areas or counties but to their native provinces – a concession to regional feeling.[19]

Despite its elite image, the constabulary experienced periodic recruiting difficulties relating to emigration patterns, the political situation, and dissatisfaction with wages and benefits. A paucity of first-class candidates was evident in the early 1870s, the mid-1880s, and prior to the First World War. Several officers complained in 1872 that a relative shortage of preferred recruits was bringing more farm labourers, as opposed to farmers' sons, into the force.[20] Roughly 1,500 men resigned from 1870 to 1872 and nearly 700, most of them Catholic, from 1907 to October 1912. Chamberlain opined in 1914 that many young recruits were "distinctly inferior material" in terms of physique and education. County inspectors attributed the attrition of personnel and the shortage of recruits to political uncertainty, the increasing cost of living, better opportunities in British and colonial police forces, and the desire of farmers who had purchased their farms to keep their sons on as labourers. Inspector General Stewart Wood noted in 1872 that many young constables, after five years of experience, left for America or the colonies or were recruited by English police forces. Years later an unofficial organ, the *Constabulary Gazette,* portrayed England, America, and the empire as an "El Dorado" for young Irish policemen.[21]

The NWMP, in the planning stages, was envisioned as a Native force. Prior to the first Métis resistance of 1869-70, Prime Minister Macdonald had thought of the Mounted Police as largely Métis or mixed-blood, following British practice in India, the West Indies, and Africa, where security forces were officered by Europeans but recruited from the local population. The establishment of Riel's provisional government, the execution of Canadian Thomas Scott, and continued tensions between mixed-bloods and Ontario settlers made this plan politically untenable. A few Métis and Natives were hired as NWMP scouts, guides, and interpreters. Neither the armed Indian scouts who accompanied patrols in the late 1880s (and made a small number of arrests) nor the "specials" on Poundmaker's Cree reserve were regarded as real police. In the 1890s, only trustworthy Bloods and Blackfoot were employed as scouts. The NWMP commissioner found them "zealous and useful in every way." Despite the employment of special constables, Canada never developed a tradition of Native policing as found in the United States and Australia.[22]

The NWMP consisted principally of Canadians as well as British immigrants and a few Americans. The popular image was that of an imperial foreign legion, and three of the first five commissioners were British born. Yet the NWMP tended to be native born. Ethnically, the police included "the strong blood of the Anglo-Saxon" with "a dash of the Teuton or the Gaul."[23] Despite this last reference, French Canadian recruits, the government admitted on more than one occasion, were rare.[24]

The Mounties, as their romanticizers suggested, were hand picked but usually within the context of contemporary public employment channels;

patronage generally was not handed out to immigrants just off the boat. The memoirs of Superintendent Burton Deane (himself a beneficiary of "connections") mention that many Conservatives left the force after the 1896 Liberal victory and that senior officers were often political appointees. In his opinion, the force had developed into a "philanthropic organization" for friends of the government. Both Commissioners Herchmer and Perry were appointed for reasons of political influence, and under the Liberals (1896-1911) the Territories "were a sort of private game reserve operated principally in the interests of the Sifton family, the prominent member of which was the Minister of the Interior in the Dominion Cabinet."[25] Prospective recruits who travelled beyond Ontario were less beholden to MPs, party fundraisers, newspaper editors, and other patronage brokers.[26]

The physical requirements for service in the Mounties were more onerous than those of the British army. Canada's militia commandant favoured rural recruits "who are better fitted for the rough-and-ready open-air than those from the town." In Major General Selby Smith's view, clerks and "decayed" gentlemen were unsuitable.[27] Recruiters emphasized size, strength, and health. The wife of an officer offered a Kiplingesque depiction of the average constable in the 1890s. One of "nature's children," he loved horses, dogs, guns, athletics, and fighting. The Mountie's barrack-room vices of drink, habitual gambling, and "heart-rendering" language were more than compensated for by his resourcefulness, bravery, and sense of duty.[28]

Of enlistees in the original six NWMP divisions of 1874, a majority claimed military, militia, or police experience (some of the militiamen had been posted in Manitoba). All recruits in theory had to possess equestrian skills, but many appear "to have rated their abilities in this line too highly." Many of the several hundred constables hired following the troubles of 1885 were "unable to ride, and unaccustomed to horses."[29] As was the case with Union cavalry recruits during the Civil War, rural and urban Canadians did not ride horses but used them to pull wagons and other conveyances.

The NWMP, a fraction of the size of the RIC, required few replacements in a given year. In 1882, following complaints that many recruits were "mere lads," the minimum age was raised to twenty-one. Previously, the government had raised the term of enlistment from three to five years in order to make the recruit both "a thorough cavalry soldier" and an efficient policeman.[30]

Compared to the RIC (but not to many English constabularies), the Mounties were somewhat mixed in terms of previous occupations. The top three backgrounds of recruits until the early 1900s were skilled worker, farmer, and clerk. Together these categories formed over 70 percent of the total.[31]

The composition of the force was partly related to the timing of recruitment. During periods of rapid expansion, or high wages, standards declined. The dominion government augmented the force to 500 in the early 1880s, then to over 1,000 in the late 1880s because of Métis and First Nations unrest. Edward Blake in 1882 offered the standard Liberal critique that the NWMP was too large, that the white population of the west must police itself, and that the militia could be relied upon in emergencies.[32]

In the late 1890s, after the NWMP expansion into the Yukon Territory and with police enlisting to serve in the South African War, there were fewer than 800 men in all ranks. Annual "wastage" was 10 percent. The early Yukon detachments depleted experienced men from the Prairies. During the 1890s, the force depended largely on re-enlistments to maintain its strength (66 percent of "new" men in the period 1895-99); recruits who survived the probationary period were a minority. After 1885, many recruits were British born. By the early twentieth century, first-class candidates became increasingly difficult to find. Dismissal and desertion rates climbed, and many experienced men purchased their discharges. Two-thirds of the force in 1905 had served under five years, half of it for less than four. During the pre–First World War boom, with civilian wages high, the force experienced a shortage of re-enlistments and first-class recruits. The RNWMP obtained special permission to recruit in Britain. In 1912 and 1913, a majority of nearly 500 new members had been born in Great Britain, and most of them appear to have been English rather than Scots or Irish.[33]

Compared to the RIC, the Mounties were relatively top heavy. Because of the NWMP's military organization and capabilities, its officer corps was somewhat socially exclusive. Commissions went to militia leaders, Royal Military College graduates, ex–British army officers, and other "gentlemen." Senior officers, until the early twentieth century, were assigned servants. Young men belonging to better families were more likely to enjoy personal and political connections. Individuals with gentlemanly qualities were preferred. The NWMP partly followed the English and North American pattern of advancement through the ranks, but its lower ranks included many "respectable" noncommissioned officers (NCOs) and officer candidates (see the section on promotion below).[34]

Training

Both forces had extensive training regimens compared to Anglo-American urban police. The emphasis on indoctrination and detailed training reflected the military ethos of senior officers. The RIC inspectors general were, with one exception, military men. The emphasis on drill, field exercises, and rifle and bayonet proficiency did not always sit well with rankers. The RIC had a reputation for being overly bureaucratic and obsessed with formalities, such as keeping the barracks diary and memorizing acts of Parliament (commentators also poked fun at the excessive paperwork of the Mounted Police, whose patrol sheets had to be signed by settlers).[35]

Prospective RIC recruits first applied to the local barracks. If successful, they were examined medically and subjected to six months of training, which included military and physical drill, firearms proficiency, police duties, and first aid. Constables were expected to continue to study the constabulary code and law on a daily basis. Officer cadets, who tended to come from professional, judicial, and clerical families, were trained more systematically at "the first police academy in the British Isles" in Dublin. After passing a competitive examination drawing on knowledge of Latin, French, English, mathematics, and law, cadets were quartered at the Phoenix Park depot – with one orderly for every four gentlemen. Here they were instructed in riding, veterinary science, musket and company drill, accounting, shorthand, and report writing.

Social life at the depot was particularly important and included cricket, football, and racquet sports and mess activities, pranks, and hazing rituals. Much of the cadet training appears to have been dedicated to inculcating confidence, a casual, gentlemanly style, and an attitude of *noblesse oblige* that would curry favour with the local gentry, clergy, and professionals. Officers were mounted and provided with a personal orderly. Following his formal training, the cadet was apprenticed for a time under a county inspector. Freshly minted district inspectors appear to have relied heavily on their head constables.[36]

Training in the NWMP took on a more militaristic tone with the opening of the Regina depot in 1882. Recruits trained for six months at Regina, and British NCOs (royal marines and cavalry) were the preferred instructors. In the 1890s, enlistees were trained in all aspects of riding, harnessing, shoeing, and saddling horses; veterinary science; firearms; drill; general police duties; and the *Criminal Code,* criminal statutes, and prosecutions. As an "efficient prairie man," the Mountie also had to know how to cook, mend, and repair.[37] Mounted infantry drill was introduced by Commissioner Herchmer. John Donkin, who had served with the 17th Lancers in Ireland, found the discipline strict at Regina and the winter an "everlasting program" of drilling and riding.[38]

Promotion

The RIC, as the British Empire's largest constabulary, had a constant turnover in personnel and corresponding chances for promotion. In 1905, it consisted of the inspector general; the deputy inspector general and 3 assistants; 37 county inspectors; 200 district inspectors; and roughly 10,000 head constables, sergeants, acting sergeants, and constables. According to one witness in 1901, promotion was more common in disaffected counties such as Clare, Galway, Kerry, Mayo, and Wicklow. Rank-and-file resentment over advancement often fixated on the officer class, which, although becoming more open in the mid-1890s, continued to perpetuate "rigid social distinctions between officers and men."[39]

The most important officers were the county inspectors, who, in the words of Chamberlain, acted as "the executive officers of the government in a county." Prior to the mid-1840s, all officers were commissioned. The cadet system was introduced to fill the rank of subinspectors. Most cadets were Anglo-Irish; their critics (who included their own NCOs) portrayed them as callow and pompous rejects from British military schools. The head constables believed that they themselves provided the real continuity in rural districts. By the 1870s, more "rankers" were succeeding to the rank of subinspector, but most officers clung to an elitist view. Subinspector Henry Arthur Blake, Tipperary, testified in 1872 that an educated officer class ensured that "police supervision does not become police tyranny." Others argued that magistrates would lose confidence in officers appointed from the ranks. After the reforms of 1895, one-half of the commissioned ranks came from the rank and file. Yet at the elite level, the traditions of the officer class persisted, fuelling rank-and-file discontent.[40]

"Rankers" tended to endorse the classic trade union doctrine of promotion by seniority and appointment of officers from the ranks. The Monck Commission, aware of the success of the English police model, suggested greater reliance on the lower ranks, if only for purposes of economy. The typical constable received his sergeant's promotion after fifteen years of service; a district inspector waited roughly twenty-five years before promotion to county inspector.[41] Because RIC detachments were so numerous, there was a high demand for sergeants. Appointment to the upper ranks was more elusive. The traditional view, found in the 1882 committee report, favoured a predominance of officer cadets possessing "habits of command and perfect tact, qualities with which education and social training have a good deal to say."[42] Others suggested that rankers lacked the casual attitude that characterized a true officer. Subconstable Patrick McKeon of County Sligo explained that officers from the ranks were not gentlemen and hence annoyed the men. Chamberlain personally favoured promotion from the ranks but not at the expense of the controversial "P list," a pool of promising junior constables fast-tracked into more responsible positions. The 1914 commissioners balked at suggestions that promotions be made totally on the basis of seniority.[43]

The inquiries of 1872, 1882, 1901, and 1914 indicate that advancements to sergeant and head constable were matters of intense interest to the rank and file. Although competitive exams were instituted, Catholics complained that Protestants held an unfair advantage.[44] According to a 1906 pamphleteer, county and district inspectors (whose recommendations were crucial for constables' promotions) tended to support fellow Protestants. So did the "Protestant and Freemason influence" (gentry, ministers, professionals) of the counties: "We find every Protestant becoming a Freemason as soon as he begins to think of promotion." Membership in secret societies was officially banned, but Catholics, prohibited by their church from joining the Masonic order, were convinced that Masons enjoyed promotions and favourable transfers. The chief secretary attempted to increase the number of Catholic district inspectors in the late 1890s, but, in the opinion of the pamphleteer, Dublin Castle "set about rendering the new system as ineffective as possible."[45] According to an Antrim-based constable, recruits in the north by 1914 were usually "rabid Orangemen or low-class Ribbonmen."[46]

The NWMP, despite its popular reputation, was not a pure meritocracy. Many officers and NCOs, like most ambitious Protestants in Canada, were Freemasons (hence the sobriquet "Royal Canadian Masonic Police").[47] Religious tensions, for example over issues such as separate schools, were not unknown in the North-West. Nevertheless, as in the London Metropolitan Police, once the force was established many officers were promoted by "merit." The latter, of course, was decided by members of the federal cabinet in Ottawa.[48] Macdonald explained in 1889 that "we take from the non-commissioned officers the most deserving." NCOs, the prime minister explained, were knowledgeable about the west and Indians and their customs. Roughly half of the officers (nonmedical officers then numbered fewer than fifty) had been appointed from the ranks. Others came from the active militia or Canada's Royal Military College. Rankers formed a similar proportion of the officer cadre two decades later, a pattern that paralleled that of the Irish Constabulary. The limited number of officer positions probably generated much bitterness over commissions and promotions; one superintendent wrote that Royal Irish Constabulary officers were in a much better position in terms of advancement.[49] It was not socially demeaning for a middle-class Canadian to join the Mounted Police. The NWMP, in contrast to the RIC and most other police forces, accepted "sons of gentlemen" and educated individuals in the ranks. This, according to Macdonald, made it a *corps d'élite*.[50]

Conditions of Service

Historical accounts offer conflicting assessments of the policeman's lot in Ireland. On the one hand, there is the image of a highly regimented and isolated gendarmerie subjected to a bureaucracy that allowed constables "less freedom than a ticket-of-leave suspect."[51] In theory, the Victorian RIC were never off duty or allowed to don civilian garb. Constables were forbidden from marrying during their first seven years, and prospective wives were screened by senior officers. The police could not play cards in barracks and prior to the early 1900s, unlike the English police, were prohibited from entering public houses except in the line of duty. Their wives were not allowed to engage in trade, such as dressmaking or store keeping, and their families could not take in lodgers. Single men had to live in the barracks. Moreover, the Irish police were subjected to a constant round of inconvenient and costly transfers.[52]

On the other hand, because the RIC was so numerous and a barrack-based organization, a typical day was not physically demanding. Rural policemen, who patrolled at the most four hours each day, were idle most of the time. A Newmarket district inspector described the two-man patrol as "practically a walking exercise." The remainder of the day was spent in drill, parade, report writing, and other station duties. Rural night patrol was rare. The pub rule was widely disobeyed. Urban postings, in Belfast and Derry, and to a lesser extent Cork, Limerick, and Waterford, were more exacting. The district inspector visited periodically; the county inspector arrived but a few times each year. The memoirs of Constable Jeremiah Mee suggest that station sergeants told Dublin Castle "what it wanted to hear" in terms of official reports. In the words of William Britton, who joined in 1918, "it all depends, in a small station, on the sergeant." Life in the typical rural barracks was anything but exciting – at least during periods of relative calm. There were other benefits as well. Single men lived in the barracks for free prior to 1883, and all RIC members and their families were eligible for free medical attendance. Paid leave was introduced in 1901.[53]

By 1909, roughly 1,400 constabulary posts dotted Ireland. The barracks was as much a disciplinary device as shelter from a hostile populace. Some of the urban barracks were large and generated considerable economic spin-offs; each of Belfast's two dozen stations in the 1880s, for example, had its own baker, butcher, grocer, fuel supplier, and servants. The typical rural or village barracks, housing a sergeant and three men, was a rented dwelling containing a kitchen, a messroom, a day room, and sleeping quarters. By 1914, nearly half of the stations housed between five and nine men each, and two-fifths held fewer than five each. Only one family (usually the sergeant's) was allowed to a barracks. Premises were often crowded, unsanitary, and very public. Urban police families rubbed elbows with drunks and prostitutes. Again conditions in the countryside were different. As is portrayed in the play *Upstarts,* set in a rural *Garda* station in the 1950s, the lockup was probably the least important room in the barracks.[54]

Testimony before the committees of 1882 and 1901 suggests that married men experienced considerable difficulties. Recruits were not free to marry until advancing from subconstable to constable. In 1882, the RIC contained 3,600 married men; four-sevenths of them lived out of and the remainder in the barracks with their families. Teenage daughters were forced to board outside. According to witnesses in 1882 and 1901, urban posts were more popular for family reasons; the rural barracks were isolated, and schooling was more difficult to arrange. Married men (obliged to reside in proximity to the station and report every few hours), although given a housing allowance, complained of high rents, costly provisions, and indebtedness. The incidence of marriage rose with rank; in 1882, six-sevenths of the subconstables were unmarried, compared to only one-third of the constables.[55] According to one county inspector in 1901, a married man's status depended on "the character of the wife's arrangement" (dowry/inheritance) and the number of children. Officers believed that they should discourage "improvident" marriages. In 1880s Belfast, the police, attempting to remain respectable, tended to avoid marrying into the millworker class. The depot commandant suggested in 1901 that policemen often married "the wrong sort" – shop girls, dressmakers, and schoolteachers, who were allegedly inferior housekeepers.[56]

The Irish police force was considered desirable employment for much of the late-Victorian period; its attrition rate was far below that of the English police force. Yet the rank and file grumbled about pay and benefits.[57] Administrators and British politicians tended to respond that Ireland was largely an agricultural, low-wage country and that remuneration should be governed accordingly. They also pointed out that the police pension (the service pension dated back to 1836) brought an element of security unknown to most Irish workers. The rank and file employed their elite reputation to demand parity with English constabularies and pension reform. Retirement on full pay necessitated thirty years of service; by 1883, retirement on two-thirds pay was possible after twenty-five years.[58]

In 1883, the rank and file lobbied for a raise to the level of "the artisan class" and to compensate for the severity of police duties. The commissioners concluded that pay rates were adequate because of the low cost of living and rejected the artisan analogy, arguing that the police wages were virtually guaranteed. There were slight increments for senior constables and sergeants in 1908, but the rank and file continued to remonstrate for a major raise. Two witnesses in 1914 cited Pope Leo XIII on the social and moral obligations of paying workers a living wage.[59]

Discipline was a source of grievance in all police forces, largely for its impact on promotion. The RIC disciplinary code was detailed and extended to the employee's private life. One cause of unfavourable records, for example, was indebtedness. The 1882 hearings reflected the rankers' dissatisfaction with fines and records of punishment for interfering with promotion, favourable transfer, pensions, and widows' gratuities. Some rankers supported the right of the accused at disciplinary tribunals to be represented by legal counsel with power to examine and cross-examine witnesses. The rank and file also appear to have resented the authority of the resident magistrates.[60]

The NWMP operated through militaristic internal regulations adapted from the RIC's. Policemen could not only be fined but also arrested and jailed for disciplinary infractions.[61] Despite such controls, drunkenness, desertion, and other problems were not unknown. In less than three years, two-thirds of the "originals" resigned, deserted, or were dismissed. In 1883, poor rations, conditions, and morale at Fort Macleod resulted in a near mutiny by the ranks; earlier a French Canadian inspector had lost control of his men at Fort Calgary.[62] Although actual disciplinary policy was mild, NWMP members were never given the chance to speak at formal hearings, as were Irish police. Instead, they looked to sympathetic politicians and journalists. In the late 1880s, N.F. Davin, MP, made the strict disciplinary style of the force the basis of his attack on Commissioner L.W. Herchmer. Under the *Mounted Police Act,* he charged, the commissioner had enormous powers; individuals had been imprisoned for twelve months for drunkenness, then dismissed.[63]

According to NWMP historian J.P. Turner, the "bubble" burst in 1891-92 when the accumulated grievances of both officers and men against Herchmer led to a judicial inquiry. Among the over one hundred allegations were that the commissioner had displayed political partisanship, promoted inexperienced over senior members, interfered with an officer's magisterial duties, and sent spies to check on district commanders. In a speech in Parliament, Davin suggested that the force discriminated against French Canadians. Although the judge cleared Herchmer of any major malfeasance, the reputation of Canada's "finest" suffered.[64]

The remuneration of the NWMP, although superior to that of the RIC, in the context of Canadian society was not overly generous, particularly after the pay cut of the early 1880s. Constables in 1884 earned between fifty and seventy-five cents per day, sergeants up to one dollar. Each troop was provided with a number of artisans, such as carpenter, baker, tailor, and blacksmith, but frontier conditions required the Mounties to be self-sufficient. Fatigue duty, according to Donkin, was heavy. Although barracks food was plentiful, constables lost weight when on patrol.[65] The strenuous nature of Mounted Police life and the resulting numerous applications for purchasing discharges were cited by Macdonald in 1885 when he announced that the force would be doubled in size.[66] Of the 663 men who exited between 1895 and 1899, one-fifth purchased discharges, and one-half left upon expiry of their enlistment terms.[67]

The NWMP, like the RIC, discriminated against married men. Recruits had to serve seven years before seeking permission to marry, and commanders could conduct background checks on their prospective brides. Those men who did marry, according to Davin in 1891, were burdened with disruptive and expensive transfers from post to post. Post life was hard on women. Like those of RIC families, Mounted Police family quarters often included cells for prisoners.[68]

RIC veterans differed in one important respect from English, Canadian, and American policemen: their chances of a second career were limited.

This became more and more apparent by the early twentieth century. Rank-and-file testimony before the commissions of inquiry echoes this complaint and indicates that policemen began planning for civilian life several years before retirement. Outside Ulster, many potential employers were hostile toward police pensioners. If the latter worked at all, it was usually a socially demeaning occupation such as messenger, process server, gatekeeper, custodian, janitor, or porter. Of the roughly 5,500 pensioners who lived beyond Dublin in 1901, only half were employed, and half of them ran their own businesses such as shops or pubs. Some inherited or purchased farms from parents or in-laws. As of 1914, there were 1,000 additional pensioners outside Dublin, and the proportion of unemployed, employed, and self-employed remained the same. As one constable explained to the 1901 commissioners, RIC duties were often directed not at criminals but at "men of good social and political position" (i.e., nationalists), a factor that lessened prospects in "after life." The fact that pensioners had to report to the local barracks on a regular basis probably did not endear them to the local population, which regarded them as possible informers. Employment prospects were slight in the west of Ireland, particularly after land reform. According to a Donegal policeman, by 1914 the breaking up of the great estates and the decline of the gentry "deprived the country of a good many persons who might employ the police in the old days."[69]

The opportunities for veterans of the NWMP could hardly have been more different. Many, if not most, recruits did not enter the force in search of a career in policing. The government consistently viewed discharged police veterans as desirable settlers in the region. Original enlistees were promised land grants at the end of their terms. William Francis Butler, in *The Great Lone Land* (1872), had suggested that ex-police given land as "military settlers" would form a reserve security force.[70] Opponents of pay increases and pensions traditionally opined that men enlisted principally to establish themselves in farming, ranching, or business in the west. Economy-minded Liberal MPs from Ontario preferred this constant turnover to a rigid and expensive pension system that would make career constables "utterly unfit" for civilian employment. By the turn of the century, an estimated 4,000 individuals had been recruited into the organization, and many had settled in the North-West. In 1913, during a period of high wages, 10 percent of the force purchased discharges "to work in civilian life." Another 7 percent deserted.[71]

One attempt at lessening turnover and raising morale was the 1889 NWMP pension bill, modelled on RIC policy. At this time, retirees had only a modest gratuity based on years of service, and men injured in the line of duty benefited from a small fund.[72] Of the officers who left the force from 1873 to 1909, 42 percent resigned, 23 percent died, 19.6 percent retired with a gratuity, and only 6.5 percent received a pension.[73]

Relations with the Public

The size of the NWMP patrol area was often vast by European standards; outposts manned by NCOs and constables could be a hundred miles from the nearest officer. The commissioner wrote in 1899 that his men could be "trusted anywhere without supervision." During the frontier stage, such isolation made the police "virtually a separate government."[74] The late-Victorian Mounted Police, however, were not thin on the ground in terms of population. In 1896, the force numbered 750, including 70 "specials" (dog drivers, cooks, artisans, and guides – white, First Nations, and Métis). Expansion in the Yukon Territory in the late 1890s, whose population surged to 20,000, caused a further reduction on the Prairies, where the population had doubled during the decade. In 1900, the ratio of police to white population in the Yukon met "police state" proportions of 1 to 79. The ratio of police to population for the "organized" North-West Territories in 1901 was 1 to 350 according to Commissioner Perry. By 1905, there were ten divisional headquarters containing over a hundred permanent outposts.[75]

The NWMP shared another important characteristic with the RIC: it was armed. Popular culture suggested that the archetypal Mountie regarded use of guns as "un-British"; anecdotal evidence suggests otherwise.[76] The original weapons were the Snider carbine and Adams revolver (part of the column on the Great March carried lances). These were followed in the 1880s by Winchester repeating rifles and Enfield revolvers. Prior to the Riel Rebellion, the force was equipped with four small field guns and two mortars. The police arsenal in the Yukon in 1896 included machine guns, Winchester and Lee-Metford carbines, and Enfield and Smith and Wesson revolvers. In 1903, the government decided to issue the controversial Canadian-made Ross rifle. In the early years, recruits were better at shooting than they were at riding. According to Chambers, Canadians had "natural aptitude" with firearms, yet target practice occurred only once each year.[77]

The Mounties tended to categorize the west's population into three groups: First Nations, Métis, and white settlers. The immediate task of the police in 1874 was to stop the cross-border liquor traffic ravaging the First Nations. From 1878 to 1884, nonwhites, although an absolute majority in the west, constituted less than 30 percent of the "criminal and other cases" registered by the NWMP. In other words, in the early years, most recorded crime was committed by the settlers – another contrast with the situation in Ireland. Most accounts suggest that Indian crime was both underreported and underprosecuted. This discretionary response to Aboriginal misbehaviour continued in later years.[78]

Depictions of First Nations and mixed-blood individuals in Donkin's *Trooper and Redskin in the Far Northwest* (1889) are negative at worst, romanticized at best.[79] Yet official reports reflect ongoing sympathy with the First Nations, except for leaders who caused political or security trouble. The

Indian question, as far as the police were concerned, was two-sided. In keeping with the force's original mandate, First Nations had to be protected from violent or predatory whites. Throughout the 1870s, the NWMP helped to expedite the treaty-making process; it would continue to escort bands to reserves, help distribute annuities and other payments, periodically enforce the reserve pass system, and generally aid the Indian agents. It also assisted with emergency rations and vaccinations and helped Métis with jobs and food on an ad hoc basis.[80]

Prior to the 1885 rebellion, there were worries that the NWMP's decentralized deployment would make it militarily ineffective in a genuine crisis. During the early 1880s, police reports had warned Ottawa of the suffering and dissatisfaction of First Nations and the economic and cultural anxieties of Métis. The shooting started near Duck Lake when a police/volunteer party attempted to secure stores. Métis fighters defeated the police but allowed them to evacuate Fort Pitt. Seventy-five Mounties fought against the Cree at Cutknife Hill; others skirmished north of Frenchman's Butte. Total police casualties during the resistance amounted to eight dead and six wounded.[81]

The direct military contribution of the police was limited, but their role in managing, largely by default, the powerful Blackfoot Confederacy of southern Alberta was an important strategic determinant in 1885. The conditions that created First Nations unrest in the 1880s, namely the disappearance of the Canadian buffalo and the arrival of the railway, ultimately guaranteed the success of the police. Indian agents empowered as magistrates, working directly or through chiefs, also provided a police function on reserves in the post-1885 period. The commissioner in 1897 suggested a greater use of Indian special constables, and First Nations constables hired by the Indian Department, but for reserve populations the NWMP remained the ultimate coercive threat.[82]

The Conservative government successfully connected the NWMP to the overall National Policy strategy for western development. In 1879, returning from opposition, the Tories transferred responsibility for the police from Justice to the Department of the Interior, which also oversaw dominion lands, western territories, and Indian affairs. Opposition Liberals called for scaling down or dismantling what they viewed as a wasteful, authoritarian patronage machine. By the 1890s, the argument went, a system of treaties, reserves, Indian agents, farm instructors, and schools effectively controlled the Prairie First Nations. Yet the minister of the interior in 1892 pointed to the American Ghost Dance movement as proof of the need for further vigilance. Indians, Commissioner Herchmer noted, were peaceful for the most part, but many persisted in carrying large ammunition belts and repeater rifles. In 1888, after the British Columbia government asked for federal assistance in dealing with the Kootenai First Nation, the NWMP located a temporary force in the area. The Charcoal and Almighty Voice murders (the latter killed three policemen) added to continuing anxieties about frontier security. The Conservatives, and NWMP commanders, repeated Macdonald's favourite argument that it was much cheaper to contain the tribes through a small police than through a large, provocative military establishment such as the United States cavalry.[83]

The police buffer also assisted settlers and ranchers and protected railway construction crews and Hudson's Bay Company posts from Indian interference. Part of this work involved scouting for lost and stolen horses and cattle and generally exploring for water, timber, and other resources. Indians were escorted from ranchland, and stolen livestock in their possession was returned without charges. In the 1880s and 1890s, the police assisted the Canadian Pacific Railway in protecting road crews and quelling labour troubles, but it also intervened on behalf of workers' wage disputes. Rounding up stray cattle, providing veterinary services, distributing seed grain and rations to distressed settlers, fighting prairie fires, and nursing sick children rounded out the force's service activities. Such administrative duties, which the modern police professional finds objectionable, actually enhanced the power of the Mounted Police. Like RIC documents filed away in Dublin Castle, NWMP district reports were sent to divisional headquarters and the commissioner on a regular basis.[84]

The overrepresentation in arrest statistics of whites, at first a minority in the North-West, seems to fly in the face of the model of a colonial police force, which was supposed to reinforce minority rule. Culturally, the police were identical to the mass of white settlers, with whom they were genuinely popular. Haydon, writing at the high tide of imperialism, attributed this popular response to the style of policing. The NWMP, in the best traditions of the "British race," did its work "silently, unostentatiously and efficiently."[85] The police, increasingly, were living in closer proximity to greater numbers of white settlers, who, the commissioner noted, rustled far more cattle than did the Indians.[86]

Police culture, barracks life, and a militaristic ethos created typical occupational distance from the public. Donkin confided that the police "nurtured a most thorough contempt for civilians." Yet the police force was not a self-contained institution: a large number of time-expired men "contributed to the North-West some of its very best settlers and citizens." Canteens eventually were introduced partly as a control device to shield off-duty police from civilians. The gulf between police and civilians widened when the government recruited Galician, Doukhobor, and other non-British settlers. By the early twentieth century, police reports would differentiate between Canadian and British settlers and "foreigners."[87]

The one exception to the force's positive relations with settlers was its enforcement of the North-West Territories liquor law, originally enacted to prevent the sale of alcohol to the Indians. The more settled the west became, the greater the difficulties in enforcing the dry law. As in other jurisdictions, the police relied on informers for successful prosecutions. Most division commanders, however, personally opposed the prohibition ordinance as damaging to police legitimacy.[88] The issue was complicated by the fact that senior police officers doubled as magistrates, a situation common in nonwhite colonial situations but rare in Canada. NWMP supporters such as Sir John Thompson cited the fact that police officers performed the bulk of magisterial duties in the territory as one of the reasons to prolong the life of the institution. A parliamentary critic responded that this system was more suited "to a country under military law."[89]

Mounted Police duties increased with settlement and greater prosperity. In the 1890s, patrols visited individual farms and ranches and generally reported on the condition of the district, noting details such as crop yields, floods, and wage levels for farm labourers. With security issues relating to First Nations and Métis receding in importance, the police shouldered "more civil undertakings." For the Manitoba border patrol in the early 1890s, these duties included acting as subcollectors and preventive officers for the Customs Department. The Departments of Agriculture and the Interior, as well as the Indian Department, were also assisted. When agricultural settlement moved into the Peace and Mackenzie River districts, the police were there. Prime Minister Laurier explained the reversal of Liberal policy toward the force in utilitarian terms: "The duties of these men are not those of ordinary policemen."[90]

The service function was coupled with order maintenance and crime control. From 1900 to 1909, peak years in the settling of the "Last Best West," convictions outside Manitoba rose by a factor of sixteen. Like their urban counterparts, the NWMP were secure in the knowledge that magistrates (often their own officers) and juries, in 80-90 percent of the cases, would validate their initial arrest or summons with a conviction.[91]

At first glance, relations between the constabulary and the bulk of the Irish people seem to have been straightforward: mistrust, alienation, hostility, and violence. Victorian Ireland, after all, was the most heavily policed society in the British Empire, and the constabulary was viewed as a quasi-garrison. Although the population declined dramatically after 1849, the constabulary remained large, directly as a result of Britain's Irish policy. The RIC, Brady wrote, was "the backbone of British administration in rural Ireland for over a hundred years."[92] Chief Constable Walter Davis of Birkenhead was more circumspect: "The population of Ireland is less amenable to direction and control than that of England."[93] RIC men recognized their highly political role and attempted to use it to settle their pay, promotion, and pension grievances. Sergeant James McCawley of Dromore, County Down, stated in 1901 that the RIC was "doing the work of an army of occupation as well as a police force."[94]

Physical danger was a reality of RIC service, although its incidence can be exaggerated. Over time, the constabulary, like its Canadian counterpart, became less militaristic. Violence between police and populace peaked during the land agitations of the 1870s and 1880s. In 1887 at Mitchelstown, County Cork, the RIC fired on a disorderly crowd, killing two. After this incident, the police were instructed to first use their truncheons, and their carbines and bayonets only as a last resort.[95] Violence declined during the relatively peaceful 1890s and early 1900s, then increased dramatically when resistance turned into a shooting war. Scores of "old RIC" men (excluding the notorious Black and Tans recruited after the First World War) were killed or wounded during the Anglo-Irish War.

Carbines and bayonets were standard issue for the rank and file, and officers were equipped with swords and revolvers. Despite the RIC's acquisition of heavy arms and fortified barracks after 1916, its image as a heavily armed gendarmerie must be qualified. Even during rent strikes and eviction duty, the police were more apt to complain about billets, rations, and pay than violent opposition and injuries. By the 1880s, "musket" practice was conducted only once a year, and marksmanship appears to have been indifferent. The carrying of arms was common during the Land War and in 1890s Belfast, but the turn-of-the-century constable sported only a truncheon.[96] In Lowe's analysis, by this point the RIC (by now largely a Catholic body) had lost its earlier military edge. According to a witness before the 1901 inquiry, the dangers in Ireland were almost entirely agrarian and political. This was unfortunate for the police: violence of this type was legitimate conduct in the eyes of the rural classes. The police, for good reason, patrolled in pairs or larger groups.[97]

Where Protestants were in the majority, the police, who were largely Catholic, operated under no less anxiety. In Belfast, both Protestants and Catholics considered the RIC partisan. Edwards describes the constabulary as a "tough, not too scrupulous organization, whose personnel was necessarily embittered by the extent of its isolation from Irish life." But he concludes that the RIC, despite its overall mandate, had "certain standards" and "qualities of impartiality."[98] The latter were not always possible in the highly charged atmosphere of Belfast, where the RIC took over policing following sectarian riots in 1864. According to one officer, Belfast duty at the best of times was unpleasant: "tramping stones, breathing bad air and never seeing the sun except through smoke." Despite a heavy police presence, further disturbances took place in 1872, 1883, 1886, and 1907. The city had, in the words of one RIC sergeant, "an excitable public," particularly during the summer marching season.[99]

Catholics were convinced that the police were guilty of "flagrant partisanship" in favour of Protestants and resented the heavy representation of

Protestants above the rank of constable. The sectarian balance in the Belfast RIC, especially as of 1912, was a delicate matter. In a letter to the Catholic Vigilance Committee, the Belfast commissioner asserted that local promotions and postings were made on merit only, although related correspondence shows that senior officers were acutely conscious of "party feeling" in various neighbourhoods.[100] In the 1880s, according to one policeman, the substantial millworking class was openly hostile to the police, denying it access to the Shankhill area during sectarian rioting. A generation later antipathy against the police among the Protestant working class, and members of the Ulster Volunteer Force (UVF), was clearly visible. The UVF, fearing the implementation of home rule in 1913, planned to arrest the constabulary and seize its arms. The fledgling Ulster government in 1921 complained that the police were under the control of "an alien institution, namely Dublin Castle."[101]

A colonial police force, as Brewer explains, is identified more by an "operational role designed to impose an alien political authority" than "a benign service function or conventional crime fighting."[102] Policemen cognizant of their unpopularity argued that not all of it stemmed from grand political issues. The 1870 constabulary regulations advised police to round up vagrants and drunks, take deserted children to the workhouse, and prevent boys from whipping tops and rolling hoops in the public streets. One subinspector advised the Monck Commission that police enforcement of the road nuisance laws was counterproductive to building good relations with farmers.[103] Dublin Castle clearly valued the constabulary's political intelligence capabilities, but its other functions were no less important. In fact, the two intertwined. As Lowe notes, the RIC, like police elsewhere, was assigned a number of civil functions that drew it deeply into rural administration. These duties included conducting the census, preparing agricultural returns, suppressing swine fever and rabies, escorting convicts and prisoners, enumerating emigrants, combatting illicit distillation, enforcing customs regulations, inspecting weights and measures, assisting Congested Districts Boards, and enforcing a multitude of acts of Parliament. And criminal law, not political surveillance, seems to have "occupied a central place in the day-to-day activities of the police."[104]

The RIC was neither universally despised as traditional nationalism would have us believe nor as above reproach as imperial literature suggested. But as an institution operating "on the surface of Irish society," it was distant from the people.[105] The officer class was especially isolated. Social distance, although not as apparent in Ulster, was part of the occupational culture and part of the rank and file's argument for increased remuneration and benefits. The 1914 constabulary inquiry was informed that juries did not convict persons prosecuted as a result of police action, that citizens were loath to lend assistance, and that police were ostracized, forbidden from taking part in athletic competitions, for example. The growth of nationalist organizations such as Sinn Fein, the Gaelic League, and the Gaelic Athletic Association pushed the police further to the margins of society.[106]

As of 1912, the future of the Irish Constabulary seemed to be assured; on many levels, the force was a success. Yet when the political climate heated up again, the rank and file came under more and more stress. The home rule bills of 1912 and 1913 would have placed the police under the Irish government within several years. As late as 1921, after the RIC had been boycotted, targeted by republican violence, and further discredited by the actions of the Black and Tans, the *Constabulary Gazette* still nourished the hope that the RIC would have a role to play in a new Ireland. Toward the end of the Anglo-Irish War, the *Gazette* editor grew more pessimistic, sensing that Britain would abandon the Irish police to ill treatment by the victorious nationalists. Now predicting the demise of the force, the editor believed that "the same objections to RIC men would not apply in Canada, South Africa or Australia."[107] But objections there were. The government of Canada, five of its provinces, and Newfoundland replied negatively in 1922 to a British government suggestion that experienced RIC constables be hired by the dominions. Canada and Newfoundland each had unemployment problems of their own.[108]

The North-West Mounted Police, meanwhile, had survived the greatest threat to its own survival – provincial status for Alberta and Saskatchewan in 1905. The simple explanation was that it had become deeply interwoven in the institutional structure of settler society. Mounties were bush rangers, colonization agents, roving bureaucrats, and sometimes policemen. In both the Yukon and the Prairies, Canada's federal police "found themselves involved in a far wider range of roles than other forces based on the English *or* Irish models."[109]

Without the contracts negotiated to provide rural law enforcement in the two new provinces, the force would have been reduced by 70 percent. Legal or constitutional legitimacy was now derived from provincial governments. In the fall of 1914, the dominion government, to keep the peace in Alberta and Saskatchewan, which contained many Austro-Hungarian Empire and German immigrants, increased the RNWMP by 500. In 1917, citing wartime exigencies, Ottawa would withdraw from the western policing contracts, leading to the creation of provincial constabularies on the Prairies. But in 1920, as the RIC was on its last legs politically, the RNWMP expanded its jurisdiction and profile as the Royal Canadian Mounted Police.[110]

Ireland rejected control from Westminster; the RIC, identified with foreign domination, was doomed. With independence, Britain's legal institution frontier in most of Ireland came to an end. The Canadian west, although alive with regional discontent, never rejected partial control from Ottawa, particularly when it benefited provincial taxpayers. The fact that the RNWMP was a de facto regional force identified with the frontier only enhanced its legitimacy.[111]

Conclusion

We return to the two images from the opening of this chapter: the map of Ireland perforated by birdshot, and cobwebs covering the Canadian plains. Both are visual representations of surveillance and regulation of rural populations by central state agencies. The police of the two imperial frontiers shared certain characteristics. Both lived in barracks, were armed, and organized along paramilitary lines. Both developed a distinct esprit de corps or corporate identity, the key to which was controlling crime. Finally, the service role in both Ireland and Canada was important. But there were also fundamental contrasts. One was the principal internal dynamic of the institutions: ethnicity and language versus religion and nationality. The NWMP contained few French Canadians; the rank and file of the constabulary in 1895 was 80 percent Catholic, while 60 percent of the officers were Protestant. The social background of NWMP recruits, in contrast to the peasant origins of their RIC counterparts, were more middle class. Mounted Police officers, who exercised magisterial duties, were in many ways more powerful than their Irish counterparts.[112]

The Mounties operated initially "where there are no roads, no fences, not even wagon tracks," a frontier principally natural or physical.[113] That faced by the RIC was political and, eventually, military. There was little that was subtle about the constabulary presence in Ireland; the shotgun blast is an apt analogy. Its religious makeup and mundane daily activities could not detract from its overtly political mandate. In contrast, as the west was transformed from a colony into a white settler society, the "web," the social and institutional entanglement of the Mounties, was mostly depoliticized and therefore successful in the long run. In the 1990s, Disney was not marketing T-shirts, mugs, or bric-a-brac bearing the logo RUC or, for that matter, *Garda Siochana*. The RNWMP was so effective that when its disbandment was proposed the majority population of the region protested. In this case, the rule of the state coincided with the rule of law.[114]

Acknowledgments

I would like to acknowledge the support of the Social Sciences and Humanities Council of Canada and express thanks to John Phyne for reading previous versions of this chapter. The comments of the anonymous readers were also appreciated.

Notes

1 Sir Francis B. Head, *A Fortnight in Ireland* (London: J. Murray, 1852), 45-56.

2 Ernest J. Chambers, *The Royal North-West Mounted Police: A Corps History* (Montreal: Mortimer Press, 1906), 156.

3 S.W. Horrall, "Sir John A. Macdonald and the Mounted Police Force for the Northwest Territories," *Canadian Historical Review* 53, 2 (1972): 179-200; Greg Marquis, "Towards a Canadian Police Historiography," in *Law, Society, and the State: Essays in Legal History,* ed. L.A. Knafla and Susan Binnie (Toronto: Law Society of Upper Canada, 1995), 477-95; Carl Betke, "Police and Pioneers on the Canadian Prairies, 1885-1914," in *Lawful Authority: Readings in the History of Criminal Justice in Canada,* ed. R.C. Macleod (Toronto: Copp, Clarke, Pitman, 1988), 98-119; R.C. Macleod, *The North-West Mounted Police and Law Enforcement, 1873-1905* (Toronto: University of Toronto Press, 1976); David Cruise and Alison Griffiths, *The Great Adventure: How the Mounties Conquered the West* (Toronto: Viking, 1996); Donovan T. Saul, ed., *Red Serge and Stetsons: A Hundred Years of Mounties' Memories* (Victoria: Horsdal and Schubart, 1993); William Baker, ed., *The Mounted Police and Prairie Society 1873-1919* (Regina: Canadian Plains Research Center, 1998); William Behean and Stan Horrall, *Red Coats on the Prairies: The North-West Mounted Police, 1886-1900* (Regina: Centax Books, 1998).

4 Richard Hawkins, "The 'Irish Model' and the Empire: A Case for Reassessment," in *Policing the Empire: Government, Authority, and Control, 1830-1940,* ed. David Anderson and David Killingray (New York: Oxford University Press, 1991), chapter 2; Stanley Palmer, *Police and Protest in England and Ireland, 1750-1870* (New York: Oxford University Press, 1988), 542-43; R.I. Mawby, *Comparative Policing Issues: The British and American Experience in International Perspective* (Boston: Unwin Hyman, 1990), 27-38, chapter 5; Greg Marquis, "The 'Irish Model' and Nineteenth-Century Canadian Policing," *Journal of Imperial and Commonwealth History* 25 (1997): 193-218; Chambers, *The Royal North-West Mounted Police,* 152.

5 Keith Walden, *Visions of Order: The Canadian Mounties in Symbol and Myth* (Toronto: Butterworth, 1982).

6 Robert Thacker, "Canada's Mounted: The Evolution of a Legend," *Journal of Popular Culture* 14 (1980): 298-312; Gerald Friesen, *The Canadian Prairies: A History* (Toronto: University of Toronto Press, 1984), 163-71; Macleod, *The North-West Mounted Police,* 51; Michael Dawson, *The Mountie from Dime Novel to Disney* (Toronto: Between the Lines, 1998).

7 Lorne Browne, "The RCMP and Its Ancestors: Over 100 Years of Willing Service," in *Rethinking the Administration of Justice,* ed. Dawn Currie and Brian D. Maclean (Halifax: Fernwood Publishing, 1992), 185-213 at 192; Greg Marquis, *Policing Canada's Century: A History of the Canadian Association of Chiefs of Police* (Toronto: University of Toronto Press, 1993); Walden, *Visions of Order;* W.R. Morrison, *Showing the Flag: The Mounted Police and Canadian Sovereignty in the North 1894-1925* (Vancouver: UBC Press, 1985), 2; R.C. Macleod, "Law and Order on the Western Canada Frontier," in *Law for the Beaver, Law for the Elephant: Essays in the Legal History of the North American West,* ed. John McLaren, Hamar Foster, and Chet Orloff (Regina: Canadian Plains Research Center, 1992), 90-105; William Baker, "The Mounties and the Miners: The Royal North-West Mounted Police and the 1906 Lethbridge Strike," *Labour/Le Travail* 27 (1991): 55-91. The relationship with Disney is discussed in Dawson, *The Mountie.*

8 Marquis, "The 'Irish Model.'" The Irish Constabulary was a model for England's county police. See C. Steedman, *Policing the Victorian Community: The Formation of English Provincial Police Forces, 1856-80* (Boston: Routledge and Kegan Paul, 1984), 21-24.

9 A recent exception is John Brewer's *The Royal Irish Constabulary: An Oral History* (Belfast: Institute of Irish Studies, 1990). Brewer is based in Northern Ireland. See also Ian Bridgeman, "The Constabulary and the Criminal Justice System in Nineteenth-Century Ireland," *Criminal Justice History* 15 (1994): 95-126.

10 Royal Irish Constabulary/Dublin Metropolitan Police, *Report of the Committee of Inquiry 1914* [1914 Inquiry] (Dublin: A. Thom, 1914), Evidence, 219; G. Marquis, "Working Men in Uniform: The Early Twentieth-Century Toronto Police," *Histoire sociale* 20 (1987): 259-77 at 265-66.

11 Connor Brady, *Guardians of the Peace* (Dublin: Gill and MacMillan, 1974), 2.

12 Britain, House of Commons, *Civil Service (in Ireland) Inquiry Commission: Dublin Metropolitan Police Report 1873, Sessional Paper,* (1873) [1873 Inquiry], 22, 81-82; C.W. Leatham, *Sketches and Stories of the Royal Irish Constabulary* (Dublin: Edward Ponsonby, 1909), 7; Royal Irish Constabulary, *Report of the Commission of Inquiry 1882-83* (London: Harrison and Sons, 1883) [1882 Inquiry], "Evidence," 167, 178, 364-65; *Royal Irish Constabulary: Report of the*

Commission of Inquiry 1901 (Dublin: Alex Thom and Company, 1902), Report, 10 [1901 Inquiry]; W.J. Lowe, "'Employment of a Very Desirable and Much-Needed Character': The Irish Constabulary, 1837-1922," unpublished paper, Chicago State University, 1989, 21. Recruits, at least prior to the early 1900s, tended to be young.

13 1914 Inquiry, Evidence, 189.

14 C. Townshend, *Political Violence in Ireland* (Oxford: Clarendon Press, 1983), 83.

15 Leatham, *Sketches,* 20-21.

16 1914 Inquiry, Evidence, 220.

17 Lowe, "'Employment,'" 23-24; Seamus Breathnach, *The Irish Police: From Earliest Times to the Present Day* (Dublin: Anvil Press, 1974), 149.

18 1882 Inquiry, Evidence, 10.

19 1914 Inquiry, Evidence, 63.

20 1873 Inquiry, 148, 180.

21 1873 Inquiry, 263; Ireland, State Paper Office, Chief Secretary's Records Office Papers, 1914/6466, Fiat Justitia to Chief Secretary, 23 March 1914; 1914/1720, Parliamentary question 31 October 1912; 1914 Inquiry, Report 6-7, Evidence, 31, 50, 61, 97, 111.

22 Canada, "Annual Report of the Commissioner of the North-West Mounted Police," 1897, *Sessional Papers* (Ottawa: Government Printers, 1898); Canada, House of Commons, *Debates,* 1891, 4824; Macleod, *The North-West Mounted Police,* 9, chapter 2; Hawkins, "The 'Irish Model,'" 4; Chambers, *The Royal North-West Mounted Police,* 107; L.E. Skinner, *Police of the Pastoral Frontier: Native Police 1849-59* (St. Lucis, Queensland: University of Queensland Press, 1975). For native policing, see David Barlow, "Minorities Policing Minorities as a Strategy of Social Control: A Historical Analysis of Tribal Police in the United States," *Criminal Justice History* 15 (1994): 141-63.

23 Bertie W. Antrobus, "Reminiscences of Fort Macleod in 1885," *Canadian Magazine* 8 (1896): 11-12.

24 House of Commons, *Debates,* 1884, 1295; Mawby, *Comparative Policing Issues,* 81; Macleod, *The North-West Mounted Police,* 78-79.

25 R.B. Deane, *Mounted Police Life in Canada: A Record of Thirty-One Years' Service* (London: Cassell, 1916), 9-10, 87-88, 135. Supplying the force with buildings, transport, food, clothing, forage, animals, tools, et cetera offered other opportunities for political patronage: House of Commons, *Debates,* 1889, 1451.

26 Macleod, *The North-West Mounted Police,* 59-60, 84-85; Cruise and Griffiths, *The Great Adventure,* 29.

27 A.L. Haydon, *The Riders of the Plains: Adventures and Romance with the North-West Mounted Police* (Toronto: Copp, Clark, 1910), 45; Chambers, *The Royal North-West Mounted Police,* 36; John Peter Turner, *The North-West Mounted Police 1873-1893,* vol. 2 (Ottawa: King's Printer, 1950), 308-9.

28 Antrobus, "Reminiscences," 13-14.

29 Chambers, *The Royal North-West Mounted Police,* 21n4, 104. See also Cruise and Griffiths, *The Great Adventure,* 176.

30 Haydon, *The Riders of the Plains,* chapter 20; House of Commons, *Debates,* 1879, 88; Nora Kelly and William Kelly, *The Royal Canadian Mounted Police: A Century of History* (Edmonton: Hurtig, 1973), 21.

31 Macleod, *The North-West Mounted Police,* 86; Steedman, *Policing the Victorian Community.*

32 House of Commons, *Debates,* 1882, 544-45.

33 House of Commons, *Debates,* 1914, 709; "Annual Report," 1895-1900, 1905, 1910; Macleod, *The North-West Mounted Police,* 82. The total NWMP contribution to the South African War was 245 men. Following the failure of recruiting in Manitoba and Ontario, 98 men (half of them ex-soldiers) were hired in England (out of 1,300 applicants).

34 Macleod, *The North-West Mounted Police;* Friesen, *The Canadian Prairies,* 168-69; Palmer, *Police and Protest,* 537. In 1884, Macdonald spoke of the difficulty of attracting cadets from the Royal Military College; see House of Commons, *Debates,* 1295.

35 Robert Curtis, *The History of the Royal Irish Constabulary* (Dublin: Moffat and Co., 1869), 99; *Royal Constabulary Manual: The Constabulary Manual, or Guide to the Discharge of Police Duties* (Dublin: Alex. Thom, 1870); A. Bain, *Police Duties and Drill* (Dublin: Alex. Thom, 1894).

36 1873 Inquiry, 191-92; 1914 Inquiry, Evidence, 63; G. Garrow Green, *In the Royal Irish Constabulary* (Dublin: Hodges and Figgis, n.d.), chapter 1; Leatham, *Sketches and Stories,* 10; Palmer, *Police and Protest,* 363; Brewer, *The Royal Irish Constabulary,* 5.

37 Haydon, *The Riders of the Plains,* chapter 20.

38 John G. Donkin, *Trooper and Redskin in the North-West: Mounted Police Life in Canada, 1884-1888* (1889; Toronto: Coles Publishing, 1973), 228, 238-39.

39 1914 Inquiry, Evidence, 10, 20; Brady, *Guardians,* 12.

40 1873 Inquiry, 182, 205, 228; 1882 Inquiry, Evidence, 70; 1914 Inquiry, Evidence, 230-31; Brady, *Guardians,* 12-13; Palmer, *Police and Protest,* 537.

41 1873 Inquiry, 134; 1882 Inquiry, Evidence, 37, 57-58; 1901 Inquiry, Evidence, 104; Leatham, *Sketches and Stories,* 8.

42 1882 Inquiry, Report, 17.

43 Ibid. at Evidence, 136. See also 304, 359; 1914 Inquiry, Report, 16-18.

44 1873 Inquiry, 166-67, 172.

45 *Promotion in the Royal Irish Constabulary* (Dublin: n.p., 1906), 21; 1882 Inquiry, Evidence, 197, 216.

46 1914 Inquiry, Evidence, 136.

47 For police Freemasonry and Orangeism, see Marquis, "Working Men in Uniform."

48 Macleod, *The North-West Mounted Police,* 93-95.

49 House of Commons, *Debates,* 1889, 1212; 1900, 4788-90; Turner, *The North-West Mounted Police,* vol. 2: 457; Palmer, *Police and Protest,* 538.

50 House of Commons, *Debates,* 1889, 1210-12; 1900, 4788-90; 1914, 710-14; Haydon, *The Riders of the Plains,* appendices. In 1909, 11 percent of the officer corps was French Canadian, possibly a reflection of the Laurier government's political base in Quebec.

51 J. Gaughan, ed., *Memoirs of Constable Jeremiah Mee, RIC* (Dublin: Anvil Books, 1975), 32.

52 1882 Inquiry, Report, 14.

53 1882 Inquiry, Report, 7; 1901 Inquiry, Evidence, 187; Green, *In the Royal Irish Constabulary,* 99; Brewer, *The Royal Irish Constabulary,* 56.

54 1882 Inquiry, Evidence, 10; 1901 Inquiry, Evidence, 19-20; 1914 Inquiry, Evidence, appendix 12.

55 Palmer, *Police and Protest,* 536; 1882 Inquiry, Evidence, 52, appendix 1(3); 1901 Inquiry, Evidence, 14-25, 37. Constables later became sergeants, and subconstables became constables.

56 1882 Inquiry, Evidence, 323; 1901 Inquiry, Evidence, 21, 119, 149; 1914 Inquiry, Evidence, 185. For the importance of dowry and related matters in rural Ireland, see Conrad Arensburg and Solon T. Kimball, *Family and Community in Ireland* (Cambridge, MA: Harvard University Press, 1968).

57 Lowe, "'Employment,'" 10-11; Palmer, *Police and Protest,* 535-46.

58 1882 Inquiry, Report, 10-11, Evidence, 183.

59 1882 Inquiry, Report, 3, 5-7, Evidence, 26; 1914 Inquiry, Report, 19-21, Evidence, 150-60.

60 1873 Inquiry, 138; 1882 Inquiry, Report, 19-21, Evidence, 154, 159, 165, 301, 434; 1914 Inquiry, Evidence, 177-78, 221.

61 Chambers, *The Royal North-West Mounted Police,* 154. NWMP regulations were prepared under Justice Minister A.A. Dorion of Mackenzie's Liberal government in 1875; see Turner, *The North-West Mounted Police,* 1: 253.

62 Macleod, *The North-West Mounted Police,* 53-54; R.B. Nevitt, *A Winter at Fort Macleod,* ed. Hugh Dempsey (n.p.: McClelland and Stewart West, 1974), 12; House of Commons, *Debates,* 1894, 4678-79; Turner, *The North-West Mounted Police,* 2: 27-28; Cruise and Griffiths, *The Great Adventure,* 364; Bruce Dawson, "Mutiny at Fort Macleod," *Alberta History* 43, 3 (1995): 21-25.

63 House of Commons, *Debates,* 1889, 429-32; 1899, 21; "Annual Report," 1889, appendices P and V.

64 Turner, *The North-West Mounted Police,* 2: 518; House of Commons, *Debates,* 1891, 2915-23.

65 House of Commons, *Debates,* 1884, 770-72; Donkin, *Trooper and Redskin,* 277; Haydon, *The Riders of the Plains,* appendices. By 1910, constables with nine years of service could earn one dollar per day. The concentrated nature of the pre-1885 NWMP meant longer individual patrols; see Macleod, *The North-West Mounted Police,* 21-22.

66 House of Commons, *Debates,* 1885, 2402-3.

67 "Annual Report," 1895-99.

68 House of Commons, *Debates,* 1891, 1269-70; Saul, *Red Serge,* 112, 118.

69 1882 Inquiry, Report, 28-9, Evidence, 129, 156, 328; 1901 Inquiry, Evidence, 19, Report, 26-7; 1914 Inquiry, Report, 9-10, Evidence, 37, 62. According to Arensburg and Kimball's *Family and Community,* early-twentieth-century rural society was obsessed with land, property, and job security. Both rural and urban residents of County Clare were also obsessed with social rank.

70 Palmer, *Police and Protest,* 535-36; William Francis Butler, *The Great Lone Land: A Tale of Travel and Adventure in the North-West of America* (1872; Toronto: Musson Books, 1924), 378-79; House of Commons, *Debates,* 1890, 2687. By the late nineteenth century, two-thirds of RIC recruits had been on the force twenty or more years. Adventure was a motive for many recruits; see Jean D'Artigue, *Six Years in the Canadian North-West* (Toronto: Hunter, Rose and Company, 1882).

71 House of Commons, *Debates,* 1889, 770-71, 1269-74; 1900, 6095; 1902, 808; Deane, *Mounted Police Life in Canada,* 8. Desertion from 1879-89 averaged 6 percent per year; see Macleod, *The North-West Mounted Police,* 83.

72 House of Commons, *Debates,* 1889, 769-70; chapter 26, *An Act to Authorize the Granting of Pensions to Members of the North-West Mounted Police Force,* S.C., 1889.

73 Haydon, *The Riders of the Plains,* appendices.

74 "Annual Report," 1899, 4; Bob Beal and R.C. Macleod, *Prairie Fire: The 1885 North-West Rebellion* (Edmonton: Hurtig Publishers, 1984), 28.

75 Turner, *The North-West Mounted Police,* 2: 428, 455; Chambers, *The Royal North-West Mounted Police,* 131; "Annual Report," 1901.

76 At various times, the commissioner and district superintendents reported on the need for men on patrol to be able to quickly deploy their carbines and revolvers; see Turner, *The North-West Mounted Police,* 2: 355-56; and "Annual Report," 1883.

77 Chambers, *The Royal North-West Mounted Police,* 148-50; Donkin, *Trooper and Redskin,* 277. See also "Annual Report," 1889, appendix L. Another problem was the poor quality of NWMP ammunition.

78 "Annual Report," 1878-84; Macleod, *The North-West Mounted Police,* 145-48. The cases include those prosecuted by the NWMP and private individuals, including First Nations and Métis. Police officers served as magistrates in most of these cases. In the early 1870s, whites were about 4-5 percent of the total population of the North-West Territories; see Friesen, *The Canadian Prairies,* 137. For more on this topic, see R.C. Macleod and Heather Rollason, "'Restrain the Lawless Savages': Native Defendants in the Criminal Courts of the North West Territories, 1878-1885," *Journal of Historical Sociology* 10 (1997): 157-83.

79 Donkin, *Trooper and Redskin.*

80 House of Commons, *Debates,* 1885, 2421-27; 1899, 5930-31; "Annual Report," 1889, appendix K; Beal and Macleod, *Prairie Fire,* 61. Emergency rations were also given to indigent Métis. See also House of Commons, *Debates,* 1899, 75, 89; "Annual Report," 1905, 65.

81 House of Commons, *Debates,* 1885, 2408; Haydon, *The Riders of the Plains;* Beal and Macleod, *Prairie Fire.* Charges were laid in the case of one police death only.

82 "Annual Report," 1897-1900; Macleod, *The North-West Mounted Police,* 104-5, 145-48, and chapter 3, 11. In 1900, one out of seven convictions registered by the NWMP was under the *Indian Act.* Part of the strategy of the treaties was to use chiefs and headmen to secure indirect rule. See Marquis, "The 'Irish Model.'"

83 House of Commons, *Debates,* 1892, 2668-92; "Annual Report," 1888, 1895; Macleod, *The North-West Mounted Police,* 57-60.

84 Betke, *Police and Pioneers;* "Annual Report," 1897.

85 Haydon, *The Riders of the Plains,* vii.

86 "Annual Report," 1895.

87 Chambers, *The Royal North-West Mounted Police,* 156; Donkin, *Trooper and Redskin,* 84; Macleod, *The North-West Mounted Police,* 150-56.

88 "Annual Report," 1889, appendices K and L; House of Commons, *Debates,* 1894, 4667-78; Chambers, *The Royal North-West Mounted Police,* 111-12; Macleod, *The North-West Mounted Police,* chapter 11.

89 House of Commons, *Debates,* 1894, 4630, 4664-65. In Ireland, prosecution and judicial duties were carried out by resident magistrates and Crown prosecutors; see Bridgeman, "The Constabulary."

90 Turner, *The North-West Mounted Police,* 2: 551; House of Commons, *Debates,* 1891, 1701-3; 1901, 3443; 1903, 8657-59.

91 Haydon, *The Riders of the Plains,* appendices; Marquis, *Policing Canada's Century,* chapter 1.

92 Brady, *Guardians,* 1.

93 1901 Inquiry, Evidence, 211.

94 Ibid. at 180.

95 Palmer, *Police and Protest,* 552; Townshend, *Political Violence,* 143-44; L.P. Curtis Jr., *Coercion and Consent in Ireland 1880-1892: A Study in Conservative Unionism* (Princeton: Princeton University Press, 1963), 198-200.

96 1882 Inquiry, Evidence, 66, 393; 1901 Inquiry, Evidence, 115; 1914 Inquiry, Evidence, 189. See also W.J. Lowe and E. Malcolm, "The Domestication of the Irish Constabulary, 1836-1922," *Irish Economic and Social History* 19 (1992): 26-48.

97 Lowe, "'Employment,'" 8; 1901 Inquiry, Evidence, 297; Palmer, *Police and Protest,* 520, 536.

98 Owen Dudley Edwards, *The Sins of Our Fathers: Roots of Conflict in Northern Ireland* (Dublin: Gill and MacMillan, 1970), 109.

99 1901 Inquiry, Evidence, 112-13; 1914 Inquiry, Evidence, 86, 148.

100 Chief Secretary's Records Office Papers, 1912/15222, Reverend McCotter to Chief Secretary, 24 August 1912; 1912/16964, Commissioner Belfast RIC to Chief Secretary's Office, 26 September 1912; 1912/20607, J.B. Dougherty to Secretary, Catholic Vigilance Committee, 26 November 1912.

101 1882 Inquiry, Evidence, 327; Townshend, *Political Violence,* 252; *Constabulary Gazette,* 5 November 1921. See also Brewer, *The Royal Irish Constabulary,* 11.

102 Brewer, *The Royal Irish Constabulary,* 13.

103 *The Constabulary Manual* (1870); 1873 Inquiry, 211.

104 Lowe, "'Employment'"; Bridgeman, "The Constabulary," 118.

105 Palmer, *Police and Protest,* 375.

106 1882 Inquiry, Evidence, 195, 248, Report, 20-1; 1914 Inquiry, Evidence, 94, 149, 171, 180.

107 *Constabulary Gazette,* 17 September 1921.

108 Kent Fedorowich, "The Problems of Disbandment: The Royal Irish Constabulary and Imperial Migration, 1919-29," *Irish Historical Studies* 30 (1996): 99-100.

109 Mawby, *Comparative Policing Issues,* 75; Morrison, *Showing the Flag,* 38, 50-51. Under the agreement of 1905, Ottawa paid two-thirds of the costs of rural policing, setting a precedent for a police contact system that eventually would extend to eight provinces.

110 Betke, "Police and Pioneers"; Stan Horrall, "The Royal North-West Mounted Police and Labour Unrest in Western Canada, 1919," in *Lawful Authority,* ed. Macleod, 133-60.

111 Mawby, *Comparative Policing Issues,* 27-28; Horrall, "The Royal North-West Mounted Police." By the 1980s, the RCMP, through provincial and municipal contracts, policed over 70 percent of the population of British Columbia, more than 50 percent in Saskatchewan, over 40 percent in Alberta, and over 30 percent in Manitoba; see Marquis, *Policing Canada's Century,* 380.

112 Palmer, *Police and Protest,* 538.

113 Turner, *The North-West Mounted Police,* 2: 469.

114 Macleod, *The North-West Mounted Police,* 61-63; Dawson, *The Mountie,* 145-47, 166-67, 171-72. The insightful theme of "community entanglement" is developed by John Weaver in *Crimes, Constables, and Courts: Order and Transgression in a Canadian City, 1816-1970* (Montreal and Kingston: McGill-Queen's University Press, 1995).

7

The Common Law and Justices of the Supreme Court of the North-West Territories: The First Generation, 1887-1907

Roderick G. Martin

The history of the common law and judiciary of the North-West Territories (NWT) has received scant critical attention from legal historians. In fact, Louis Knafla has suggested that the legal history of western Canada "has been a haphazard affair ... lacking a critical context and focus."[1] Indeed, much of the work has been anecdotal, prosopographical, devoted to the chronological reconstruction of political and legal developments, or concerned with questions such as "when was English law received on the Prairies?"[2] This absence of an incisive Prairie legal historiography has been especially unfortunate since Knafla's own examination of the "legal and cultural milieu" of the west revealed that Prairie judges "worked hard to establish the independence of the judicial regime and local control over a rapidly expanding society and economy."[3] Although not endeavouring to provide a detailed analysis of the Supreme Court of the North-West Territories (SCNWT), and thus fill this gap in our historical knowledge, this chapter analyzes some of the important social, political, economic, and cultural issues that coloured the legal context of the court's early years from 1887 to 1907. Although relatively brief, the following discussion reveals the profound influence exerted by the SCNWT during Prairie society's formative years and, it is hoped, raises a series of intriguing questions that will prove useful to scholars who wish to compare the events and developments examined here with those of other settler societies.

This chapter examines the more notable civil actions that came before the SCNWT and intimates the importance of the decisions made by the first generation of justices in shaping common law precedents for the NWT. At the same time, it is revealed that civil law proceedings, occupying 85 percent of the court's docket, dominated the court's activities and provided a fertile environment for the development of the local legal profession.[4] Indeed, the first seven volumes of the *Territorial Law Reports,* covering the period from June 1887 to May 1907, reflect this predominance of civil actions. The 521 civil cases recorded include procedural applications, company law and private law issues, actions for damages, negligence, breaches of contract, sale of goods, corporate or municipal taxation assessments, master and servant relations, real estate, mortgages and land titles, liens for wages, wrongful dismissal, libel, alimony, the *Medical and Legal Professions Act,* the *Canada Evidence Act,* and Admiralty law. The ninety-three criminal cases included reference writs of *certiorari,* substantive law, rules of law, rules of court, and appeal cases in murder, theft of cattle, fraud, polygamy, perjury, seduction of a female under the age of twenty-one, assault, obstruction, midwifery, wilfully causing fires, illegally selling liquor, discrimination, and conspiracy to defraud.

While the *Territorial Reports* do not contain the entirety of the SCNWT's caseload during these years, they do represent an excellent cross-section of the substantive issues that were heard by the court and that were relevant to its "bench and bar" at that time.[5] Although editors Nicholas Du Bois Dominic Beck of Calgary, O.M. Biggar of Edmonton, and T.D. Brown of Regina all left their respective marks on legal reportage on the Prairies, arguably Beck's contribution was the most profound. Born and raised in Cobourg, Ontario, Beck graduated from Osgoode Hall Law School in 1881, practised law in Ontario, Manitoba, and Calgary in the North-West Territories, was appointed to the Supreme Court of Alberta in 1907, and remained on the bench until 1928. As principal editor from 1900 to 1910, Beck's name appears on virtually every report.[6] Toronto-born Oliver Mowat Biggar practised private and public sector law and helped to edit several volumes of the *Reports.* His notoriety, however, was acquired as a member of the Military Service Council that implemented conscription, 1917-18, and from 1918 to 1919, as the judge advocate general and chief counsel for the Canadian military.[7] Thomas Dowrick Brown was from Port Hope, Ontario, and was called to the NWT bar in 1906. Helping to edit several volumes of the *Reports,* Brown practised law in Moosomin, North-West Territories, until 1907, when the firm of Brown, Thompson and Mclean was established in Regina.[8]

The Supreme Court of the North-West Territories was created in 1886 in concert with a declaration by the lieutenant governor in council that the laws of the NWT were the laws of England as of 15 July 1870.[9] Initially created without a chief justice, the court was composed of five members, three of whom, James F. Macleod, Charles-B. Rouleau, and Hugh Richardson, were already established as stipendiary magistrates (SM). Newcomers to the court were Edward L. Wetmore and Thomas H. McGuire.[10]

Scottish-born Macleod immigrated to Upper Canada with his family in 1845, where he attended Upper Canada College and Osgoode Hall. After graduation, he practised law at Bowmanville, Ontario, for a decade before eventually becoming a commissioner of the North-West Mounted Police (NWMP) in 1876.[11] Rouleau was born in Quebec in 1840, educated at Laval University, and had been a police magistrate (PM) in Ottawa before coming

Justice James F. Macleod, ca. 1887-94. *Glenbow Archives, NA-2258-1*

to the Prairies.[12] Richardson was born in London, England, and came to Canada at the age of five. Admitted to the Upper Canada bar in 1847, he practised at Woodstock from 1852 to 1872, served as Crown counsel from 1856 to 1862, and in 1872 joined the Department of Justice in Ottawa as chief clerk. Like Macleod, Richardson was also a lieutenant colonel in the militia and in 1876 was appointed an SM.[13] One of the new appointees to the SCNWT was from New Brunswick. Wetmore had been a solicitor from 1863 to 1881, the mayor of Fredericton for three years beginning in 1881, a commissioner overseeing the consolidation of the New Brunswick statutes, and a member of the provincial legislature from 1883 to 1886.[14] The other appointee, McGuire, was from Kingston, Ontario, where he practised as a barrister.

During the court's twenty-year existence, Wetmore was the most active jurist. He presided over 192 civil and criminal assize appeal cases, although almost all were exclusively on the civil side. Noted practitioner C.C. McCaul described Wetmore as the strongest member of the court, a view reflected in the fact that the third volume of the *Reports* is replete with his judgments. Justice Stuart, on the other hand, presided over five civil cases, although he was a late arrival, joining the court only in 1906. Scott presided over eighty-three criminal and civil cases, Richardson over twenty-seven, Rouleau over fifteen, Newlands over fourteen, McGuire over eight, and Harvey over six. The remaining members – including Macleod, Prendergast, Sifton, and Johnstone – do not appear in the assize appeal reports. All the justices, however, appear at one time or another presiding *en banc*. The "ebb and flow" of these appeal cases to the SCNWT culminated in 1907, when the court divided into the Supreme Courts of Alberta and Saskatchewan.[15]

Although each member presided over his own district, the court sat *en banc* twice a year in Regina.[16] The original five districts of the NWT were eastern and western Assiniboia, with judicial headquarters at Moosomin and Regina respectively; the districts of southern and northern Alberta, with headquarters at Fort Macleod and Calgary; and the district of Saskatchewan, headquartered at the town of Battleford.[17] Each justice presided as a judge "of a Superior Court of civil and criminal jurisdiction ... with jurisdiction throughout the Territories," and, on assize, the justices presided over summary trials, jury trials, or appeals from the decisions of the lower Territorial courts.[18] The cases that came before the justices *en banc* were generally lower court appeals, including Courts of Revision, SMs, justices of the peace (JPs), and reference or appeal cases from the justices on their assize circuits.[19]

The evidence gleaned from the *Territorial Reports,* judicial notebooks, and assize files also suggests that on assize and *en banc* the justices maintained a rigorous schedule.[20] The first seven volumes of the *Reports* catalogued over 614 recorded proceedings for June 1887-May 1907, and the judicial notebooks of Macleod, Rouleau, and Scott indicate that the *Reports* are not exhaustive. Furthermore, for each of the cases heard *en banc,* there had previously been a summary or jury trial that was appealed.[21] An examination of the number of cases on assize that did not appear on the court *en banc* calendar reveals that a minority of these cases made it to the appeal court.[22] Leave to appeal had to be granted by the court as if it was the court of final appeal or last resort, and its decisions were binding on all courts in the NWT.[23] Thus, the legal principles, doctrines, precedents, and law flowing from the proceedings of the SCNWT *en banc* became the common and precedent law of the NWT.

Perhaps the most influential element in the growth and evolution of the commercial component of Territorial civil law was the Canadian Pacific Railway (CPR). The CPR's arrival, and in time the influx of settlers, made breaches of both common and Territorial laws increasingly frequent. The bulk of both civil and criminal cases were heard and determined by NWMP

First Supreme Court judiciary, North-West Territories (later Saskatchewan and Alberta), ca. 1890. *Left to right:* Sheriff James H. Benson, Justice E.L. Wetmore, Colonel James F. Macleod, Hugh Richardson (chief), Charles B. Rouleau, T.H. McGuire, "Dixie" Watson, clerk of the court. *Glenbow Archives, NB-16-239*

commissioned officer magistrates in police courts of first instance.[24] However, when there were appeals from a lower court, or if a substantive legal question was at stake, the SCNWT justices held exclusive jurisdiction. In that regard, the evidence reveals that the number of civil cases heard *en banc,* on assize, or in chambers was nearly six times greater than criminal cases.[25]

Arguably, the absence of any alternative civil dispute resolution process at a time of extensive commercial and economic growth meant that, during this early period, civil litigation dominated the superior court's calendar, and the CPR was involved in many important cases. In fact, between 1887 and 1907, the CPR was a party to fourteen civil cases on assize and *en banc.*[26] Several included claims for injuries caused by the negligence of the company, for animals destroyed by its trains, and a suit for negligence when a train engineer travelled at a dangerous speed through a municipality.[27] In many ways, the CPR cases broke new legal ground in the Territories, and such was the case in 1887 when the court *en banc* heard one of its first appeal cases, *Walters et al v. The Canadian Pacific Railway Company.*[28]

The *Walters* case was an action for nondelivery of the plaintiff's goods that had been stored in a CPR warehouse. The company had acted both as common carrier and as warehouseman, and the issue turned on whether the CPR had discharged its duty and liability before the loss of the goods. This case was legally significant in that, since the CPR was the main source of rapid transportation in the Prairies, an adverse decision could have been devastating. In finding for the company, the court drew upon a number of English precedents. For his part, Justice McGuire cited eleven English cases in framing his written opinion. The court also cited an Ontario precedent in favour of the railway that, in warehousing goods with the railway, the risk remained with the owner.[29] The court also cited a Supreme Court of Canada (SCC) precedent on property in transit that the Territorial court deemed applicable to common carriers and warehousemen on the Prairies.[30] From this foundation, the court defined the common law responsibilities of the CPR as a common carrier and warehouseman in the region and thus framed a precedent for future disputes. This case also clearly shows how the court adopted, adapted, and applied judgments, doctrines, and precedents from jurisdictions outside the NWT.[31]

English precedents continued to shape legal interpretations on the Prairies, as evidenced in the 1902 case of *Kenny v. The CPR*.[32] Heard by then Chief Justice McGuire, the case was an action for damages by the plaintiff for injuries alleged as a passenger on a Calgary to Edmonton train. When the train derailed into a ravine, Kenny suffered a number of severe injuries. In deciding the case, McGuire referred to numerous English cases that assisted him in determining that the CPR had a duty to carry the plaintiff in a safe manner and that agents of the company were liable for the safe running of a train while CPR tracks and bridges were in an unsafe condition.[33] Again, a precedent for the NWT was rooted in the English precedents but made amendable to conditions in the Prairies.

A similar course of action was found in the case of *Eggleston v. The CPR,* heard *en banc* in 1905.[34] A CPR train near Wetaskiwin had overtaken 250 horses that had been running at large on the unfenced CPR line, and 44 horses had been struck and killed. At issue was whether the CPR was negligent or whether the plaintiff had been grossly negligent in allowing the horses to wander onto the tracks in the first place. Once again the court drew upon English and Canadian cases in holding that Judge Scott's findings against the company should not be reversed.[35] The decision was consistent with the common law principle that a trial judge was in the best position to determine "the credibility ... of all the evidence" and that an appeal court ought not to reverse such decisions "unless it is shewn [sic] to be clearly wrong upon the evidence so taken."[36] On appeal, the SCC reversed that decision while, in essence, agreeing with the trial judge and the SCNWT.[37] Yet, at the same time, the SCC held that the lower courts had ignored mitigating circumstances that affected the case: a thick blanket of fog had obscured the engineer's vision until seconds before the accident. Therefore, the CPR could not be held liable.

It is evident that the Territorial justices exercised discretionary justice in applying legal precedent.[38] Interestingly, in cases where injury occurred or negligence was determined on the part of the CPR, the decisions often went against the company.[39] Yet cases related to CPR business – matters such as taxation, business locale, or status as a common carrier – were usually decided in favour of the company.[40] In cases where the decisions went against the CPR, they also appear to have gone against precedent, an inclination that demonstrated the independence of these early judges. For example, in *Eggleston,* where the court ruled against the CPR, it was the SCC that reversed the decision and affirmed the company's rights and status. In the least, the case suggests that as late as 1905 the court was still coming to terms with its authority regarding Parliament and the unsettled civil law on the Prairies.

As the CPR cases demonstrated, the court's role in the development of law and society in the North-West Territories was pivotal, and in few places was this felt more acutely than in the administration, establishment, and endorsement of rules and standards for land registration. Borrowed from Australia, the Torrens system was introduced in the Canadian Prairies by the *Territories Real Property Act* of 1887.[41] Not surprisingly in a settler society, sorting out questions of land title was an important facet of the court's business, especially once the tide of immigration began to rise in the 1890s. For example, the case of *Wilkie et al. v. Jellett et al.* in 1895 raised a series of questions concerning land registration and title to property.[42]

In early March 1891, the Edmonton and Saskatchewan Land Company of Canada sold some land to Wilkie, who, in turn, failed to register the title until December 1893. In the interim between Wilkie's acquisition and his registration of title, Jellett obtained a judgment against the company and registered a claim against the land. Therefore, when Wilkie finally registered his title, he was confronted with the writ of execution clouding clear title. Wilkie brought the matter to court in an attempt to remove the execution order that Jellett had obtained. Justice Rouleau, in considering the question, denied Wilkie the relief he sought and ruled in favour of Jellett.

The subsequent appeal to the SCNWT turned on whether the "execution against lands duly delivered to the register [was] binding as against a prior but unregistered transfer for value to a *bona fide* purchaser."[43] The court *en banc* not only reversed Rouleau's decision but also ordered the registrar of lands to remove the entries from the land register. Basing its decision on English, Canadian, and Australian case law, and thus enjoining the sheriff from selling the land in question (and thus protecting the plaintiff Wilkie), the court articulated a common law precedent upholding the proprietary rights of the landholder. Described by Wilbur Bowker as a "leading case," *Wilkie v. Jellett* showed the justices' "real concern with making the system work."[44] The decision also suggests that, when confronted with administrative procedures that did not conform to the court's sense of the law, the judges did not hesitate to change those procedures or stipulate how the land registration system ought to operate.

Wilkie, and other cases like it, also reflected the inevitable disparities in registration because of the volume of land transfers and title registrations in the North-West Territories. These cases demonstrate how the SCNWT established common law administrative rules and regulations concerning what could and could not be done in the land title registration system. Again the justices exercised their judicial discretion to institute a common law regime for land titles that, in turn, imparted administrative and regulatory certainty to the system. Judgments on administrative law, however, were not restricted to land registration, and there were numerous appeals arising from Court of Revision decisions.

One such case, *Angus et al. v. The Board of School Trustees of the School District of Calgary,* was heard in 1886.[45] Appealed by Angus from the Court of Revision regarding lands that had been sold by the CPR, the case involved the question of whether the company's former lands were exempt from taxation by such a board. The court ruled that a school board possessed no authority to undertake a taxation assessment for schools in the municipality of Calgary. Citing section 127 of the *Municipal Ordinance* authorizing municipalities to raise taxes, the court *en banc* allowed the appeal, and the assessment against the appellants was set aside.

In another taxation case, a series of disputes against the Battleford School District went before the full court on appeal after having been appealed from the Court of Revision and then referred by Justice McGuire.[46] At issue were the interpretation of the *School Ordinance* and the location of debts incurred by the Hudson's Bay Company (HBC). Having considered the matter, the court *en banc* decided that, even though the HBC headquarters was in London, England, and thus outside the NWT, a substantial portion of the company's business was conducted in the North-West Territories. Therefore, the company was subject to school taxes. The court again was innovative and creative in finding precedents to substantiate its reasoning. It stated that the company had debts that were "situs" and "may be said to be 'situated' in some place ... within the limits of the said school district."[47]

As part of its role as the high court located on the Prairies, the SCNWT also dealt with private civil matters such as family law, and in this regard the first recorded alimony case in the Territories was heard in January 1895. Brought by Mrs. Harris, whose divorce from her husband had not yet been granted, the request for alimony was based on the argument that, while her husband had abandoned her, she maintained rights in relation to implied authority in his affairs.[48] In viewing the case, Judge Wetmore chose not to establish precedent regarding the court's authority in matters of alimony. While it was true that the court possessed original jurisdiction, it was nonetheless limited to "the powers and authorities exercised by the Courts of Common Law, Chancery and Probate in England on July 15, 1870, and consequently in the absence of express legislation there [was] no jurisdiction to entertain a suit for alimony."[49] In effect, Wetmore denied Harris alimony because imperial or dominion statutes were silent on the matter. Furthermore, he was disinclined to seek a remedy from jurisdictions beyond England and Canada that could have supported Mrs. Harris' claim. Ultimately, his finding suggests that he had no judicial choice in the matter.

Clearly, within the boundaries of the NWT, the Supreme Court possessed authority to preside over and adjudge on any matter that it chose.[50] Although imperial and dominion statutes limited Wetmore's judicial authority, the *Harris* decision apparently sent an explicit message to the NWT legislature. Thus, on 30 September 1895, some eight months after the *Harris* hearing, the Territorial Council passed *Ordinance 14,* which responded to Wetmore's decision and the implicit inadequacy of the law.[51] The ordinance conferred jurisdiction upon the court in matters of alimony. Consequently, in October 1896, Mrs. Harris brought a second action seeking alimony.[52] Wetmore presided over this application and decided that the facts did not establish her claim. He reasoned that, despite the circumstances of her abandonment, Mrs. Harris had not been deserted by her husband and was not entitled to either a decree for divorce or, as a consequence, alimony.[53]

Arguably, Wetmore's ruling in the initial case had been authored with the specific intent of raising awareness about, and drawing legislative attention to, the absence of statutory provisions framing alimony. The case also appears to be the first occasion in which a Territorial judge overtly influenced the legislature to enact new law that would address an important social issue. Indeed, by remaining true to the rule of law, Wetmore influenced both the creation and the implementation of a new statute that recognized a novel situation in the region. As it turned out, this would not be the only occasion in which Wetmore demonstrated similar influence.

Presiding over the case of *R. v. Simpson* on 3 June 1898, Wetmore was confronted with a writ of *certiorari* seeking to quash a conviction handed down by a JP.[54] The accused had been convicted of using insulting language when describing one James May as being a "damned liar." The JP convicted and fined him $10.00 plus $8.15 in costs. In default of the fine, a distress warrant was issued, and subsequently two cows were seized and sold for $61. Wetmore determined that, in the absence of a statute covering "insulting language," the JP was without authority to convict, and thus the conviction was quashed.[55] Furthermore, not only had the JP erred, but he had also compounded the matter by overcollecting for the fine. Finally, while

Wetmore did not believe that the JP had been guilty of wilful misconduct, the judge nonetheless pointed out that the JP would not be protected from a civil suit if May launched such an action.[56] Wetmore, in acting as he did, not only reinforced the role that judicial review could play on the Prairies but also established the precedent that a judicial official of an inferior court was not immune from subsequent legal action flowing from the performance of his official duties.[57]

A similar instance that struck somewhat closer to home involved a case tried before Justice Rouleau that, upon appeal, was reversed by the SCNWT. Heard in 1899, the matter of Constable Nettleship raised the awkward question of whether NWMP officers were biased judicial officials, especially when it came to questions of adjudicating cases of desertion.[58] The original issue on appeal to Rouleau concerned the proceedings and verdict of an NWMP military service court that was constituted to inquire into a charge of desertion levelled against Constable Nettleship. The evidence revealed that Nettleship, having deserted his post, was placed on the deserters' list by Superintendent R. Burton Deane. The result of Deane's actions meant that Nettleship could be arrested on sight.

Nettleship's counsel applied for, and was granted, a writ of prohibition by Justice Rouleau, which prevented any arrest from taking place. On appeal by the NWMP to the court *en banc,* Rouleau's action was overturned on the argument that, during the service court hearing, the officers of the NWMP had acted as *quasi-judicial* officials and had properly exercised their judicial authority within the terms and conditions of the *NWMP Act.* Not only had Nettleship been legitimately placed on the deserters' list, but it had been Deane's duty to act in the manner that he had. Ultimately, the court determined that this duty did not disqualify an officer from subsequently conducting a fair service court hearing.

This case upheld several rules of law and created new precedents. It affirmed the SCNWT jurisdiction as an appeal court of last resort from another judicial body, albeit an NWMP judicial body and Rouleau's assize court. In fact, the SCNWT labelled Rouleau's decision as "incautious" and "premature."[59] The case also affirmed the court's jurisdiction to hear any matter brought before it on appeal. In exercising its judicial discretion, the court was innovative and cited numerous English and Canadian case law precedents and statutes, including the *NWMP Act* of 1894, which it termed analogous to the *British Army Mutiny Act.*[60] It was the first case in which a superior court upheld the authority of commissioned officers and the validity of the *NWMP Act* as a statute governing NWMP internal matters. The court also affirmed the common law judicial authority of NWMP officers and adjudged the fairness of the police service court law and practice in their own system.

A similar willingness to address the question of fairness in law and policy was demonstrated by Justice Scott in the 1903 case of *Song Lee v. The Town of*

Edmonton, a case involving a municipal bylaw imposing a fee of twenty-five dollars on every person operating a laundry.[61] The plaintiff, Song Lee, ran a small laundry that provided her with a picayune amount of money. Citing several English cases in concert with a Canadian case relating to the powers of municipalities to enact ordinances, Scott determined that the fee discriminated against "many women in destitute circumstances who earn a meager support by taking in washing," and as a result the bylaw was quashed because it was deemed oppressive and unfair.[62]

In one respect, this decision affirmed the legal status of women, their subservient role in society, and their right to earn a meagre income. Ten years earlier in the *Harris* case, Wetmore had also followed the rule of law in denying Mrs. Harris alimony and equality before the law. As such, *Harris* is an example of the triumph of the principle of law, whereas in the *Simpson* and *Song Lee* cases, laws, rules, doctrines, and precedents were applied to meet the particular circumstances of a case. Neither Wetmore nor Scott undermined the rule of law or the applicability of the common law. Rather, they adhered to the rule of law in creating new common law or in affecting the creation of new statute law.

Yet to the degree that these cases suggest a willingness to chart a new path shaped by the North-West Territories, it is equally true that this willingness was also tempered by conservatism. For example, in the case of *Martin v. Reilly* in 1889, the court *en banc* presided over an appeal from a trial jury decision.[63] At issue was the recovery of $1,250 between former business partners. The appeal court affirmed the jury verdict and held fast to the English rule that a jury decision should not be disturbed, "even assuming that the learned Judge did mis-direct the jury as complained of." Thus, "in the absence of any substantial wrong or miscarriage ... in the trial," the court held that "a new trial should not be granted."[64]

A similar course of action was taken in the 1891 case of *Sexsmith v. Murphy et al.,* an action of detinue for recovery of personal chattels.[65] Following the discovery of fresh evidence, leave to appeal was granted, although ultimately the court of appeal dismissed the case in citing the Australian precedent of *The Commissioner for Railways v. Brown.*[66] In that case, the court had held "that where the question is one of fact, and there is evidence on both sides properly submitted to the jury, the verdict of the jury once found ought to stand; and that setting aside such a verdict should be of rare and exceptional occurrence."[67]

Not surprisingly, judicial conservatism was in evidence in a number of areas and, as the *Harris* case suggested, in areas where notions of Victorian morality were at play. For example, in the 1899 case of *Ings v. Calgary General Hospital,* Justice Scott was confronted with a suit for wrongful dismissal and libel, which was entangled in more profound questions swirling around the subordinate status of women in the NWT and allegations of marital infidelity.[68] The plaintiff Ings was a Calgary physician who had been living for several years in an adulterous relationship with Mrs. Annie Grant. In his role as a physician at the General Hospital, Ings had recommended Grant for a nursing position, and she had been subsequently hired. However, when the relationship was exposed, both Ings and Grant were terminated because "the plaintiff [was] living in adultery ... [and this was] ... relevant because it tends to show not only that the latter [female] was not a fit and proper person for a nurse, but also that he must have been aware of the fact."[69] Obviously, while the subsequent case involved allegations of wrongful dismissal and libel, the fact that Ings was involved in a relationship with a woman who was not his wife was an integral ingredient in how the events had played themselves out.

Furthermore, the case highlighted the disparity between women's public and private roles and their actual status in society as well as before the courts. Although a trained nurse and a valued member of the medical community, Annie Grant lived in adultery and therefore was deemed not a "fit and proper person" to be a nurse. Nurses were to be virtuous models of the ideal Victorian female persona, responsible, subservient, and dutiful to doctors and tender and caring toward patients, husbands, and children. In the least, Grant did not "fit" that role. Moreover, both Grant and Ings had abandoned their respective families in Nova Scotia. Given the nature of these factors, it is less than surprising that the hospital dismissed them and that, on appeal, the court took particular notice of the evidence showing that Grant "had been living in adultery or leading an immoral life," which, in the court's opinion, had particular bearing on the issue at hand.[70]

The result was the first instance wherein the court articulated a common law rule that licentious behaviour rendered a woman to be unfit to perform nursing duties. Indeed, the decision supported the stereotype of dangerous or threatening women who lived outside the standards of acceptable behaviour. The case also revealed the extent to which the court was a product of its era, of its social, political, cultural, and economic boundaries. Moreover, it is evident that on many issues the court was not willing to entertain any form of judicial activism whatsoever.

A similar conservative bent can be seen in *Shorey et al. v. Stobart et al.*, which had been tried by Justice Rouleau on assize and then appealed to the Supreme Court sitting *en banc*. In a rather tangled case, the original ruling of March 1888 was gained by a fraudulent scheme concocted by E.H. Riley, a businessman unable to pay his debts and his mother, Georgina Riley, with the express intent of defeating and defrauding the plaintiffs and defendants out of their claims against E.H. Riley.[71] The ruse succeeded, and Mrs. Riley was subsequently awarded a settlement of $2,541.42, although E.H. Riley was not indebted to her whatsoever. A writ of execution was placed on the judgment; then the sheriff sold a large portion of E.H. Riley's goods to recover the monies owing. Shortly after 19 March 1888, the plaintiffs and defendants then applied and recovered judgment on their respective claims against E.H. Riley, claiming that the original judgment had been obtained by fraud and collusion. In a further twist, the defendants (Stobart, Sons, and Company), with the intent of aiding the Rileys in their scheme against the plaintiffs (Shorey et al.), entered into an agreement with the Rileys, outside the court proceedings, to abandon their claim, and in return Mrs. Riley would assign them her judgment. The agreement was carried out, and subsequently in the proceedings before Rouleau he voided the judgment and declared that it had been obtained by fraud, aided and abetted through the efforts of Stobart to defeat the creditors (Shorey et al.).

On appeal by the defendants, the court *en banc* was made aware of the fraudulent nature of the evidence presented in the lower court. What is more, the justices had never encountered similar circumstances, and lacking a Territorial or Canadian example to shape their response they adopted and applied English common law principles regarding abuse of the judicial process. They concurred with Rouleau's judgment that reversed the original finding, which, if allowed to stand, "would be a gross abuse [of the judicial process] to allow such a judgment to have validity."[72] The court adopted, adapted, and applied English law, in concert with its common law and judicial duty, in order to create appropriate precedents, and it thus prevented the administration of justice in the NWT from being brought into disrepute.

This understandable hostility toward fraudulent behaviour was also in evidence in the December 1893 appeal court's handling of *Bonin v. Robertson,* which involved the fraudulent conversion of a span of horses.[73] Apparently, an Elizabeth Malette had mortgaged some horses in the United States and then brought the animals to south Edmonton, where she sold them to the plaintiff without advising the buyer of the mortgage encumbrance. The issue in this case turned on whether an American chattel mortgage was enforceable in the NWT. The court *en banc* determined that it possessed sufficient discretion as to the reach of foreign laws in the NWT. Framed by that context, its ruling concluded that the mortgage was void since it had been neither filed nor registered in the Territories. In both *Shorey et al. v. Stobart et al.* and *Bonin v. Robertson,* the court had refused to exercise its judicial discretion so as to facilitate an injustice. Yet at the same time, by excluding evidence, drawing upon foreign decisions, and invoking common law, both cases are excellent examples in which the members of the SCNWT exercised judicial discretion. This fine line between judicial activism and judicial restraint was also retraced in 1899.

Tried before Justices Scott and Rouleau, *Kelly v. The Alaska Mining and Trading Company* concerned a lien for wages. In charting a course through the issues at stake, Scott and Rouleau referred to Maritime law in deciding in favour of the plaintiff, who had been employed on the ships *Alpha* and

M.M. Chessron operating on the Athabasca, Slave, and Mackenzie Rivers.[74] In framing their decision, the judges decided that in England the Courts of Chancery had jurisdiction in cases of necessaries and wages on which a lien might be created. They thus determined that a similar jurisdiction existed in the NWT. Furthermore, Admiralty law was consulted because the plaintiff had been employed as a seaman within the meaning of the *Inland Water Seamen's Act*.[75]

Finally, the court concluded that "Imperial and Canadian Acts show that the general maritime law is applicable to inland non-tidal waters[,] and the Court of Exchequer has constantly exercised its Admiralty jurisdiction on that assumption," and that "this Court has equal concurrent jurisdiction in Admiralty matters."[76] The result was that the case would be determined by this latticework of English and eastern Canadian rules and common law precedents in an attempt to fashion a Territorial legal remedy.[77] Certainly, the *Kelly* case reveals the extent to which the justices could be innovative in locating precedents to meet the particular circumstances of a litigating party. Indeed, it appears as if Rouleau and Scott went out of their way to find for the plaintiff's claim for $450 (plus interest) in wages.

In another notable instance, the court's willingness to be resourceful in finding precedents, and thus to engage in a form of activism, was laid bare in the reference case of *Re: Edmonton By-Law* that came before the court *en banc* in December 1900.[78] Submitted directly to the court by Lieutenant Governor Amedee Emmanuel Forget through the auspices of Attorney General F.W.G. Haultain, the reference asked the court to decide if a bylaw was valid prior to gaining the lieutenant governor's assent. The bylaw in question provided for the postponement of the payment of funds and was essentially a scheme by the town, disguised as a bylaw, to avoid payment of the principal of a debenture by equal instalments. Not only did the court rule against the bylaw, but it also did not shy away from criticizing the lieutenant governor: "The Lieutenant-Governor in Council cannot be a proper party to a cause or matter, and therefore the entertaining of a stated case such as is presented to the Court is simply making the Court or Judges the legal advisers of the Executive."[79]

In reaching the decision, the court reflected upon its own authority to determine such a matter under the *Judicature Ordinance*. It invoked the rule of law and suggested that there was no legislation that required a ruling on reference cases. It did, however, acknowledge the supremacy of the legislative council in reviewing the matter and determining that the bylaw was inappropriate. Justice Richardson's parting comments reflect the annoyance of the court. Richardson stated that "should a case of similar character be hereafter submitted to us we will consider fully, before investigating the question submitted, whether the case is properly before the Court."[80] By reviewing and deciding the bylaw case, the court promoted the common law precedent of judicial review by a court of last resort that had definitive authority in all statute and common law matters.

Judicial review affirmed the court's status as a supreme court and, in and of itself, was important for the court's members. At the same time, reference cases also provided the government with an effective mechanism to obtain a conclusive legal opinion and ruling prior to enacting laws. Any challenges to the legality of bylaws or ordinances that had already been considered by the SCNWT on reference were, effectively, challenges to the tribunal's established opinion. It is thus possible to conclude that perhaps reference cases reduced the amount of litigation after such legislation had been enacted.

Finally, throughout the early period of the court's jurisprudence, the justices also drew upon their own decisions in building up a body of Territorial jurisprudence.[81] The matter of *Turriff v. McHugh* in 1889 involved the question of responsibility for warranting the title of a horse sold to the plaintiff. In framing their ruling, the court *en banc* cited an earlier case that had established a rule regarding the sale of personal chattels by a vendor.[82] In that instance, the court declared that, upon such a sale, it was to be implied that a vendor transferred title to the chattel and, consequently, warranted the title.[83] In the *Turriff* case, however, the plaintiff had full knowledge of the "cloud on the title," and consequently the appeal was dismissed.

A similar willingness to draw upon its own reasoning in fashioning decisions for more recent disputes was revealed in 1895 when the court, sitting *en banc,* considered the cases of *Massey v. McClelland* and *Baker v. McClelland*.[84] These were references from Justice Richardson concerning land that had not been registered under the *Homestead Exemption Ordinance*.[85] In the guiding case of *Claxton,* Justice Richardson had held that an unregistered homestead was liable to seizure and sale under execution.[86] Speaking for the court *en banc* in the *Massey* case, Richardson ruled that Massey had no exemption from seizure and sale and that in the other case Baker had a temporary exemption for a later execution date. The *Claxton* case had reaffirmed the principle that Territorial legislation was valid and had full force and effect as NWT law. That rule was subsequently extrapolated to the cases at bar and thereafter became entrenched as common law. Thus, when the court cited its own rules, it not only affirmed former judicial decisions and rules of law but also demonstrated that Territorial law was living jurisprudence.

This broad selection of civil cases indicates that, in sitting on assize and court sessions constituted *en banc,* the judges of the SCNWT advanced a form of circumscribed judicial activism. They applied their relative interpretation and judicial discretion to the laws, rules, doctrines, and precedents while remaining true to the rule of law. On balance, their overriding sense of the law and possible remedy was rooted in the particular circumstances of parties appearing before the court. In so doing, they applied principles, doctrines, and precedents from English and Canadian statutes and common law. And, where applicable, they cited precedents and doctrines of the Supreme Court of Canada as well as provincial Supreme Courts while turning, on occasion, to American and Australian judicial decisions and scholarly papers and publications.[87]

Moreover, the justices' decisions emphasized finding new rules of law, fashioned for the new communities and novel situations of the Territories, while remaining true to English common law. In facilitating the growth of enduring common law doctrines while, in equal measure, fashioning a Territorial jurisprudence as a bedrock for the region's emerging economy, politics, and society, the court provided a key legacy for the emergence of Prairie society in the early years of the twentieth century. In so doing, the court gave voice to an astute mix of principle and unadorned practicality that, in time, resonated in almost every corner of this vast landscape.

Figure 7.1

SCNWT justices and dates of tenure, 1876-1926

- James Farquharson Macleod, 1 January 1876-5 September 1894
- Hugh Richardson, 22 July 1876-12 November 1903
- Charles-Borromée Rouleau, 28 September 1883-25 August 1901
- Edward Ludlow Wetmore, 18 February 1887-16 September 1907
- Thomas Horace McGuire, 25 April 1887-18 February 1902, then appointed chief justice, 18 February 1902-3 January 1903
- David Lynch Scott, 28 September 1894-26 July 1924
- James Emile Pierre Prendergast, 18 February 1902-18 March 1944
- Arthur Lewis Sifton, became chief justice, 3 January 1903-25 May 1910
- Henry William Newlands, 2 January 1904-17 February 1921
- Horace Harvey, 27 June 1904-9 September 1949
- Thomas Cook Johnstone, 8 October 1906-29 November 1913
- Charles Allan Stuart, 8 October 1906-5 March 1926

Source: This list was compiled from the *Times Law Reports*, vols. 1-7, 1887-1907. Also see Louis A. Knafla and Richard Klumpenhouwer, *Lords of the Western Bench: A Biographical History of the Judges of Alberta* (Calgary: Legal Archives Society of Alberta, 1997).

Figure 7.2

SCNWT appeal proceedings, 1887-1907

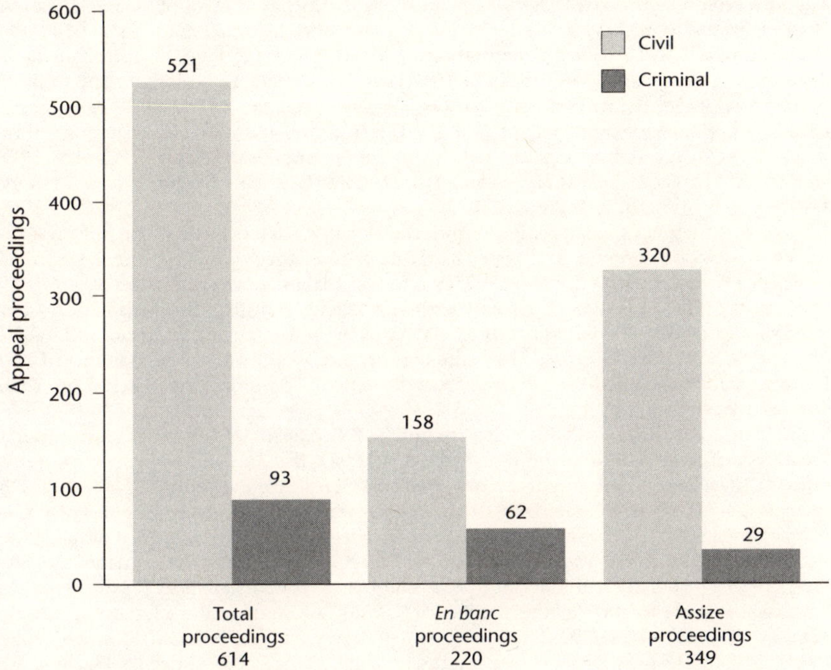

Notes

1 Louis A. Knafla, "From Oral to Written Memory: The Common Law Tradition in Western Canada," in *Law and Justice in a New Land: Essays in Western Canadian Legal History,* ed. Louis A. Knafla (Calgary and Toronto: Carswell, 1986), 31-77.

2 See Louis A. Knafla and Richard Klumpenhouwer, *Lords of the Western Bench: A Biographical History of the Supreme and District Courts of Alberta, 1876-1990* (Calgary: Legal Archives Society of Alberta, 1997); Wilbur F. Bowker, *A Consolidation of Fifty Years of Legal Writings 1938-1988,* ed. Marjorie Bowker (Edmonton: Faculty of Law, University of Alberta, 1989), 691-734; D. Colwyn Williams, "The Dawn of Law on the Prairies," *Saskatchewan Bar Review* 27, 4 (1962): 126-33; and 28, 1 (1962): 17-69. Also see D. Colwyn Williams, "Law and Institutions in the North West Territories, 1869-1905," *Saskatchewan Bar Review* 28, 3 (1963): 109-18; 29, 2 (1964): 51-60; 29, 3 (1964): 83-101; and 30, 2 (1965): 51-66; J.E. Cote, "The Introduction of English Law into Alberta," *Alberta Law Review* 3 (1964): 262-92; W.P Ward, "Administration of Justice in the North-West Territories, 1870-1887" (Edmonton: University of Alberta, 1966); E.C. Morgan, "The North-West Mounted Police, 1873-1883" (Regina: University of Saskatchewan, 1970); T.M. Reynolds, "Justices of the Peace in the North-West Territories, 1870-1905" (Regina: University of Regina, 1978); and Roderick G. Martin, "The North West Mounted Police and Frontier Justice" (PhD thesis, University of Calgary, 2005), for an extensive review of law's reception.

3 Knafla, "From Oral to Written Memory," 59.

4 See Figure 7.2 for a breakdown of the SCNWT's appeal workload.

5 This phrase is coined from C.C. McCaul, "Precursors of the Bench and Bar in the Western Provinces," *Canadian Bar Review* 3 (1925): 25-40.

6 See Roderick G. Martin, "The Common Law and the Justices of the SCNWT, 1887-1907" (master's thesis, University of Calgary, 1997), 145.

7 Norman Hillmer, "Biggar, Oliver Mowat," in *The Canadian Encyclopedia,* vol. 1, ed. James H. Marsh (Edmonton: Hurtig Publishers, 1985), 171.

8 The firm would later boast W.F.A. Turgeon, KC and attorney general of Saskatchewan; see *Who's Who and Why,* vols. 6-7, ed. C.W. Parker (Toronto: International Press, 1914), 794.

9 W.G. Morrow, "An Historical Examination of Alberta's Legal System," *Alberta Law Review* 29, 2 (1981): 148-70, n3. See also *North-West Territories (NWT) Act,* c. 50, in "The Constitutional Development of the Prairie Provinces," in *The Canadian North-West: Its Early Development and Legislative Records,* vols. 1 and 2, ed. E.H. Oliver (Ottawa: Government Printing Bureau, 1914), n.p. Oliver's published documents contain the former *NWT Act* (1875), chapter 49, *An Act to Amend and Consolidate the Laws Respecting the North-West Territories,* assented to 8 April 1875, 1075.

10 1 T.L.R. vi, "Judges of the Supreme Court of the North-West Territories." The jurisdiction of the court was both original and appellate. Section 14 of the *NWT Act* conferred upon the court the powers of a superior court of civil and criminal jurisdiction. Section 5 of the *NWT Ordinances* (1886) was also congruent with the federal statute. "The jurisdiction of the SCNWT ... shall be exercised as nearly as may be as in the High Court of Justice in England" (7). The SCNWT then acquired the same competence as the Courts of Common Law in England, which included the Court of Queen's Bench, Common Pleas, Exchequer, Chancery, and Probate.

11 See Martin, "The Common Law." Also see Roderick G. Martin, "Macleod at Law: A Judicial Biography of James Farquharson Macleod, 1874-1894," in *People and Place: Historical Influences on Legal Culture,* ed. Jonathan Swainger and Constance Backhouse (Vancouver: UBC Press, 2003), 37-59; R.C. Macleod's article in *Dictionary of Canadian Biography,* vol. 12, ed. Frances G. Halpenny (Toronto: University of Toronto Press, 1990), 672-75; Captain Ernest J. Chambers, *The Royal North-West Mounted Police: A Corps History* (Montreal: Mortimer Press, 1906), 5-160; Sherrill MacLaren, *Braehead: Three Founding Families in Nineteenth Century Canada* (Toronto: McClelland and Stewart, 1986), 264; and "Colonel James Farquharson Macleod, C.M.G.," in *R.C.M.P. Quarterly* 1, 4 (Ottawa: Royal Canadian Mounted Police, 1944), 141-42. For his judicial career, see the judicial notebooks of Justice J.F. Macleod, files 74.1/252, 253, 254, 255, 256, and 257, at the Provincial Archives of Alberta (PAA), Edmonton; and vols. 1-7 for the years 1889-91; and the Supreme Court Sittings, 1890-94, file M776, Glenbow Alberta Archives. For Macleod's appeal cases, see T.L.R., vols. 1-2. Macleod had a rigorous, active, and interesting police and judicial career. He had been a practising lawyer, a lieutenant colonel in the militia, a superintendent, an assistant commissioner, and a JP in the NWMP, 1874-76; a civilian SM, January-July 1876; a commissioner of the NWMP, an SM, and a member of the NWT Council, July 1876-80; and in 1877 a special Indian commissioner, NWT, who negotiated Treaty 7. He was then appointed a full-time civilian SM, 1880-85; a judge of the High Court of Justice with precedence, 1885-87; and justice of the SCNWT, 1887-94. He died in September 1894 at Calgary.

12 Knafla and Klumpenhouwer, *Lords of the Western Bench,* 160-61.

13 Ibid. at 158-59.

14 Bowker, *Legal Writings,* 722.

15 See Figure 7.1 for details of the court's membership.

16 Sections 15 and 17 of the *NWT Act.* On assize, the justices also heard appeals from inferior courts.

17 1 T.L.R. xix; and Bowker, *Legal Writings,* 719.

18 Section 8 of the *NWT Act.* The legacy of the travelling judge was deeply rooted in English legal historical tradition. In the NWT, the first travelling judges were NWMP commissioned officer JPs and SMs, whose authority was *ex officio,* and by virtue of the *NWT Act.* English assize judges' authority stemmed from royal commissions, and as Crown representatives they brought royal justice to the counties. The SCNWT justices were also travelling judges who brought the administration of the law and justice to local NWT towns.

19 Courts of Revision decided municipal, school, and county taxation assessments. See 5 T.L.R. 192 in *"Re: Canadian Pacific Railways and Town of Macleod";* 5 T.L.R. 459 in *"Re: P. Heiminch v. The Town of Edmonton";* and 5 T.L.R. 462 in *"Re: Isabella Heiminch and the Town of Edmonton."*

20 This conclusion was substantiated from the review of the primary source materials that included T.L.R., vols. 1-7, and the judicial notebooks of Justices Macleod, Rouleau, and Scott in accession file 79.266 at PAA. Also, the NWMP "Annual Reports," 1887-1907, contain a number of assize cases.

21 From a total of 220, 158 were civil and 62 were criminal cases. The rest were assize appeals and other issues.

22 PAA, accession file 79.266, 27 May 1887-9 January 1891, for the Northern Alberta Judicial District, where there were 1,064 civil assize cases.

23 See Henry Campbell Black, *Black's Law Dictionary,* 6th ed. (St. Paul: West Publishing Co., 1990), at 96, 890. Leave to appeal means "permission or authorization to do something" (890).

24 Martin, "Macleod at Law," 37-59; "The North West Mounted Police and Frontier Justice," 169-70. Contemporary interpretation would suggest that NWMP courts were not, or never could be, courts of first instance. The *NWT Act* (1873) and *Administration of Justice NWT Act,* chapter 35, and 1877 *NWT Act* amended, however, provided that SMs and JPs would act as summary trial judges, or two JPs or a JP and an SM in more serious matters. Furthermore, in the courts of first instance between 1874 and 1898, there were over 13,788 cases heard, and in numerous proceedings a case that came before the summary conviction court might contain a number of individuals charged with offences. NWMP officer judges sat on 7,989 (58 percent) of those cases. The majority of the civilian cases without the NWMP magistrates were heard by local town JPs. The only year in which civilian magistrates or judges of the high court presided over more cases (364 versus 263) was 1885, and that was significant for a variety of reasons, including NWMP involvement in the Riel Rebellion and the treason trials.

25 T.L.R., vols. 1-7. The cumulative results reveal that SCNWT justices heard 521 cases in civil or commercial law and 93 cases in criminal law.

26 See T.L.R. for the CPR civil cases. They are 1 T.L.R. 88, 4 T.L.R. 227, 5 T.L.R. 60, 5 T.L.R. 123, 5 T.L.R. 143, 5 T.L.R. 187, 5 T.L.R. 190, 5 T.L.R. 420, 5 T.L.R. 503, 6 T.L.R. 168, 6 T.L.R. 420, 6 T.L.R. 423, 7 T.L.R. 56, and 7 T.L.R. 327.

27 For negligence of the company, see *Finlay v. CPR,* 5 T.L.R. 143 and *Kenny v. The CPR,* 5 T.L.R. 420. For animals, see *Eggleston v. CPR,* 6 T.L.R. 168. For speed through a municipality, see *Andreas v. Canadian Pacific Railway Co.*, 7 T.L.R. 327.

28 1 T.L.R. 88.

29 *Mayer v. Grand Trunk RR* (1880), 31 U.C.C.P. 248.

30 *Grand Trunk RR v. Vogel* (1885), 11 S.C.R. 612.

31 In the absence of NWT case law precedent.

32 5 T.L.R. 420.

33 For the English cases informing McGuire's decision, see *Foulkes v. Metropolitan Ry. Co.*, 49 L.J.C.P. 361; *Bretherton v. Wood,* 6 Moore (1821) at 141; 3 Br. & B. 54; 9 Price 408; and 23 R.R. 556. For *Collett v. London & N.W.R. Co.*, see (1851), 16 Q.B. 984; 20 L.J.Q.B. 411; 15 Jur. 1053. For the Kenny case, see *Kenny v. The CPR* (1902), 5 T.L.R. 420.

34 6 T.L.R. 168, 1 W.L.R. 356, Rev. 36 S.C.R. 641.

35 6 T.L.R. 168. The SCNWT cited the binding case of *Village of Granby v. Menard* (1900), 31 S.C.R. 14.

36 Ibid. at 169.

37 36 S.C.R. 641.

38 Also see the Consolidated Rules of the Supreme Court of the NWT regarding judicial authority. In *Jackson v. Canadian Pacific Railway* (1907), 6 T.L.R. 423, Justice Wetmore proclaimed the all-encompassing and extensive authority of the court *en banc.*

39 See *Kenny v. The CPR,* 5 T.L.R. 420; *Hansen v. CPR,* 6 T.L.R. 420; *Andreas v. CPR,* 7 T.L.R. 327; *Eggleston v. The CPR,* 6 T.L.R. 168, reversed on appeal to the SCC.

40 See 1 T.L.R. 88, 4 T.L.R. 227, 5 T.L.R. 60, 5 T.L.R. 123, 5 T.L.R. 143, 5 T.L.R. 187, 5 T.L.R. 192, 5 T.L.R. 503, 6 T.L.R. 168; for reversal by the SCC, see 36 S.C.R. 641, 6 T.L.R. 423, 7 T.L.R. 56.

41 Bowker, *Legal Writings,* 63. The Torrens system was introduced to the NWT on 1 January 1887, through the *Territories Real Property Act.* It was later modified by amendments to the act through the *Land Titles Act* of 1894. Documents registered pre-Torrens were brought forward into the Torrens system. The land registration system operated only upon land for

which a patent from the Crown had been issued. See Kirk N. Lambrecht, *The Administration of Dominion Lands, 1870-1930* (Winnipeg: Hignell Printing, 1991), 13. Also see 1 T.L.R. xviii, *An Act Respecting Real Property in the Territories* (49 Vic. c. 26, Dom.). Parliament had originally established the Torrens system in 1886.

42 2 T.L.R. 133.

43 Ibid. at 140-41.

44 Bowker, *Legal Writings,* 720. He also suggested that court rulings were "sound and fair."

45 1 T.L.R. 111.

46 4 T.L.R. 285.

47 Ibid. at 293.

48 See *Harris v. Harris,* 3 T.L.R. 289.

49 Section 8, *NWT Act,* R.S.C. 1886, c. 50, and the *Harris* case, 289.

50 Ibid. at 290. Original jurisdiction was conferred upon the SCNWT justices by section 8 (the *Judicature Ordinance,* chapter 21) of the *NWT Act* (see note 10). The court had the authority exercised by the English courts of common law as of 15 July 1870. The English courts, however, had no jurisdiction in alimony. Judicial authority over alimony cases was exercised by the Courts for Divorce and Matrimonial Causes.

51 Harris (no. 2), 3 T.L.R. 416. Also see 57 & 58 Vic. (1894), c. 17, s. 20, of the *Dominion Acts:* "This section gave the Legislative Assembly power to confer on the Territorial Courts jurisdiction in matters of alimony."

52 Harris (no. 2) at 416. Also see the *Ordinance Respecting Alimony,* chapter 29 in *The Ordinances of the North-West Territories* (Edmonton: Government Printer, 1896), 387: "The Supreme Court of the [NWT] shall have jurisdiction to grant alimony to any wife who would be entitled to alimony by the law of England, or to any wife who would be entitled by the law of England to a divorce ... or to any wife whose husband lives separate from her without sufficient cause."

53 *Harris v. Harris* (no. 2), 3 T.L.R. 428-29.

54 *R. v. Simpson,* 3 T.L.R. 475. The justice of the peace was not named in the report.

55 3 T.L.R. 476.

56 *Regina v. Banks,* 2 T.L.R. 81, deals with intentional misconduct of a judicial official.

57 *Black's Law Dictionary,* 885. Law is derived from judicial precedents, legislation, or custom. Wetmore quashed the conviction as a nonexistent offence and re-established the rule of common law.

58 4 T.L.R. 148.

59 Ibid. at 164 and 168.

60 Ibid. at 156.

61 5 T.L.R. 466.

62 Ibid. at 466, 468, 470.

63 1 T.L.R. 217.

64 Ibid. at 223.

65 1 T.L.R. 311.

66 *Black's Law Dictionary,* 450. Detinue, a "possessory action for recovery of personal chattels unjustly detained." See *The Commissioner for Railways v. Brown* (1887), 13 Ap. Cas. 133, 57 L.J.P.C. 72, 57 L.T. 895 (New South Wales).

67 Cited in *Sexsmith v. Murphy et al.* and in *MacDonnell et al. v. Robertson,* 1 T.L.R. 438. *The Commissioner for Railways v. Brown,* 13 Ap. Cas. 133, 57 L.J.P.C. 72, 57 L.T. 895, as per C.J. Tindal (1841), was cited and affirmed.

68 4 T.L.R. 58.

69 Ibid. at 63.

70 Ibid. at 58; see the headnotes.

71 1 T.L.R. 262.

72 Ibid. at 279.

73 2 T.L.R. 21.

74 4 T.L.R. 18. See the headnotes for this case. Maritime law and the *Inland Water Seaman's Act* were utilized as authorities by the SCNWT. The court had concurrent jurisdiction with the

Exchequer Court of Canada in Admiralty matters inasmuch as the Court of Chancery in England had concurrent jurisdiction with the Court of Admiralty on 15 July 1870.

75 *The Inland Seamen's Act,* R.S.C., c. 75.

76 See 4 T.L.R. 21.

77 Ibid. at 18-27. The case revealed that the justices could be quite innovative and creative in finding precedent and law to meet the particular or individual circumstances of a litigating party. They referred to obscure rules and precedents of law, including a number of Maritime and Admiralty acts applicable in Canada that included *Smith's Admiralty Practice and Maritime Law, The Inland Water Seaman's Act,* R.S.C., c. 75; *The Merchant's Shipping Act,* 1854, 17 & 18 Vic. c. 104 (Imp.); *The Colonial Courts of Admiralty Act,* 1890, 53 & 54 Vic. c. 27 (Imp.); *The Maritime Jurisdiction Act,* 1877, and *The Canadian Admiralty Act,* 1891, 54 & 55 Vic. c. 29.

78 4 T.L.R. 450. Reference cases were a government practice in which a superior court was asked to rule on controversial or uncertain issues prior to any stated case coming before the court. This was challenged in 1894. See James G. Snell and Frederick Vaughan, *The Supreme Court of Canada: History of the Institution* (Toronto: Osgoode Society, 1985), 136. "The federal Conservative governments of the 1890's sent five reported cases to the Court on reference" (293).

79 See *Re: Edmonton By-Law,* 4 T.L.R. 455. The court *en banc* advised the lieutenant governor not to give his assent to the bylaw.

80 Ibid.

81 1 T.L.R. 83, *Dickie v. Dunn.*

82 1 T.L.R. 186: "The court only applies the rule of law that a sale of personal chattels implies an affirmation by the vendor that the chattel is his, and therefore he warrants title" (187).

83 There was an implied warranty with the title that the vendor transfers to the buyer: "The court only implies an affirmation by the vendor that the chattel is his, and therefore he warrants the title" (1 T.L.R. 187).

84 2 T.L.R. 179.

85 See the *Homestead Exemption Ordinance,* 57 & 58 Vic., c. 29. Also see the *Territorial Real Property Act,* Vict. (1888), s. 16 of 51, c. 20; and Vict. (1894), 57 & 58, c. 29.

86 1 T.L.R. 282.

87 *The Territorial Law Reports,* vols. 1-7 (Toronto: Carswell, 1900-12).

8

The Implications of a Provincial Police Force in Alberta and Saskatchewan

Zhiqiu Lin and Augustine Brannigan

The Advent of the Prairie Provincial Police in Alberta and Saskatchewan

The North-West Mounted Police (NWMP) were the first public police force responsible for maintenance of law and order in western Canada. In 1905, when Alberta and Saskatchewan became provinces, they had the power under the *BNA Act* (1867) to create their own provincial forces, as had already been done elsewhere. Quebec formed its own police force as early as 1870, British Columbia and Manitoba in 1880, and Ontario in 1896, although these forces existed more on paper than in reality. The Royal North-West Mounted Police (RNWMP) commissioner, A. Bowen Perry, anticipated the organization of provincial police by the newly established governments.[1] Due to financial considerations, both governments decided to continue with RNWMP services. In 1917, the federal government withdrew the RNWMP from civil police duties in Alberta and Saskatchewan. The provinces were forced to organize their own forces. The withdrawal of the RNWMP was precipitated by the collapse in personnel levels as policemen resigned in great numbers to enroll for military service overseas. However, there was also some feeling that the federal service did not relish the onset of policing the new provincial prohibition legislation.[2] The new forces were established in 1917 but were fated to be short-lived. By 1928, Saskatchewan faced financial exigencies, and by 1932 Alberta faced bankruptcy.

Although the provincial forces existed only for a relatively short period, the history of the forces provides a unique opportunity to examine social and political implications of provincial policing in western Canada. Compared with the federal police, the provincial forces were more closely attuned to the concerns of the provincial governments, and provincial legislation received greater priority. During the period 1917-32, the provincial statutes, including liquor control and public order offences, enjoyed an upswing in enforcement. In addition, the provincial police were more vulnerable to interference by provincial politicians. In the case of the Saskatchewan Provincial Police (SPP), the force became at times identified with the political aspirations of the provincial Liberal Party. This connection could be attributed largely to the fact that the SPP was created out of the secret liquor police. In contrast, the Alberta Provincial Police (APP) enjoyed a more autonomous organizational structure from the start; it formed the first provincial police commission to distance the force from the executive branch of the provincial government. It was this organizational foundation, not the larger social and political differences between the provinces, that explained the subsequent different career trajectories of the two forces.

Organizational Structure of the Provincial Police and Police Independence

In the history of policing, two of the key changes in police institutions were the adoption of a quasi-military bureaucratic hierarchy and the rise in political autonomy of the police. In the case of the provincial forces, their development simply built on the legacy of the Mounties. The RNWMP influenced the provincial police considerably in terms of their organizational structure and the impartial enforcement of law.[3] The regulations of the Alberta Provincial Police stipulated that, "towards the attainment of complete police efficiency, it is essential that the members of the Force should cultivate and maintain the good opinion of the country at large, by prompt obedience to all lawful commands, by pursuing a steady and impartial line of conduct in the discharge of their duties, by their cleanly, sober and orderly habits, and by a civil and respectful bearing to all classes."[4] How did this emphasis on impartiality work in practice? Stationing police in barracks situated outside the community was not feasible in western Canada. In fact, the barracks of the police forces were typically rented houses or buildings on the main streets of the towns or rural municipalities. According to the police regulations, the constables were subject to periodic changes in their districts or detachments. In practice, these regulations were rarely implemented as the transfers were very expensive. Nevertheless, the change of a detachment was a common measure for a constable against whom a complaint had been filed. The police regulations prohibited a police constable from serving in a district in which he had family connections or from taking part in the liquor trade or other kinds of business. The case of Constable Harper of the APP suggests that the APP followed this rule closely. Harper was transferred out of the detachment at Vulcan because he was the son of a local justice of the peace and was well known in that community.[5] However, this rule could not be observed without difficulties. Unlike in the RNWMP, most of the members of the provincial police were married men. In Saskatchewan, the policy was not followed at all or only rarely. The family of Inspector Simpson, commander of the Weyburn Division, ran a small business in the same district. The inspector's family supplied milk to the

Weyburn Mental Hospital in his wife's name. To return the favour to the hospital, he frequently violated the police regulations by acting as a coroner for the hospital when a civilian coroner was not available.[6]

Police constables were also prohibited from declaring their political affiliation. Provincial police acts treated "wearing a society or party emblem whilst on duty" and "manifesting any political partisanship" as serious offences.[7] Political interference seemed not to be so serious an issue with the APP. But the independence of the SPP in law enforcement had been seriously questioned, especially after Mr. Cross became the attorney general of the province in 1921.

The Saskatchewan Provincial Police adopted the commissioner system modelled on that of the RNWMP. The Saskatchewan government used the Saskatchewan Secret Service (an undercover anti-liquor squad) as an organizational basis for the provincial police. The former head of the Secret Service, Charles Augustus Mahony, was appointed as the commissioner of the SPP. Under this system, the provincial police were controlled and managed directly by the commissioner and assistant commissioner. However, they were also subject to the control, orders, and authority of the attorney general of the province.[8] There were no regulations specifying the power of the attorney general. The system opened the door for the politicians to manipulate the police for political purposes. During the period 1917-21, when Turgeon was the attorney general, the commissioner of the SPP enjoyed considerable autonomy in managing the police. However, after 1922, James Cross, the attorney general, reversed Turgeon's hands-off policy. Cross was especially interested in the police and assumed an active role in the administration of the force. Consequently, Commissioner Mahony's authority was subverted, and Mahony became "a cog in the wheel," in his own words.[9] And the assistant commissioner, Tracey, commented that "the policy was a mistaken one and did not operate to the best interests of either the police force or of the government, because it brought the administration of the police in such proximity to the political side of the Government as to be too likely to encourage designing persons to try and affect it on political grounds, while it laid the government too easily open to the imputation that the police were subject to political control."[10] Indeed, so gross and open was the political interference with the force that in 1930 the Saskatchewan government established a royal commission to inquire into the problem. Inspector Duckworth testified that for some Liberal politicians "it was of prime importance that a member of the Force should be politically fit, that he should exercise his influence and office for the advancement of party interests."[11] Under this circumstance, some constables were actively engaged in political work in some federal or provincial elections; others became unofficial Liberal Party workers.[12] Inspector Duckworth pointed out that as a result "members of the Saskatchewan Provincial Police force dabbled in politics and were encouraged and in some cases required to do so by 'heelers' and the greater their efficiency in this respect rather than in their abilities as police officers was what frequently counted when it came to promotions. For the same reason men who had shown themselves unfit for the service could not be dismissed or transferred to some other point."[13]

Improper political influence was exercised personally by Attorney General Cross and his deputy attorney general. They interfered not only with the appointment, dismissal, or placement of constables but also with how they performed their duties. During elections, constables were frequently ordered to refrain from normal law enforcement with a view to benefiting the Liberal Party.[14] The 1930 royal commission inquiry showed that political interference with the SPP was serious and extensive. The commission investigated seventeen cases of political interference for the benefit of the Liberals.

Compared with the SPP, the APP did not experience serious problems with political interference. The first step to promote the independence of the Alberta Provincial Police taken by the Alberta government was to create a board of commissioners as a commanding body of the APP, the first of its kind for a provincial force in Canada. The idea of a board of the commissioners was associated with the development of the city police.[15] The *Alberta Police Act* did not offer an explicit statement that the mandate of the board was to remove the police from political control, but this was implied. The board was composed of two members of the lower judiciary (Gilbert Saunders, police magistrate for the city of Calgary, and Philip Carteret Hill Primrose, police magistrate for the city of Edmonton, who served as chairman) and a senior civil servant (Arthur George Browning, deputy attorney general for the Province of Alberta, who served as the secretary).[16] The board possessed a considerable degree of autonomy in its decision making.[17]

However, the board was short-lived. After a two-year operation, it was abolished by the *Police Act* of 1919. Control and management of the force were transferred to the attorney general. The major reason for its abolition was that it enjoyed little popularity because of a series of controversies surrounding the force. In its first year, some sixty-six new recruits resigned. According to Superintendent McDonnell, "a considerable number left shortly after engagement presumably after finding themselves unsuited to the work." Others claimed that they were unable to live on their pay.[18] Other evidence suggested that there was considerable dissatisfaction among the constables, with incompetent management by the superintendent and disappointment with city-police-style uniforms, of extremely inferior quality and an embarrassment to the rank and file.

The large number of resignations and the controversies surrounding the superintendent induced some criticism of the management of the force. In the provincial legislature, the government was compelled to defend the force and the board against attacks from the opposition. On 28 February 1918, MLAs A.E. Ewing and J.W.S. Kemmis demanded a public investigation into the administration and operation of the provincial force because of "the unsatisfactory conditions" prevailing among the police.[19]

One week later, after the APP became a controversial topic in the provincial legislature, Superintendent McDonnell tendered his resignation on the ground of ill health. At the same time, he accepted a position of inspector at Peace River. However, McDonnell's resignation did not change the unfavourable perception of the force, which was associated with the enforcement of the unpopular prohibition laws.[20] The government finally abolished the board altogether and reorganized the force to improve its public credibility.

In Saskatchewan, why was the SPP so prone to manipulation by the politicians for political purposes? For the twenty-four years (1905-29) after the creation of the province, Saskatchewan was under the government of the Liberal Party. The first premier of the province, Walter Scott (1905-16), had a reputation for awarding jobs and contracts to political supporters. Although Premier William Martin (1916-22) tried to move toward the ideals of more efficient government, later premiers Charles Dunning (1922-26) and James Gardiner (1926-29) reverted to Liberal form. In retrospect, it appears that the lack of an effective political opposition failed to check the co-optation of government jobs and contracts for political advantage by those in power.

In Alberta, the Liberals also formed the government for a long period (1905-21) and used patronage appointments to reward political supporters, but not to the same extent as their Saskatchewan counterparts.[21] During the period 1921-35, the United Farmers of Alberta formed the provincial government. Monto reports that they adopted a policy according to which "the elected members should not have anything to do with operating the political (i.e., electoral) machinery."[22] This political pluralism appears to have countered political exploitation of the civil service. The provincial police, unlike the previous federal force, were more vulnerable to political interference from provincial politicians. The Saskatchewan case also implies that the attainment of police autonomy depends not only on an ideal rule of law but also on the political culture in which they operate and the mechanisms employed to ensure police autonomy. Concerns with professionalism within the forces may mitigate the extent to which they could be manipulated politically. But it was not a factor that could alter the ultimate fate of a police force in the face of a political machine with little concern for autonomy. Concern with professionalism among officers themselves may be a significant factor in the struggle over the autonomy and independence of police organization, as in nineteenth-century Toronto, but it is not determinative by itself.[23]

Transitions in Policing and Changes in Priorities

If there is evidence that the APP and SPP as provincial institutions were under a stronger sphere of political influence, is it possible that this affected in some aggregate or macrosociological way the nature of law enforcement in each province? To research this question, we examined the annual reports of the RNWMP, the respective provincial forces, and the RCMP over the period 1905-40 to determine if there were any discernible shifts in the kinds and rates of crimes associated with these changes in policing.[24] This section reports the results of this analysis. As we shall see, a close study of the trends in serious crime and public order offences during this period reveals that there were discernible shifts in law enforcement patterns in the transition points from the RNWMP to the provincial police and to the RCMP. In the next section, we attempt to capture some of the flavour of policing by describing at a microsociological level the sorts of things that confronted the provincial forces and that may help us to interpret the patterns of enforcement associated with their regimes.

Two important themes in historical criminology are of some relevance here. The history of policing suggests that the modern police forces emerged in urban areas coincidentally with the rise of the large classes of urban paupers pushed off the land by agricultural closures and drawn to the cities by industrialization. The English police developed as a rational institution as a way of controlling the "dangerous classes," the poor, and the marginal fringes of society. That is the first point. However, as North America was settled, the model of an urban police force responsible to civic authority diffused to newly established towns and cities often as an alternative to vigilante rule. In other words, they emerged in the absence of riots and without threats from a large, hostile underclass. Over time, the object of control shifted from "class control" to "crime control." That is the second point. Monkkonnen traced this process in the large US cities from 1860 to 1920. He discovered that over time control of public order, which dominated policing agendas at the start of his series, gradually gave way to a preoccupation with victimization and that a concern over drunkenness and disorderly conduct was superseded by a concern for property and personal offences.[25] What do the provincial trends in Alberta and Saskatchewan reveal?

Figure 8.1 is based on the annual reports from the respective police forces. It shows the rates of arrest for *Criminal Code* infractions recorded annually for the provincial nonurban sector. It suggests very little in terms of overall trends. There is no overall direction. The rates represent a random walk – at least ostensibly. The numbers in Figure 8.1 are standardized as arrests per

Figure 8.1

Arrests for *Criminal Code* offences by province per 100,000 population, 1906-40

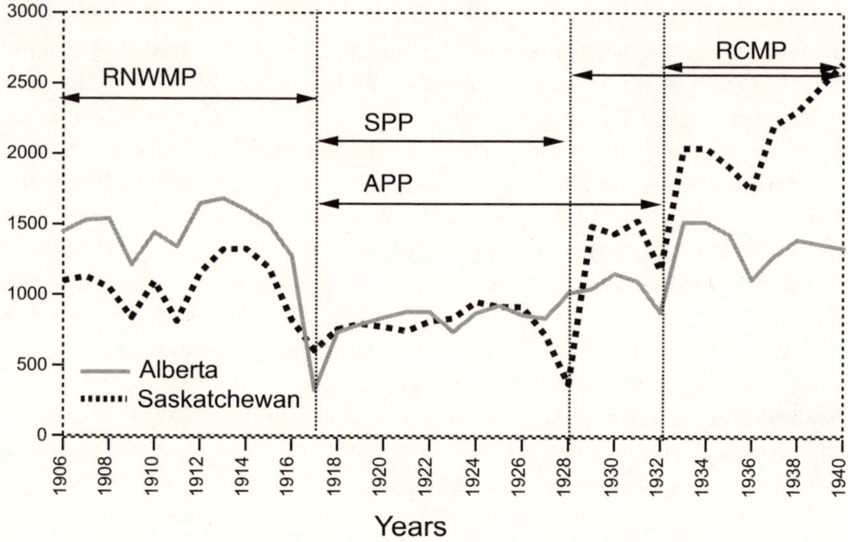

100,000 population. In the early part of the sequence, crimes appear to peak in 1913-14 and quickly dive to a low point in 1917. The pattern is identical in both provinces. Afterward, crime rates climb gradually upward in the 1920s and 1930s, more sharply in Saskatchewan than in Alberta. This period saw three dramatic, overlapping societal changes: the Great War (1914-18), the massive Prairie immigration project (from 1910 to 1913, over 1,200,000 were settled, this at a time when the entire Canadian population was only about seven million people, increasing the population by 20 percent in half a decade), and the rise of alcohol prohibition (adopted by Parliament in 1916 and initiated in most provinces the following year). Immigration was halted by the war. The war created animosity toward the huge non-British immigrant population, and prohibition, as well as questions of national loyalty, gave police reasons for intrusive scrutiny of the newcomers.[26]

Official rates of crime are often unreliable indicators of the actual amount of crime in any society because they are subject to so many unexamined sources of distortion. One of the key factors is change in the number of police actually employed in the jurisdiction. Again, turning to the annual reports, it is possible to estimate the changing levels of policing in the prov-

Figure 8.2

Police strength per 100,000 population in Alberta and Saskatchewan, 1906-40

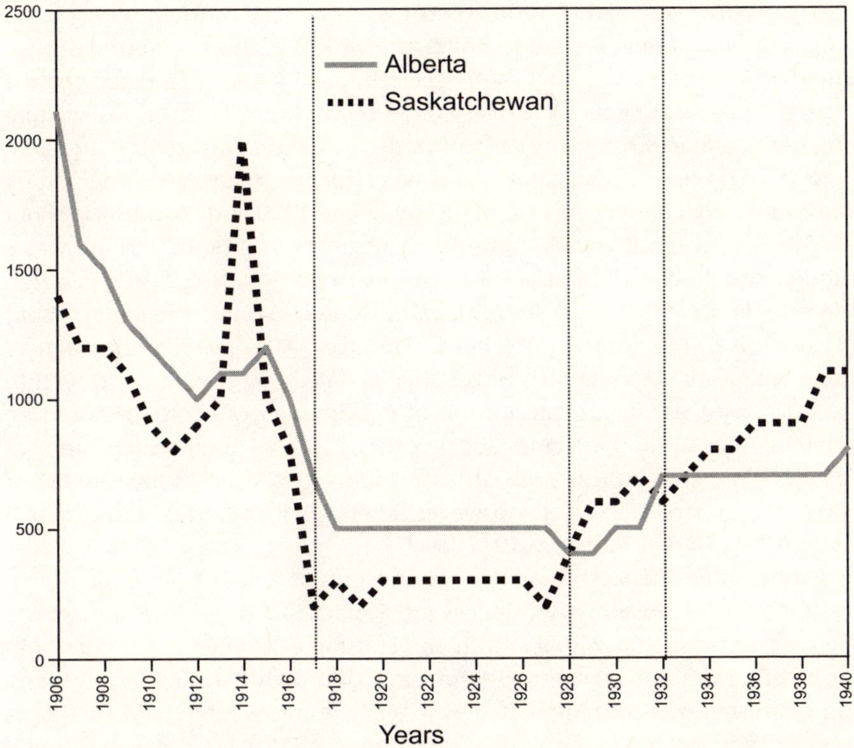

inces over the period of interest to us here. Figure 8.2 reports the police strength per 100,000 population in both Alberta and Saskatchewan.

Most of the period during which the "provos" were commissioned appears as a statistical trough dwarfed on either side by higher long-term trends. Throughout the war, the number of police per capita appears to decline – sharply at the start of the war until 1917, the year in which the provincial forces were created. Relative to federal manpower levels, the provincial police were staffed at significantly lower levels. In addition, the staffing levels do not appear to have changed perceptibly over the lives of the forces. The points where the per capita rates increase coincide more or less with the reversion to federal control in each province.

The actual numbers of police are not always a good measure of their productivity. Two other important processes must be considered. Policing has a large discretionary component, especially in the area of public order. Public order offences are a most unstable category of crime. They frequently reflect the values and norms of social elites and religious groups in society. Some scholars do not regard these offences as "real" crimes at all. In Alberta, arrest rates for public order offences show a steady decreasing trend during the thirty-five-year period 1906-40. At the turn of the century, public order offences were closely related to liquor consumption. If we examine the annual crime reports prepared by the Dominion Bureau of Statistics for the period 1886-1930, there were over 2,173,000 summary convictions, excluding traffic offences.[27] Seventy percent of these offences consisted of drunkenness (51.6 percent) and vagrancy (18.5 percent). According to Thorner, drunk and disorderly conduct rose dramatically before 1900 and constituted about 40-50 percent of all crimes committed in southern Alberta.[28] There was a similar situation in rural Alberta in the first two decades of the twentieth century. From 1906 to 1917, drunk and disorderly conduct made up about 23 percent of the annual public order offences. After 1917, these offences were chargeable as violations of the *Alberta Liquor Act,* which continued to account for a significant proportion of public order offences. In addition, vagrancy constituted a significant percentage of the public order offences (about 14 percent) at this time, although from 1917 to 1923 the number of vagrants arrested decreased. However, after 1924, the arrest rate for this offence rebounded to its pre-1917 level.

Public order offences are subject to an unusual amount of police discretion. This is because many offences are a matter of degree and reflect the perception of the individual citizen and constable. At what point does public inebriation amount to public "drunk and disorderly conduct"? How many times must citizens be confronted by a needy homeless man before requests for personal assistance amount to "vagrancy"? Both are matters of judgment. In addition, many crimes, particularly public order offences, can be resolved without arrest or detention. The drunkard can be put to bed. The needy can be run out of town or turned over to a church or charitable organization. A lot of offences are not worth the paperwork and court time that arrest entails. And the part-time magistrates who were created under provincial laws and who were paid from the fines collected from offenders were not likely to relish sentencing a lot of vagrants with little means to pay the court costs. In addition, as the security needs of the public forced police attention toward incidents of violence, personal victimization, and property crimes, the discretionary attention to public order offences was progressively overshadowed. That appears to have been the process that Monkkonnen identified in US data. What do the provincial data suggest? Figure 8.3 reports the rate of arrests for public order offences per constable in the two provinces over thirty-five years. Even though the actual number of constables was in a stepwise decline during the heyday of the provincial forces (see Figure 8.2), the provincial constabularies were actually making

Figure 8.3

Arrests for public order offences per police officer by province, 1906-40

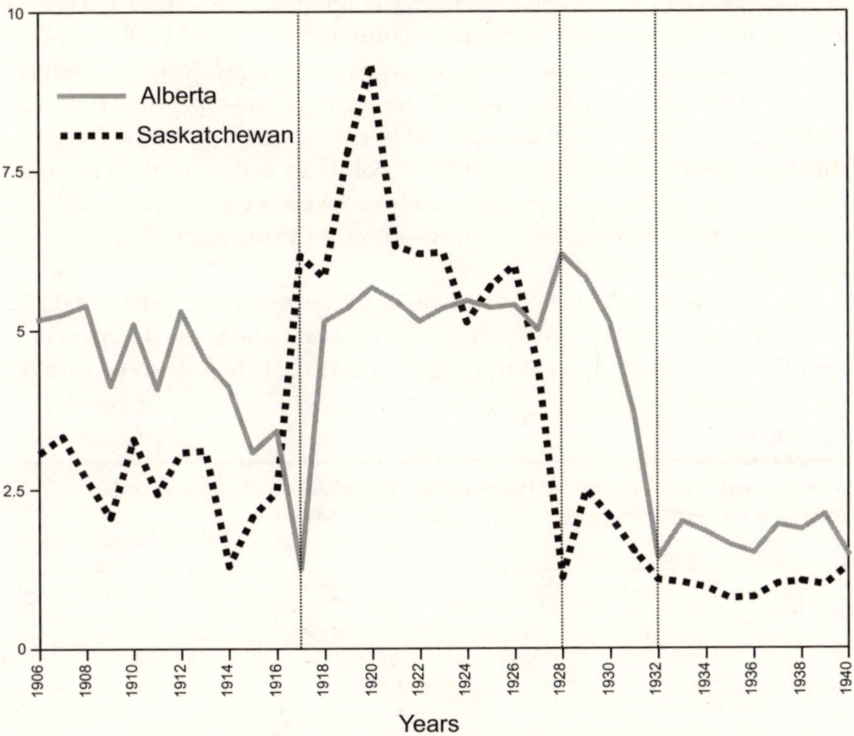

many *more* arrests per person for public order offences than either the RNWMP or the RCMP. This is true in both provinces, and the rate declined after the RCMP transition in each province. The decline coincided precisely with the shift in police administration.

How can we explain this? It may be that the average number of arrests for public order offences jumped during the period of provincial control because the rate of crime was stable and the number of officers employed to deter it declined. However, in Saskatchewan prior to 1917, when there were clearly more constables, there were still significantly fewer arrests for public order offences. And the decline afterward appears to be a stepwise change. Did public order offenders simply behave themselves, with the result that arrests dropped in a stepwise fashion when the Mounties took over with a larger complement of officers? That seems improbable. In our view, there were policy considerations in the provincial forces that made public order a higher priority. This interpretation is further supported when we examine the degree to which the federal and provincial forces upheld the enforcement of provincial statutes. Some statutes covered the same misconduct provincially and federally. Drunkenness could be charged either as a provincial offence or as a federal offence. The provinces also regulated school attendance, labour relations, family maintenance, billiard halls, domestic animals, game, mines, prairie fires, restaurants, theatres, workers' compensation, and so on. Figures 8.4 and 8.5 show arrests under provincial statutes versus arrests under federal public order offences. Again they reveal stepwise shifts that coincide with the transition points to and from the provincial jurisdiction in policing. Figures 8.4 and 8.5 reveal a clear shift toward provincial statutes following the commissioning of the provincial forces in each province.

The RNWMP traditionally obtained little satisfaction from control of public order offences. The data concerning the relationship between the arrest rates for *Criminal Code* offences and those for provincial statutes show that the

Figure 8.4

Arrests under provincial statutes versus *Criminal Code* public order offences per 100,000 population in Alberta, 1906-40

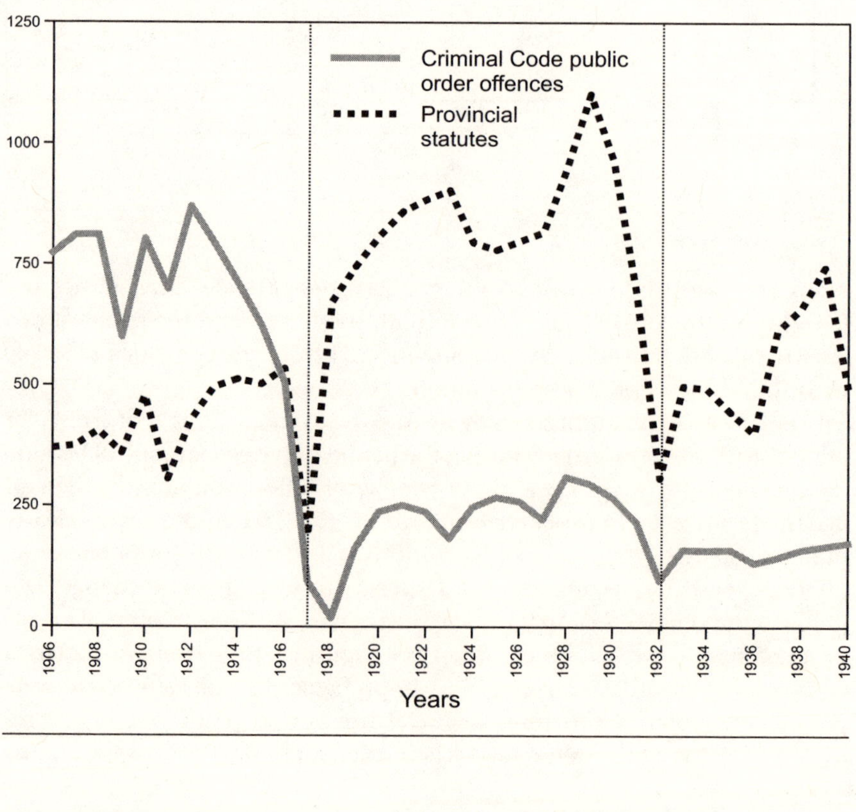

Figure 8.5

Arrests under provincial statutes versus *Criminal Code* public order offences per 100,000 population in Saskatchewan, 1906-40

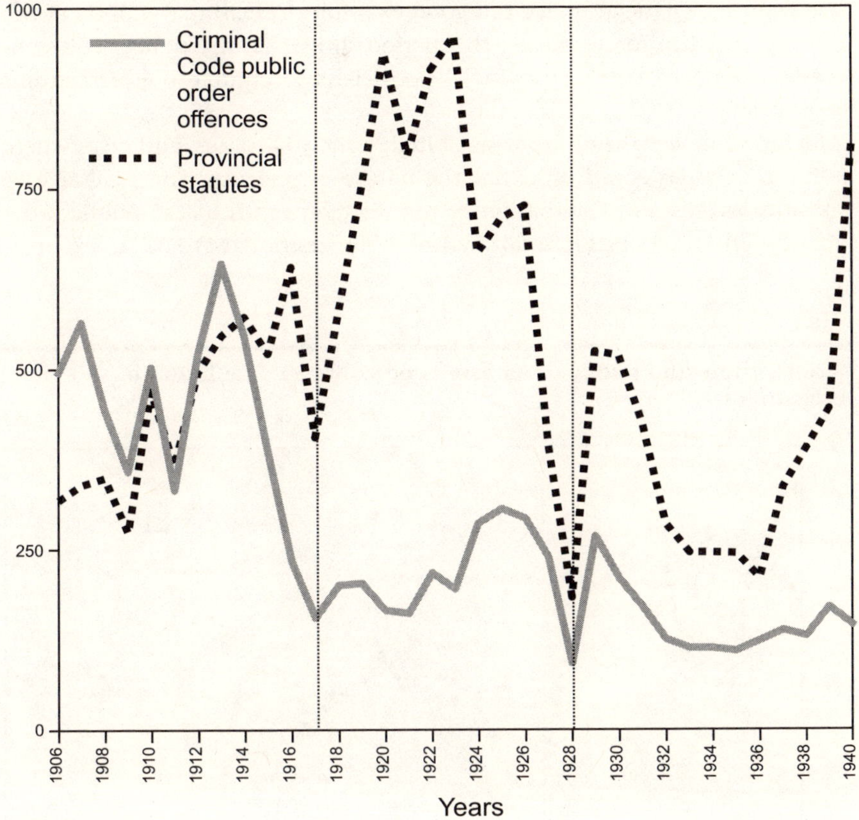

provincial police gave greater priority to enforcement of provincial statutes over the *Criminal Code* of Canada. This does not mean that the provincial police let serious criminals "get away with murder." Rather, there were many public order offences in the *Criminal Code,* such as vagrancy, drunk and disorderly conduct, offences concerning houses of ill repute, and so on. The evidence indicates that after 1917 there was an immediate increase in arrests for offences under provincial statutes, while public order offences under the *Criminal Code* decreased in both provinces. This *suggests* that in exercising their discretion the provincial police gave more attention to public order offences stipulated under the provincial statutes than to the public order offences in the *Criminal Code.*

Under the provincial mandate, the police appear not only to have received instructions to enforce certain provincial statutes vigorously but also to have felt more pressure from both the public and the politicians to enforce policy-related provincial statutes. The enforcement of liquor legislation by the provincial police is a good example. The annual reports of the provincial police forces during this period show that the police were constantly pressured by the provincial politicians to enforce the prohibition legislation.

So far we have focused on areas of high police discretion and areas where political agendas could influence the nature of policing. The final area to consider entails an examination of the relative trends in the public order offences and the trends in serious crimes that are thought to be far less open

Figure 8.6

Serious crime and public order arrests per 100,000 population in Alberta, 1906-40

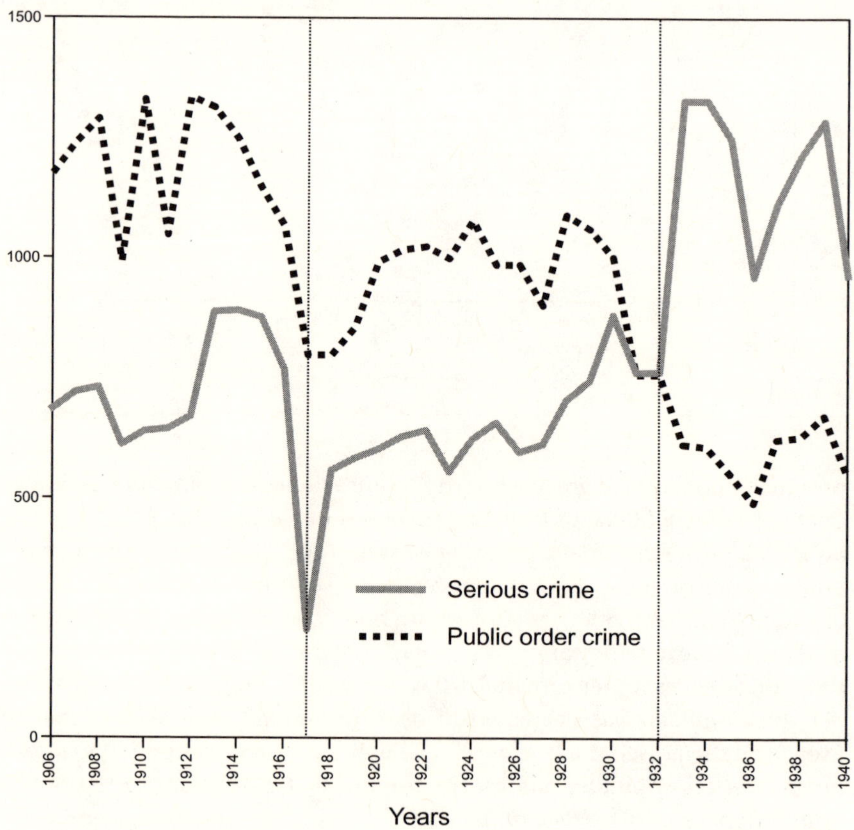

Figure 8.7

Serious crime and public order arrests per 100,000 population in Saskatchewan, 1906-40

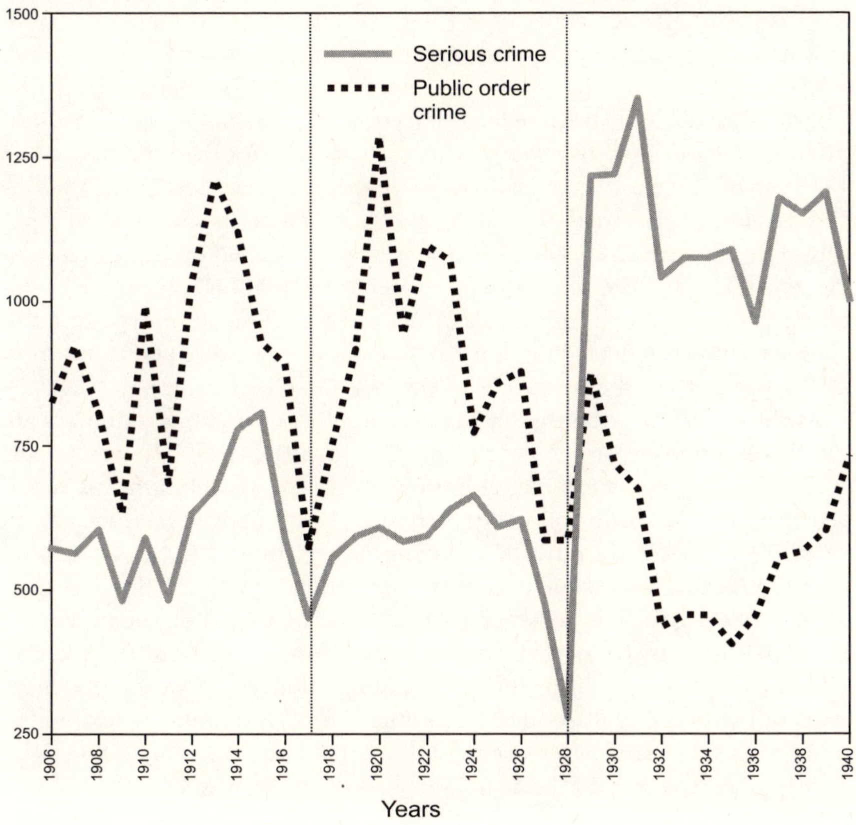

to informal dispositions. In Figures 8.6 and 8.7, we compare the rates of public order offences versus serious crimes separately for Alberta and Saskatchewan. Serious crimes included indictable offences against persons and property. These trends clearly show that the transition to the RCMP was marked by a crossover in which serious crimes replaced public order offences as the dominant reason for arrest. Notably, the crossover occurs at different years in each province, reflecting the different points of police transition.

It is difficult to fully untangle the reasons for the crossovers reported in these figures. In Alberta, it is clear that there was a gradual increase in serious crime during the 1920s. The introduction of higher numbers of constables after the RCMP transition probably increased the ability of the system to process cases. However, the transition is confounded by the sharp economic instability in society associated with the onset of the Depression. The Depression led to widespread destitution and unemployment. The Prairies, due to repeated droughts, were especially hard hit. The dramatic increase in serious crime in Saskatchewan and Alberta was due almost entirely to changes in charges of personal theft. Assault charges did not change in this period. *Specific* areas of theft – cattle rustling, breaking and entering, forgery, etc., which were recorded separately – did not change. This does not mean that people became more larcenous because of the economic situation. In fact, in Saskatchewan, the *conviction* levels for theft did not reflect the stepwise increase in arrests. They remained more or less the same over the transition. This suggests that the new force, with its untarnished reputation, borrowing on its earlier Prairie legacy, was called on aggressively by citizens when the economy threatened and applied the law with a gradually increasing number of officers. The aggregate statistics moved upward. In our view, this reflected more the behaviour of the police and the worries of the public than the behaviour of the offending sectors.

As the transitions occurred in the two provinces, the three dominant social forces discussed earlier receded into the past. The Great War was a tragic memory. The Depression halted immigration. And prohibition was superseded by the state-controlled liquor trade. These changes significantly altered the nature of policing. What had policing entailed for the provincial forces? What were the areas of tension and tribulation during their heyday? After reviewing the annual reports for both forces, including the individual divisional reports, we believe that one could not understand the work of policing without recognizing the role of immigration, with its associated problems of cultural pluralism, labour conflict during economic development, and the social trauma of resettlement. We will discuss the evidence on these points with reference to the annual reports of the provincial police.

Provincial Police Activities in Controlling the "Dangerous Classes"

Over the period 1917-32, provincial police work was mainly concerned with what historians call the "dangerous classes" in addition to serious crime. In the first quarter of the twentieth century, foreign immigrants of non-British origin represented over 35 percent of the total population in Alberta and Saskatchewan, as shown in every national census conducted between 1901 and 1931. In 1911, there were 1,128,941 immigrants in the Prairie provinces who were from the United States, the British Isles, and continental Europe.

As suggested in Tables 8.1 and 8.2, many of these immigrants were from southern and east-central Europe. The largest groups of immigrants were Russian, Polish, German, and Austrian. The term "foreign immigrants" was often used to refer to those peoples whose origins were non-British and non-English-speaking: that is, mostly from southern and east-central Europe.

Table 8.1

Total population by origin in Alberta

Birthplace	1901	1911	1921	1931
Canada	41,782	161,869	315,090	425,867
British Isles	7,643	68,252	97,505	106,781
Foreign-born				
Austria	5,712	10,583	9,981	4,083
Germany	1,186	6,102	4,606	8,148
Russia	2,439	10,011	11,572	15,561
Poland	–	5,816	3,073	8,202
Sweden	1,609	6,345	6,535	7,431
Norway	–	5,761	6,681	8,820
Denmark	302	1,380	2,353	5,500
Other	12,186	96,713	129,171	139,228
Total	72,859	372,832	586,567	729,621

Source: These figures are from the *Census of Canada* reports for 1901, 1911, 1921, and 1931 (Ottawa: Dominion Bureau of Statistics).

Table 8.2

Total population by origin in Saskatchewan

Birthplace	1901	1911	1921	1931
Canada	55,084	248,751	457,833	603,240
British Isles	10,506	80,177	99,166	99,730
Foreign-born				
Austria	7,695	15,878	17,039	11,382
Germany	992	8,300	6,409	9,832
Russia	12,146	23,084	28,315	31,382
Poland	–	8,797	12,989	29,594
Sweden	484	6,209	7,381	7,580
Norway	–	7,625	9,240	10,721
Denmark	67	982	1,515	2,947
Other	4,173	91,735	116,434	114,106
Total	91,147	491,538	756,321	920,514

Source: These figures are from the *Census of Canada* reports for 1901, 1911, 1921, and 1931 (Ottawa: Dominion Bureau of Statistics).

One of the major concerns of the provincial police was the fact that foreign immigrants were ignorant of Canadian law and order. Commissioner Bryan of the APP in 1921 stated that "the province of Alberta owing to its cosmopolitan population is hard to police, alien settlements being scattered all over it. These people banded together as they are, and in a good many instances retaining the customs and mode of life they lived in their own countries before coming to Canada, are not as yet educating themselves with regard to the laws of this country, it is impossible to obtain evidence from them, and they are too prone to look upon any policeman as an enemy instead of a friend."[29] The police believed that an important method of educating the immigrants to observe laws was to enforce laws among them. This approach often led the immigrants to complain about justices of the peace and police constables who punished them severely over trivial disputes among them. The demand to remove Justice of the Peace Woolly and Constable Varzari by local residents in Andrew, Alberta, in 1917 was a case in point. A report by the inspector of Edmonton division from the investigation into the complaint concluded that the justice of the peace and the constable had only carried out their routine duties involving prosecutions and trials of cases concerning local Russian nationals: "I am informed that the petition circulated and signed was done at the instance of certain parties who are in opposition to the proper enforcement of the Canadian law among the Russian People ... In this district there is a large community of extremely ignorant people. Administer the law as it is administered among our Canadian people, and these people may some day be spoken of as intelligent. Cease to administer it ... [and] these people will never be *good* citizens or have any respect for the laws of the country."[30] Opposition to enforcement of laws only strengthened the police belief that foreign immigrants had to be educated (i.e., arrested) to establish the rule of law. This explains in part the dramatic increase in the use of public order law as well as provincial statutes, especially in the period following the Great War.

The immigration booms from 1896 to 1914 in the North-West Territories and the Prairie provinces triggered three interrelated social and moral reform movements: the social gospel movement, the prohibition movement, and the women's rights movement. The urban middle-class Anglo-Canadians who led these movements argued that the new immigrants possessed a series of social and moral defects. They were more inclined toward crime, violence, prostitution, family breakdown, and political corruption than the rest of the population. In Alberta, the Ukrainians gained a reputation for being particularly crime prone, a fact that Gregory Robinson traced to the demographic dominance of unattached males in rival gangs in the immigrant settlements.[31]

Frequently, the police suggested that immigrants were inclined to crime since they had little sense of law and order. The police argued that the level of immigration was a predominant factor that determined the levels of various crimes in different districts. Higher crime rates in districts were correlated with higher levels of foreign immigration.[32] The increase in the number of both serious crimes (e.g., murder, assault, and theft) and public order offences was attributed primarily to the foreign population. APP inspector

J.S. Piper of Division A in the Edmonton area reported to the commissioner in 1928 that "the increase in the number of both murder and stealing can be attributed to the foreign population mostly, who often think they have the right to take the law into their own hands, and settle any dispute that may happen to arise."[33] Commissioner Mahony of the SPP in his 1919 annual report to the attorney general expressed a similar view. He claimed that "a *large* percentage of the crimes committed can be traced to persons of foreign extraction."[34]

These views had policy implications. Police detachments were located to ensure surveillance of immigrants. In the mining communities where foreign immigrants were concentrated, the police deployed more detachments and had more policemen in each detachment than in any other places. However, the control of foreigners was actually quite complex. This is seen especially in the handling of strikers, vagrants, and radicals and their relationship to the immigration question.

Industrial Action, the Provincial Police, and Foreign Immigrants

Strikes in mining communities in both provinces, especially in Alberta, were fairly common. Immigrant workers played a prominent role in those strikes. Because few English-speaking Canadians were interested in such socially undesirable work, immigrants made up a large proportion of the miners. As a result, they played a prominent role in strikes. Concurrently, radical organizations realized that working-class communities with their large numbers of foreign components provided good grounds for organizing. APP superintendent McDonnell pointed out in 1919 that many strikes in coal-mining districts were organized "by agitators of the [One Big Union] who visited all the mines in the district holding meetings and they soon had the foreign element in line with them, the latter being in the majority in the unions."[35]

Consequently, in Alberta and Saskatchewan, mining communities became a central concern of the police.[36] In his 1918 annual report, APP inspector Brankley in the Calgary region called mining towns such as Drumheller "hot bed[s] of the disease"[37] because the foreign immigrants repeatedly precipitated the industrial strikes in those areas. For the police, labour unrest posed significant difficulties for law enforcement and the maintenance of order. However, their role was not one of simple suppression. To win the confidence of the workers, the police also played the role of industrial mediators. This is shown in the "rules of engagement" during strikes.

The policemen involved in maintaining order in strike areas were frequently instructed to abstain from all acts of interference in the labour disputes. Their duties in connection with a strike were strictly to protect life and prevent the destruction of property. The SPP constables were specifically instructed not to display their sidearms unless threatened by a riot.[38]

Historical evidence suggests that the police identified with the property owners. Many policemen regarded strikes as harassment of property owners that they would have strictly forbidden. APP inspector Brankley, in charge of the Calgary division, suggested in 1918 that there had been few strikes and that the mining industry had been operating in full swing. This was not because the miners had become more reasonable but because the operators had conceded to practically all the demands levied by employees, who had been anything but reasonable. The inspector reported that "in fact the operators are practically at the mercy of the Miners Union, which, when consideration is given to the fact that same is composed almost wholly of alien enemies, is a most regrettable state of affairs to be tolerated."[39]

Although the police were sympathetic with the property owners in the industrial disputes, this did not mean that they acted *only* in the interests of property owners or managers during such disputes. The owners and operators of the mines under a strike often requested police protection. However, for the police, the occurrence of a strike was not a sufficient reason to send constables to the area. One of the important criteria for providing police protection was the existence of threats to life and destruction of property. Typically, mine operators complained that they did not receive enough protection from the police. The police believed that the mine operators frequently exaggerated their situations and were trying to use the police to break picket lines. These differences of perception certainly caused friction between the police and the mine management. Sometimes mine operators directly petitioned police protection or complained to the press or the premiers of the provinces about the inaction of provincial police. When this occurred, the police believed that mine operators were trying to embarrass them politically.[40]

Frequently, the police did gather a few constables from the vicinity detachments and send them to the strike areas. The police presence often had the effect of pacifying the strikers. Subsequently, the police had to explain to the mine operators that they could not station the constables any further as there were no threats to life or property.

Given these tensions, the police were forced to present themselves as a neutral mediator. They often informed the workers that they were allowed to form a picket line as long as there was no violence involved. In 1925, APP commissioner Bryan advised a group of miners from the Red Deer Valley Miners Union, including the well-known union activists Jenkins, Hall, and Metcalfe, that, "as long as no force or violence was attempted, they would be allowed to walk along the road in the vicinity of the mines but that law and order would be maintained if it took a thousand men to do it."[41] Occasionally, the police gave some practical advice to the union leaders concerning how a labour impasse could be solved. In the Drumheller mining strikes of 1925, the commissioner of the APP advised radical union leaders to step down in order to achieve settlements with the operators.[42]

There were occasions when the police acted more as suppressors than as mediators. On the morning of 4 January 1923, a picket line was formed by eighty men and forty women at the public road to the Bush Mines in the Edmonton area. The picket line was eventually driven back. During this melée, Constable Engel was struck over the head and lost consciousness, and Constable Keen was struck in the face. When the order was given to the mounted section to clear the strikers away, several mounted men were struck by rocks. Constable Farthing sustained a deep cut over the eye and one on the nose. Constable Marks had a serious cut on the head. Batons were used freely by the mounted and dismounted policemen. The strikers were eventually dispersed. Obviously, many strikers were also injured. But these injuries were not recorded in the police records.[43]

One important tactic that the police used to break strikes and to arrest their organizers was to connect industrial action to the Communist Party of Canada. This approach resonated with the fears of class warfare among the middle- and upper-class Anglo-Canadians aroused by the Bolshevik Revolution. Strikers and political radicals were often viewed as part of the criminal classes. Such a characterization justified the use of greater force than the public might have accepted otherwise and led to the frequent detention of strikers and their leaders. The 1930 annual report from the headquarters of the APP states that the strikers at Mercoal were composed mostly of a very radical element and communist leaders from Toronto.[44] The report from Division A referred to the same group of workers as the "mob." To break the picket line and reduce potential violence, the police arrested five workers on charges of membership in an unlawful assembly. They were found guilty of the charge and sentenced to one month in Fort Saskatchewan Jail and a fine of fifty dollars. In addition, some of them were found guilty of common assault, riotous conduct, and obstructing a peace officer. These punishments had the effect of quelling all the radical elements in the mining areas in the province.[45] Avery also points out that this tactic was strongly supported "by the mine managers of the region, who seized upon the illegitimate status of the [Communist Party of Canada] and [Industrial Workers of the World] to discard all collective bargaining procedures."[46]

In fact, the police also implicated communists in violent criminal behaviour. Two cases in point were the dynamiting of a fan house and box car loader in the Elgon Mine of Alberta in 1927 and the dynamiting of William Hopkin's house near Newcastle Mine in 1925. In spite of the most strenuous investigations involving several police officers, no evidence was discovered that incriminated labour activists. But the police firmly believed that communist activists were responsible for the action.[47]

The police role vis-à-vis the mining community was complicated. The police were required to permit lawful strikes and to act impartially during them. However, they were opposed to industrial mass action and were frequently exposed to danger in suppressing it. In addition, there was deep animosity toward the union because of its foreign elements and communist sympathies. This combination in fact exacerbated conflicts and fomented violence in labour struggles. On the other hand, the police resented manipulation of their function by the mine owners who attempted to co-opt police control to break strikes and, when that failed, to embarrass the police politically. The outcome was a situation in which the police were drawn into suppression of unionists during periods of conflict while trying to maintain a semblance of neutrality and occasionally mediating tensions to forestall violence.

In contrast, police activities in controlling the unemployed and vagrants were concerned primarily with maintaining public order and preventing serious crime. For the police, there was a close correlation between vagrancy, unemployment, and crime: vagrancy involved the unemployed foreign elements. As a result, the provincial police made vagrancy a priority.

Vagrancy, Radicals, and Foreign Immigrants

In rural areas, charges for vagrancy were seasonal, associated with harvesting and threshing periods. Usually, a large number of harvesters floated into rural areas during the fall from the cities and from other provinces. Toward the end of the season, the provincial police expected the harvesters to leave for home. Arrests for vagrancy usually increased after the end of harvesting season since there were always some harvesters who drifted without a fixed address. The police attributed the vagrancy problem to two factors. First was the policy of neighbouring provinces toward the floating or unemployed elements of their populations. In 1924, APP inspector E.W. Bavin in the Lethbridge area explained that, "owing to the fact the large cities in B.C. and Manitoba have been endeavouring to keep their unemployed moving, they have been drifting through the west, and a number of them are a very useless type. Consequently, we show an increase in the number of vagrants handled."[48] The second factor was the availability of government relief. When seasonal work was finished, some labourers remained in the provinces because they intended to collect relief from the provincial governments or look for new employment.[49] In either case, they were unwelcome.

Enforcement of the vagrancy law suggests that the police must have been aware that enforcement was not only to maintain public order but also to discipline labourers. When other jobs were available at the end of the harvest, the police laid charges for vagrancy against men who refused to accept such jobs, usually in mining or lumbering. However, in those years when inclement weather reduced harvesters' income to the extent that there were few jobs available to them, the police were actually sympathetic toward them and reported that many of them deserved government relief.[50] Despite limited amounts of relief, the police were reluctant to turn away the deserving applicants. On the contrary, they always rejected applications from persons who refused to accept a job or who were found drunk.[51]

In controlling unemployed foreign immigrants, the police were quick to link the activities of the unemployed directly to the Communist Party of Canada. In 1928, about 800 men turned up in Edmonton demanding government relief. The police estimated that over 85 percent of the protesters were foreign immigrants from central European countries.[52] The police believed that the protest would cause social disorder because the organizations had "red elements."[53] The report from the commissioner of the APP emphasized that radicals were dangerous to the maintenance of public peace. They intended to exploit the situation of the poor and unemployed by fomenting trouble among the working class. It was said that the radicals even intended to educate children in communist ideology. The police noted that, "while our men were marching, mounted or dismounted, out to where they were training at Drumheller, children would line up on the sidewalk and sing the *redflag*."[54] For the police, one way to reduce the influence and potential danger of social unrest by foreign immigrants was to increase the proportion of English-speaking employees who would offset the effect of foreign immigrants in industrial and mining communities.[55]

"Canadianizing" Foreign Immigrants: Educating Children, Regulating Adults

The police had a more general and unwritten mandate to impose Anglo-Canadian values and norms on immigrants to assimilate them into Canadian society. Similar to the police in nineteenth-century England, the provincial police committed great time and resources to controlling immigrants' leisure time. Leisure activities, such as drinking, gambling, and dancing, were monitored to meet Anglo-Canadian moral standards. The police routinely attended public activities, such as fairs, picnics, roundups and stampedes, dances, and boxing bouts. Pool and billiard rooms were inspected regularly. Enforcement of the *School Attendance Act* and the *Liquor Act* is the most interesting area in which we can see not only the police attitudes and activities in enforcing moralistic law but also the reactions of the population to the imposition of morality by the state.

Many Anglo-Canadians held that the major defect of central and eastern Europeans was their lack of education. The assimilation of the immigrants would have to be achieved through enforced attendance in the Canadian school system. This was required by the *School Attendance Act* in Saskatchewan and the *Truancy Act* in Alberta. These laws made parents accountable for the failure of children to attend school.[56] The laws were not popular pieces of legislation for many citizens of the provinces. Many immigrant parents from central and eastern Europe disliked sending their children to tax-supported denominational or public schools where only English was taught.

The police did not enjoy enforcing the school laws either, particularly in Saskatchewan. During the early period of the force, the SPP investigated and prosecuted as many as 1,500 cases annually.[57] This consumed a considerable amount of police time and resources. Several division inspectors complained that the enforcement of the law should not be part of police duties. For instance, the inspector of the Weyburn Division argued that "prosecutions of this nature do not enhance the good name of the police force ... People begin to think that the police are running around looking for this kind of petty case instead of looking after cases of a serious nature."[58] In answering the request of the Banff School Board for the enforcement of the *Truancy Act* of Alberta, the board of commissioners of the APP also indicated that the APP could enforce the act only "so long as such work did not interfere with the regular duties of the constables."[59]

Liquor Enforcement by the "Provos"

The police inspectors did not have a better attitude toward the enforcement of prohibition. The Alberta *Liquor Act* of 1916 was violated by so many people and so frequently that Inspector Piper in the Edmonton area in 1918 expressed his doubt that prohibition was a proper way to alter people's drinking habits. SPP commissioner Charles Mahony seemed to hold a more positive attitude toward enforcement of the prohibition law in Saskatchewan. He apparently believed that enforcement was necessary to reduce crime since crime was correlated with the consumption of liquor. He said that "the use of intoxicating liquor and noxious drugs is indirectly responsible for about 50 percent of all crime committed in the province."[60]

Although at the onset of prohibition official attitudes toward the law differed somewhat between the provinces, the actual enforcement of the law was rather similar. Both the SPP and the APP adopted a reactive policing strategy. This was because most policemen in the forces were known to the bootleggers. Even new undercover policemen, who acted as special constables, could not get evidence because few bootleggers were naive enough to sell liquor to strangers.

Police investigations typically arose from complaints about persons who were selling or keeping liquor illegally. Many of these complaints were lodged initially with various high-level authorities, including the attorneys general of the provinces. They would turn these complaints over to the police commissioners and instruct them to investigate. The majority of these complaints provided very little information about the offenders and were often anonymous and may have come from temperance activists. On occasion, the persons who signed the complaints wanted their names withheld. The police investigation of such complaints was not only extremely costly in terms of time and money but also often bore little fruit. Many complaints consisted of hearsay evidence or arose from personal grudges. When the police successfully identified the location of an alleged bootlegging operation, they often obtained little assistance from local citizens.[61] As a result, they had little success in getting evidence against bootleggers, and most of the charges and convictions secured by the police were actually against the people who purchased liquor from the bootleggers.

The difficulties that the police experienced in enforcing the laws were multiplied by tactics used by bootleggers to circumvent the liquor law and to avoid police detection. These included spying, bribing, and the use of trains to conceal the distribution of illegal liquor as mislabelled freight. The spy system was so effective that the bootleggers must have spent substantial money to support it. The movement of the police was noted by spotters and telephoned from one locale to another. Even with undercover policemen, it was impossible to stop the traffic.[62]

The bootleggers were able to trace police movement because the primary means of transportation used by the police was the railway. The railway men, as informers for the bootleggers, were frequently able to identify the undercover liquor branch officers travelling on trains to investigate liquor cases throughout the provinces. The engineers would wire information ahead about police movement to various points along the line. As a result of this system of counter-espionage, bootleggers could identify undercover policemen and foil their raids.

Another effective tactic used by bootleggers was bribery. In the 1921 annual report, the APP reported that, among twenty-seven constables engaged in policing the liquor traffic, six were convicted or dismissed for corruption – almost one-quarter! The case of Constable Smith illustrates just how vulnerable the police were to bribes. Police were offered bribes that were sometimes worth more than forty times their monthly salary ($120). Stationed at Coutts in 1918, Constable Smith was offered $5,000 to absent himself from his detachment for two days to leave the border unmanned.[63] Nevertheless, he refused the offer.

Bootleggers were also able to recruit city and town police and other officials to work in their espionage system. In the Crow's Nest Pass, the mayors and the chiefs of police of some towns committed themselves to watching strangers and provincial police coming into their towns.[64] A more disturbing fact was that the names of some mayors and chiefs of police of some towns were found among the list of the convicted bootleggers. The provincial police charged and convicted the mayor of Coleman, Mr. Johnson, twice for illegally selling liquor. The chief of police of St. Albert was convicted and fined $100 for bootlegging. The town councils did not remove the offenders from their official positions even after their convictions. This showed that the violation of the liquor law was not only extensive but also publicly acceptable.

In counterattacking the bootleggers' espionage system, the APP established a Liquor Branch (LB) in 1919, and the government of Saskatchewan formed the Liquor Commission (LC) by an amendment to the *Temperance Act* in 1920. These new branches of the attorneys general explicitly provided for social control by using the plainclothes policemen to replace the uniformed officers to enforce the law.

The establishment of the LB and the LC largely relieved the uniformed policemen from liquor law enforcement. The new agencies were designed for two purposes. First, the plainclothes recruits, consisting mostly of special constables, were thought initially to be better able to avoid detection by the bootleggers. Second, the transfer of responsibility to the LB and the LC was supposed to shift public hostility away from the uniformed police and enable them to regain some popularity so as to perform other duties more effectively. In reality, there was little evidence to indicate that the new organizations achieved either purpose.

Matters were not helped by the fact that the special constables had an unsavoury reputation. Because the liquor law and its enforcement were extremely unpopular, the special constables were viewed with suspicion. As a result, those who took the jobs were often men of "less than exemplary character." Inspector Hodgkins of the LB apologetically said that the kind of work the members of the Liquor Branch had to do led them into all kinds of temptation, and "the work is of such a nature that it is very difficult to get the better class of men to do the work."[65]

Establishment of the new agencies required a considerable amount of government expenditure. In 1921, the Liquor Branch of the APP spent about $19,413.18 (out of a total budget of $478,855.79).[66] In 1923, the SPP spent a total of $10,039.00 (out of its total budget of about $300,000.00) to assist with the enforcement of the liquor law. While historians have noted the costs of liquor law enforcement, the laws were also a rich source of revenue for the government.[67] In 1921, the police attached to the Liquor Branch of the APP collected $64,722 in fines and confiscated $62,800 worth of liquor. This is in contrast to the $23,000 required to purchase the building for the Weyburn Divisional Headquarters of the SPP. The inspector of the Weyburn division noted that it could easily be paid for by $24,231 worth of liquor seized by the police in that division in 1920.[68] After 1920, this income was removed from the police and placed at the disposal of the government.

In the early 1920s, the police began to use automobiles for transportation whenever they wanted to make a raid on bootleggers. Initially, they hired taxis for this purpose. Many policemen bought private vehicles and used them to do police work. Police tactics used to control bootlegging were very much shaped by their reactions to the bootleggers' innovations to circumvent the law and avoid police detection.

Due to the lack of strength in the Liquor Branch of the APP and the difficulties in enforcing the *Liquor Act,* the APP eagerly sought to pass the duties of enforcing the law in cities to municipal police. In 1918, the board of commissioners of the APP adopted a policy recognizing the jurisdiction of municipal police in Edmonton, Calgary, Lethbridge, and Medicine Hat over liquor infractions in their cities. This had been provided for in the 1918 amendments to the *Liquor Act* of 1916.[69] According to the APP, it was more appropriate for the city police to check on violations of the act in liquor stores and hotels since most of them were located in the cities. But the city police of Calgary questioned the legality of this new obligation. The board of commissioners recorded in 1918 that the city commissioners "refuse[d] to be primarily responsible for the enforcement of the law in connection with liquor."[70] The evidence also suggested that the rank and file of the city police had no interest in enforcing these laws. In 1924, Calgary municipal authorities called upon the APP to crack down on violations of the liquor laws. The Calgary press were skeptical about the ability of the city police to enforce the laws.[71]

On the other hand, the power of city police to enforce the prohibition law in city jurisdictions led to a certain amount of resentment in smaller towns and villages that remained under provincial police jurisdiction. The people who lived in small centres were aware that, since the large cities managed their own affairs concerning the *Liquor Act* (referred to as "home rule" by some local people), the people living in the cities were allowed to drink whatever they wanted. In the country, where the APP enforced the act, the only liquor available was home-brewed moonshine. This amounted to discrimination and fostered resentment. The police observed that because of this resentment the complaints about violations of the *Liquor Act* from small towns fell off in 1921. By 1922, in order to appease the resentment, many small-town police requested and received authority from the attorney general to enforce liquor laws locally.[72]

According to the Alberta *Liquor Act,* and the Saskatchewan *Temperance Act,* private dwelling houses were permitted to have any quantity of liquor on the premises. Many bootleggers took advantage of this and converted their cellars into large trading warehouses. Legally, the liquor in private dwellings could be imported from other provinces through mail order. The police found that this was not always the case. Much of it came from liquor export warehouses within the provinces that were diverting supplies manufactured for export into the local market. At the same time, the police also complained that the prohibition laws created many criminals. From the beginning of the prohibition era, medical professionals, including physicians, druggists, and veterinary surgeons, quickly turned to bootlegging. In fact, it was suggested in the annual reports of the LB that doctors and druggists were among "the worst offenders" of the prohibition laws.[73] Everybody knew that much of the liquor consumed in the provinces was sold legally by prescription.

Police difficulties in enforcing the liquor law were primarily created by the loopholes and the complexity of the prohibition legislation and by the large number of people who participated in the illicit liquor trade. A substantial proportion of the population simply did not support the law. APP inspector Brankley in the Calgary area reported in 1921 that "the enforcing of [the *Liquor Act*] is a bone of contention with us. The act is on the Statute Books, and has to be enforced, but where you have pretty nearly 50 per cent of the population against you, and throwing every barrier in the road to frustrate Justice and to shield guilty parties, make it very arduous for us."[74]

Even the "better" class of citizens who never violated any laws showed no hesitation in violating the liquor legislation. APP inspector Fisher of the Red Deer district noted that the *Liquor Act* was so unpopular that it appeared to be "more honoured in the breach than in observance in the public."[75] Most of the public actually did not think that the violation of the liquor regulation was a crime. Inspector Brankley (Calgary area) reported in 1921 that "I have had on more occasions than one some of the very best citizens tell me that they did not think it a crime or offence to break this act – in fact, they loved to do so."[76] It was "smart" to circumvent the prohibition law and get a drink or bottle of whisky. The law had little or no moral authority attached to it.

In spite of public resistance, the police were required to enforce the laws in both provinces. However unpopular, the laws were on the provincial statute books, and some politicians from strong prohibitionist constituencies often urged the police to enforce the acts vigorously. At the same time, many people complained about liquor violations in their towns and villages.

The police often found themselves in the centre of conflicts between the prohibitionists and the anti-prohibitionists. Typically, the police were instructed by the attorneys general of the provinces to investigate violations of the prohibition laws when a complaint was lodged. When the police got to the localities, they often could get no assistance, even from the complainants. Sometimes they faced violent opposition from townspeople. In the 1921 report, APP inspector Stott remarked that "we have had complaints from people about the *terrible conditions* that exist in their town, and when we have investigated the complaint and caught the offenders, the whole town was up in arms, wanting to hang, draw, and quarter the detective who was responsible."[77] A direct consequence of the hostile public attitude toward the laws and their enforcement was that the police failed efficiently to enforce the law because they could not get evidence that could be adequately presented in the courts to secure convictions. Inspector Hodgkins of the Liquor Branch of the APP noted that, in his two-year experience working in the branch, there was not a single person willing to provide information about the violation of the *Liquor Act* and give evidence supporting a prosecution.[78] The results of most police investigations were disappointing.

If the public was reluctant to co-operate in investigating liquor offences, magistrates and justices of the peace were barely lukewarm in trying such cases. Justices of the peace often dismissed cases because the police could not provide sufficient evidence or because the evidence was secured using improper methods. Furthermore, justices of the peace often refused to convict the accused on the verbal evidence collected by special constables or informants hired by the Saskatchewan Liquor Commission since these hired informers or special constables were crooked men themselves who had dubious credibility. When this happened, some justices of the peace did not restrain themselves from criticizing the police. In 1921, the superintendent of the APP complained in his annual report to the attorney general that in several instances justices of the peace took opportunities to censure police constables in the presence of the persons who were charged with violations of the *Liquor Act.* He believed that their attitudes toward the police were detrimental to enforcement of the law in general and prohibition legislation in particular. They tended to encourage law offenders and discourage police enforcement. In Saskatchewan, the Liquor Commission decided that the liquor inspectors were to work in pairs so that the evidence obtained by them would be more likely to be accepted by the courts.

Where guilt was established, the police often accused the justices of the peace and magistrates of being too lenient on the offenders since they imposed only minimum fines. This was because they either shared the public's anti-prohibition sentiment or did not want to be unpopular in the town or village where they lived. The police explained that the court's reluctance to dispense justice was associated closely with its pecuniary interest. Most justices of the peace received only twenty-five dollars per month. It was necessary for them to have their own businesses in the towns where they lived. Thus, they were afraid for business reasons to dispense justice vigorously.[79] In order to solve these problems, the police suggested the appointment of travelling magistrates with a relatively higher salary.

The efforts of the APP and the SPP to enforce prohibition legislation resulted in public contempt for the police. The police were referred to as "spotters" and "whisky sleuths." The relationship between the police and the public was seriously undermined.

Enforcement of the prohibition law was detrimental to the police in both provinces. The governments gradually recognized that total prohibition was impossible to enforce and that the attempts were exposing the police to danger as well as ridicule. The governments in Alberta and Saskatchewan adopted a new approach in 1924. Control by licence replaced retail prohibition. The Liquor Branch of the APP in Alberta and the Saskatchewan Liquor Commission were disbanded. Liquor Control Boards were established in both provinces to administer the *Licence Act.* Many public places, such as beer halls, hotels, and restaurants, were allowed to sell intoxicating alcoholic beverages under government-regulated licences. The police had a very positive attitude toward the new changes, and the 1924 annual report of the APP suggested that the changes received the wholehearted support of most citizens.[80] The police began to regain their popularity.

Conclusion: Return of the Mounties

In recent years, provincial critics of the federal government have proposed the re-establishment of the provincial police force in Alberta as part of a larger political "firewall" strategy.[81] Certainly, the implications of previous provincial police forces in the two provinces should be taken into consideration in the current debates on the pros and cons of having once again such a police force. Our examination of the development of the two provincial police forces and their activities led us to conclude that, compared with the federal police, the provincial forces were more likely to be influenced by provincial governments and politics; the provincial statutes, including the controversial prohibition laws, received greater priority. As a result, the forces concerned themselves mainly with policing the "dangerous classes," who were largely foreign immigrants, although crime control became increasingly important in their routine policing activities. The police devoted considerable amounts of their time and resources to immigrant-related industrial unrest, floating immigration populations, liquor law enforcement, and "Canadianization" of the children of foreign immigrants through enforcement of truancy laws. Furthermore, differences in the organizational structures in the two provinces provided less of a check on political interference in Saskatchewan than Alberta, although, in the end, it was provincial finances as opposed to provincial politics that ended the colourful histories of these two organizations.

From the longer-term perspective and in spite of their best efforts to maintain law and order for more than a decade, neither force achieved a very memorable legacy. During the lives of the provincial police forces, several crises eroded their legacies. During the prohibition movement, because the laws had no moral authority, a large segment of the population defied them. Police enforcement of the law resulted in a crisis in public confidence in the impartiality and effectiveness of the law. At the same time, because of continuous financial difficulties, the police were often overstretching their ability to perform various duties.

The forces were finally disbanded mainly because of financial exigencies (Saskatchewan, 1928) and bankruptcy (Alberta, 1932). Although the press anticipated that the provinces would remember the police efforts to maintain law and order "for a long time," the population seems to have forgotten the existence of the forces as soon as they were dissolved.

If the NWMP was created in 1873 to open up and settle the west as part of Canada, the second coming of the federal force probably had a similar symbolic implication for the federal government. The return of the Mounties reflected the political re-integration of the west more fully into the federal sphere of influence. The replacement of provincial institutions with a national institution was not without symbolic importance. Ironically, when it was created in 1873, the NWMP was only a regional police force. Its jurisdiction was limited to the North-West Territories until 1905, when the new provinces were established. Then the administration of justice fell to the attorneys general of the provinces. Due to financial difficulties, a temporary arrangement was made between the provinces and the federal government providing that the federal government maintained the NWMP in the west in return for payment by the provinces. In 1917, because of the war, the federal government terminated the agreement. During wartime, the force was employed to patrol the international border with a small number of men, 485 in 1917 including all ranks.[82]

However, right after the war, the federal government amended the *RNWMP Act*. Contrary to the English tradition that cherishes the idea of locally autonomous police, the 1919 (July) amendment transformed the RNWMP into a national police force. According to the amendment, the members of the RNWMP were constables in every part of Canada for the purpose of carrying out the criminal and other laws of Canada.[83] This amendment empowered the RNWMP to extend its jurisdiction over and to be employed legally in any part of Canada. In November 1919, the Royal North-West Mounted Police were renamed the Royal Canadian Mounted Police in order to reflect their new status.[84]

Establishment of the national police force was an important development in the government's nation building. The RCMP was no longer treated simply as a law enforcement agency. It had established a reputation as an important institution carrying Canadian national identity. Up to 1932, the RCMP absorbed six provincial police forces to assist the provinces with their financial difficulties. These included the provincial police forces of Alberta, Saskatchewan, Nova Scotia, New Brunswick, Prince Edward Island, and Manitoba.

When the Provinces of Alberta and Saskatchewan were created, provincial politicians set out to build them as independent local societies. One step in creating a distinct provincial identity was the creation of local police forces to exercise authority over provincial priorities. The Saskatchewan legislature passed legislation to create provincial police in 1906; Alberta followed in 1908. Alberta in particular recognized the importance of using the police to implement provincial government policies. These plans came to fruition only in 1917. By that time, provincial politics were seized by the problems of prohibition and regulating the newly arrived settlers.

We have referred to factors that tended to put the provincial forces in a bad light. By the same token, it can be argued that the federal government in effect avoided performing all of the unpopular tasks initiated by the local governments, including the prohibition and liquor laws, the control of immigrants from central and eastern Europe, and the surveillance of labour unrest during the 1920s. This state of affairs enabled the RCMP to maintain its popularity in the western provinces.

In 1994, the Province of Alberta commissioned a feasibility report to explore the creation of a new provincial police force to replace the RCMP contract services. The report was never made public, and the plans were judged ill-advised on two grounds. First, the prospect of an increase in the provincial civil service of approximately 1,000 new police officers at a time when the government was engaged in massive downsizing appeared to be politically contradictory. Second, the government feared public resistance to the provincial abolition of the red tunics. Public admiration for the Mounties is sometimes referred to as "scarlet fever." Trifling with such an important symbol of Canadian nationalism was not worth the potential savings that might have eventuated, and the plans were put to rest.[85] However, a decade later the idea continues to be discussed in the context of "western alienation."

Acknowledgments

This research was made possible by a grant from SSHRCC. We wish to acknowledge the useful comments of Rod Macleod and Clive Emsley.

Notes

1 Canada, Sessional Papers, No. 28, Annual Report of the Royal Northwest Mounted Police, from the Headquarters, 1905, 2.

2 The drop in numbers was documented by Duncan F. Robertson, "The Saskatchewan Provincial Police 1917-1928" (master's thesis, University of Saskatchewan, 1976), and "The Saskatchewan Provincial Police 1917-1928," *Saskatchewan History* 31, 3 (1978): 1-11. The case of the fear over prohibition is mentioned by Howard Palmer and Ramara Palmer, *Alberta: A New History* (Edmonton: Hurtig, 1990), 176.

3 In 1904, the North-West Mounted Police were granted the right to use the prefix "royal" in recognition of their services during the Boer War in South Africa (1899-1902). At that time, the NWMP became the RNWMP. For more on the critical role of the police in the peaceable settlement of the Prairies, see Roderick Macleod, *The North-West Mounted Police and Law Enforcement 1873-1905* (Toronto: University of Toronto Press, 1976). Macleod also notes how the existence of the Mounties helped to expedite the evolution of the provincial police. See R.C. Macleod, "The RCMP and the Evolution of Provincial Policing," in *Police Powers in Canada: The Evolution and Practice of Authority,* ed. R.C. Macleod and David Schneiderman (Toronto: University of Toronto Press, 1996), 44-56.

4 "Alberta Provincial Police Regulations," s. 3, Statutes of Alberta, 1931; "Regulations of the Saskatchewan Provincial Police," s. 9, Statutes of Saskatchewan, 1919-20; and "Rules and

Regulations for the Government and Guidelines of the Royal Northwest Mounted Police Force of Canada," s. 24 (Ottawa: Government Printing Bureau, 1909).

5 Noted in the attorney general's files in a memo for Superintendent McDonnell, 15 June 1917, Provincial Archives of Alberta (PAA), accession no. 66.166, 498a.

6 Government of Saskatchewan, *Report of the Royal Commission to Inquire into Statements Made in Statutory Declarations and Other Matters* [the Royal Commission Report] (Regina: Roland S. Garrett, King's Printer, 1931), 21.

7 Statutes of Alberta, *The Alberta Provincial Police Act,* c. 26, 1919; Statutes of Saskatchewan, *The Saskatchewan Provincial Police Act,* c. 19, 1920.

8 *The Saskatchewan Provincial Police Act,* c. 19, 1920; *The Alberta Provincial Police Act,* c. 26, 1919.

9 The Royal Commission Report, 69.

10 Ibid.

11 Ibid. at 14.

12 Ibid. at 176.

13 Ibid. at 12.

14 Ibid. at 176.

15 See Philip C. Stenning, "The Role of Police Boards and Commissions as Institutions of Municipal Police Governance," in *Understanding Policing,* ed. K.R.E. McCormick and L.A. Visano (Toronto: Scholars Press, 1992), 433-87.

16 These appointments and the duties of the board were stipulated in the 1917 *Alberta Provincial Police Act.*

17 Ibid. at c. 4.

18 The Attorney General Files, the Superintendent to the Board of the Commissioners, PAA, accession no. 70.414, 243.

19 Journal of the Legislative Assembly of Alberta, 28 February 1918, 22.

20 Another problem with the force in the public mind concerned the enforcement of the liquor laws. This is suggested in Keith Hart's unpublished paper "The Formation of the Alberta Provincial Police, 1917-1919," Provincial Archives of Alberta (PAA). Hart refers to a discussion of this point in the *Morning Albertan* of 20 February 1919.

21 See L.G. Thomas, *The Liberal Party in Alberta: A History of Politics in the Province of Alberta 1905-1921* (Toronto: University of Toronto Press, 1959). The Saskatchewan situation is described by Norman Ward and David Smith, *Jimmy Gardiner: Relentless Liberal* (Toronto: University of Toronto Press, 1990). Also see David Smith, *Prairie Liberalism: The Liberal Party in Saskatchewan 1905-1971* (Toronto: University of Toronto Press, 1975).

22 Tom Monto, *The United Farmers of Alberta: A Movement, a Government* (Edmonton: Grant Publishing, 1989).

23 See Helen H. Boritch, "Conflict, Compromise, and Administrative Convenience: The Police Organization in Nineteenth-Century Toronto," *Canadian Journal of Law and Society* 3 (1988): 141-74; and Helen H. Boritch and John Hagan, "Crime and the Changing Forms of Class Control: Policing Public Order in Toronto the Good," *Social Forces* 66, 2 (1987): 307-35.

24 The provincial rates that we employed do not reflect the trends recorded by the city police in cities such as Calgary, Edmonton, and Regina, which staffed their own municipal forces that kept the city tallies. As a result, the provincial trends are largely rural crime trends taken from the annual reports of the provincial and federal forces and thus reflect the trends in small towns, villages, and rural municipalities.

25 Eric H. Monkkonen, *Police in Urban America, 1860-1920* (New York: Cambridge University Press, 1981). Also see E.H. Monkkonen, "A Disorderly People? Urban Order in the Nineteenth and Twentieth Centuries," *Journal of American History* 68, 3 (1981): 539-59.

26 There were significant demographic factors associated with policing during the war. The first and most immediate was the removal from the population of large numbers of young men, those at gravest risk of offending. However, the police appear to have shifted their attention to some degree to juveniles and females, whose conviction records experienced a stepwise rise and decline associated with the period of hostilities. See Augustine Brannigan,

"Mystification of the Innocents: Comics and Delinquency in Canada 1931-1949," *Criminal Justice History* 7 (1986): 111-44.

27 These Dominion Bureau of Statistics summaries are reported in the *Annual Year Books of Canada* (Ottawa: Queen's Printer, various years). They are based on the annual survey of the courts and report convictions and acquittals by charge category. See Augustine Brannigan and Zhiqiu Lin, "'Where East Meets West': Police, Immigration and Public Order Crime in the Settlement of Canada from 1896 to 1940," *Canadian Journal of Sociology* 24, 1 (1999): 87-108.

28 See Thomas Thorner, "The Incidence of Crime in Southern Alberta," in *Law and Society in Canada in Historical Perspective,* ed. D.J. Bercuson and L.A. Knafla (Calgary: History Department, University of Calgary, 1979), 53-88.

29 Annual Report of the APP, Division A, 1921, 76.

30 "A Report by the Inspector of 'A' Division on August 10th, 1917 Referring to the Inquiry of Deputy Attorney General as to Conditions at Andrew," PAA, accession no. 66.166, 498a.

31 Gregory Robinson, "'Rougher than Any Other Nationality': Ukrainian Canadians and Crime in Alberta, 1915-29," *Journal of Ukrainian Studies* 16, 1-2 (1991): 147-79.

32 Annual Report of the APP, Division A, 1929, 97.

33 Annual Report of the APP, Division A, 1928, 17. A report from Red Deer showed that the lower crime rate in the area occurred because the district was composed of a greater proportion of older settlers relative to the foreign-speaking population. Annual Report of the APP, Division B, 1920, 4.

34 Annual Report of the SPP, Headquarters, 1919, 1.

35 Annual Report of the APP, Headquarters, 1919, 47.

36 Annual Report of the APP, Division D, 1922, 3; Division C, 1920, 53; Annual Report of the SPP, Regina Division, 1920, 47-50.

37 Annual Report of the APP, Division C, 1918, 9.

38 Ibid.

39 Annual Report of the APP, Division A, 1918, 2.

40 Annual Report of the APP, Headquarters, 1925, 93.

41 Ibid.

42 Ibid. at 94.

43 Annual Report of the APP, Headquarters, 1923, 76.

44 Annual Report of the APP, Headquarters, 1930, 69.

45 Annual Report of the APP, Division A, 1930, 19.

46 See Donald Avery, *Dangerous Classes: European Immigrant Workers and Labour Radicalism in Canada 1896-1932* (Toronto: McClelland and Stewart, 1979), 124. The role of American police in suppressing labour is discussed in Bruce C. Johnson, "Taking Care of Labour: The Police in American Politics," in *Understanding Policing,* ed. McCormick and Visano, 491-516.

47 Annual Report of the APP, Division C, 1927, 34; 1925, 39.

48 Annual Report of the APP, Division D, 1924, 12.

49 Annual Report of the APP, Division B, 1923, 19.

50 Annual Report of the APP, Headquarters, 1926, 74.

51 Annual Report of the APP, Headquarters, 1927, 34.

52 This large percentage of the unemployed who were refused government relief might also suggest that the police treated some immigrants badly in the allocation of relief, particularly when they were identified with radical elements and engaged in mass actions that threatened to breach the peace. Otherwise, the role of the police in distributing relief does not appear to have been a controversial or high-profile element of their official role, at least as evident from the annual records.

53 Annual Report of the APP, Headquarters, 1928, 66; 1925, 97.

54 Annual Report of the APP, Headquarters, 1925, 99.

55 Annual Report of the APP, Division C, 1918, 8.

56 Annual Report of the SPP, Saskatoon Division, 1918, 6; Headquarters, 1920, 1; Annual Report of the APP, Division C, 1920, 43.

57 Annual Reports of the SPP, Headquarters, 1917, 1918, 1919.

58 Annual Report of the SPP, Weyburn Division, 1917, 5.

59 Meeting of the Board of Commissioners, APP, 7 January 1918, PAA, accession no. 66.166, 1288.
60 Annual Report of the SPP, Headquarters, 1920, 1.
61 Annual Report of the APP, Liquor Branch, 1920, 10; Annual Report of the SPP, Detective Division, 1917, 3.
62 Annual Report of the APP, Headquarters, 1918, 21.
63 Annual Report of the APP, Headquarters, 1918, 23.
64 Annual Report of the APP, Liquor Branch, 1920, 6.
65 Ibid. at 10.
66 The total expenses by the APP for enforcement of the liquor law were $55,153.94. PAA, accession no. 75.370/box, 72.270/56.
67 See Chris Stewart and Lynn Hudson's popular histories, *Mahony's Minute Men: Saga of the Saskatchewan Provincial Police 1917-1928* (Saskatoon: Modem Press, 1978), and *Murder in Uniform* (Saskatoon: Modem Press, 1978). Two popular histories of the period of prohibition on the Prairies are told by Frank W. Anderson, *The Rum Runners* (Aldergrove: Frontier Publishing, 1972); and James Gray, *Booze: The Impact of Whiskey on the Prairie West* (Toronto: Macmillan, 1972).
68 Annual Report of the SPP, Weyburn Division, 1920, 6.
69 Meeting of the Board of Commissioners, APP, 1 April 1918, PAA, accession no. 66.166, 1288.
70 Meeting of the Board of Commissioners, APP, 13 May 1918, PAA, accession no. 66.166, 1288.
71 Annual Report of the APP, Liquor Branch, 1924, 9.
72 Annual Report of the APP, Division C, 1922, 43.
73 Annual Report of the APP, Division C, 1921, 14.
74 Ibid. at 28.
75 Annual Report of the APP, Division B, 1920, the last page of the report, which is not numbered.
76 Annual Report of the APP, Division C, 1921 28.
77 Annual Report of the APP, Liquor Branch, 1921, 10.
78 Annual Report of the APP, Liquor Branch, 1920, 1.
79 Annual Report of the APP, Liquor Branch, 1921, 9.
80 Annual Report of the APP, Division D, 1924, 1.
81 See Barry Cooper and Royce Koop, "Policing Alberta: An Analysis of the Alternatives to the Federal Provision of Police Services," Fraser Institute Occasional Paper, *Public Policy Sources* 72 (2003): 3-18.
82 Reports of the RCMP, Headquarters, 1917, 1920.
83 The *RCMP Act* in Report of the RCMP, s. 12, ss. 3, 1920, 7.
84 Ibid.
85 According to Robert Dunster, ADM Justice (Public Security), the report was called the "Hahn Report" after its chair, Edward Hahn. The report was never filed with the library of the provincial legislature, although some paragraphs were made available to the opposition parties. While the government decided not to resurrect the provincial police, the mere existence of the report resulted in greater flexibility in the federal-provincial negotiations over costs and services in the RCMP contract.

9
The Development of Prairie Canada's Water Law, 1870-1940

Tristan M. Goodman

The early development of Prairie water law systems in the sixty years after the mid-nineteenth century witnessed a profound erosion of common law riparian rights in response to social, economic, and political forces across the region. Indeed, it can be argued that the development of a western Canadian water regime is a unique chapter in the nation's legal history. During this period, fundamental changes occurred within the region's legal system. But, more specifically, dramatic alterations took place in how water law was conceived, administered, and enforced. In effect, when disputes erupted over access to usable and clean water supplies, it is certain that these contests were played out within an informal means of dispute resolution. Indeed, an extralegal system of negotiation and compromise was applied more often than not in the early years of the ranching frontier in the foothills of the Canadian Rockies. And this was the approach that set the mould for the subsequent history of water rights on the Prairies.[1]

External Influences

Prairie water law did not develop in a vacuum. Not surprisingly, the physical proximity, experiments, and developments in the American west exerted considerable influence on the initiatives of Canadian legislators. Canadians, in turning to the American example, recognized some of the perceived weaknesses in the American legal system and adapted some of its strengths to better suit the unique needs on the Canadian Prairies. For example, the uncertainty that flowed from unclear title in relation to resource ownership, and the associated flood of litigation that followed, were consciously addressed in Prairie legislation. Indeed, the heavy reliance on court action in the United States is a striking point of contrast between the two nations.[2] Unlike the American system, which relied upon courts to settle disputes under the first-come, first-served system of prior appropriation, that of Canada placed the determination of what constituted "beneficial use" in the control of a centralized government authority.[3] As a result, in Canada the issuance of a government approval, in the form of a water licence, was the starting point of almost all water rights, whereas the American system relied upon court decisions that determined whether beneficial use or riparian rights governed a particular situation.[4] David Percy states that what constitutes beneficial use and the allocation of water is unique in that a more "disguised approach to allocation and administration" is found in the Canadian system of water law.[5]

Another aspect of comparison between the two systems is found in the question of whether a dual system of riparian rights and prior use was in place.[6] In the United States, water law was allowed to develop with a strong dualistic approach – containing both riparian water rights and prior use rights – that has remained largely intact to the present day.[7] In spite of the reliance on common law principles in the American west, legislation came to recognize customary mining practices "where not in conflict with the constitution and laws" of the country.[8] From the Canadian perspective, this ambiguity invariably fostered uncertainty as to which law or practice shaped a given situation. This particular concern would have important considerations for the manner in which Canadian legislators approached their own water law regime, opting for a system with greater security of title.

Still another point of comparison between the United States and Canada pertained to the particular challenges of dealing with water in their respective western regions. Both countries had problems dealing with the complex relationship between regionalized values and the reallocation of water resources. Despite sharing similar challenges, the two countries approached the question from different perspectives. In the United States, the inability to make room for new users was a product of court decisions protecting riparian rights and, as a consequence, setting in place nontransferable water rights. Furthermore, a shortage of water in many areas of southern California also contributed to the development of western American water law.[9] Canada, while having similar problems in dealing with the allocation of water resources for more recent and often more highly valued users, theoretically should not have suffered the same fate as the United States. Unfortunately, Canadians were not spared these difficulties. While problems did not arise from the courts in protecting common law riparian rights, there was a laxity in how the system was applied and administered. Specifically, government licences in Canada tended to be issued for lengthy periods of time with little regard for future possible use.[10]

Australian Influences and Comparisons

Australia has for many years placed control of water resources with the government and not with the courts. It is generally acknowledged to have some of the earliest government allocation systems for water resources.[11] While English origins were at the root of Australian water law, Australians' dissatisfaction with the riparian system grew from needs that were strikingly similar to those of western Canada. This unease initially stemmed from the economic needs of the Australian mining community but soon spread to broader concerns over the distribution of water in large arid regions.[12] As a consequence, the initial moves toward government control and distribution of water rights came in the early 1840s.[13] Yet unlike that of the western United States, the Victoria government in Australia moved in anticipation of the development of a mining culture seen to be imminent.[14] The Australian drive toward a government allocation system of water law would be completed in 1884. The Australian Royal Commission of Inquiry into Irrigation was chaired by Alfred Deakin, who travelled extensively to other English colonies to examine their water law systems. Both the American and the English mining communities had significant influence on his decisions and on his subsequent conclusion that the state "should exercise the supreme control of ownership over all water other than springs [groundwater] on private land."[15]

This drive to establish government control of water resources in an allocation-based manner foretold similar initiatives in the Canadian North-West Territories.[16] Indeed, by mimicking this pre-emptive strike by establishing full governmental control over the allocation or appropriation of water resources, the 1894 *North-West Irrigation Act* of Canada echoed Australia's 1857 *Gold Fields Act* by framing legislation in anticipation of future development.[17] In effect, the Australian situation served as a model of action designed to prevent future problems with incoming Prairie settlers.[18]

Other similarities occurred in the introduction of conservation measures by both the Australian and the Canadian systems. The Australian *Public Works Act* of 1865 provided the Board of Lands and Works with the authority to remove water rights if the grantee was wasting or misusing water.[19] Similar measures were later introduced in Canada, first by the *British Columbia Land Ordinance* and decades later by the *North-West Irrigation Act.*[20] Although these had differing degrees of use, effect, and administration, similar principles existed within the three pieces of legislation. Given the Australian legislation and water law system that developed from the early 1840s to the 1870s, there is little question that Australian initiatives exerted considerable influence on the subsequent development of water law on the Prairies.

Western Canadian Water Law, 1870-94

The development of a western Canadian water regime is a unique aspect of the nation's legal history and natural resource development. This period from 1870 to 1894 witnessed both fundamental changes within the legal system and, more specifically, dramatic alterations to the system of water law used on the Prairies. The North-West Territories officially received formal water law in 1870 with the reception of English common law.[21] Yet despite this reception date, we know little of its actual application until the early 1880s. Initial disputes concerned the degradation of land that in turn could affect the water resources of the local area rather than involved direct conflicts over riparian rights.

These disputes involved the broadly dispersed ranching community and the various types of livestock that were grazed near watercourse areas.[22] Sheep and a number of other animals were especially hard on the local environment because they cropped grazing areas to a lower level than did cattle. This had a more detrimental effect on the delicate prairie landscape. In cropping the local grasses to a lower level, these animals exposed the soil to strong winds that carried off much of the nutrients. Thus, not only was the land stripped of its potential to sustain local grasses and livestock, but also the shifting soil altered land formations, affected groundwater, and in time degraded other water supplies by muddying rivers and streams.[23]

The increase in ranching during the 1880s did more than exacerbate the problems created by grazing behaviours. Rising demand also accentuated the region's poor drainage, small lake areas, evaporation basins, permanent sloughs, and unique glacial till plains.[24] Furthermore, the smaller streams feeding or being fed by the Bow, Oldman, South Saskatchewan, and Red Deer Rivers were often affected by snow melts from the Rocky Mountains and extremes of low volumes or high turbidity. Some streams in the foothills, such as Highwood River, Willow Creek, and Oldman River, often flooded and created innumerable problems for both ranchers and travellers. Moreover, sudden chinooks in the winter months also created difficulties that in turn sparked disputes between neighbours over concerns related to drainage and water quality. In other circumstances, downstream ranchers were invariably upset with upstream users because of animal waste fouling the water in the lower-volume streams. Not surprisingly, all of these conditions gave rise to disputes over access to usable and clean water supplies. While conflicts over water rights did occur, the research that has examined these contests reveals the existence of an informal means of dispute resolution. Indeed, an extralegal form of negotiation and compromise was applied more often than not during these early years of relatively sparse settlement in the North-West Territories.

One of the first pieces of Canadian legislation to indirectly affect water rights on the Prairies was the *Dominion Lands Act (DLA)* of 1872.[25] Emphasizing land and enacted broadly to aid in the development and settlement of the Territories, this legislation nonetheless had an important effect on water use and, to a lesser degree, on water rights in the region. In addressing questions of water law and water rights, the framers had two options: they could either apply the British riparian doctrine, or they could turn to the American notion of prior appropriation. The British riparian approach, rooted in the common law, meant that riparian owners were entitled to receive the flow of water to their property with little or no decrease in quantity or quality. Riparian owners also had a right to use the water for domestic and nondomestic purposes connected to their riparian land.[26] However, the nondomestic purpose could not noticeably diminish the water quantity or quality of other riparian owners. The American alternative of prior appropriation followed a first-come, first served principle that protected the interests of those who had established first use of the resource. In practice, this meant that the first or prior users enjoyed a legal advantage over new entrants into the region because of greater security of title.[27] Faced with this choice, the authors of the *DLA* embraced the American prior appropriation policy. From a number of perspectives – those of settlers, local governments, and the Canadian Pacific Railway Company – prior appropriation, or prior allocation as it came to be known in Canada, was preferable for the stability and clarity of water rights.

However, to the minor extent that the *DLA* incorporated prior allocation as the guiding principle of water law on the Prairies, the historic influence of the common law riparian doctrine remained, although it was gradually eroded. Specifically, the riparian doctrine presented several problems not encountered in other regions of the country. The inability to remove large quantities of water for irrigation, problems with some landowners not being directly connected to a watercourse, and the instability of common law water rights resulted in the dominion government's acquiring more regulatory control over the resource. Indeed, settlers' increasing economic reliance on water required increased government involvement.

The problem was that settlers, governments, and companies were wary of investing capital in any water development project because of the inability to guarantee secure and stable water supplies under the riparian system. Furthermore, during times of shortage, those who had established long-term use enjoyed no protection in cutbacks or withdrawals of access to water. In effect, under the riparian system, all users suffered equally. With a prior allocation regime, cuts were prioritized so that the most recent users would be affected first, thus protecting the interests of older ones. This rule ensured that rights and their individual application were clearly understood by all interested parties. Inasmuch as these practical considerations undermined common law riparian practice, the administrative application and judicial interpretation of the *DLA* served to further such erosion. The cumulative effect was that the act, in common with the piecemeal decisions of ranchers, farmers, and local governments, signalled the first successful dilution of common law riparian rights on the Prairies.

The indirect erosion of riparian rights under the *DLA* was reflected in later occasions when the act was subjected to judicial interpretation. For example, in *The King v. Alberta Railway and Irrigation Company* (1912), the case turned on to what extent, if any, riparian rights were retained in an irrigation canal constructed by the defendant. Delivering its ruling in December 1909, the Alberta Supreme Court found that, despite the riparian land being in the lawful hands of the defendant, the water and benefits of that water could not interfere with other areas.[28] Since the *North-West Irrigation Act* had been passed in 1894, the company's riparian claims were adjudged to be invalid. Thus, through the power of the *DLA,* the right to proceed with little or no regard for external users of the land or water was revoked. The company no longer had the right to construct irrigation works without the consent of the government.

A more direct indication of the same rationale can be seen in the 1921 case of *The King v. Alberta Railway and Irrigation Company.*[29] Although adjudicated over two decades after passage of the *North-West Irrigation Act,* the case set out the land and its benefits as being within the rights of the original possessor.[30] Those benefits included an irrigation ditch and the water contained therein as belonging to the Crown as original "owner." While some chose to view riparian rights as having been attached to the disputed land, it was successfully argued that the *DLA* overrode any riparian claim. Finally, in the Saskatchewan case of *Cain v. Copeland* determined a year later, it was held that, under the framework of the *DLA,* the first resident of a disputed area enjoyed a right to the land in question and the attached benefits. In this particular case, those benefits included drainage areas and irrigation ditches.[31]

The apparent dismantling of these common law riparian rights reflected the need to institute a new legal regime that would prevent conflicts over water erupting both between ranchers and settlers and within settler communities. Furthermore, agricultural conditions and those improvements needed to foster economic growth dictated that irrigation projects had to be undertaken. After all, the Prairies were unlike either British Columbia or central Canada, where water was plentiful. Simply put, if the region was to support large-scale agricultural production and come to occupy a key place in the nation's economy, irrigation was an essential first step. Indeed, Thomas Mayne Daly, the Conservative MP representing the Selkirk riding in Manitoba, enthusiastically supported any measure that would hasten the arrival of irrigation on the Prairies.[32]

Addressing the House of Commons on 25 June 1894 as minister of the interior and superintendent general of Indian Affairs, Daly noted that he had agreed "with the Irrigation League of Calgary in their passing of a resolution that this government recognize the importance and great benefits of irrigation to the North-West Territories."[33] Although prairie lands were found to produce poor crops in their natural state, the added application of water could provide some of the best agricultural land in North America. Without irrigation, Prairie Canada would have a very different historic evolution and economic value. And in relation to water rights, Daly argued that, insofar as riparian rights were concerned, they had been "done away entirely" by the *North-West Irrigation Act*.[34] Clearly, from the dominion government's perspective, the preservation of common law riparian rights would not be allowed to stand in the way of settlement or economic development on the Prairies.

The proposed *North-West Irrigation Act (NWIA)* of 1894 was also portrayed as a preventative measure to avoid the frequency of litigation that had been seen for many years in California. Specifically, because of the rapid growth first in mining and then in agriculture, California's dual system spawned an inordinate amount of litigation. Moreover, the lack of clarity over questions of water ownership was a constant obstacle to economic development.[35] Indeed, Catherine Miller demonstrates that, thanks in part to systemic uncertainty over water rights, companies in the sunshine state wasted little time in seeking legal recourse to settle water questions.[36] The desire by the dominion government to prevent a similar situation in Canada is evident through statements in the House of Commons. As stated by an MP, "it has been found in regard to irrigation in California that the question of riparian rights has given rise to more litigation than any other matter, millions have been expended on it."[37] The goal of stability and continued economic growth in the Prairies was to be achieved through settlement and development, and from the dominion government's perspective this necessitated strong measures.

While committed to its legislative agenda and the results expected, the governing Conservatives were not deaf to criticisms. Under pressure from opposition MPs, the act's provisions applied only to surface water since groundwater remained outside the scope of the *NWIA*. William Mulock, Liberal MP, gave voice to the particular opposition concern that the legislation "will do more [than establish reliable irrigation]. They [the clauses of the act] will interfere with a man owning a well on his own lot." Notably, Liberal opposition was centred on the extensive range of the legislation rather than on the nature of the proposed change. In effect, the government's attempt to remove completely common law riparian rights was felt to be too extensive and an interference with landowners' rights. Resistance to including groundwater was also founded on a contemporary legal question. What constituted groundwater as distinct from surface water was uncertain. Indeed, only two years earlier a Canadian court had ruled "that where the courses of subterranean waters are known they are covered by the same rule as surface waters." Perhaps owing to both the opposition and the continuing debate over what constituted groundwater, the Conservatives relented and removed groundwater from the act. Although the removal may have quieted some criticism, it inadvertently re-opened the door for common law riparian rights and future challenges based on them.[38]

That groundwater would be excluded from the *NWIA*'s provisions exposes the limits of nineteenth-century knowledge in relation to water resources. Specifically, the direct relationship between ground- and surface water was not appreciated.[39] As a result, the realization that surface water fed groundwater and that groundwater fed surface water had not yet been made. Therefore, under the auspices of the act, groundwater pumping led to a significant depletion of surface water, and the pollution of surface water eventually led to groundwater contamination.

The *NWIA* reflected the interests of ranchers, farmers, local governments, and the dominion government as well as served the interests of the Canadian Pacific Railway (CPR). Describing the CPR "as a catalyst for settlement and economic development" in the Prairies, Brian Osborne and Susan Wurtele note that reforms to water law aided the railway company and its activities as a developer and landowner.[40] Furthermore, Harold Innis' 1923 seminal work on the CPR details the company's involvement in the establishment of irrigation schemes across the region.[41] Aided by government subsidies, favourable legislation, and its considerable influence as the most powerful private landowner in the region, by 1903 the company was able to establish the Irrigation Block of the Canadian Pacific in Alberta, which at that time was the largest irrigation project in North America.[42]

The present agricultural conditions in Alberta and parts of Saskatchewan and Manitoba have solid roots in these developments. The Department of the Interior gave the CPR great leniency in choosing the sections of land it was to be granted, and in turn the company was never hesitant about requesting specific land. In submitting requests for a number of the more southern sections, it recognized that should its schemes for irrigation fail the lands would be almost worthless. Thus, because of the importance of irrigation in the company's attempts to promote settlement, it energetically lobbied the government for increased control over land and resource use in the North-West Territories.[43]

Passage of the *NWIA* heralded a new era of water law on the Prairies and continues to provide the basis for the system of water law across the region. By placing "the right to use all water at anytime in any river ... in every case" under control of the federal Crown, the act set in place a licensing process that controlled access to water.[44] Although similar to the American prior appropriation system, the Prairie variant had several key differences. Prior allocation in Canada vested ownership of the resource in the Crown and not in individuals. Moreover, the Crown retained authority to remove a licence or institute any action deemed necessary in relation to water resources. Most importantly, it was hoped that Crown ownership of all water and the imposition of a licensing system would avoid a repetition of the situation in California.[45] Whether the increase in government control actually resulted in a decrease in litigation compared to California is difficult to speculate upon without further research into the exact number and types of court proceedings concerning water resources in the early twentieth century. My initial speculation suggests that it did decrease litigation, but a thorough examination of all court cases is needed to reach a reliable conclusion.

Moreover, despite the *NWIA*'s attempt, common law riparian rights remained part of the region's legal heritage, although the strength of common law was underestimated by those opposed to riparian rights (e.g., the CPR and the framers of the act). Notably, the permanent removal of riparian rights was far from certain, and the legal cases of the future would show how in some instances the strength and wide approach of the legislation had not completely removed riparian rights. This act and similar future ones were challenged on a number of legal fronts. The first challenge came from landowners' concerns based on the loss of rights attached to an individual's land. These cases do not appear to have entered the superior courts and had little success in challenging the basic removal of common law riparian rights. The second challenge came from surface water problems from groundwater removals. Limited evidence suggests that these removals were at times so great that the surface water was affected in a negative quantity manner.[46] Further research is needed in this area before conclusions can be reached. The third and final challenge came from the premise that the act had not in fact removed all riparian rights from common law. Despite the government's goal of full and complete removal of riparian rights, success was not achieved. A small degree of riparian rights did remain in the common law. Challenges would be mounted against this and later similar legislation.

One such challenge in 1907 revealed that, despite the *NWIA*'s strong legislative approach to water resources, it had not completely alleviated all common law riparian rights. In fact, the Alberta Court of Appeal, comprised of Chief Justice A.L. Sifton, Mr. Justice Horace Harvey, Mr. Justice David Scott, and Mr. Justice Nicholas Beck, opined that, where the act was unclear or when gaps existed because of unique situations, the common law applied with the original riparian right to water and its use. And in the case then before the court, the ditches of a riparian owner were found to be protected from harm or change by a municipality, despite the municipality complying fully with the licensing requirements of the act.[47]

Over three-quarters of a century later, riparian rights were still being upheld. For example, in the case of *R. (Alberta) v. Very* (1983), the persistence of riparian rights was a central element at issue.[48] In defending his refusal to seek a licence for the use of water from a "slough" located on the surface of his land, Roland A. Very claimed that he possessed a common law right to the slough and that, as such, his right was unaffected by any legislative enactment. Very's counsel argued that this slough did not fall under the *NWIA* for two reasons. First, it had no presence of a bed and no well-defined banks with reasonable permanence of water. Second, it did not contain water that was of benefit to society as a whole for purposes such as fishing, navigation, or recreation, and its only value was for the personal and seasonal watering of livestock. In deciding the case, the court found that the wording of "the act is applied to all water bodies ... including any other water bodies" not directly specified in the act and thus was too extensive.[49] In making his decision, Judge J. Egbert drew upon a number of earlier cases in finding for Very's common law riparian rights.[50] The court based its decision on a "common law riparian right of a slough" and thus confirmed Very's contention that he did not require a Crown licence to draw on the slough as a water resource.[51]

The *NWIA* was a powerful piece of legislative water law that brought great change to a riparian owner's claim to the water flowing past his or her land. In general, the courts accepted the principles of the legislation. But they did not apply its sweeping government control without questioning the facts of each specific case. Therefore, riparian rights can be seen to have survived in specific situations under the heavy cover of legislation. Although not as evenly split between common law and legislation as in California, the two systems still had respective weight in the courts of the North-West Territories by the turn of the twentieth century.

Prairie Water Legislation in a Post–Common-Law Period: 1894-1930

With the passing of the *North-West Irrigation Act,* an important change in western Canada's legal system had occurred. Other coordinate pieces of legislation, such as the amendments to the *North-West Irrigation Act,* the *Dominion Water Power Act* of 1919, the *Irrigation Act* of 1906 (amended in 1927), and the *Natural Resource Transfer Agreements* and their amendments in 1938 were eventually passed. The result was a uniform system of water law covering the areas of modern-day Alberta, Saskatchewan, and large sections of Manitoba that had developed during the first four decades of the twentieth century. This system resulted from the retention by the dominion government of all ungranted natural resources within the boundaries of the Prairie provinces. With the 1912 *Manitoba Boundaries Extension Act* and the 1930s *Natural Resources Transfer Agreements (NRTA),* they assumed full control of their own water resources.[52] Although there was some initial confusion over the *NRTA*'s inclusion of water resources, this was settled in 1938 with an amendment specifically including water resources in the transfer. Made retroactive to 1930, the amendment ended any controversy over control and ownership of water resources in the Prairies and confirmed the uninterrupted authority of the prior allocation system.

While the 1938 amendment clarified that the Crown had indeed transferred its interests "in waters and water-powers within the provinces" to Alberta and Saskatchewan, it was uncertain as to who controlled the water in the intervening years between 1930 and 1938.[53] On balance, the record indicated that the question was of limited interest to the Province of Alberta, which, under the assumption of having been granted full rights and ownership of the resource, passed its own water law legislation in 1931.[54] Arguably, the *Alberta Water Act* was representative of other early attempts by the provinces to exercise their newly granted powers. In effect, it was a consolidation of the federal legislation. In practice, the transfer did not usher in a new era of Prairie water law.

Another important piece of federal legislation was the *Dominion Irrigation Act (DIA)* of 1927.[55] Because the newly created Provinces of Alberta and Saskatchewan did not receive control of water resources until after 1930, this act affected them for three years. Unlike earlier legislation that can be understood to remove or diminish common law riparian rights, the *DIA* seemingly established a small justification for common law riparian water rights. Section 11 specifically states that riparians were not to be deprived of water for domestic purposes and that this right was not specific to a legislative right. However, unlike the relatively new *Alberta Water Resources Act,* or similar provincial enactments across the region, the nature of domestic usage was not clearly elaborated in the 1927 *Irrigation Act.*[56]

Although there does not appear to have been any litigation in which section 11 was at issue, the question of what comprised "domestic" was debated in both Alberta and Ontario.[57] The 1927 act was important to the degree that it clarified some forms of common law riparian rights. Furthermore, in leaving the character of domestic usage unclear, the act seemingly provided fertile ground for future controversy. As it turned out, however, this did not prove to be the case. By 1930, both Alberta and Saskatchewan acquired control over their water resources, and the *DIA* was rarely resorted to for redress or clarification. Despite this lack of use, the act remains important for its limited re-establishment of common law riparian rights, and in time provincial legislatures would incorporate these notions into their own legal regimes.

A final ingredient in the composition of Prairie water law during these years was the effect of international controversies pertaining to cross-border water resources. During the turn of the twentieth century, there were international problems in central Canada (the Niagara area), with similar difficulties in Prairie Canada (the Milk River region). It is possible that the government's removal of a large portion of riparian rights on the Prairies was, to a small degree, an attempt to gain control of water resources in order to prevent international problems with the United States. Indeed, it is difficult to ignore the Boundary Waters Treaty of 1909 that, under articles V, VI, and VII, specifically reduced riparian rights in boundary regions.[58] Furthermore, the riparian rights affected by articles V and VI established target volumes for water allocation on both sides of the border. Thus, it removed any landowner's riparian right beyond the specific volume limits put in place by the treaty.[59] The International Joint Commission (IJC), established by article VII to adjudicate disputes under the treaty, also had potential to undermine riparian rights.[60] In handling any question that arose under the treaty, the IJC was to frame its decisions in reference to international law that was taken to be paramount to both common law and domestic statutes. The idea was to ensure that the binding nature of IJC decisions would be enforced without difficulty or undue delay. At the same time, this mandate allowed the IJC to remove riparian rights in a specific area under the justification of international co-operation and law. This could not be done without government consent; however, once committed, governments had obligations under the treaty to implement IJC advice.

Conclusion

The early legislative developments of the dominion government's movement from riparian common law rights to a statute-based water law follow a clear pattern. While it is certain that common law riparian rights were eroded after 1872, this erosion was not constant, nor was it always permanent. Indeed, during the early part of the twentieth century, judicial decisions in favour of riparian rights were echoed by limited legislative protection of a riparian right as it pertained to a nebulous notion of domestic use. Although the specific extent of these rights is difficult to gauge, it is undeniable that the dual system existing in the western United States was not allowed to take hold on the Canadian Prairies. Although common law riparian rights were, to some extent, rejuvenated in the early twentieth century, their application in law remained weak and limited to specific cases.

The development of water law in the Prairies stemmed from the economic and social conditions of the era. The goal of settlement in the national interest drove the dominion government and the CPR to push for legal changes in water law. The system's development was greatly affected by examining other countries' successes and failures. History demonstrates that situations unique to the Canadian Prairies determined the water law regime that it would adopt. The law of water rights came from English legal traditions, but at the same time these traditions were rooted in the medieval period and conveyed through earlier colonial experiences. In effect, the water law that developed on the Prairies was very much a product of that region's peculiar historic experience while, in equal measure, reflecting the aspirations for what the region might become.

Notes

1 Edward Brado, *Cattle Kingdom: Early Ranching in Alberta* (Toronto: Douglas and McIntyre, 1984), 76, 185.

2 Catherine Miller details the dramatic extent to which the water law of the western United States was influenced by a heavy stream of litigation; see M. Catherine Miller, *Flooding the Courtrooms* (Lincoln and London: University of Nebraska Press, 1993).

3 Marie Ann Bowden, "Comparing Canadian and U.S. Water Law," *Border Waters: Proceedings of a Conference on U.S./Canada Transboundary Water Management* (Bozeman, MT: 49th Parallel Institute for Canadian-American Relations, 1987), 55.

4 John D. Leshy, "The Prior Appropriation Doctrine of Water Law in the West: An Emperor with Few Clothes," *Journal of the West* 3, 29 (1990): 5-13 at 7.

5 David Percy, "Principles of Western Canadian Water Law," in *Border Waters,* 51.

6 Norris Hundley Jr., *The Great Thirst: Californians and Water, 1770s-1990s* (Berkeley: University of California Press, 1992), 69.

7 Marc Reisner, *Cadillac Desert: The American West and Its Disappearing Water* (New York: Penguin Books, 1987), 45.

8 *California Practice Act* (1851), *California Statutes,* s. 621.

9 Hundley, *The Great Thirst,* 7.

10 David Percy, *The Framework of Water Rights Legislation in Canada* (Calgary: Canadian Institute of Resources Law, 1988), 12.

11 J.M. Powell, *Watering the Western Third: Water, Land, and Community in Western Australia, 1826-1998* (Perth: Waters and Rivers Commission, 1998), 6.

12 Sandford D. Clark and Ian A. Renard, "The Riparian Doctrine and Australian Legislation," *Melbourne University Law Review* 7 (1970): 475-506 at 475.

13 *Melbourne Corporation Act,* (Victoria Statutes, Australia, 1842), 6 Victoria, s. 88.

14 Powell, *Watering the Western Third,* 18.

15 "First Progress Report, Victorian Royal Commission on Water Supply" (Melbourne: Government of Victoria, 1884), 54-55.

16 Howard Palmer, *Alberta: A New History* (Edmonton: Hurtig Publishers, 1990), 57.

17 *North-West Irrigation Act* (Canada, 1894), c. 30; *Australian Gold Fields Act* (Victoria Statutes, 1857), 21 Victoria.

18 Canada, *House of Commons Debates* (1894), 25 June 1894, vol. 1, 4950.

19 *Public Works Statute* (Australia, 1865), s. 231.

20 *Lands Ordinance* (British Columbia, 1870), no. 144, s.37; *North-West Irrigation Act* (Canada, 1894).

21 Chester Martin, ed., *Dominion Lands Policy* (Toronto: McClelland and Stewart, 1973), 199.

22 *Harris v. Rankin* (1887), 4 Manitoba Law Review 115.

23 Brado, *Cattle Kingdom,* 33.

24 Ibid. at 32.

25 *Dominion Lands Act* (Canada, 1872), c. 31.

26 Ludwik A. Teclaff, *Water Law in Historical Perspective* (New York: William S. Hein Company, 1985), 6.

27 Ibid. at 21.

28 *The King v. Alberta Railway and Irrigation Company* (1912), in *Law Reports of the House of Lords, Judicial Committee of the Privy Council and Peerage Cases* (London: , 1912), 828.

29 Ibid. at 827.

30 *Dominion Lands Act* (Canada, 1872), c. 31, sec. 23.

31 *Cain v. Copeland* (1922), 2 Western Weekly Reporter 1025.

32 See John Kendle, "Thomas Mayne Daly," *Dictionary of Canadian Biography,* vol. 14, *1911 to 1920,* ed. Jean Hamelin (Toronto: University of Toronto Press, 1998).

33 Canada, *House of Commons Debates* (1894), 25 June 1894, vol. 1, 4950.
34 Ibid.
35 Hundley, *The Great Thirst,* 120.
36 Miller, *Flooding the Courtrooms,* 20.
37 Mr. Daly, in Canada, *House of Commons Debates* (1894), 25 June 1894, vol. 1, 4950.
38 Canada, *House of Commons Debates* (1894), 29 June 1894, vol. 1, 5064.
39 Elizabeth Kay Berner and Robert A. Berner, *The Global Water Cycle: Geochemistry and Environment* (Englewood Cliffs, NJ: Pearson Education Publishing, 1987), 30.
40 Brian Osborne and Susan E. Wurtele, "The Other Railway: Canadian National's Department of Colonization and Agriculture," *Prairie Forum* 20, 2 (1995): 231-53 at 231.
41 See, generally, Harold Innis, *A History of the Canadian Pacific Railway* (London: P.S. King and Sons, 1923).
42 James Hedges, *The Federal Railway Land Subsidy Policy of Canada* (Cambridge, MA: Harvard University Press, 1934), 66.
43 Ibid. at 65.
44 *North-West Irrigation Act,* c. 30, s. 4.
45 Canada, *House of Common Debates* (1894), 25 June 1894, vol. 1, 4950.
46 E.B. Swindlehurst, *Alberta Agriculture: A Short History* (Edmonton: Alberta Ministry of Agriculture, 1968), 28.
47 *Robertson v. Town of High River* (1907), 6 Western Law Reports 767.
48 *R. (Alberta) v. Very* (1983), 6 Western Weekly Reports 143.
49 *North-West Irrigation Act,* c. 30, s. 4.
50 *A.G. Can. v. Hallet and Carey Ltd.* (1952), Appeal Cases 427; *C.P.R. v. R.* (1906), 38 Supreme Court Reports 137; *Flewelling v. Johnston* (1921), 16 Alberta Law Reports 409; *Would v. Herrington* (1932), 40 Manitoba Law Reports 365.
51 *R. (Alberta) v. Very,* 145.
52 *The Manitoba Boundaries Extension Act* (Canada, 1912), c. 32, s. 6; and the "Natural Resources Transfer Agreements" that can be found in the *Constitution Act* (U.K., 1930), c. 26, schedule 2, s. 1.
53 *The Natural Resources Transfer (Amendment) Act* (Canada, 1938), c. 36.
54 *Water Act* (Alberta, 1931), c. 71.
55 *Irrigation Act* (Canada, 1927), c. 104.
56 See the *Water Resources Act* (Alberta, 1996), c. W-3.5, s. 21, ss. 1.
57 See *Tottrup v. Queen (in Alberta)* (1979), Alberta Supreme Court, 79 Dominion Law Reports (3d) 533.
58 *Boundary Waters Treaty* (UK, 1909), 36 Stat. 2448; Treaty Series 548 (1909), 319-27.
59 Treaty Series 548 (1909), 322.
60 Ibid. at 323.

10

Monopolies and State Regulation: The Calgary Power Company, Utilities, and the Alberta Public Utilities Board, 1910-30

Janice Erion

Legal historians have traditionally analyzed law from the formal legal paradigm that focuses on the criminal justice system, the formal court process, legislation, and the legal profession consisting of lawyers and judges. Legal historian H.W. Arthurs has convincingly argued that law is pluralistic and extends beyond the formal paradigm to include many different systems and a wide range of influences, in particular administrative law.[1] He indicates that, while administrative law and state regulation are vehicles of state intervention, they cannot be reduced to politics. They transcend politics to become law. Although governments have traditionally hesitated to intervene in the economy, governments in England and Canada created boards, commissions, and tribunals in the nineteenth century because the formal court system could not perform the necessary social tasks and functions of regulating the economy, preserving culture, resources, and amenities, and controlling powerful interests. Administrative law is created by statutes. However, their often vague language allowed boards and tribunals wide discretion in their decisions, creating new norms, procedures, and ultimately a unique system of law.

During the early twentieth century, the Alberta prairies were still being settled, and communities were built not only with incoming settlers but also with the crucial infrastructure of roads, railway lines, sewer, water, telephones, and electricity. The supply of electrical power was critical for the successful development of the Canadian Prairies, and southern Alberta was no exception. Electricity was necessary to establish industries such as cement plants and lumber mills, which were not only essential to the economy but also provided the basic materials to build the communities. Electricity was also necessary to operate cable cars for transportation and to provide street and indoor lighting. As electric and other utilities developed, Prairie governments adopted the regulatory models created in Britain, the United States, and eastern Canada by establishing boards to regulate these utilities and control the pricing and supply of their essential commodities.

The supply of electricity has three main components. The first one is the generation of power. In the case of hydroelectric power, generation occurs at the site of a suitable water source. The second component is the transmission of power from the generation source to a market such as a city, town, or industrial site. The third one is the local distribution of power to various industries, businesses, and residential consumers. Despite the different components, the supply of electricity in Alberta developed into highly capitalized monopolies controlling both the production and the supply of electricity.

The electric industry in Canada generally developed into highly capitalized monopolies during the early twentieth century. This was largely due to the high capital costs of developing generation facilities and transmission lines. Nevertheless, the forms of monopolies that developed were divergent, with some provinces, such as Ontario, choosing public ownership and other provinces, such as Quebec and Alberta, allowing private enterprise. Provinces such as Ontario, through Ontario Hydro, chose public ownership to gain control of the electric industry and to protect what was viewed as an essential public resource. In regions where governments allowed private enterprise monopolies to develop, the governments generally argued that regulation would protect the public interest and simulate competitive market forces by controlling prices and regulating supply. Economist F.M. Scherer summarizes the rationale as follows: "The most traditional economic case for regulation assumes the existence of natural monopoly – that is, where economics of scale are so persistent that a single firm can serve the market at lower unit costs than two or more firms. Reasonably clear examples include electric power and gas distribution [and] local telephone service ... Regulation is said to be necessary in such instances to protect consumers from the monopoly pricing behaviour that achieving all scale economies renders virtually inevitable."[2]

However, Christopher Armstrong and H.V. Nelles, in their study of the organization and regulation of Canadian utilities from 1830 to 1930, argue that regulation in Canada has historically failed to protect public interests and effectively control utility monopolies.[3] They hold that the creation of Canadian utility regulation boards was the means by which powerful utility corporations participated in a legitimizing process by appearing to render themselves accountable to some judgment other than that of owners.[4] This chapter will investigate the interrelationship between the development of the Calgary Power Company electricity monopoly between 1910 and 1930 and the early history of the Alberta Board of Public Utility Commissioners (hereafter referred to as the Public Utilities Board or PUB).

The geographical area of Calgary has been chosen as a case study of the development of the Calgary Power Company (now TransAlta Utilities Corporation) during its earliest years of 1910-30. Although the Calgary municipal government built its own generating facilities in 1905, by 1912 approximately 70 percent of the city's electrical needs were supplied by the Calgary Power Company.[5] In Alberta, electricity was generated during this era using water, coal, or natural gas, with water or hydro power being the cheapest to produce. Between 1909 and 1912, the Calgary Power Company gained control over two major Alberta water sources for hydro power: Horseshoe Falls and Kananaskis Falls, which were located approximately sixty miles from Calgary. In 1928, the company obtained the water rights to the Ghost-Radnor site along the Bow River, twenty-eight miles west of Calgary, and built its third and largest hydro facility. The other potential water sources were either located in Banff National Park, which prohibited development, or too far inside the Rocky Mountains for viable transmission to the Calgary market. Other sites along the Bow River had the problem of low water flow after the winter freeze. Thus, this control allowed Calgary Power to control the region's cheapest generation source for electrical power and adopt a solid base to build a monopoly. By 1928, it was the only supplier of electricity to Calgary and had secured its monopoly over city and region.

This chapter also proposes to examine the role of the Public Utilities Board in regulating utilities from its creation under the *Public Utilities Act* from 1915 to 1930. Despite the traditional rationale of regulating monopolies, the Public Utilities Board played no evident role in the relationship between the city of Calgary and the Calgary Power Company. The monopoly was largely in place by 1915, and regulation legitimized and allowed the monopoly to grow unhampered in southern Alberta.

A number of issues will be addressed in this chapter. First, the justifications for regulation will be examined along with the principles of regulation behind the *Public Utilities Act*. Second, the growth of the Calgary Power Company in Calgary and the surrounding area and, third, the role and powers of the Public Utilities Board in regulating utilities will be assessed. Fourth, a comparison will be made between the development of hydroelectric utilities in Ontario, Quebec, and Alberta.

State regulation was created and justified by four major arguments still used today, and they are summarized by Stephen Breyer in his book *Regulation and Its Reform*.[6] First, regulatory bodies can ensure the efficient use of resources. Second, state regulation can control the social, political, or economic power concentrated in the hands of a single business. Third, regulatory bodies provide a forum for public grievances against a monopoly and prevent unjustifiable price discrimination between consumers. Fourth, regulation prevents a windfall of profits to the monopoly by ensuring that investors earn no more than a reasonable return on their investment.

The traditional justifications were reflected in the *Public Utilities Act* of 1915, which established a board of three commissioners. The act was passed relatively quickly in October 1915, with no opposition recorded in the

Hansard Scrapbook of 1915. Section 20 gave the board jurisdiction to hear and investigate complaints regarding rates and to disallow or change rates that were in its opinion "excessive, unjust, or unreasonable or unjustly discriminate." Section 23 gave the board the power to "fix just and reasonable rates" in such cases.[7] The traditional justifications were clearly outlined by Commissioner A.A. Carpenter in the 1917 application hearing involving Northern Alberta Natural Gas Development Company Limited and the city of Edmonton:

> The object aimed at by the Public Utilities Act is to secure efficient service by public utilities at rates that are fair and reasonable. When the question of what is fair and reasonable in regard to rate is raised, the Board is required to make a thorough inquiry into the operations of the utility and into all matters that are material so far as the determining of a proper rate is concerned. The best that a public utility can expect is to be allowed a reasonable return upon its investment. If the investigation shows that the profits of the utility are excessive and provide an unreasonable return upon the amount invested, the rate should be reduced.[8]

However admirable the regulatory principles such as fixing fair and reasonable rates and reasonable returns sound, the real question is whether the Public Utilities commissioners were able to implement the principles and traditional justifications. Some clues may be found by examining the early history of electric utilities in Calgary.

Armstrong and Nelles argue that monopolies are made and not born.[9] They reject the idea that utility monopolies naturally occurred and that utility entrepreneurs were passive instruments of economic and technological dynamics. The success of the Calgary Power Company emerged from the will to overcome any market competition. Although electricity monopolies had previously been broken, the men behind Calgary Power had the will, the vision, and the influence to establish long-term control over the Calgary market.

Before the First World War, the competition to supply electricity was provided by a number of entrepreneurs as well as the Calgary municipal electric plant. In 1889, Peter Prince, owner of the Eau Claire and Bow River Lumber Company, was granted permission by Calgary City Council to set up poles and furnish electric street lighting when he could not reach an agreement with the Calgary Electric Lighting Company for the joint use of steam boilers.[10]

Calgary had grown after the turn of the century from 4,000 in 1901 to 40,000 by 1911.[11] However, Peter Prince failed to take the opportunity to expand the electrical services with the city's growth, and the city decided to build its own generating facility in 1905 after failing to reach an agreement with Prince for expanded electrical service.[12] The city council decided that it was important to keep rates competitive. Council settled on commercial rates of 12¢-16¢ per kilowatt hour, house rates of 14¢ per kilowatt hour, and 11¢-13¢ per kilowatt hour for hotels, restaurants, and churches.[13] The Calgary Water Power Company rate was 18¢ per kilowatt hour, so the municipal rates represented a significant price reduction.[14] Council also embarked on an aggressive campaign to sign up enough customers to cover the operating expenses of the new steam-powered plant. Council encouraged the city commissioners to induce customers to the city utility through grants of "public monies or special favours."[15]

By 1907, the municipal plant had reached its limit. The city realized that it would be a number of years before a hydro project could be completed in the Kananaskis region, and it required a larger power station in the interim. As city commissioners reported to the council, "at the present time we are consuming up to the limit of our output of electrical energy at our present power station. We are still taking on all private business and intend to do so, but it is not unlikely that the street lights will have to be cut off during temporary heavy loads before we can use our new installation to relieve the situation."[16] In 1910, the city completed the Victoria Park plant with steam boilers. But it was clear that, with quick annual growth, and Peter Prince not interested in expanding his services, city facilities would not be sufficient for long. Thus, conditions were ripe in 1909-10 for the calculated risk of making an electric utility monopoly.

The founders of the Calgary Power Company maintained the highest positions in Canadian financial and political circles. The company head office was established in the financial capital of Montreal, and the early board of directors included Herbert S. Holt, Richard B. Bennett, and Max Aitken. Holt, appointed the first president in 1910, was a man with a vision to create electric utility monopolies. He was concurrently developing a hydroelectric monopoly in the Montreal region. He had become president of Montreal Light and Power in 1901, and he maintained a strategy of buying out rivals, including the acquisition of the Provincial Light, Heat and Power Company in 1906.[17]

By 1909, Bennett had become a successful and influential lawyer in Calgary with the firm Lougheed Bennett. Accordingly, he was appointed as both director and solicitor for the Calgary Power Company, and he became president in 1910 when Holt moved to the position of vice-president. During his legal career, Bennett represented major Canadian corporations such as the Hudson's Bay Company, major banks, and life insurance companies.[18] The man who would later become prime minister was also well connected politically. He was elected for a term as a member of the North-West Territories Assembly in 1898, and he was elected to the Alberta legislature in 1909. He became the Conservative member of Parliament for the Calgary East Riding in 1911. His law partner, James Lougheed, was appointed a Conservative senator in 1889 and was a federal minister without portfolio in the Borden government.

Max Aitken, who later became Lord Beaverbrook, was the most famous high financier in Canada at the time.[19] He used the Royal Securities Corporation as his investment bank for underwriting and marketing securities and bankrolling his business ventures.[20] By 1907, he had also acquired control of the Montreal Trust and Deposit Company.[21] Aitken had significant experience with utility acquisitions. He controlled the Dartmouth Electric Company and intended to merge it with the Halifax Tramway Company.[22] Through the Royal Securities Corporation, he controlled over half a dozen Caribbean and South American utility companies, including Demerara Electric, Venezuela Power Company, San Salvador Electric Light Company, and the Bolivian Power Company.[23]

By 1909, Aitken was at the peak of his financing career in Canada, completing three giant mergers within one year. He consolidated three of the largest railway car manufacturers in Canada and completed a merger of several small steel producers in southern Ontario and Montreal to create Stelco Steel. His third and largest endeavour was the Canada Cement merger that involved $13.5 million in common shares. It was so large that it presumed a monopoly position in the Canadian economy. The merger involved Western Canada Cement and International Portland Cement, both of which had operations in the Calgary area. Gregory P. Marchildon, in his comprehensive analysis of Lord Beaverbrook's career in high finance, presents convincing evidence that Aitken knew Western Canada Cement was in financial trouble and forced the directors into a merger agreement in which they would have to reduce the debt within four months. When they were unable to do so, Aitken refused to renegotiate and essentially forced the company into a position of bankruptcy. He then acquired the assets at highly discounted prices. He purchased first mortgage bonds at an 85 percent discount and second mortgage bonds at a 77 percent discount. While Aitken netted approximately $600,000 in share commissions, the directors and their families were left with $690,000 in unsecured debts. The result for consumers was that cement prices increased 40¢ per barrel in Toronto and 15¢ per barrel in Montreal.[24]

In 1908, the potential of the power business had been brought to Aitken's attention by his brother Traven, who was in Calgary to find possible investments. As Traven informed him in a letter, "you can sell 6000 horsepower in the city and that is the full capacity of the Bow River at low water. You will have the City lighting – at least you will sell the power to the city – if you want it. The cement works will take 1500 horsepower from you. P. Burns & Co. will take a large amount and a dozen other manufacturers will all take power from you. You want new business and here it is, good business."[25]

But it was his action in 1909 to create a monopoly under the Canada Cement Company merger that led primarily to Aitken's decision to pursue the Kananaskis-area hydroelectric development. The supply of cheap electricity to operate the cement plants at Exshaw and Calgary became necessary.[26] Another syndicate, operated by local businessmen W.M. Alexander and W.J. Budd, held the rights to develop a hydroelectric facility at Horseshoe Falls, but they failed to raise the necessary financing. Aitken and Bennett formed a new company, the Calgary Power Company, to buy out Alexander and Budd's Calgary Power and Transmission Company along with its hydro interests and contracts. Aitken was able to secure financing through his Royal Securities Corporation by a set of transactions that involved floating $3 million in shares.[27]

In 1910, the new company negotiated a contract with the city of Calgary to sell electrical power for the price of $30 per horsepower per year for a period of two years.[28] This was less than half the cost of operating the city steam plants.[29] In 1911, the hydro project at Horseshoe Falls was completed along with transmission lines, and the flow of electricity to Calgary began. However, the fate of the monopoly was far from settled. The river flow dried to a trickle in February and March of 1912, and it became clear that the company required another source to meet its contractual obligations with the city and new industry. The company acquired rights to a small facility at Radnor, on the Bow River west of Calgary, which supplied electricity to the Canada Cement plant, but it was not sufficient to meet Calgary Power's needs. The most viable power site was at Kananaskis Falls, located two miles upstream. This site was important not only for its potential to produce power but also because the company would be able to use its storage dam at Lake Minnewanka to augment the water flow for the facilities at both Horseshoe and Kananaskis Falls.[30]

The company directors took up the challenge of securing Kananaskis Falls, realizing its critical potential as a generation source. In the 1912 Calgary Power Company annual report, Bennett announced that, due to the "extraordinary expansion" of the city and the fact that the demand for power exceeded the resources of the company and municipal steam plant, the directors had decided to pursue the development of Kananaskis Falls. He summarized the potential of the project: "At present the only alternative the City of Calgary has to using company power is the operation of their own plant which costs $65.00 per h.p. per year."[31] The company believed that it was guaranteed a larger market share because it could generate and distribute cheaper hydro power.

As far back as 1910, the company began to pressure the federal water powers branch for the rights to Kananaskis Falls but received unexpected competition from Dr. Andrew Macphail, a wealthy Montreal doctor. Macphail had hired the influential Liberal lobbyist and lawyer Andrew

Haydon, who had negotiated the Horseshoe Falls lease. The Macphail proposal appeared to be technically superior because the Calgary Power proposal would flood some pits owned by Canada Cement and require the CPR bridge over the Kananaskis River to be raised.[32] However, in 1911, Robert Borden and the Conservatives swept to power. Bennett, newly elected Conservative MP, was able to use his political connections to the company's advantage. Writing to Max Aitken in the spring of 1912, he said, "I have succeeded in getting the Department of the Interior to give us Kananaskis Falls and will have the lease issued in due course."[33] The department also concluded that it could be more efficient to allow one company to control the three sites of Horseshoe Falls, Kananaskis Falls, and Radnor and share staff and transmission lines. It did not even require an agreement with the Department of Indian Affairs to begin construction despite the fact that the site was located on lands of the Stoney Band.[34] Thus, the federal Department of the Interior used its discretionary power to facilitate a monopoly.

In 1913, the city of Calgary signed another contract with Calgary Power for a five-year period with an option to renew for a further five years. Under this contract, the city obtained a better price for electricity: $26 per horsepower per year for the minimum requirement of 5,000 horsepower and $20 per horsepower over 10,000 horsepower.[35] The price reduction was most likely the result of several factors. First, the Kananaskis Falls plant gave the company additional cheap power that it could sell to the city. The two facilities had a capacity of 32,000 horsepower.[36] Second, the city was considering an expansion of municipal facilities to supply Calgary's own power needs. Montreal engineer R.A. Ross had previously recommended an expansion of the Victoria Park plant in a report to city council.[37] City commissioner A.G. Graves and engineers R.A. Brown and James McCall also proposed an expansion of the city steam plant, arguing that the increase in load factor would decrease the electrical cost to an amount only slightly higher than Calgary Power rates.[38] The recommendation was implemented in 1914. This threat to expand municipal facilities probably influenced Calgary Power to lower its rates.

The city was clearly in a good bargaining position. Fluctuations in the level of the Bow River caused interruptions in the supply of hydro power to the city. As a result, it was able to negotiate a penalty clause against Calgary Power for interruptions in service. The city's good bargaining position was also evidenced by the fact that the contract between Calgary Power and the village of Cochrane set a much higher price for electricity. The 1915 Cochrane contract set the price at $4.1675 per horsepower per month, approximately $50 per horsepower per year.[39] This rate was almost double the rate paid by the city of Calgary.

The city reached its best bargaining position in 1915. The Bow River was unusually low, and there was a major machine failure at one of Calgary

Power's hydro plants. Under a one-year supplementary agreement, Calgary Power was allowed to operate and maintain the municipal power facility at Victoria Park. In exchange, the company agreed to provide all of the city's electrical requirements for a sum of $190,000 for the year.[40] The cost of electricity was approximately $20 per horsepower after operation and maintenance costs for the Victoria Park facility were paid to the city.[41] City commissioners Brown and McCall estimated that $35,000 was saved during the contract year.[42]

In 1916, the city also tried to induce Calgary Power to reduce prices during the summer months when the Bow River was high and electricity generation plentiful. The city proposed that the company sell power over the minimum purchase requirement of 5,000 horsepower for $13 per horsepower. However, Bennett took a strong stand against any further price cuts for the city and announced in the company's annual report that it would not depart from the original 1913 contract still in effect.[43] The city appeared to be content enough with the terms of the 1913 contract that in 1918 council exercised its option to extend the contract until 1923. However, the city still had its municipal facilities and the ability to develop other methods of cost savings. City engineers tested the efficiency of running the municipal facilities at a higher load for a seventeen-hour period. They determined that the most efficient and least costly arrangement was to use the city steam power plant for peak demand and hydro power at constant levels throughout the day.[44]

Competition was threatened from a number of hydro project proposals, but Calgary Power was able to fend off any major rival. In 1912, railway and hydraulic engineer Zephir Malhiot proposed to build a hydro facility along the Bow River south of Calgary. Bennett and Calgary Power were so concerned about the competition that Bennett paid Malhiot $1,000 for a forty-day option to buy out the rival project.[45] However, Malhiot was unable to secure the necessary financing and support for the project, and he clearly blamed Calgary Power and Bennett for using their influence to defeat the competition. He stated in 1920 that "I had been for so long studiously and faithfully endeavouring to start the development of my Hydro-Electric power plans, with the aid of local capitalists. I found that the rivalry of the Calgary Power Company, espoused by the Member of Parliament and followers/influences, subdued so many who would have desired to see my plans succeed."[46] He clearly saw a link between the political power that Bennett had acquired as a federal MP and the development of a business monopoly.

The city also considered undertaking a hydro project at Spray Lakes when the 1923 power contract ended. However, Calgary Power offered reasonable contract prices at $15 per horsepower (55¢/kWh), which the council decided to accept.[47] The Alberta government also considered developing a provincial hydro project at Spray Lakes and creating public utilities during the 1920s, but the estimated costs of financing such a project and buying out the existing Calgary Power facilities proved prohibitive. Calgary Power evidently calculated that, by offering a competitive rate, it could sell more power in the growing city and still increase profits. As the company reported, "1924 was the first full year under the contract entered into with the City of Calgary in 1923, and it is gratifying to note the increases shown in the profits of the company resulting from the operation of the contract."[48] The result was that Calgary Power's net profits in 1924 were $158,342.70, up from $119,605.72 in 1923.[49]

By the early 1920s, the Calgary Power Company effectively had a monopoly over the city of Calgary. Although the city continued to operate its municipal facility, most of the power demands were met by Calgary Power as the city continued to grow during the 1920s. Purchasing hydro power was cheaper than building more facilities for steam power generation. The Calgary Water and Power Company continued to offer potential competition, but in reality neither this company nor the city's municipal plant could meet the growing demand for electricity in the city. Thus, in 1928, the city renewed the contract with Calgary Power. The 1928 contract set the price of electricity at 74¢/kWh for the first eighty million kWh and 65¢/kWh for additional electricity.[50] It is probably not coincidental that the price increases occurred the year that Calgary Power solidified its monopoly. In 1928, the city leased the Victoria Park plant to Calgary Power and never operated municipal power facilities again. Both the 1923 and the 1928 agreements were approved by the Public Utilities Board without any conditions or changes.

Calgary Power also purchased the assets of Peter Prince's Calgary Water and Power Company in 1928 for $600,000.[51] The elimination of this competition was a calculated decision by the Calgary Power board of directors. They approved the purchase in May 1928, stating that Prince's company was supplying electricity to a "substantial part of the city." Acquisition of the company, along with the lease of the city's steam plant, would result in Calgary Power "having full control of the power supply in the City of Calgary."[52]

The rates paid by Calgary residents were comparable to those of other western cities but higher than centres that had hydroelectric power.[53] For example, in 1925, an average monthly electric bill in Calgary was $2.16 based on forty kWh per month. Edmonton's average was significantly higher at $3.04; however, in Winnipeg, where hydro power was used, the average was $1.20 per month. Electricity was slightly more expensive in Calgary than the national average of $2.04. The price was high enough for Calgary Power to make healthy profits but not too high to make it feasible for competitors to build rival hydro or steam plants. The company actively created a monopoly by using its influence in Ottawa to obtain the rights to Kananaskis Falls, by eliminating rival projects, and by buying out competition.

Electric Utilities in Alberta

The development of electrical utilities in the area surrounding Calgary mirrored the city's experience. Until approximately 1928, electricity was primarily generated and supplied to a town or village by a local entrepreneur granted an exclusive franchise to set up a small generating facility. For example, Thomas A. Weeks, trading under the Hardisty Electric Light Company, contracted to supply electricity to the town of Hardisty.[54] The town of Olds had a ten-year franchise agreement with A.N. Bilton and R.A. Brown to sell light and power to the town.[55] H.H. McGordie of Edson supplied electricity to his town.[56] Albert Metz and Paul Whittock of Vulcan established the Vulcan Electric Light Supply company that supplied electric power to their town.[57] Verle A. McCarty supplied electric light to the village of Bashaw.[58] In northern Alberta, Joseph Boudreau supplied electricity to St. Paul de Métis,[59] and William Johnson and J. Edward supplied electricity to Lloydminster.[60]

In Alberta, electricity was generated by water, coal, or natural gas. Hydroelectric power was the cheapest to produce, but there was a limited number of suitable sites, and they were controlled primarily by Calgary Power. Thus, local entrepreneurs were left with the more expensive alternatives of coal- and gas-powered generation. During the 1920s, numerous small utilities faced financial ruin because they could not balance the difficult task of trying to produce power at rates that were low enough for local customers to afford but high enough to make a profit. The PUB warned the Vimy Light, Heat and Power Company that its proposal to use flat rates instead of meters had been unprofitable for other companies in the past.[61] This utility's venture eventually failed as the town of Big Valley entered into a franchise agreement with George Scott several years later.[62] Okotoks Electric fell into financial trouble and applied to the PUB for an increase in rates. However, the board rejected the application because, in their opinion, an increase would reduce consumption and further reduce the company's profits.[63] The Crane-Cassidy Company plunged into a financial crisis because its rates were insufficient for the company to be profitable, and the town of Magrath had to apply to the PUB for an order that the company continue its electrical service.[64] The Weno Power and Light Company also applied for a rate increase, but it was refused because its small number of customers could not absorb it. The PUB required the company to continue service for a minimum of forty-five days.[65]

The instability of the smaller utility companies was also evidenced by takeovers. In 1919, the Drumheller Power Company purchased the interests of Northwestern Engineering and Supply Company to supply electricity to the town of Drumheller, despite the town's objections to the PUB.[66] In 1923, the Drumheller Power Company was taken over by the Union Power Company, and in 1925 Union Power also took over the Mine Power Company and expanded its service to the villages of Morrin and Munson.[67] A larger takeover occurred in 1924 when United Electric and Engineering took over the assets of Western Canadian Collieries, which had been supplying power to the town of Blairmore.[68] The company also signed franchise agreements with the village of Cluny and the town of Gleichen, both located east of Calgary, during the same year. This company was eventually taken over by Calgary Power in 1929.[69]

Cities such as Calgary, Lethbridge, and Edmonton were able to develop their own municipal plants. A 1928 survey of electric utilities in Alberta indicated that Edmonton had the largest steam plant in the province with a capacity of 25,000 horsepower. The Calgary steam plant had a capacity of 14,000 horsepower, and the Lethbridge one had a capacity of 3,500 horsepower.[70] The municipalities operated their plants independently and did not move to integrate their power systems with each other. This was likely due to the distances between them and the need for several hundred kilometres of transmission lines. Several other centres took over local utilities that ran into financial trouble or did not provide satisfactory service. The city of Red Deer had a series of long-standing disputes with the local Western General Electric Company. The first complaint filed with the PUB was in February 1916 by the city, disputing the company's charges for light and meter rates and telephone.[71] In October 1916, the village of North Red Deer also complained that the company had failed to extend its service to certain residents.[72] The strained relations between Red Deer and the company continued until 1925, when the city finally agreed to purchase the utility's assets. And on 15 May 1917, the PUB approved a $5,000 debenture for the town of Gleichen to purchase the electric light plant in town from local owner F.C. Vigar.[73]

Despite the expert advice in the 1928 provincial government-commissioned survey recommending a province-wide plan to develop other potential water sources in Alberta, and integration of existing facilities to provide the most efficient and cheapest overall service, the government took no action.[74] Therefore, conditions were ripe for Calgary Power to expand its monopoly beyond Calgary. There were no competitors that had the influence, the large core market, the capital, and the cheap source of power possessed by Calgary Power.

Into the mid-1920s, Calgary Power had three main customers: the city of Calgary, the village of Cochrane, and the Canada Cement plant at Exshaw. In 1926, the board of directors made the bold decision to begin an aggressive expansion policy in the province. Transmission was extended south to Lethbridge in the next year, with an interchange agreement between the city and Calgary Power.[75] And in the same year, the company made arrangements with the dominion government to develop the Ghost-Radnor hydro power site located on the Bow River twenty-eight miles west of Calgary.[76] The plant was completed in December 1929 with a capacity of 36,000 horsepower and was by far the largest generation facility in the province. In 1929, the company also entered into an interchange contract with the city of Edmonton and began building a transmission line from the new plant to Edmonton.[77] The company concentrated on linking as many towns as possible to the main transmission lines. The line to Edmonton allowed the company to expand into northern Alberta. While the company had 1,000 miles of transmission lines in Alberta in 1927,[78] it had 1,865 miles by 1930.[79] The company was serving five out of six cities in the province and 130 communities by 1929,[80] and it reached 148 communities by 1930.[81] The company also brought power to rural farmers by charging an extension fee to connect them to company lines.[82]

To finance the expansion, the company issued a further $7 million in stock.[83] This calculated risk paid off handsomely, and company profits skyrocketed. In 1928, net profits rose to $251,197.62,[84] increasing to $525,774.39 in 1929[85] and to $627,777.60 in 1930.[86] The company's 1930 annual report confirmed that the significant increase in profits was due to the enlargement of the company's field of operation and savings in operating expenses through closing down the more expensive auxiliary steam plants following the development of the Ghost-Radnor facility.[87] The men behind Calgary Power accomplished an incredible expansion program in a very short period of time to build a successful utility and provide many communities in Alberta with electricity by 1930.

Regulation under the Public Utilities Board

What was the impact of the Public Utilities Board and its powers of regulation on the Calgary Power Company, and did the commissioners fulfill the expectations of the traditional arguments for regulation? Because regulatory bodies are statutory creations, their regulatory powers depend upon the vision of the legislators and the enabling language of the statute. Although all regulation involves some form of state intervention, the degree of intervention or regulation that the legislators choose can vary significantly. Regulation can be as direct and significant as establishing rates by statute, as in the case of the Crow Rates that set rail rates for the shipment of western Canadian grain from the Prairies.[88] A less direct but significant form of intervention is to have the administrative body establish or approve all rates. In the case of railway regulation during this era, railways could not negotiate contracts with individual shippers. Railways were required to produce public tariffs listing all their rates for the transportation of specific goods on various routes and submit the tariffs to the applicable federal or provincial boards for approval.

Alberta legislators chose a lesser degree of regulation by allowing electric utility companies the freedom to negotiate contracts and all terms and conditions with the local distributor and then submit the contract to the PUB for approval. The reasons for this choice are not readily apparent, except that the main impetus behind the legislation was to regulate municipal borrowing powers, not electric utilities or monopolies. The Alberta minister of municipal affairs, Wilfred Garlepy, pushed for a local government board to regulate municipal borrowing in his annual report and moved the issue onto the government agenda.[89] The Sifton government then decided to form a multipurpose board to regulate municipal borrowing, similar to the local government board in Saskatchewan, and to regulate utilities like Manitoba Public Utilities Commission.[90] The board was appointed on 20 October 1915 with three commissioners: G.H.V. Bulyea (chair), A.A. Carpenter, and J. Stocks. The board's jurisdiction over provincial utilities included telephone and telegraph companies, railways, tramways, companies furnishing water, gas, heat, light, or power to the public, and the provincial government telephone system.[91]

The ability of the PUB to fulfill the traditional justifications for regulation was limited by the legislation that defined its mandate, the Alberta courts, and its workload in overseeing numerous other matters. The board's ability to deal with price discrimination was limited by legislation. For example, the 1915 *Public Utilities Act* excluded contracts entered into prior to 1915. It also excluded utilities owned and operated by a municipality unless the municipality specifically brought itself under board jurisdiction.[92] The large number of independent electric utility operators, and different sources of generation, meant that there would be divergent rates unless the independent utilities were integrated.

The board was also powerless to deal proactively with issues involving rates and price discrimination because it could only adjust prices when there was an application to the board. Even when an application was brought to the board, its jurisdiction was limited by the specific questions raised by the complaint or application. In 1922, the town of Magrath filed a complaint that the Crane-Cassidy Company was not complying with their contract. The board concluded that the real problem was insufficient rates for the company to earn a fair return. However, because the question of rates was not referred to the board, it was powerless to adjudicate the rate matter.[93]

The board's ability to ensure efficient use of resources was impeded by the fact that the dominion government controlled important water resources such as those at Kananaskis Falls and Spray Lakes and by the fact that the board did not have the legislative mandate to integrate the many electric utilities operating in the province, which could have ensured a more efficient distribution of power. The board's inability to regulate the efficient use of resources was clearly evidenced in the area of natural gas regulation. By 1920, the original natural gas reserves in southern Alberta, in particular the Bow Island field, were being rapidly depleted. There was no effective conservation regulation in place, and there was a serious problem of overproduction and gas wastage. The excess was generally burned or "flared." In a 1928 report for the Brownlee government, Commissioner A.A. Carpenter determined that there was annual gas wastage of twenty-five billion cubic feet.[94]

Most of the utility-related applications before the PUB involved gas utility companies that requested increases in their rates because the rapid depletion of fields necessitated the expense of developing new fields and constructing additional pipelines. The PUB could deal with rates, but it had no power to deal with the underlying problems of resource wastage and depletion. The problems became even more evident during the 1930s. In 1931, the city of Calgary brought an application before the PUB for a reduction in natural gas rates. Calgary consumers had become impatient over high rates when millions of cubic feet of gas were being burned off as waste.[95] The government was slow to respond but eventually created a separate regulatory board in 1938, the Gas Conservation Board, to deal with the problem of inefficient use of natural gas resources.

Although the PUB reviewed electric supply contracts submitted for approval, even when contracts were rejected it had little impact on the overall development of electric utilities in the province. For example, in 1919, the board rejected an arbitration clause in an electrical contract between Albert Lindstrom and the town of Hanna because rate charges were always subject to board jurisdiction.[96] It is interesting to note that Lindstrom had been supplying electricity to the town for "some considerable time" before the agreement was submitted to the PUB. This not only calls into question the influence of the board if utilities were operating without approval but also raises the question of how many other utility suppliers may have been operating outside the regulatory framework. The board also rejected a clause in a contract between the Grand Prairie Electric Company and the town because it was only charging the company nominal rent for the power house building. This was held to be a violation of the town act but again had little impact regarding the larger questions of how utilities would develop in the province.[97]

The powers of the PUB, including its power to fix rates, were also limited by the courts. In 1919, the Appellate Division of the Alberta Supreme Court limited the board's ability to interfere with contract rates even when an application was made.[98] The court held that the PUB had no jurisdiction to interfere with a rate fixed by contract, only one unilaterally imposed by the company. Justice William Simmons stated, "to hold that sub-section (C) of section 23 of the Public Utilities Act gave the Board power to alter this agreement in so important a feature as to change the maximum price contracted for would be tantamount to holding that the Board could make an agreement between the parties. This would be a wide power indeed and it would require clear legislative direction, assuming (which is open to argument) that the legislature could delegate such extensive power, to confer such upon the Board."[99] However, the court could have arrived at a different conclusion. In response to the decision, the board noted that such issues did not even arise under American statutes because the jurisdiction of public utility commissions over contracts in the United States was supreme.[100] While a survey of US administrative jurisprudence is beyond the scope of this chapter, there were ample precedents to allow the PUB a more active role in regulating utilities. In *Re Orleans Electric Light and Power Company,*[101] the Indiana Public Service Commission held that it had the power to establish a rate for utility service, notwithstanding a contract between the utility and the patron. In *Re Consolidated Gas, Electric Light & Power Company,*[102] the Maryland Public Service Commission held that the availability of a cheap source of supply should be to the benefit of consumers of a gas and electric company. However, the Alberta courts clearly viewed the legislature as having limited jurisdiction to delegate such powers to the PUB.

As a result of the numerous limitations on the board's mandate and powers, it is not surprising that there was very little interaction between the PUB and Calgary Power. The PUB approved all of the contracts between the city of Calgary and Calgary Power between 1915 and 1930. There was only one case where the PUB rejected a Calgary Power contract during this era, and it was rejected in favour of a local monopoly. The Calgary Power Company entered a contract to supply electricity to several mines in the District of Carbon that were being serviced by another local utility company. The board refused to approve the contract with Calgary Power, stating that a competing company should not be allowed "to invade the territory already serviced by another company" merely because it offers lower rates.[103] An applicant would have to show "exorbitant" rates to replace an existing service. This legal threshold indicates that the board was not particularly interested in fostering competition and market forces within the industry. Ironically, when Calgary Power was building and solidifying its monopoly and submitted numerous contracts to the board in 1929, its annual report stated that "no matters of outstanding importance in connection with public utility matters came before the board."[104]

The PUB carried a heavy workload in this era with other administrative matters, and only a small portion of its work involved regulating electric utilities. The majority of work that fell into the category of utilities involved approving provincial railway tariffs. The board administered numerous pieces of provincial legislation, including the *Railways Act,* the *Sale of Shares Act, An Act Respecting Subdivisions,* and the *Coal Miners Wages Securities Act.* Aside from regulating utilities, the PUB's work involved four other main areas: regulating borrowings on debentures by local authorities, the cancellation of subdivision plans and compromises of tax arrears,[105] the withdrawal of lands from cities and towns, and the administration of the *Sale of Shares Act.*[106]

These areas reflected the board's necessary role in regulating the development of Albertan communities. The supervision of loans by way of debentures sought to be raised by cities, towns, villages, rural municipalities, and school districts was crucial during this era. There were frequently 150-200 applications per year. Communities were in need of funds to build the necessary infrastructure, and applications were made for debentures to build water and sewer lines, power and telephone lines, roads, sidewalks, parks, schools, libraries, and firehalls. However, these needs had to be balanced and regulated against the municipality's financial position and revenues. The commissioners stated that great care was exercised in passing municipal borrowings due to the serious problems of not collecting taxes and running into deficits as a result of the war, inflation, and speculation.[107] The board had detailed investigative powers and expertise to regulate matters arising from the development of communities that the formal court system did not have the time, procedures, or expertise to handle.

The work of the board was also valuable in a number of other aspects. It was able to take the vague terms of "fixing just and reasonable rates" and implement rules, procedures, and formulas to adjudicate applications and determine what specific price was reasonable for the utility buyer. A.A. Carpenter, on the board throughout this era, had an unrivalled knowledge of corporate accounting and rate structure formulation in the province.[108] The rate structure formulation involved determining the present value of the utility's plant(s) and operations, including the distribution system. Experts also factored in the accepted accounting variable for contingencies, depreciation, and new development in order to establish the appropriate base rate. The board generally set a pricing rate that allowed the utility a healthy 8-10 percent rate of return on investment.

The number of adjudications per year varied from no hearings in 1917 to seven in 1924. There were normally only a few per year, and they involved either natural gas or electric utilities. One illuminating case involved an application by the city of Calgary to order Canadian Western Natural Gas, Light, Heat and Power to augment its supply of natural gas and to fix a reasonable gas rate.[109] The city had entered into two contracts for the supply of natural gas. The main source at Bow Island was being rapidly depleted, and the gas companies needed to develop new fields. After unsuccessful negotiations for a rate increase, the Calgary Gas Company notified the city that it would discontinue business on 31 May 1920. Simultaneously, the other supplier, Canadian Western Natural Gas, announced high rate increases that would have made the use of gas "except for cooking and hot water heating practically prohibitive."[110] The board carefully considered the procedures and decisions from a number of US utility commissions, including Indiana, California, Maryland, Wisconsin, and Oregon, to determine appropriate values for the rate base. It also considered the expense of developing new sources of natural gas and pipelines from other natural gas fields in southern Alberta such as Foremost, Turner Valley, and Redcliff. The board rejected the company's argument to set the base rate using the highest valuation of reproduction cost rather than the present value. However, it allowed an 8.5 percent rate of return and raised the price from the present one of approximately 35¢ per 1,000 cubic feet to 48¢. The increase was based on the condition that the company augment its gas supply to meet the city's needs.

The board was also able to facilitate several settlements between disputing parties. In 1924, the city of Red Deer and the Western General Electric Company reached an arbitrated agreement whereby the city agreed to purchase the utility's assets at the value determined the previous year by the PUB.[111] Ironically, the board had dismissed the city's application for a decrease in rates earlier in 1924,[112] but its determination of the assets and expenses did facilitate a final settlement. On one occasion in 1921, the board brought its own motion in which it called on Canadian Western Natural Gas, Light, Heat and Power to show cause why the rate increase allowed between the company and the city of Edmonton in 1920 should not be decreased to the previous rate. The hearing was suspended as the motion prompted the company to reach a settlement with the city.[113]

Establishment of the PUB also had the critical effect of shifting the focus away from the question of whether public or private interest monopolies should control utilities and toward the forum of debate regarding the jurisdiction and powers of the PUB. Several parties that lost their applications in front of the board chose to appeal the decisions by challenging its jurisdiction. There were several reported decisions between 1916 and 1929 involving natural gas suppliers and one case challenging the cancellation of a subdivision plan. As previously indicated, in 1919 the city of Edmonton was successful at the Appellate Court in limiting the board's jurisdiction to amend the contract price set with Northern Alberta Natural Gas. The debate then spilled over to the legislature as to whether the PUB should have the power to interfere with contracts and eventually resulted in a new *Public Utilities Act* in 1923 that gave the PUB power to increase rates above the contract price.[114]

In 1924, when the PUB utilized its new power and allowed Canadian Western Natural Gas, Light, Heat and Power to increase its gas rates to the city of Lethbridge from the existing contract price of 35¢ per 1,000 cubic feet to 48¢ per 1,000 cubic feet, the debate over the PUB's powers again arose in the legislature. The Conservative MLA for Lethbridge, Dr. Stewart, brought a motion to take away the PUB's powers to vary contract prices. He emphasized the need to restore the sanctity of contracts and the 35¢ contract price,[115] but he argued on a broader philosophical level that the PUB had more power than the courts to alter contracts and that its "arbitrary" powers should be removed.[116] This discourse served no doubt to identify state regulation and the PUB, rather than any monopoly, as arbitrary enemies that needed to be controlled. The *Edmonton Journal* reported that, although Dr. Stewart's motion was defeated by a vote of nineteen to twenty-eight, it stood "as one of the most keenly contested [debates] for several sessions past."[117]

In March 1927, the legislature again became embroiled in the debate over the process for appeals from the PUB. The Conservative Party claimed that the *Public Utilities Act* was not clear on the machinery for appeals. A Conservative MLA, D.M. Duggan, brought forward a bill providing that appeals from the board on questions of fact should be taken to the cabinet and that appeals on questions of law should be heard by the Appellate Division of the Supreme Court of Alberta.[118] The resulting debate degenerated into arguments challenging the commissioners' ability to decide questions of law and renewed the debate over the 1923 act, which allowed the board to increase contract gas rates. The debate focused attention on trying to limit the board's powers while neglecting the larger issues of regulating monopolies, the efficient use of resources, and, most importantly, who should control power resources.

There was debate throughout the 1920s regarding public versus private ownership and whether the province should develop power facilities. But the government's approach was to deflect the matter by referring it to studies and reports. There was no move to actively implement any concrete plans. On 14 April 1923, the legislature passed a resolution to enter negotiations with the dominion government to secure water power rights for the Spray Lakes to develop hydroelectric power.[119] The dominion government was noncommittal in granting the province these rights, and as a result the legislature commissioned a report that was received on 19 February 1925. Upon reading the report, Premier Greenfield cautioned that the undertaking at Spray Lakes was so expensive (in the range of $12-$14 million) that the gravest consideration was needed, particularly as the province was facing financial problems.[120] The project was so expensive because it involved purchasing the present facilities operated by the Calgary Power Company. The government took the position that more study was required, including further consultations with municipalities to determine the market for power and their willingness to participate in its distribution.

The Brownlee government stated throughout the 1920s that in principle it was in favour of public ownership but continued to delay any action due to the costs involved. Labour leader Fred J. White spearheaded the most vocal crusade for public ownership, maintaining the straightforward position that "the gifts of nature [were] for the people."[121] He was a sharp critic of the provincial government and charged that "after dickering with the subject for seven years [the government] ought to be in a position to make a definite pronouncement."[122] He argued that there would be more development under public ownership and that power would be cheaper since power in Ontario was cheaper than in the United States. Liberal leader Shaw also brought resolutions for the government to investigate public ownership. But in the end, neither Liberal nor Labour Party was able to move the government to take positive steps toward public ownership of power resources.

In March 1929, Premier Brownlee tabled a memorandum of a 1928 power survey of Alberta, known as the Baxter Report.[123] The report identified that electric power was limited to domestic purposes, mining operations, grain elevators, and a few industries. It stated that electrical use would become more widespread if rates were lower: "Rates in effect discourage the use of power in many places and for that reason power is not being used to the extent it might be in Alberta if conditions were more favourable."[124] The Baxter Report recommended further development of potential hydro power sites in the province, including Spray Lakes and Lake Minnewanka, and transmission lines to link communities in a provincial power scheme. The report concluded that many communities would benefit from lower rates if the cheaper hydro power plants were integrated with existing steam plants. The government failed to act on the recommendations, and Calgary Power took up the challenge by developing the Ghost-Radnor power site, building transmission lines, and integrating power facilities.

An Edmonton Labour MLA, C.L. Gibbs, warned the government not to delay in moving toward public ownership of utilities. He stated that "already the wise men from the east are lying awake at nights trying to find the key to the natural resources combination, and wondering how to get on the blind side of the government."[125] He went on to comment that, although the Calgary Power Company had benefited the province by providing cheap power for northern Alberta farmers, the government should not delay long enough to allow Calgary Power to "ripen a melon at our expense" before undertaking public development of power resources.[126] In 1929, White took a stand against monopolies and made a plea for public ownership. He argued that the mere fact that Public Utilities commissioners had been appointed to regulate rates charged by private utilities proved conclusively that private corporations had not dealt fairly with the public. He stated, "if we are to have a power monopoly, by all means let it be a state and not a private monopoly."[127] The leader of the Conservative Party, A.A. McGillivray, took the opposite position that public ownership was unnecessary since the PUB had been appointed. He stated, "at one time people were at the mercy of large corporations in the power business, today the authority of utilities boards to examine into the company's affairs and to fix rates that are just and fair as between the producer and consumer of power does away with this danger." He gave numerous reasons why the government should not become involved in the power business, ranging from the tremendous cost of taking over the assets of existing power companies to the argument that public ownership was "a step toward communism."[128]

The legislature finally passed a resolution in favour of public ownership in 1930, but the resolution also called for "no embarkation upon a development scheme at the present time."[129] White expressed his frustration that four reports had been submitted to the province yet no definite plan had been formulated. He warned that, "while the government has hesitated, private enterprise had gone ahead until its ramifications covered the entire province."[130] Premier Brownlee defended the government's inaction in developing public utilities since coming into office in 1921. He argued that the government was not justified in making the necessary capital expenditure until it was relieved of some of its financial burden. He also blamed the dominion government that, until powers over natural resources were returned to the province, it was not in a position to utilize the resources and take over the Calgary Power Company, operating under a dominion franchise.[131] Brownlee continued his course of inaction by stating that the government was now consulting another expert from Johns Hopkins University and that a scheme should not be embarked on all at once.[132] The onset of the Depression in 1930 brought a final blow against establishing public ownership over electric utilities during this era. By 1932, the government faced such extensive financial difficulties that it could no longer even afford to continue a power survey. Brownlee said that the survey was dropped when the Depression arrived due to the government's financial difficulties.[133] As a postscript, in 1935 the Social Credit Party swept to power in Alberta with its strong free-enterprise philosophy and belief that government should stay out of business. Len Stahl indicates in his book *A Record of Service* that the party and its philosophy were a likely reason why Alberta remained one of the few areas in Canada where privately owned electric utilities operated rather than government-owned utilities.[134]

Comparison with Ontario and Quebec

Armstrong and Nelles provide a useful comparison of the development of public hydroelectric utilities in Ontario with the private hydroelectric monopoly that emerged in Quebec and identify four variables that influenced the choice of public ownership versus allowing a private monopoly.[135] First is the organization of the industry. Montreal had sufficient investors to promote rival hydro projects during the late 1800s and early 1900s. Actual or potential competition operated against Herbert Holt's Montreal Light and Power Company into the 1920s from the Montreal Tramway and Power group and Shawinigan Water and Power. Holt's strategy was to charge relatively high rates to consumers and small commercial businesses but lower rates to industrial users, keeping the business community on side.[136] By the mid-1920s, Holt had secured a monopoly by the lack of opposition from the business community and an aggressive policy of buying out rivals.

In contrast, there was a lack of competition in the Toronto region. The Toronto financial community was a cohesive group of personal friends who exerted peer pressure to prevent competition. A popular movement was started by consumers who experienced high rates and poor service and were determined to break the monopoly of the Toronto Electric Lighting Company. Local businessmen and manufacturers believed that cheaper and more reliable power was needed to promote further industrialization in the region and that public ownership was the means. In 1905, manufacturer and politician Adam Beck took up the cause of "power at cost," and using his political position he established Ontario Hydro in 1910.[137]

The Calgary situation was similar to that of Montreal. In fact, Holt was involved in both private monopolies. There was competition from the city of Calgary facilities, and potential for competition into the 1920s, but the Calgary Power Company succeeded in gradually eliminating it. The cost of building competing facilities made competition unfeasible by the 1920s. The Calgary Power Company recognized the need to develop a utility with reasonable and reliable power and pushed to acquire the rights to Kananaskis Falls after the inadequate performance of the Horseshoe Falls facility and later the rights to Ghost Lake.

The second factor is the degree of unified control that city corporations exercised over the metropolitan area. The Montreal region was made up of many independent municipalities that never united regarding public ownership of utilities. Holt was able to exploit their weaknesses and divisions. Toronto was a much more unified region as it aggressively annexed new suburbs, and its Board of Control provided strong leadership against the private utilities.[138] Calgary did not appear to experience the same conflict and disunity as Montreal. However, there were few viable alternatives as the Calgary Power Company controlled the largest and reasonably cheap hydroelectric sites. The municipal plants initially provided bargaining power, but over time this position was lessened by the increasing costs of developing other municipal power plants. This factor is seen more clearly in the province of Alberta, where small independent utilities developed and did not unite to support a public utility scheme. They were unable to individually compete with the resources of Calgary Power.

The third factor is the degree of co-operation between governments. In Ontario, municipalities co-operated in the development and distribution of power. The provincial government also co-operated in passing legislation quickly to approve the municipality's contracts with Ontario Hydro when the Toronto Electric Light monopoly tried to challenge the competition. Ontario Hydro was also able to draw heavily on the credit of the province for its bond guarantees. In contrast, there was often conflict between Montreal and the provincial government in Quebec City. The province kept a strict watch on municipal spending and would not allow municipalities sufficient capital to build or buy hydroelectric facilities. Holt had inflated the value of his company assets, which made a buyout by the city unaffordable. Rather than support and finance public ownership, the provincial government set up the Public Utilities Commission in 1909. Armstrong and Nelles conclude that the PUC legitimized the Holt monopoly by appearing to protect public interest with statutory powers to fix "reasonable rates." It posed no threat to private utilities by simply approving rate increases. The board had no powers of expropriation and no sizable staff. Thus, the establishment of a regulatory board diverted conflict into the quasi-judicial process and away from the real issue of public control over utilities and power at the lowest possible cost.[139]

The Montreal scenario closely resembled that of Calgary in terms of the provincial government attempting to tightly control municipal spending. The dual purposes of the commission had the potential to work against the public interest, controlling municipal borrowing on the one hand and allowing the growth of a private utility monopoly on the other. By the 1920s, the governments could not afford to purchase the private utilities. The provincial government failed to take leadership in uniting communities and developing a provincial power scheme, but it also did not receive enthusiastic cooperation from the federal government to obtain waters to develop hydroelectric facilities. The federal government chose to favour the Calgary Power Company with water rights.

The fourth factor is the availability of water.[140] In Quebec, the abundant water supply initially facilitated private competition. There was not a sense of urgency for municipalities to unite and share the resources. The Toronto region was limited to Niagara Falls as the only major water power source. The limited water power sources available fuelled public fears about a private monopoly controlling a scarce resource. The Calgary Power Company, through its political allies in Ottawa, was able to control the major water power sources near the Calgary region. Alberta did not have the abundant water supply of Quebec, but the possibility of development at Spray Lakes and Lake Minnewanka by the provincial government deflected the sense of urgency regarding Calgary Power's control over water power sources. The matter of developing a provincial public utility system moved slowly through a series of studies and reports until the Depression put an end to the studies themselves.

Conclusion

The Public Utility Board did not play a significant role in the development and regulation of electric utilities during this era. Both the legislators and the courts limited its ability to interfere with contract rates and to ensure the efficient use of resources. The PUB did not appear to take an active role in stimulating market forces but spent much of its time regulating municipal and school district expenditures and the sale of shares. The small, private, independent electric utilities were unstable, lacking the capital and the core market to provide any real competition for the Calgary Power Company. The concentration of power in the hands of Calgary Power was unhindered by regulation. The board did provide a forum for public grievances, but the effect was to shift any conflict into the quasi-judicial arena. The debate was often deflected to discussions of the board's power and jurisdiction and away from the debate of public ownership of power resources and electric utilities.

In Alberta, there was no charismatic leader in the provincial government such as Adam Beck, who founded Ontario Hydro. The public utility was able to pursue a much broader mandate than a utility board. It ensured the efficient use of water power and integrated the various municipalities to provide the lowest possible cost and prevent price discrimination. Through public ownership of utilities, it prevented social, political, and economic power from being concentrated in the hands of a monopoly. The Alberta government failed to take a leadership role in developing a public utility scheme and integrating the various existing power plants to ensure the maximum and most efficient use of the province's power resources. While the government continued its course of debate and inaction, Calgary Power rose to the challenge of developing the water resources and integrating power resources in Alberta. The company brought power to rural Alberta and more reasonable power to communities with independent facilities. The success of the monopoly is evidenced by the present existence of TransAlta Utilities. Herbert Holt, Lord Beaverbrook, and R.B. Bennett would be proud.

Acknowledgments

I wish to thank Louis Knafla, Jonathan Swainger, Nigel Banks, John McLaren, and Paul Brand for their comments and suggestions; Diane Erion and Shawn McReavey for assisting me; and the archives and staff at the City of Calgary Archives, the Glenbow Alberta Institute Library, and the Provincial Archives of Alberta for their courteous service in my research endeavours.

Notes

1 H.W. Arthurs, *"Without the Law": Administrative Justice and Legal Pluralism in Nineteenth-Century England* (Toronto: University of Toronto Press, 1985).

2 F.M. Scherer, *Industrial Market Structure and Economic Performance,* as cited in *Unnatural Monopolies: The Case for Deregulating Public Utilities,* ed. Robert W. Poole Jr. (Lexington, MA: D.C. Heath and Company, 1985), 1.

3 Christopher Armstrong and H.V. Nelles, *Monopolies Moment: The Organization and Regulation of Canadian Utilities, 1839-1930* (Philadelphia: Temple University Press, 1986).

4 Ibid. at xiv.

5 W.E. Hawkins, *Electrifying Calgary: A Century of Public and Private Power* (Calgary: University of Calgary Press, 1987), 97.

6 Stephen Breyer, *Regulation and Its Reform* (Cambridge, MA: Harvard University Press, 1982).

7 *Public Utilities Act,* Statutes of Alberta (1915), c. 6.

8 Provincial Archives of Alberta (PAA), Annual Report of the Board of Public Utility Commissioners of Alberta [PUB Annual Report] (1917), 6.

9 Armstrong and Nelles, *Monopolies Moment,* 93.

10 "Council Meeting," *Calgary Herald,* 3 July 1889, 8.

11 Hawkins, *Electrifying Calgary,* 58.

12 "The Light Plant Plans Will Be Rushed," *Calgary Herald,* 22 April 1905, 1. Prince's company continued to supply electricity to some customers in Calgary until its assets were purchased by the Calgary Power Company in 1928.

13 Hawkins, *Electrifying Calgary,* 75.

14 City of Calgary Archives (CCA), Board of Commissioner Papers, series 1, box 69, file Out of Town Correspondence January to August D-M, "Letter Mayor to *Idaho Daily Statesman,*" 15 February 1916.

15 CCA, Council Minutes (20 May 1906), 352-53.

16 CCA, Council Minutes, "Letter Commissioners to Mayor" (22 October 1910), 241.

17 Christopher Armstrong and H.V. Nelles, "Contrasting Development of the Hydro-Electric Industry in the Montreal and Toronto Regions, 1900-1930," *Journal of Canadian Studies* 18, 1 (1983): 5-27 at 14-15.

18 For a detailed description of R.B. Bennett's early legal career, see Louis A. Knafla, "Richard 'Bonfire' Bennett: The Legal Practice of a Prairie Corporate Lawyer, 1898 to 1913," in *Essays in Canadian Law,* vol. 4, *Beyond the Law: Lawyers and Business in Canada, 1830-1930,* ed. Carol Wilton (Toronto: Osgoode Society, 1990), 320-76.

19 For a detailed analysis of Lord Beaverbrook's career in high finance, see Gregory P. Marchildon, *Profits and Politics: Beaverbrook and the Gilded Age of Canadian Finance* (Toronto: University of Toronto Press, 1996).

20 Ibid. at 241.

21 Ibid. at 79.

22 Christopher Armstrong and H.V. Nelles, "Competition v. Convenience: Federal Administration of Box River Waterpowers, 1903-1913," in *The Canadian West: Social Change and Economic Development,* ed. Henry C. Klassen (Calgary: Comprint Publishing, 1977), 163-180 at 165.

23 Marchildon, *Profits and Politics,* 80n2.

24 Ibid. at 182-86, 151-53, 176-78, 212.

25 Hawkins, *Electrifying Calgary,* 141.

26 Knafla, "Richard 'Bonfire' Bennett," 355-58.

27 Glenbow-Alberta Institute (GAI), Calgary Power Company Papers (CPCP), M1546, box 1, file 3, Minute Book (11 June 1913), 7.

28 Ibid. at box 12, file 72, "Agreements with the City of Calgary 1910-1944."

29 The 1912 Calgary Power Company Annual Report stated that the city of Calgary steam plant cost approximately $65 per horsepower to operate. Ibid. at box 3, file 6, 1.

30 Ibid.

31 Ibid.

32 Armstrong and Nelles, "Competition v. Convenience," 173-75.

33 Ibid. at 176.

34 The Department of Indian Affairs finally brokered a deal in 1914 between the Calgary Power Company and the Stoney Band that consisted of $9,000 to purchase ninety-four acres, with $7,500 in rent from 1914-19 and $1,500 in annual rent after 1919. Ironically, the department had to put up the money initially because the company alleged that it did not have the finances. Ibid. at 178.
35 GAI, CPCP, M1546, box 12, file 172, "Contract between Calgary Power and the City of Calgary, 1913."
36 *Hansard Scrapbook,* 6th legislature, 3rd session, 31 January 1929-20 March 1929; "Number of Important Water Power Sites Not Developed within 200 Miles of Edmonton," *Edmonton Journal,* 1 March 1929, 94.
37 CCA, Council Minutes, "Ross Report" (1910), 186.
38 CCA, City Annual Report, "Report of Chief Engineer" (1912), 187-88.
39 GAI, CPCP, M1546, box 7, file 67, "Contract between Calgary Power Company and the Village of Cochrane."
40 GAI, M1546, box 3, file 6, Annual Report (1916), 3.
41 CCA, Board of Commissioners Papers, series 1, box 60, file Out of Town Correspondence, July to December D-M, 7 December 1915, "Correspondence Mayor to Lorenzo Dow, Tacoma."
42 CCA, Council Minutes (31 May 1915), 463-64.
43 GAI, M1546, box 3, file 6, Annual Report (1916), 3.
44 Hawkins, *Electrifying Calgary,* 165.
45 GAI, Zephir Malhiot, "Seventy Years of Growth with Canada: 1854-1948" (typescript diary), red page no. 428.
46 Ibid. at red page no. 561.
47 CCA, Council Minutes (6 August 1923), 319.
48 GAI, M1546, box 3, file 6, Annual Report (1924), 1.
49 Ibid.
50 Ibid. at box 12, file 172, "Agreements between Calgary Power and City of Calgary."
51 Ibid. at box 2, file 4, Minute Book (30 May 1928), 19.
52 Ibid. at 19-20.
53 See Armstrong and Nelles, *Monopolies Moment,* 307. Appendix 1 provides a very informative comparison of utility rates across Canada.
54 The parties submitted the contract to the PUB for approval in 1916. The board initially rejected two clauses in the contract involving rate jurisdiction and a renewal clause. The contract was resubmitted and approved on 17 August 1916, with the board specifically stating that it had the jurisdiction over rates. PAA, PUB Annual Report (1916), 16-17.
55 The contract was approved by the PUB on 3 July 1917. Ibid. (1917) at 47.
56 The PUB approved a ten-year franchise agreement between the parties on 22 February 1919. Ibid. (1919) at 12.
57 The parties submitted an agreement that the company would provide steam power to the town for three years, which the PUB approved on 21 June 1920. Ibid. (1920) at 38.
58 The village of Bashaw granted a ten-year exclusive franchise to McCarty for the supply of electric light to the village. The PUB approved the agreement on 15 March 1920. Ibid. at 19.
59 Joseph Boudreau was granted a franchise to supply electric light to the town for ten years, and the agreement received PUB approval on 24 October 1921. Ibid. (1921) at 81.
60 The PUB approved the parties' agreement on 11 April 1923. Ibid. (1923) at 5.
61 The PUB approved the ten-year franchise on 10 June 1921 despite their warning. Ibid. (1921) at 49.
62 Ibid. (1925) at 12.
63 Ibid. (1922) at 25.
64 The town of Magrath complained to the PUB in 1922 that the company was not complying with their agreement. The PUB was able to bring the parties together, and they reached a one-year tentative agreement. Ibid. at 25.
65 The board refused the application for increased rates on 17 December 1925 and required a continuation of service until 1 February 1926. Ibid. (1925) at 12.

66 Ibid. (1919) at 46.
67 Ibid. (1925) at 10-11.
68 Ibid. (1924) at 45.
69 Ibid. (1929) at 10. The Calgary Power Minute Book indicates that United Electric and Engineering operated 100 miles of transmission lines and distributed power to Strathmore, Gleichen, Bassano, and a number of surrounding villages. The purchase was in the form of a stock exchange, whereby ten UEEC shares (based on a par value of $10) were exchanged for every Calgary Power share (valued at $100). GAI, CPCP, Minute Book, box 2, file 4 (29 August 1928), 21.
70 *Hansard Scrapbook,* "Number of Important Water Power Sites" (1 March 1929), 94.
71 PAA, PUB Annual Report (1916), 31.
72 Ibid. at 32.
73 Ibid. (1917) at 31.
74 *Hansard Scrapbook,* "Number of Important Water Power Sites" (1 March 1929), 94.
75 GAI, CPCP, Annual Report (1927), 1.
76 Ibid.
77 Ibid. (1929) at 1-2.
78 Ibid. (1927) at 1.
79 Ibid. (1930) at 2.
80 Ibid. (1929) at 2.
81 Ibid. (1930) at 2.
82 Farmers were charged the cost of the line, whether on road allowances or on private property, used to supply power in their districts. The company assumed the care of its equipment and the maintenance and operation of lines. *Hansard Scrapbook,* "Number of Important Water Power Sites" (1 March 1929), 94.
83 The issue of a further $7 million in stock was officially approved at the directors' meeting on 5 October 1928. GAI, CPCP, Minute Book (5 October 1928), 23.
84 Ibid., Annual Report (1928) at 4.
85 Ibid. (1929) at 4.
86 Ibid. (1930) at 4.
87 Ibid. at 1.
88 See *An Act to Authorize a Subsidy for a Railway through the Crow's Nest Pass,* 60-61 Victoria (1897), c. 5.
89 *Hansard Scrapbook,* 3rd legislature, 3rd session, 2 February 1915-17 April 1915, "Alberta Public Utilities Act Placed before House Controls Civic Borrowings" (2 April 1915), 46.
90 Ibid.
91 PAA, PUB Annual Report (1916), 1.
92 Ibid. (1919) at 73.
93 Fortunately, the board informally brought the parties together, and a tentative one-year agreement was reached. Ibid. (1922) at 25.
94 David Breen, *Alberta's Petroleum Industry and the Conservation Board* (Edmonton: University of Alberta Press, 1993), 56.
95 Ibid. at 70.
96 PAA, PUB Annual Report (1919), 11.
97 Ibid. at 80.
98 *Re Public Utilities Act: Northern Alberta Natural Gas Development Company Ltd. v. City of Edmonton* (1919), 15 Alta. L. Rev. 416.
99 Ibid. at 435.
100 PAA, PUB Annual Report (1924), 8.
101 (1919) P.U.R. 1919D, 979.
102 (1921) P.U.R. 1921D, 705.
103 PAA, PUB Annual Report (1928), 9.
104 Ibid. (1929) at 2.
105 This time period was an unpredictable age of land speculation, and the board played an important role through its powers to provide relief from taxes and through the cancellation of subdivision plans. In years such as 1924, there were almost two hundred orders

cancelling subdivisions in the province. In 1929, the board was also appointed as arbitrator for compensation claims by landowners affected by replotting schemes.

106 The board played a major role in regulating the many speculators who were attracted to the Prairie economy in Alberta. Any company share offering in the province had to be approved by the PUB. Its annual reports indicate that a considerable amount of the board's time was spent on investigating and approving share offerings. It was particularly busy between 1917 and 1923 because it sought to regulate federally incorporated companies offering shares within the province in addition to provincially incorporated ones. The board enjoyed emphasizing the importance of its role and stated in the 1920 annual report that it had undoubtedly eliminated the sale of shares in "a large number of wild cat projects." Ibid. (1920) at 4. However, the Supreme Court of Canada eventually ruled that the PUB did not have jurisdiction over federally incorporated companies, and this workload decreased after 1923.

107 Ibid. (1919) at 4.

108 Breen, *Alberta's Petroleum Industry,* 55.

109 PAA, PUB Annual Report (1921), 67-80.

110 Ibid. at 69.

111 See PAA, "Report of the Public Utility Commissioners Re: City of Red Deer and Western General Electric Co Ltd. the Lieutenant Governor in Council" (26 November 1924).

112 PAA, PUB Annual Report (1924), 19-30.

113 Ibid. (1922) at 1.

114 *Statutes of Alberta,* 1923, c. 53. Section 54 gave the board powers to increase or decrease prices but exempted contracts entered into before the passage of the new act in 1923.

115 *Hansard Scrapbook,* 5th legislature, 5th session, 19 February 1925-6 August 1925; "Stewart Loses Brave Battle for Cheaper Gas for Lethbridge," *Edmonton Journal,* 9 April 1925, 85.

116 "Utilities Board Has Power Denied Highest Courts in Dominion," *Edmonton Journal,* 8 April 1925, 82.

117 "Stewart Loses Brave Battle."

118 *Hansard Scrapbook,* 6th legislature, 1st session, 10 February 1927-2 April 1927; "Bill to Curb Powers of Utility Board Is Doomed to Failure," *Edmonton Journal,* 26 March 1927, 108.

119 *Hansard Scrapbook,* 5th legislature, 5th session, 19 February 1925-6 August 1925; "To Hold Conference with Municipalities on Spray Lakes," *Edmonton Journal,* 9 April 1925, 84.

120 Ibid.

121 *Hansard Scrapbook,* 6th legislature, 3rd session, 31 January 1929-20 March 1929; "Liberal Leader Demands Thorough Investigation [of] Alberta Power Resources," *Edmonton Journal,* 9 March 1929, 119.

122 *Hansard Scrapbook,* 6th legislature, 4th session, 30 January 1930-3 April 1930; "Public Ownership of Power in Alberta Approved," *Edmonton Bulletin,* 19 March 1930, 89.

123 R. Bruce Baxter, the deputy minister of telephones, left the government after completing the report and was appointed managing director for the Calgary Power Company in Alberta and Saskatchewan: *Edmonton Bulletin,* 1 March 1929, 94. He was appointed as a director on 3 December 1928: GAI, CPCP, Minute Book (3 December 1928), 56.

124 "Number of Important Water Power Sites," *Edmonton Bulletin,* 1 March 1929, 94.

125 *Hansard Scrapbook,* 6th legislature, 4th session, 30 January 1930-3 April 1930; "C.L. Gibbs Tells Government Public Ownership Is Vital," *Edmonton Journal,* 7 February 1930, 25.

126 Ibid.

127 "Liberal Leader Demands Thorough Investigation," *Edmonton Bulletin,* 9 March 1929, 120.

128 Ibid.

129 "Public Ownership of Power in Alberta Approved," *Edmonton Bulletin,* 19 March 1930, 89.

130 *Hansard Scrapbook,* 6th legislature, 4th session, 30 January 1930-3 April 1930; "Legislature Shows Approval [of] Public Ownership Principle: Only One Dissenting Voter," *Edmonton Journal,* 19 March 1930, 109.

131 "Public Ownership of Power in Alberta Approved," *Edmonton Bulletin,* 19 March 1930, 89.

132 "Legislature Shows Approval [of] Public Ownership Principle," *Edmonton Journal,* 19 March 1930, 109.

133 *Hansard Scrapbook,* 7th legislature, 2nd session, 4 February 1932-6 April 1932; "Power Study Costs Bring Criticism," *Edmonton Journal,* 28 March 1932, 130.
134 Len Stahl, *A Record of Service: The History of Western Canada's Pioneer Gas and Electric Utilities* (Edmonton: Canadian Utilities Limited, 1987), 55.
135 Armstrong and Nelles, "Contrasting Development of the Hydro-Electric Industry," 5-27.
136 Ibid. at 16.
137 Ibid. at 8-13.
138 Ibid. at 17-18.
139 Ibid. at 20-22.
140 Ibid. at 23.

11

The Law and Public Nudity: Prairie and West Coast Reactions to the Sons of Freedom, 1929-32

John McLaren

On 1 May 1932, 100 Sons of Freedom were arrested in the village of Thrums, British Columbia, for parading in the nude.[1] This turned out to be the prelude to arrests for public nudity in Nelson on 9 May and Grand Forks on 13 May. By mid-June, close to 600 adult protesters of both sexes had been arrested, convicted, and almost all sentenced to three years in jail for this offence.[2] They were incarcerated in a special penal colony established hastily on Piers Island, at the top end of the Saanich Peninsula. Over 300 of the children of Freedomite parents in detention were apprehended and labelled as destitute, still in theory under the legal guardianship of their parents.[3] In fact, without any sort of hearing or parental consent, they were put into industrial schools, orphanages, and foster care in the Lower Mainland and on Vancouver Island for purposes of their resocialization as "good Canadians."

Some fifty-five Sons of Freedom were arrested in the Yorkton area of eastern Saskatchewan in July and August of the same year. The first group, charged with vagrancy in July, were all released and told by Magistrate Alexander MacDonald to go home and behave themselves. Out of a slightly larger group charged with and convicted of public nudity in August, only the leaders were sent to jail for the maximum term. Much-reduced sentences were handed down by MacDonald to mothers with children. They were given two days in jail, in part to ensure that they could care for their families. As a result, no attempt was made to apprehend the children left in their homes.[4]

The law in both provinces was the same. An amendment to the *Criminal Code* in 1930 had been introduced by the R.B. Bennett government, under pressure by the Tory administrations of Simon Fraser Tolmie in British Columbia and John Anderson of Saskatchewan to make public nudity a serious offence.[5] The amendment substituted a maximum penalty of three years in jail for the previous maximum of six months. The provision, section 205A, effectively made public nudity a political crime. The change was designed to "solve" the Sons of Freedom problem once and for all by putting the adults away for long enough so that in their absence the children could be remoulded to accept and practise Canadian values.[6]

The bones of contention for the Sons of Freedom in both provinces were the same: a rejection of state pressure for compulsory school attendance and criticism of Peter Petrovich Verigin, the second Doukhobor leader in Canada, for his support for public education for the Doukhobor community.[7] Verigin was also in bad odour because he had forced Freedomites off community land in reaction to their displays of public nudity and the involvement of some in the burning down of schoolhouses in both provinces.[8]

Education has featured episodically in Canadian history as a site of conflict over cultural definition and national identity. In the early decades of this century, education policy and law were viewed by many among the political and social elite in English-speaking Canada as crucial tools in the establishment of a Protestant Christian, Anglo-Saxon identity for Canada.[9] The community at large, it was asserted, must be loyal to the empire. A shared commitment to British traditions and institutions was essential to the country's material and moral welfare as a virtuous and progressive nation. These sentiments were at their height in western Canada during the period from 1910 to 1940. Politicians representing significant segments of the English-speaking population of the region sought to exert control and direction over those elements of the population who were not English speaking and seemed to want to preserve their own "crude" traditions and values.[10] Education was at the core of this assimilative strategy. The provincial Tory governments in power in both British Columbia and Saskatchewan in 1932 were totally committed to a policy of compulsory public education in the cause of Protestant Canadian nationalism. Moreover, they were on record as having no patience with, let alone understanding of, sectarian claims to autonomy in matters of education.[11] The presence of a group within the community that seemed to reject education out of hand was particularly irksome to these politicians and their supporters.

What, then, explains the difference in response by justice officials in the two provinces when faced with the propensity of the Sons of Freedom to strip as a challenge to state authority, especially in resistance to compulsory education? I argue that the difference is a reflection of the particular educational histories of the two provinces, of their distinctive ethnic demographics, of the makeup of the Doukhobor population in each, and of diversity in the mix of ideologies of nation building evident in the general political climate and discourse of those jurisdictions.

The political and social history of the North-West Territories from which Saskatchewan was carved in 1905 was marked by ethnic, cultural, and linguistic tension from the very start.[12] The values and aspirations of both Métis inhabitants of the region and French-speaking immigrants clashed with those of English-speaking settlers drawn from Ontario, the Maritime provinces, Europe, and the United States. As time went on, any vision of this part of Canada reflecting and accommodating a truly bicultural, bilingual society was to fade given the overwhelming numbers of English-speaking settlers and the pro-settlement policies of Ottawa. However, the presence of a French-speaking minority and a sizable Roman Catholic population drawn from both linguistic groups was to have a marked effect on the schooling legislation passed in the Territories and later adopted in Saskatchewan.

After considerable debate and controversy, the educational system constructed in the Territories placed a heavy emphasis on local initiative and control in getting school districts established and reposed considerable power over the running of the schools in the local school boards and their elected trustees.[13] Since the initiative for setting up school districts came from the local community, governance of the schools reflected to a degree the composition and cultural mix of the population in those areas. Under school legislation, it was the majority religion that counted, so that public school and separate school districts could be either Protestant or Roman Catholic depending on the relative numbers of adherents to each faith tradition present in a district. Although the Territorial Council of Public Instruction, and subsequently the provincial Department of Education, exercised general supervision of the system and intervened in the case of disputes, it was normally the school boards that were responsible for hiring and firing teachers, opening and closing schools, taxation, and attendance.[14] Furthermore, despite a requirement that general instruction be in English, as a modest concession to linguistic realities primary grades could be taught in French.[15] Moreover, other languages could be offered if parents whose mother tongue was not English so desired, as long as such classes did not disrupt the rest of the program in the school.[16] Although the system was officially "public" and thus nonsectarian in theory, the *Schools Act* provided that religious instruction could take place, but only in the last half hour of each day and with the consent of parents of the children participating.[17] School attendance that was compulsory on paper, except where a child and family fell within a list of designated exemptions, was often not in practice. This was because the legislation did not run to rural or village districts where children resided more than a mile from the schoolhouse.[18] Furthermore, enforcement depended on school boards making regulations to police and enforce the truancy provisions, which not all of them did.[19] In these particulars, the law relating to school attendance remained unchanged until 1917.

This was the educational system that an increasing number of non-English-speaking immigrants experienced in the years after 1896, when the expansive immigration policies of Clifford Sifton and the federal Liberal government began to take hold. Increasingly, the ethnic mix in Saskatchewan was to include German, Russian, and Ukrainian settlers as well as the

Doukhobor colonies established in 1899.[20] There was within the school system some room for children from ethnic communities to learn in their mother tongue and for their religious beliefs to be recognized. The inherited *Schools Act* was one to which successive Liberal governments in Saskatchewan from 1905 to 1929 were committed in general terms and that the educational bureaucracy in Regina was by and large ready to support and apply.[21] The provincial Liberals were identified by the members of minority immigrant communities with the policies of Sifton that had enabled them to migrate to Canada. As a result, the party drew heavily on the support of non-English-speaking immigrants.

This is not to say that the education system in Saskatchewan was unaffected by trends in educational policy and rhetoric in Canada generally that were directed toward nation building through the inculcation of cultural homogeneity.[22] Territorial and later provincial educational administrators saw education as an important tool in securing the assimilation of non-English-speaking ethnic groups.[23] Moreover, there were political forces in Saskatchewan, from the Tory party to the Orange lodges, with support within the Anglo-Saxon and Scandinavian communities that, as time went on, became more and more vocal in challenging existing school law and policy. These groups were one in calling for the exclusivity of a public school system, taught only in English, that disseminated Canadian values and made no concessions to the demands of particular religious denominations. This pressure built up with the approach of the First World War and strengthened in the war years and thereafter as nativism among English-speaking settlers grew in intensity.[24] The effects were felt in changes to school legislation. The Liberal government of W.M. Martin moved to make school attendance compulsory in 1917, with penalties including fines and enforcement by seizure of goods in distraint where parents failed to comply.[25] A year later the language option for non-English-speaking students was dropped, and French instruction was limited to French-speaking students in grade one.[26] In the 1919-20 legislative session, amendments to the *Schools Act* were passed requiring school trustees to take an oath of allegiance and be British subjects by birth or naturalization or, if not yet naturalized, to intend to apply for it.[27] One distinctive ethnic and cultural minority did suffer at the hands of the state in Saskatchewan as a result of the drive to compulsory education, the strict Mennonites. They rejected public schooling out of hand. Many were prosecuted, and some of them went to prison for their beliefs.[28]

Despite the legislative changes, the educational regime operating in the province was administered overall in a relatively tolerant way, which proved important in coaxing Doukhobor parents to send their children to school and to keep them there. The first schools in Doukhobor communities in Saskatchewan had been private foundations, established by their Quaker supporters and by Herbert Archer, an English Tolstoyan who had committed himself to living and working with them.[29] That it was outsiders who took the initiative in setting up schools reflects very well the low priority given by Doukhobors to academic and formal education as opposed to practical and religious training, their fears about education sponsored by the state, and the ambivalence of their leaders about encouraging the growth of a literate community.[30]

School districts were slowly established in predominantly Doukhobor communities. However, in some districts, Doukhobors sat as school trustees and thus influenced the policies of the local school authorities. The earliest examples of school boards with Doukhobor representation were in communities in which the immigrants had departed from the leadership of Peter Vasylevich Verigin and lived and farmed as independents.[31] The process of setting up school districts hastened after a significant number of the followers of Verigin and members of the Christian Community of Universal Brotherhood (CCUB) moved with their leader to British Columbia between 1908 and 1913. This exodus left their independent brothers and sisters as the majority in many Saskatchewan Doukhobor settlements.[32]

Ironically, difficulties with including Doukhobor communities within new school districts flowed in the main from the unreasonable and discriminatory stance taken by members of the non-Doukhobor community. So in the school district of Devil's Lake established in 1899, just before four Doukhobor villages were established in the area, the trustees who were non-Doukhobor sought to deny Doukhobor children access to the school while requiring their parents to pay school taxes. Frustration in Regina at this situation led to the appointment of an official trustee, and the Doukhobors were persuaded to take advantage of the school while paying back taxes.[33]

In 1903, in the Rosthern school district, an independent Doukhobor stronghold, the non-Doukhobor trustees, as a cost-cutting device, decided to deny Doukhobor children further entry to the school.[34] This wilful act was to persuade some independent parents that they should accept an offer by the Quakers to take a group of young people to Philadelphia for their education.

After 1907, when the trek by many community Doukhobors to British Columbia began, the Saskatchewan Department of Education attempted more directly to induce those Doukhobors still in the province to accept and become involved in the public school system. This was a period during which, largely through the efforts of Joseph Megas, who had encouraged Ukrainian communities to accept public education, attempts were made to open up more school districts and to train teachers from non-English-speaking immigrant communities.[35] The department took a dim view of non-Doukhobors who objected to the inclusion of Doukhobor children in schools and showed that it was ready to respond positively to the Doukhobor desire to share in the local administration of education. It did this, for example, in 1912 in the case of the Bear's Head school district. There an unholy alliance of other settlers and community Doukhobors tried to have the school closed down and access denied to the children of independents.[36] The department responded sympathetically to pressure from Herbert Archer and his friends for substitution of an elected school board for the official trustee who was then running the district.

By the outbreak of the First World War in 1914, the independent Doukhobors, who had willingly assimilated in other ways and were influenced by the attitudes of other settlers, not least the Mennonites, many of whom supported education, had generally accepted public schooling for their children. Moreover, the first Doukhobor had been licensed as a teacher – Peter Makaroff, soon to become Canada's first Doukhobor lawyer.[37]

Despite increasing pressure on the Doukhobors to conform in matters of education after 1914, and the introduction of compulsory school attendance in 1917, there was little or no adverse reaction on the part of the independents. A dispute in the Blaine Lake school district over the singing of patriotic songs in 1915 seems to have blown over.[38] The community Doukhobors who had remained in Saskatchewan were more suspicious of education sponsored by the state and took more time to comply with school attendance laws. During the period from 1912 to 1915, when community Doukhobor children were out of school in British Columbia, attendance of orthodox children in the Verigin region of eastern Saskatchewan, where the CCUB was strongest, was negligible. The Saskatchewan leadership of the CCUB, while appearing to favour Doukhobor involvement in public education, was clearly advising otherwise in the community itself. In the face of this manoeuvring, the department seems to have exercised tolerance and circumspection, which were easier because of the school attendance exemptions in place at that time.[39] However, even after the passage of the *School Attendance Act* in 1917, a policy of restraint was practised in Regina. While boys from the orthodox group began to attend school regularly, girls were notable by their absence. In 1923, when the department was contacted by the Verigin school board on what to do about this problem, the department advised that space should be made for the children but that the law should not be enforced, pending a departmental inquiry. The latter appears never to have taken place.[40]

What did finally persuade community parents to send all of their children to primary school in Saskatchewan was the announcement in 1925 by the new leader, Peter Petrovich Verigin, at that time still in the Soviet Union, that Doukhobors should send their children to school.[41] From that date, CCUB Doukhobors in Saskatchewan effectively made their peace with the public school system and discovered that by being involved they could exercise influence on the policies of local school boards where their numbers made that possible.

From early days, the philosophy and practice of government in Canada's most westerly province had emphasized power at the centre. If British conceptions of law and order were to take root in this rugged, sparsely settled terrain, it was supposed, then this would be achieved only by erecting and maintaining a system in which control over governance and administration was exercised from Victoria. True stability and order were, of course, dependent upon what the agents of the state did in local communities, but it had to be clear that their authority flowed from the centre and that they were responsible for carrying out the policies of the provincial government.[42] This was as true in education as it was in other areas of public and social policy.

Educational policy was made in Victoria and administered in the hinterland of British Columbia by provincial officials according to directions from the Department of Education. The exercise of local discretion was not viewed with favour, especially if it seemed to undercut general policy fashioned by the bureaucrats in the capital.[43]

The state educational system in British Columbia was public in nature. There was no recognition at law of separate schools that would accommodate the educational, religious, and linguistic needs of minority communities.[44] If parents wanted their children educated differently, then that had to be done as a private initiative while they continued to pay taxes to the public system. By the time of the arrival of the Doukhobors, education was compulsory throughout the province, with limited exceptions for those who could prove that their children were educated adequately elsewhere or where geographic barriers prevented attendance.[45] Given the province's distinctly British or American settler heritage, there was also never any doubt that the language of instruction was English and only English.

Such a system was both structurally and ideologically opposed to minority claims for linguistic and cultural autonomy in education as a matter of state policy. Compliance with the demands of the law, including school attendance laws, was the watchword. Furthermore, the department was capable of vigorous reaction to resisting communities, such as the Doukhobors, most of whom were at best ambivalent about the advantages of state education and some of whom were opposed to formal education in any form.[46]

The effects of the combination of centralized power and unerring commitment to instilling British values and culture in British Columbia's public schools are evident in the reaction of the system and the government in Victoria to Doukhobor resistance to public education.[47] After a brief honeymoon on education in 1911, when some Doukhobor children attended school at the behest of Peter Vasylevich Verigin, the leader of the community, education quickly became a point of conflict between the CCUB and the provincial government.[48] Doukhobor parents refused to send their children to school as long as members of the community were charged and convicted with failing to comply with vital statistics laws.[49] Victoria, under pressure from disgruntled non-Doukhobors in the Kootenays to make the immigrants comply with Canadian law, contemplated enforcing school attendance as well as registration of births, deaths, and marriages by imposing criminal responsibility on the community for breaches of the law under the odious *Community Regulation Act*.[50] Fortunately, a truce was reached before the legislation was actually invoked. In 1915, probably because neither side wanted things to come to a head during wartime conditions, a pact was reached between Verigin and Attorney General William Bowser, whereby Doukhobor children went to school but were exempted from military drill.[51]

Conflict was to re-emerge with a vengeance, however, in the early 1920s, a period of intense nativism and nostalgic patriotism in British Columbia, when the Liberal government of John Oliver initiated a vigorous and unbending policy of enforcing the truancy laws.[52] By legislative amendments, they also targeted "recalcitrant" Doukhobor parents and communities by penalizing school districts where school attendance was "unreasonably" low and imposing assessments on Doukhobor families to support school building, whether they wanted it or not.[53] While there was the odd voice of an education official counselling caution and patience in coaxing the Doukhobors to accept public education, such as that of A.E. Miller, school inspector for the Revelstoke region, these sentiments were lost in a headlong rush by the Department of Education to force compliance and realize the ideal of assimilation of a noisome, unruly, alien community.[54] The guiding hand, it seems, was supplied by Saskatchewan's director of education among "new Canadians," James T. Anderson. In his 1918 book *The Education of the New Canadian*,[55] Anderson had argued that assimilation of non-English-speaking immigrants, which was essential to nation building in Canada, could be achieved only by indoctrinating immigrant children to respect the country and to act as virtuous Canadians. This message was received with enthusiasm in educational circles in British Columbia.

The reaction of some Doukhobor parents to these new pressures from the state was to resist and to keep or take their children out of school. The provincial government responded by enforcing the community regulation legislation and penalizing the collectivity for the failure of parents to pay their fines for the truancy of their children.[56] This was done by distraining CCUB property. Some Freedomites were persuaded that more vigorous resistance to Mammon was called for. They protested in the nude on several occasions, and a small number initiated a campaign of burning schools. The Doukhobor leader professed himself powerless to stop these depredations, and the government was seemingly more interested in punishing parents under the *Community Regulation Act* than in bringing the arsonists to book.[57]

Relative peace returned, and school attendance increased in the Doukhobor communities of southeast British Columbia between 1925 and 1928, as it did in CCUB communities in Saskatchewan, as their new leader, P.P. Verigin, counselled accommodation on school attendance. Verigin initially had visions of establishing Russian-speaking schools. They were to be run by Paul Biriukov, a Tolstoyan supporter of the Doukhobors, whom he brought with him from Russia. The leader was less than resolute, however, in developing a plan of action for the schools.[58] Part of his frustration may have been the lack of any government recognition of the validity or value of Russian-language education in British Columbia. Verigin's decision in 1928 to support public schooling for Doukhobor children led to renewed resistance and protest in both Saskatchewan and British Columbia by zealots within the Doukhobor community, now definable and organized as the Sons of Freedom.[59] How these events played out in terms of the reactions of both other Doukhobors and politicians and the bureaucracy in each province differed. This was despite the fact that both had Tory governments of a strong racist bent committed to crushing dissent among the Doukhobors and the leadership of the younger Verigin himself.[60]

In British Columbia, the no-nonsense attorney general in the Simon Fraser Tolmie government, R.H. "Harry" Pooley, determined that a "get-tough" policy was necessary with the Freedomites. When in the summer of 1929 a group of 112 paraded in the nude, they were arrested. The 104 adults were given the maximum six months in jail, and 8 children were put in the care of the Vancouver Children's Aid Society as wards of the province, to be released when their parents could care for them properly or they reached the age of majority.[61] When this hastily devised exercise in social engineering collapsed in the fall of 1929, and both parents and children were released soon after, Pooley began looking for ways and means of repeating the experiment but using criminal offences that would put the adults away and provide adequate time to re-educate the children. Among the possibilities canvassed were prosecution for riotous assembly and failure to comply with the census laws.[62]

In the Doukhobor communities of southeastern British Columbia, the effect of Freedomite disaffection and protest was to persuade some in the orthodox community that the time had come for them too to stand up against the state. As a result, support for the zealots swelled.[63] The children of these families were removed from school by their parents. In other cases, CCUB families kept their children from school out of fear of the possible repercussions within the community if they did not do so. The Doukhobor community was clearly one in stress, a reality not lost on non-Doukhobors looking for any excuse to rid the region of this troublesome population or at least to cow it into submission. Provincial politicians willingly played on these negative and exclusionary sentiments by continually conflating the activities of the Freedomites with the Doukhobor community at large, in the process converting the resistance of a minority into "the Doukhobor problem."[64] They were assisted in this by word from both Ottawa and Regina, prompted by RCMP reports, that Verigin himself was the closet leader of the Sons of Freedom as well as a dangerous Bolshevik.[65]

On the surface, the situation in Saskatchewan was equally as volatile, perhaps more so. During the late 1920s, calls from segments of the English-speaking and Scandinavian community for the assimilation and even the marginalization of the non-English-speaking peoples of the province had become more and more strident. This nativist sentiment translated into increasing support for the policies of the Tory party and, more ominously, for the campaign of the Ku Klux Klan to secure a foothold in the province.[66] When it is noted that the Klan was able to draw an estimated crowd of 10,000 people to a rally in Moose Jaw in the spring of 1927, the extent of the ferment in the English-speaking community is evident.[67] The practical effect of growing disaffection with the policies of the Martin Liberal government that were labelled as "pro-alien" was the emergence of a minority Tory government from the 1929 election.[68] This was led by none other than James Anderson, former educational ideologue, Orange lodge member, arch-Protestant, and the beneficiary of the campaign of fear whipped up by the Klan.

Anderson was as committed to the solution of the "Doukhobor" problem as his counterparts in Victoria, possibly more so. It was his government that was to take the point position in using the ill-judged and illegal behaviour of P.P. Verigin as a means to get the leader deported.[69] However, the premier and his men were working in a different political and cultural environment than that which existed in British Columbia. In the first place, it was far more difficult to confuse the problems created by Freedomite resistance to public schooling with Doukhobor intransigence in general. Despite the fact that Freedomites in Saskatchewan outnumbered those in British Columbia at the start of this period, their protests were not appreciated, and in some instances disavowed, among both the independent and the CCUB populations in the province. On the matter of schooling, Doukhobors who believed that they now had a stake in the public education system were ill-disposed to those who would interfere with schooling and even burn down schoolhouses.[70] Accordingly, whereas during the period 1929 to 1932 school attendance declined in the Doukhobor communities in British Columbia, it stayed stable or increased in Saskatchewan.[71]

But it was not only in the Doukhobor population that distinctions were made. It is clear that within the bureaucracy and among administration of justice officials there was a belief that government served and needed to be somewhat sensitive to all settler citizens of the province, whatever their cultural background. In certain quarters, the sentiment in relation to the

Doukhobors was that the problems caused by the Freedomites were the result of zealotry and should not be confused with the aspirations and anxieties of the Doukhobor population at large, which was living in relative peace with itself and its neighbours. Freedomite resentment over and resistance to public education was no reason to undo the work of getting the rest of the Doukhobor community to buy into it.[72] Despite an attempt by the Anderson government to further limit the qualifications for eligibility to be a school trustee by imposing a demanding language requirement, moderate forces in the Department of Education seem to have been able both by legislative drafting and by operational policy to effectively remove its sting.[73] In the justice and law enforcement community, the objectives were to bring those Freedomites who were arsonists to book and to avoid making a generation of martyrs out of those who chose to engage in public nudity, despite the vindictive quality of section 205A of the *Criminal Code.*[74] A combination of prosecutorial and judicial discretion was used to mitigate the law's harsh potential.

In Saskatchewan, problems associated with Doukhobor schooling had effectively disappeared by the mid-1930s. Most of the non-Freedomite population were content to send their children to public schools in the running of which they often had some say and that were no longer seen as challenging their right to follow their religious beliefs. Those Freedomite families who chose to stay in Saskatchewan relented and began sending their children to school.[75] In British Columbia, the story was very different, as the sad events of not only the mid-1930s but also the period from 1940 to 1965 bear witness. There by a twist of irony the policies of those who, like James Anderson, believed in the enforced assimilation of "alien" and "aberrational" immigrant communities remained operative for much longer. This type of thinking provided the basis for one of the most shameful experiments in Canadian legal and educational history: the snatching of Freedomite children from their homes and their incarceration and resocialization in the New Denver Detention Centre between 1954 and 1959.[76]

What this chapter suggests is the value of relating general trends in political thinking and social policy to the regional and community contexts in which they played out. There is little doubt that the thinking of both politicians and educational decision makers across Canada was wedded firmly to securing the assimilation of non-English-speaking populations outside Quebec. To one degree or another, this meant compliance with the demands of public education and school attendance laws. This was as true in Saskatchewan as in British Columbia. However, as this story suggests, the degree to which minority populations were forced to comply with the law and the strategies for securing compliance could differ depending on the history of cultural and social relations and the pattern of politics within different jurisdictions.

Notes

1 See report in *Vancouver Daily Province,* 2 May 1932, 1.

2 A sample record of convictions is found in the Provincial Jail Calendar for Grand Forks for May 1932, BCARS, GR 445, BCPP Records, Jail Calendars, 1928-32, Reel B 1975, file 40-2903. The same file also contains a list of the names of the thirty-five men and forty-three women sentenced by Magistrate Crewe of Grand Forks on 20 May.

3 Ronald Hooper, "Custodial Care of Doukhobor Children in British Columbia 1929 to 1933" (master's thesis, University of British Columbia, 1947), 37-38.

4 Saskatchewan Archives Board, R769, Police Magistrates Files 1922-68, Alexander MacDonald, Yorkton, 1931-32 (I.77.6), returns by Justice of Peace, 6-8 July, 22 August, 1932. See also John E. Lyons, "A History of Doukhobor Schooling in Saskatchewan and British Columbia 1899-1939" (master's thesis, University of Calgary, 1973), 103.

5 *Criminal Code Amendment Act,* S.C. 1931, c. 28, s. 2. Also *House of Commons Debates,* 10 July 1931, 3619; 23 July, 4131-36; 24 July, 4143-48.

6 John McLaren, "Creating 'Slaves of Satan' or 'New Canadians'? The Law, Education, and the Socialization of Doukhobor Children, 1911-1935," in *Essays in the History of Canadian Law,* vol. 6, *British Columbia and the Yukon,* ed. Hamar Foster and John McLaren (Toronto: Osgoode Society, 1995), 352-85 at 365-66.

7 Ibid. at 363.

8 Ibid. at 365.

9 See, for example, J.H. Putnam and G.M. Weir, *Survey of the School System* (Victoria: King's Printer, 1925), 38.

10 See Bill Maciejko, "Ukrainians and Prairie School Reform, 1896-1921: Ethnic and Domestic Ideologies in Modern State Formation," *Canadian Ethnic Studies* 22, 2 (1990): 16-40 at 16.

11 John Lyons, "The (Almost) Quiet Evolution: Doukhobor Schooling in Saskatchewan," *Canadian Ethnic Studies* 8 (1976): 23-37 at 31-32; McLaren, "Creating 'Slaves of Satan,'" 363-64.

12 Gerald Friesen, *The Canadian Prairies: A History* (Toronto: University of Toronto Press, 1987), 220-41.

13 D.A. Schmeiser, *Civil Liberties in Canada* (London: Oxford University Press, 1964), 169-82. See also the *Schools Ordinance,* Ordinances NWT 1901, c. 29, and the *Schools Act* RSS 1909, c. 100.

14 Lyons, "A History of Doukhobor Schooling," 73-74.

15 *Schools Ordinance,* c. 29, s. 136(1); *Schools Act,* c. 100, s. 135(1). See also Keith A. McLeod, "Politics, Schools, and the French Language, 1881-1931," in *Politics in Saskatchewan,* ed. Norman Ward and Duff Spafford (Toronto: Longmans Canada, 1968), 124-32.

16 *Schools Ordinance,* s. 136(2); *Schools Act,* s. 135(2).

17 Ibid. at s. 137; s. 136.

18 Ibid. at s. 147; s. 148.

19 Ibid. at s. 148; s. 149.

20 Friesen, *The Canadian Prairies,* 242-73.

21 Lyons, "A History of Doukhobor Schooling," 107.

22 Neil Sutherland, *Children in English-Canadian Society: Framing the Twentieth-Century Consensus* (Toronto: University of Toronto Press, 1976), 202-24.

23 Lyons, "A History of Doukhobor Schooling," 59-60, 74-75.

24 For the literature covering these tensions and challenges, see McLeod, "Politics, Schools, and the French Language"; Maciejko, "Ukrainians and Prairie School Reform"; Raymond Huel, "Pastor vs. Politician: The Reverend Murdoch MacKinnon and Premier Walter Scott's Amendment to the School Act," *Saskatchewan History* 32 (1979): 61-73 at 61; Michael Owen, "'Building the Kingdom of God on the Prairies': E.H. Oliver and Saskatchewan Education, 1913-1930," *Saskatchewan History* 40 (1987): 22-34; Clinton O. White, "Maintaining Anglo-Celtic Hegemony in Saskatchewan: Rev. E.H. Oliver, Provincial Educational Policy, and the German Catholics," *Historical Studies in Education* 6 (1994): 253-79.

25 *School Attendance Act,* S.S. 1917, c. 19.

26 *Schools Amendment Act,* S.S. 1918-19, c. 48, s. 14.

27 *Schools Amendment Act,* S.S. 1919-20, c. 37, s. 18.

28 Adolf Enns, "The Public School Crisis among the Mennonites in Saskatchewan 1916-25," in *Mennonite Images,* ed. Harry Loewen (Winnipeg: Hyperion Press, 1980), 73-81.
29 Lyons, "A History of Doukhobor Schooling," 50-59.
30 McLaren, "Creating 'Slaves of Satan,'" 352-53. See also William Blakemore, *Report of Royal Commission on Matters Relating to the Doukhobor Sect in the Province of British Columbia,* British Columbia, *Sessional Papers,* 1913, T47-55.
31 Lyons, "A History of Doukhobor Schooling," 73-86.
32 For a recent and complete account of the reasons for this migration and its effects on Saskatchewan Doukhobor villages, see Carl Tracie, *"Toil and Peaceful Life": Doukhobor Village Settlement in Saskatchewan 1899-1918* (Regina: Canadian Plains Research Center, 1996).
33 Lyons, "A History of Doukhobor Schooling," 61-63.
34 Ibid. at 63-64.
35 Ibid. at 74-75.
36 Ibid. at 78-79.
37 See W.H. McConnell, "Peter G. Makaroff, Q.C.: Canada's First Doukhobor Lawyer," *Saskatchewan History* 44 (1992): 86-102.
38 Lyons, "A History of Doukhobor Schooling," 84.
39 Ibid. at 89-90.
40 Ibid. at 90.
41 See Koozma Tarasoff, *In Search of Brotherhood: The History of the Doukhobors,* vol. 2 (Vancouver: mimeographed, 1963), 527, quoting from a letter from Harry Vereshagin and Nicholai Plotnikoff, emissaries from the CCUB, to Verigin in the USSR, in P. Maloff, *Dukhobortsy: Ikh Istoria, Zinh i Bonba* (Thrums, BC: self-published, 1948), 33.
42 On the early construction of government and law in colonial British Columbia, see Tina Loo, *Making Law, Order, and Authority in British Columbia, 1821-1871* (Toronto: University of Toronto Press, 1994).
43 See Thomas Fleming, "'Our Boys in the Field': School Inspectors, Superintendents, and the Changing Character of School Leadership in British Columbia," in *Schools in the West,* ed. Nancy Sheehan, J. Donald Wilson, and David C. Jones (Calgary: Detselig Enterprises, 1986), 285-303; and Thomas Fleming, "In the Imperial Age and After: Pattern of British Columbia School Leadership and the Institution of Superintendency," *BC Studies* 1 (1989): 50-75.
44 Putnam and Weir, *Survey of the School System,* 23.
45 *Public Schools Act,* R.S.B.C. 1911, c. 102, ss. 140-42.
46 Blakemore, *Report of Royal Commission,* 1912, T48-55.
47 On the Doukhobors and education generally in British Columbia, see Mary Ashworth, *The Forces Which Shaped Them* (Vancouver: New Star Books, 1979).
48 On the short-lived support by Verigin the Elder for public education in British Columbia, see Tarasoff, *In Search of Brotherhood,* vol. 2, quoting from a letter in the *Nelson Daily News,* 27 March 1914, written by Beulah Clarke, who had taught in the school at Brilliant, to which this first wave of Doukhobor students went.
49 McLaren, "Creating 'Slaves of Satan,'" 354-57.
50 The full title of the legislation was *An Act to Make Provision for the Welfare and Protection of Women and Children Living under Communal Conditions,* S.B.C. 1914, c. 11.
51 McLaren, "Creating 'Slaves of Satan,'" 358.
52 Ibid. at 358-59.
53 *Public Schools Amendment Act,* S.B.C. 1920, c. 82, s. 22 (inserting s. 115A into the existing act), further amended and consolidated, S.B.C. 1922, c. 64, s. 129.
54 L. Barton, "'Canadianizing the Doukhobors': Government Attempts to Enforce Compulsory Education in British Columbia, 1911-1925" (honours paper, History 404, Okanagan University College, 1993), 10-11.
55 J.T.M. Anderson, *The Education of the New Canadian: A Treatise on Canada's Greatest Education Problem* (London: J.M. Dent, 1918).
56 McLaren, "Creating 'Slaves of Satan,'" 359-61.
57 Ibid. at 361-62.
58 Lyons, "A History of Doukhobor Schooling," 92-94.
59 McLaren, "Creating 'Slaves of Satan,'" 363.

60 On the background to and working out of this two-pronged stratagem, see John McLaren, "Wrestling Spirits: The Strange Case of Peter Verigin II," *Canadian Ethnic Studies* 27 (1995): 95-130.

61 McLaren, "Creating 'Slaves of Satan,'" 364. The legislative provision invoked by the provincial child welfare authorities in communication with the attorney general was the *Infants Act,* R.S.B.C. 1924, c. 112.

62 As early as September 1929, Pooley had been advocating that the Freedomite "ringleaders" should be convicted of "rioting charges" and sent off to D'Arcy Island off Victoria; see BCARS, GR 441, Tolmie Papers, vol. 283, file 4, telegram to Tolmie, 8 September 1929. On the census offences, see BCARS, GR 1323, Attorney General's Papers, telegram from Pooley to R.B. Bennett, 29 June 1931, re co-operation with the RCMP on prosecution of census offences.

63 Lyons, *A History of Doukhobor Schooling,* 158-60.

64 See, for example, National Archives of Canada, MG 26, R.B. Bennett Papers, box 367, file 1-206, reel M1072, 242660-71, minutes of a meeting on 25 September 1931 at which representations were made to Premier Tolmie, his cabinet, and Senator Robertson, federal minister of labour, by residents of Grand Forks concerning the "Doukhobor problem."

65 McLaren, "Wrestling Spirits," 101-2. See Library and Archives Canada (LAC), RG 76, Verigin File, part 1, report from Superintendent W.P. Lindsay, RCMP, Officer Commanding the Southern District of Saskatchewan, to Colonel Cortland Starnes, Commissioner, Ottawa, 27 July 1929.

66 Patrick Kyba, "Ballots and Burning Crosses," in *Politics in Saskatchewan,* ed. Ward and Spafford, 105-23.

67 See report in *Regina Morning Leader,* 8 June 1927, 1.

68 Kyba, "Ballots and Burning Crosses," 114-23.

69 In April 1931, Anderson wrote to Premier Tolmie suggesting that the two governments should press for the deportation of Verigin; see BCARS, GR 441, Tolmie Papers, vol. 295, file 4. On the deportation fiasco, see McLaren, "Wrestling Spirits," 102-9.

70 See the account of an investigation by Saskatchewan Doukhobors of a school burning in J.F.C. Wright, *Slava Bohu: The Story of the Doukhobors* (New York: Farrar and Rinehart, 1940), 331-33.

71 Lyons, "The (Almost) Quiet Evolution," 33-34.

72 Ibid. at 34.

73 *Schools Amendment Act (No. 2),* S.S. 1930, c. 46, s. 9. In an earlier amending piece of legislation, the Anderson government had moved against public schools of non-Protestant affiliation (i.e., Roman Catholic) by outlawing the use of the "emblem of any religious faith, denomination, order, sect, society or association on public school premises during school hours" and prohibiting any person teaching in a public school "while wearing the garb of any such religious faith." *Schools Amendment Act (No. 1),* S.S. 1930, c. 45, s. 1.

74 Even Anderson and his attorney general, Major MacPherson, were at some pains to make it clear to Doukhobor representatives that they were not out to treat all members of that community as nudists and arsonists and that they were anxious to bring the school burners to book. See SAB, Minutes of Meeting between Members of Saskatchewan Government and Representatives of Named Doukhobors Headed by Mr. J.G. Bondoreff, held in Parliament Buildings, Regina, 23 March 1932.

75 Lyons, "The (Almost) Quiet Evolution," 34.

76 Margaret Hill, "The Detention of Freedomite Children, 1953-59," *Canadian Ethnic Studies* 18 (1986): 47-60.

Acknowledgments

The editors gratefully acknowledge the financial support of several institutions. The publication of the book was made possible by the financial support of the University of Northern British Columbia – Vice-President of Research, the University of Calgary, and the Alberta Historical Resources Board. Without their generous grants the work would not have been published. The Social Sciences and Humanities Research Council of Canada supported the original conference from which the essays in this volume were eventually selected and rewritten for publication.

A number of individuals gave their efforts to make the book as successful as it can be. These include the anonymous readers for UBC Press; Wes Pue, Nemetz Chair in Legal History at UBC and the general editor of the series in which this appears, who offered constant encouragement; Kirsten Olson, of the Legal Archives Society of Alberta, who contributed to the original set-up of the book; Gordon Martel for wise counsel on persevering; Maggie Knafla who read the proofs and contributed to the index; and Jennifer Sauvé for unending support. At UBC Press itself, we wish to thank the Editor, Randy Schmidt, for his enthusiasm and work on the project from the very beginning, and Production Editor Ann Macklem and her staff for their constant and efficient efforts from the initial editorial process to the finished product.

The essays which appear in this book, apart from the Introduction, were first given as papers in a conference titled "Law for the Buffalo, Law for the Musk Ox" hosted by the University of Calgary in April 1997. The eighteen papers were given by graduate students, young and older scholars before a large audience of students and academics. They were critiqued in the long discussions that followed each session, and by two prominent "external" legal historians who attended the conference to provide an international perspective to the common law world that was being written on the Prairies. Thus our appreciation to Paul Brand of All Souls College, Oxford, and to David Philips of the University of Melbourne, Australia. We also wish to thank two Canadian historians who gave useful advice: Peter Oliver of the

University of Toronto and Rod MacLeod of the University of Alberta. Some papers became part of theses and dissertations, others of articles and books. Those that were uncommitted, and fit the parameters of this collection, are published here after being rewritten several times. We wish to thank the authors for their diligence and patience.

Finally, we wish to thank the following institutions who gave us permission to publish the maps and illustrations that appear in the volume. These include the University of Toronto Press for Maps 1.1, 1.3, 1.5, and 1.7; the Glenbow Museum for the photographs in Chapter 7; and Thomson Learning and Marsha Kerr for Maps 1.2 and 1.6, which were adapted from those prepared by Donald G.G. Kerr.

Contributors

Augustine Brannigan took doctoral studies in the Sociology of Science at the University of Toronto (1978). His *Social Basis of Scientific Discoveries* (1981) attracted wide attention and numerous translations. More recently he has published an iconoclastic history of social psychology, *The Rise and Fall of Social Psychology: The Misuse of the Human Experiment* (2004). His current fieldwork concerns the Rwandan genocide of 1994 and the current judicial responses, which are reviewed in "Genocide as Government through Murder," in *Violent Crime in North America,* ed. L.A. Knafla (2003).

Janice E. Erion is a legal counsel for the Canadian Pacific Railway, Calgary. She graduated with an Honour's degree in History from the University of Calgary – winning the James Gray Medal for her thesis on women as lenders and the property regime in the judicial district of Hanna, 1919-40 – and received her LLB from the University of Calgary in 1999.

Hamar Foster is a Professor of Law at the University of Victoria. His research and teaching interests include criminal law, evidence, property, legal history, and Aboriginal law. His most recent publications include co-authored articles on the Douglas Treaties and on extradition and the death penalty. He is currently co-editing a volume of essays commemorating the thirtieth anniversary of the *Calder* decision in the Supreme Court of Canada.

Tristan Goodman is the Canadian Regulatory Coordinator for ConocoPhillips, and previously worked for the Alberta Energy and Utilities Board as an advisor in environmental, economic, and strategy fields. He has a diverse experience with multinational companies and the public sector. He holds an interdisciplinary PhD in Natural Resource Management with a background in legal history, economics, and strategic policy development. His doctoral dissertation, "Assessing the Economic, Legal, and Environmental Factors Affecting Canadian Bulk Water Exports," has been accepted for publication by the University of Calgary Press.

Sid Harring is a Professor of Law at the City University of New York Law School. He is the author of *White Man's Law: Native People in Nineteenth-Century Canadian Jurisprudence* (1998), and a number of articles and chapters on indigenous peoples and the law in Canada, the United States, Namibia, and Australia; the most recent of which is "The Wendigo Killings: The Legal Penetration of Canadian Law into the Spirit World of the Ojibwa and Cree Indians," in *Violent Crime in North America,* ed. L.A. Knafla (2003).

Louis A. Knafla is Professor of History Emeritus at the University of Calgary and Director of Socio-Legal Studies. The former editor of *Criminal Justice History,* he has published on early modern English, and Canadian, legal history. His most recent works include *Violent Crime in North America* (2003), *Policing and War in Europe* (2002), and *Gender, Class, and Sexuality in Criminal Prosecutions* (2001). He is currently working on an edition of court records for early-seventeenth-century Kent, a biography of Lord Chancellor Ellesmere, and a study of the legal culture of the Kootenays from 1870 to 1914.

Zhiqiu Lin is Associate Professor of Sociology and Anthropology at Ottawa University. He received his BA from Heilongziang University, China, and his MA and PhD from the University of Calgary. His teaching and research interests are in the sociology of law, policing and crime in Canadian history, and economic reform, corruption, and legal development in contemporary China. He co-authored, with Ronald Keith, *Law and Justice in China's New Marketplace* (2001) and has in press a co-authored book, again with Ron Keith, titled *New Crime in China* (forthcoming in 2006).

Greg Marquis is an Associate Professor of History at the University of New Brunswick, Saint John, where he teaches Canadian and criminal justice history. He is the author of many articles and chapters, as well as two books, *In Armageddon's Shadow: The Civil War and Canada's Maritime Provinces* (1998), and *Policing Canada's Century: A History of the Canadian Association of Chiefs of Police* (1993). At present he is researching alcohol control in early-twentieth-century Canada and urban issues in twentieth-century Saint John.

Rod Martin is a sessional instructor in Canadian and First Nations' history at Mount Royal College, Calgary, and has recently joined the State and Legal Studies Department at Athabasca University. He is also a contract researcher for the Alberta 2005 Centennial Project at the Glenbow Museum and Archives. He recently finished his doctoral dissertation, "The North-West Mounted Police and Frontier Justice, 1874-1898" (2005), and authored "Macleod at Law: A Judicial Biography of James Farquharson Macleod, 1874-94" in *People and Place* (2003).

John McLaren is Lansdowne Professor of Law at the University of Victoria. He teaches and researches colonial legal history, and has published widely on the legal history of vice and its regulation in Canada, of law and racial and ethnic discrimination in Canada, and of environmental law in Britain and Canada. He has co-edited volumes on the legal history of British Columbia and the Yukon, and the North American West. Recent publications include the following: co-edited with Robert Menzies and Dorothy Chunn, *Regulating Lives: Historical Essays on the State, Society, the Individual and the Law* (2002); and co-edited with A.R. Buck and Nancy Wright, *Despotic Dominion: Property Rights in British Settler Societies* (2005).

Paul Nigol is an associate with Dolden, Wallace, Folick LLP, Vancouver. A former sessional instructor in history at the University of Calgary, he worked with Legal Aid at the Faculty of Law. He holds an LLB and a PhD; his doctoral dissertation was titled "Discipline, Discretion and Control: The Private Justice System of the Hudson's Bay Company in Rupert's Land, 1670-1770" (2001).

Russell Smandych is Professor of Sociology at the University of Manitoba, where he is active in the fields of criminology and historical sociology. His primary current research interests concern the study of the development of nineteenth-century British colonial criminal law and colonial law administration. Recent writings include "To Soften the Extreme Rigor of Their Bondage: James Stephen's Attempt to Reform the Criminal Slave Laws of the West Indies, 1813-1833," *Law and History Review* (2005), and "The Cultural Imperialism of Law," in *Cultural Imperialism: Essays on the Political Economy of Cultural Domination,* edited with Bernd Hamm (2005).

Jonathan Swainger is an Associate Professor and Chair of the History Program at the University of Northern British Columbia. Intrigued by distinctions between crime and acceptable levels of disorder, he has authored articles on crime and legal culture in central Alberta and crime history in northeastern British Columbia. His first book, *The Canadian Department of Justice and the Completion of Confederation, 1867-1878* (2000), and a collection of essays, *People and Place: Historical Influences on Legal Culture* (2003) co-edited with Constance Backhouse, were published with UBC Press. Swainger is currently completing a book on crime history in the Peace River region of northeastern British Columbia which will explore a community's sense of identity and notions of crime, criminality, and disorder.

General Index

Index of Cases

Index of Ordinances, Proclamations, and Statutes

Randy K. Lippert
Sanctuary, Sovereignty, Sacrifice: Canadian Sanctuary Incidents, Power, and Law (2005)

James B. Kelly
Governing with the Charter: Legislative and Judicial Activism and Framers' Intent (2005)

Dianne Pothier and Richard Devlin (eds.)
Critical Disability Theory: Essays in Philosophy, Politics, Policy, and Law (2005)

Susan G. Drummond
Mapping Marriage Law in Spanish Gitano Communities (2005)

Louis A. Knafla and Jonathan Swainger (eds.)
Laws and Societies in the Canadian Prairie West, 1670-1940 (2005)

Ikechi Mgbeoji
Global Biopiracy: Patents, Plants, and Indigenous Knowledge (2005)

Florian Sauvageau, David Schneiderman, and David Taras,
with Ruth Klinkhammer and Pierre Trudel
The Last Word: Media Coverage of the Supreme Court of Canada (2005)

Gerald Kernerman
Multicultural Nationalism: Civilizing Difference, Constituting Community (2005)

Pamela A. Jordan
Defending Rights in Russia: Lawyers, the State, and Legal Reform in the Post-Soviet Era (2005)

Anna Pratt
Securing Borders: Detention and Deportation in Canada (2005)

Kirsten Johnson Kramar
Unwilling Mothers, Unwanted Babies: Infanticide in Canada (2005)

W.A. Bogart
Good Government? Good Citizens? Courts, Politics, and Markets in a Changing Canada (2005)

Catherine Dauvergne
Humanitarianism, Identity, and Nation: Migration Laws in Canada and Australia (2005)

Michael Lee Ross
First Nations Sacred Sites in Canada's Courts (2005)

Andrew Woolford
Between Justice and Certainty: Treaty Making in British Columbia (2005)

John McLaren, Andrew Buck, and Nancy Wright (eds.)
Despotic Dominion: Property Rights in British Settler Societies (2004)

Georges Campeau
From UI to EI: Waging War on the Welfare State (2004)

Alvin J. Esau
The Courts and the Colonies: The Litigation of Hutterite Church Disputes (2004)

Christopher N. Kendall
Gay Male Pornography: An Issue of Sex Discrimination (2004)

Roy B. Flemming
Tournament of Appeals: Granting Judicial Review in Canada (2004)

Constance Backhouse and Nancy L. Backhouse
The Heiress vs the Establishment: Mrs. Campbell's Campaign for Legal Justice (2004)

Christopher P. Manfredi
Feminist Activism in the Supreme Court: Legal Mobilization and the Women's Legal Education and Action Fund (2004)

Annalise Acorn
Compulsory Compassion: A Critique of Restorative Justice (2004)

Jonathan Swainger and Constance Backhouse (eds.)
People and Place: Historical Influences on Legal Culture (2003)

Jim Phillips and Rosemary Gartner
Murdering Holiness: The Trials of Franz Creffield and George Mitchell (2003)

David R. Boyd
Unnatural Law: Rethinking Canadian Environmental Law and Policy (2003)

Ikechi Mgbeoji
Collective Insecurity: The Liberian Crisis, Unilateralism, and Global Order (2003)

Rebecca Johnson
Taxing Choices: The Intersection of Class, Gender, Parenthood, and the Law (2002)

John McLaren, Robert Menzies, and Dorothy E. Chunn (eds.)
Regulating Lives: Historical Essays on the State, Society, the Individual, and the Law (2002)

Joan Brockman
Gender in the Legal Profession: Fitting or Breaking the Mould (2001)